Necessary Illusions

Necessary Illusions

Thought Control in Democratic Societies

Noam Chomsky

South End Press   **Boston, MA**

Manufactured in the United States

Cover by Karin Aguilar-San Juan

Library of Congress Cataloging-in-Publication Data

Chomsky, Noam.

Necessary illusions : thought control in democratic societies
Noam Comsky.

p. cm.
Includes index.
ISBN 0-89608-367-5 :   — ISBN 0-89608-366-7 (pbk) :

1. Mass media--Political aspects. 2. Mass media--Censorship.
3. Freedom of information. 4. Civil rights. I Title
P95.8.C48 1989
302.2′3--dc19   89-6074
                    CIP

Table of Contents

Preface

The five chapters that follow are modified versions of the five 1988 Massey lectures I delivered over Canadian Broadcasting Corporation radio in November 1988. These lectures suggest certain conclusions about the functioning of the most advanced democratic systems of the modern era, and particularly, about the ways in which thought and understanding are shaped in the interests of domestic privilege. Following these five chapters are appendices that are intended to serve, in effect, as extended footnotes amplifying some of the points raised, separated from the text so as not to obscure too much the continuity of the discussion. There is an appendix, divided into sections, for each chapter. Each section is identified by the part of the text to which it serves as an addendum. These appendices should be regarded merely as a sample. As references indicate, some of the topics touched upon in the text and appendices are explored in further detail elsewhere. Many of them merit serious research projects.

The issues that arise are rooted in the nature of Western industrial societies and have been debated since their origins. In capitalist democracies there is a certain tension with regard to the locus of power. In a democracy the people rule, in principle. But decision-making power over central areas of life resides in private hands, with large-scale effects throughout the social order. One way to resolve the tension would be to extend the democratic system to investment, the organization of work, and so on. That would constitute a major social revolution, which, in my view at least, would consummate the political revolutions of an earlier era and realize some of the libertarian principles on which they were partly based. Or the tension could be resolved, and sometimes is, by forcefully eliminating public interference with state and private power. In the advanced industrial societies the problem is typically approached by a variety of measures to deprive democratic political structures of substantive content, while leaving them formally intact. A large part of this task is assumed by ideological institutions that channel thought and attitudes within acceptable bounds, deflecting any potential challenge to established privilege and authority before it can take form and gather strength.

The enterprise has many facets and agents. I will be primarily concerned with one aspect: thought control, as conducted through the agency of the national media and related elements of the elite intellectual culture.

There is, in my opinion, much too little inquiry into these matters. My personal feeling is that citizens of the democratic societies should undertake a course of intellectual self-defense to protect themselves from manipulation and control, and to lay the basis for more meaningful democracy. It is this concern that motivates the material that follows, and much of the work cited in the course of the discussion.

1

Democracy and the Media

Under the heading "Brazilian bishops support plan to democratize media," a church-based South American journal describes a proposal being debated in the constituent assembly that "would open up Brazil's powerful and highly concentrated media to citizen participation." "Brazil's Catholic bishops are among the principal advocates [of this] ... legislative proposal to democratize the country's communications media," the report continues, noting that "Brazilian TV is in the hands of five big networks [while] ... eight huge multinational corporations and various state enterprises account for the majority of all communications advertising." The proposal "envisions the creation of a National Communications Council made up of civilian and government representatives [that] ... would develop a democratic communications policy and grant licenses to radio and television operations." "The Brazilian Conference of Catholic Bishops has repeatedly stressed the importance of the communications media and pushed for grassroots participation. It has chosen communications as the theme of its 1989 Lenten campaign," an annual "parish-level campaign of reflection about some social issue" initiated by the Bishops' Conference.[1]

The questions raised by the Brazilian bishops are being seriously discussed in many parts of the world. Projects exploring them are under way in several Latin American countries and elsewhere. There has been discussion of a "New World Information Order" that would diversify media access and encourage alternatives to the global media system dominated by the Western industrial powers. A UNESCO inquiry into such possibilities elicited an extremely hostile reaction in the United States.[2] The alleged concern was freedom of the press. Among the questions I would like to raise as we proceed are: just how serious is this concern, and what is its substantive content? Further questions that lie in the background have to do with a democratic communications policy: what it might be, whether it is a desideratum, and if so, whether it is attainable. And, more generally, just what kind of democratic order is it to which we aspire?

The concept of "democratizing the media" has no real meaning within the terms of political discourse in the United States. In fact, the phrase has a paradoxical or even vaguely subversive ring to it. Citizen participation would be considered an infringement on freedom of the press, a blow struck against the independence of the media that would distort the mission they have undertaken to inform the public without fear or favor. The reaction merits some thought. Underlying it are beliefs about how the media do function and how they should function within our democratic systems, and also certain implicit conceptions of the nature of democracy. Let us consider these topics in turn.

The standard image of media performance, as expressed by Judge Gurfein in a decision rejecting government efforts to bar publication of the *Pentagon Papers*, is that we have "a cantankerous press, an obstinate press, a ubiquitous press," and that these tribunes of the people "must be suffered by those in authority in order to preserve the even greater values of freedom of expression and the right of the people to know." Commenting on this decision, Anthony Lewis of the *New York Times* observes that the media were not always as independent, vigilant, and defiant of authority as they are today, but in the Vietnam and Watergate eras they learned to exercise "the power to root about in our national life, exposing what they deem right for exposure," without regard to external pressures or the demands of state or private power. This too is a commonly held belief.[3]

There has been much debate over the media during this period, but it does not deal with the problem of "democratizing the media" and freeing them from the constraints of state and private power. Rather, the issue debated is whether the media have not exceeded proper bounds in escaping such constraints, even threatening the existence of democratic institutions in their contentious and irresponsible defiance of authority. A 1975 study on "governability of democracies" by the Trilateral Commission concluded that the media have become a "notable new source of national power," one aspect of an "excess of democracy" that contributes to "the reduction of governmental authority" at home and a consequent "decline in the influence of democracy abroad." This general "crisis of democracy," the commission held, resulted from the efforts of previously marginalized sectors of the population to organize and press their demands, thereby creating an overload that prevents the democratic process from functioning properly. In earlier times, "Truman had been able to govern the country with the cooperation of a relatively small number of Wall Street lawyers and bankers," so the American *rapporteur*, Samuel Huntington of Harvard University, reflected. In that period there was no crisis of democracy, but in the 1960s, the crisis developed and reached serious proportions. The study therefore urged more "moderation in democracy" to mitigate the excess of democracy and overcome the crisis.[4]

Putting it in plain terms, the general public must be reduced to its traditional apathy and obedience, and driven from the arena of political debate and action, if democracy is to survive.

The Trilateral Commission study reflects the perceptions and values of liberal elites from the United States, Europe, and Japan, including the leading figures of the Carter administration. On the right, the perception is that democracy is threatened by the organizing efforts of those called the "special interests," a concept of contemporary political rhetoric that refers to workers, farmers, women, youth, the elderly, the handicapped, ethnic minorities, and so on—in short, the general population. In the U.S. presidential campaigns of the 1980s, the Democrats were accused of being the instrument of these special interests and thus undermining "the national interest," tacitly assumed to be represented by the one sector notably omitted from the list of special interests: corporations, financial institutions, and other business elites.

The charge that the Democrats represent the special interests has little merit. Rather, they represent other elements of the "national interest," and participated with few qualms in the right turn of the post-Vietnam era among elite groups, including the dismantling of limited state programs designed to protect the poor and deprived; the transfer of resources to the wealthy; the conversion of the state, even more than before, to a welfare state for the privileged; and the expansion of state power and the protected state sector of the economy through the military system—domestically, a device for compelling the public to subsidize high-technology industry and provide a state-guaranteed market for its waste production. A related element of the right turn was a more "activist" foreign policy to extend U.S. power through subversion, international terrorism, and aggression: the Reagan Doctrine, which the media characterize as the vigorous defense of democracy worldwide, sometimes criticizing the Reaganites for their excesses in this noble cause. In general, the Democratic opposition offered qualified support to these programs of the Reagan administration, which, in fact, were largely an extrapolation of initiatives pf the Carter years and, as polls clearly indicate, with few exceptions were strongly opposed by the general population.[5]

Challenging journalists at the Democratic Convention in July 1988 on the constant reference to Michael Dukakis as "too liberal" to win, the media watch organization Fairness and Accurary In Reporting (FAIR) cited a December 1987 *New York Times*/CBS poll showing overwhelming popular support for government guarantees of full employment, medical and day care, and a 3-to-1 margin in favor of reduction of military expenses among the 50 percent of the population who approve of a change. But the choice of a Reagan-style Democrat for vice president elicited only praise from the media for the pragmatism of the Democrats in resisting the left-wing extremists who called for policies supported by a large majority of the population. Popular attitudes, in fact, continued to move towards a kind of New Deal-style liberalism through the 1980s, while "liberal" became an unspeakable word in political rhetoric. Polls show that almost half the population believe that the U.S. Constitution—a sacred document—is the source of Marx's phrase "from each according to his ability, to each according to his need," so obviously right does the sentiment seem.[6]

One should not be misled by Reagan's "landslide" electoral victories. Reagan won the votes of less than a third of the electorate; of those who voted, a clear majority hoped that his legislative programs would not be enacted, while half the population continues to believe that the government is run "by a few big interests looking out for themselves."[7] Given a choice between the Reaganite program of damn-the-consequences Keynesian growth accompanied by jingoist flag-waving on the one hand, and the Democratic alternative of fiscal conservatism and "we approve of your goals but fear that the costs will be too high" on the other, those who took the trouble to vote preferred the former—not too surprisingly. Elite groups have the task of putting on a bold face and extolling the brilliant successes of our system: "a model democracy and a society that provides exceptionally well for the needs of its citizens," as Henry Kissinger and Cyrus Vance proclaim in outlining "Bipartisan Objectives for Foreign Policy" in the post-Reagan era. But apart from educated elites, much of the population appears to regard the government as an instrument of power beyond their influence and control; and if their experience does not suffice, a look at some comparative statistics will show how magnificently the richest society in the world, with incomparable advantages, "provides for the needs of its citizens."[8]

The Reagan phenomenon, in fact, may offer a foretaste of the directions in which capitalist democracy is heading, with the progressive elimination of labor unions, independent media, political associations, and, more generally, forms of popular organization that interfere with domination of the state by concentrated private power. Much of the outside world may have viewed Reagan as a "bizarre cowboy leader" who engaged in acts of "madness" in organizing a "band of cutthroats" to attack Nicaragua, among other exploits (in the words of Toronto *Globe and Mail* editorials),[9] but U.S. public opinion seemed to regard him as hardly more than a symbol of national unity, something like the flag, or the Queen of England. The Queen opens Parliament by reading a political program, but no one asks whether she believes it or even understands it. Correspondingly, the public seemed unconcerned over the evidence, difficult to suppress, that President Reagan had only the vaguest conception of the policies enacted in his name, or the fact that when not properly programmed by his staff, he regularly came out with statements so outlandish as to be an embarrassment, if one were to take them seriously.[10] The process of barring public interference with important matters takes a step forward when elections do not even enable the public to select among programs that originate elsewhere, but become merely a procedure for selecting a symbolic figure. It is therefore of some interest that the United States functioned virtually without a chief executive for eight years.

Returning to the media, which are charged with having fanned the ominous flames of "excess of democracy," the Trilateral Commission concluded that "broader interests of society and government" require that if journalists do not impose "standards of professionalism," "the alternative could well be regulation by the government" to the end of "restoring a balance between government and media." Reflecting similar concerns, the executive-director of Freedom House, Leonard Sussman, asked: "Must free institutions be overthrown because of the very freedom they sustain?" And John Roche, intellectual-in-residence during the Johnson administration, answered by calling for congressional investigation of "the workings of these private governments" which distorted the record so grossly in their "anti-Johnson mission," though he feared that Congress would be too "terrified of the media" to take on this urgent task.[11]

Sussman and Roche were commenting on Peter Braestrup's two-volume study, sponsored by Freedom House, of media coverage of the Tet Offensive of 1968.[12] This study was widely hailed as a landmark contribution, offering definitive proof of the irresponsibility of this "notable new source of national power." Roche described it as "one of the major pieces of investigative reporting and first-rate scholarship of the past quarter century," a "meticulous case-study of media incompetence, if not malevolence." This classic of modern scholarship was alleged to have demonstrated that in their incompetent and biased coverage reflecting the "adversary culture" of the sixties, the media in effect lost the war in Vietnam, thus harming the cause of democracy and freedom for which the United States fought in vain. The Freedom House study concluded that these failures reflect "the more volatile journalistic style—spurred by managerial exhortation or complaisance—that has become so popular since the late 1960s." The new journalism is accompanied by "an often mindless readiness to seek out conflict, to believe the worst of the government or of authority in general, and on that basis to divide up the actors on any issue into the 'good' and the 'bad'." The "bad" actors included the U.S. forces in Vietnam, the "military-industrial complex," the CIA and the U.S. government generally; and the "good," in the eyes of the media, were presumably the Communists, who, the study alleged, were consistently overpraised and protected. The study envisioned "a continuation of the current volatile styles, always with the dark possibility that, if the managers do not themselves take action, then outsiders—the courts, the Federal Communications Commission, or Congress—will seek to apply remedies of their own."

It is by now an established truth that "we tend to flagellate ourselves as Americans about various aspects of our own policies and actions we disapprove of" and that, as revealed by the Vietnam experience, "it is almost inescapable that such broad coverage will undermine support for the war effort," particularly "the often-gory pictorial reportage by television" (Landrum Bolling, at a conference he directed on the question of whether there is indeed "no way to effect some kind of balance between the advantages a totalitarian government enjoys because of its ability to control or black out unfavorable news in warfare and the disadvantages for the free society of allowing open coverage of all the wartime events").[13] The Watergate affair, in which investigative reporting "helped force a President from office" (Anthony Lewis), reinforced these dire images of impending destruction of democracy by the free-wheeling, independent, and adversarial media, as did the Iran-contra scandal. Ringing defenses of freedom of the press, such as those of Judge Gurfein and Anthony Lewis, are a response to attempts to control media excesses and impose upon them standards of responsibility.

Two kinds of questions arise in connection with these vigorous debates about the media and democracy: questions of fact and questions of value. The basic question of fact is whether the media have indeed adopted an adversarial stance, perhaps with excessive zeal; whether, in particular, they undermine the defense of freedom in wartime and threaten free institutions by "flagellating ourselves" and those in power. If so, we may then ask whether it would be proper to impose some external constraints to ensure that they keep to the bounds of responsibility, or whether we should adopt the principle expressed by Justice Holmes, in a classic dissent, that "the best test of truth is the power of the thought to get itself accepted in the competition of the market" through "free trade in ideas."[14]

The question of fact is rarely argued; the case is assumed to have been proven. Some, however, have held that the factual premises are simply false. Beginning with the broadest claims, let us consider the functioning of the free market of ideas. In his study of the mobilization of popular opinion to promote state power, Benjamin Ginsberg maintains that

> western governments have used market mechanisms to regulate popular perspectives and sentiments. The "marketplace of ideas," built during the nineteenth and twentieth centuries, effectively disseminates the beliefs and ideas of the upper classes while subverting the ideological and cultural independence of the lower classes. Through the construction of this marketplace, western governments forged firm and enduring links between socioeconomic position and ideological power, permitting upper classes to use each to buttress the other ... In the United States, in particular, the ability of the upper and upper-middle classes to dominate the marketplace of ideas has generally allowed these strata to shape the entire society's perception of political reality and the range of realistic political and social possibilities. While westerners usually equate the marketplace with freedom of opinion, the hidden hand of the market can be almost as potent an instrument of control as the iron fist of the state.[15]

Ginsberg's conclusion has some initial plausibility, on assumptions about the functioning of a guided free market that are not particularly controversial. Those segments of the media that can reach a substantial audience are major corporations and are closely integrated with even larger conglomerates. Like other businesses, they sell a product to buyers. Their market is advertisers, and the "product" is audiences, with a bias towards more wealthy audiences, which improve advertising rates.[16] Over a century ago, British Liberals observed that the market would promote those journals "enjoying the preference of the advertising public"; and today, Paul Johnson, noting the demise of a new journal of the left, blandly comments that it deserved its fate: "The market pronounced an accurate verdict at the start by declining to subscribe all the issue capital," and surely no right-thinking person could doubt that the market represents the public will.[17]

In short, the major media—particularly, the elite media that set the agenda that others generally follow—are corporations "selling" privileged audiences to other businesses. It would hardly come as a surprise if the picture of the world they present were to reflect the perspectives and interests of the sellers, the buyers, and the product. Concentration of ownership of the media is high and increasing.[18] Furthermore, those who occupy managerial positions in the media, or gain status within them as commentators, belong to the same privileged elites, and might be expected to share the perceptions, aspirations, and attitudes of their associates, reflecting their own class interests as well. Journalists entering the system are unlikely to make their way unless they conform to these ideological pressures, generally by internalizing the values; it is not easy to say one thing and believe another, and those who fail to conform will tend to be weeded out by familiar mechanisms.

The influence of advertisers is sometimes far more direct. "Projects unsuitable for corporate sponsorship tend to die on the vine," the London *Economist* observes, noting that "stations have learned to be sympathetic to the most delicate sympathies of corporations." The journal cites the case of public TV station WNET, which "lost its corporate underwriting from Gulf+Western as a result of a documentary called 'Hunger for Profit', about multinationals buying up huge tracts of land in the third world." These actions "had not been those of a friend," Gulf's chief executive wrote to the station, adding that the documentary was "virulently anti-business, if not anti-American." "Most people believe that WNET would not make the same mistake today," the *Economist* concludes.[19] Nor would others. The warning need only be implicit.

Many other factors induce the media to conform to the requirements of the state-corporate nexus.[20] To confront power is costly and difficult; high standards of evidence and argument are imposed, and critical analysis is naturally not welcomed by those who are in a position to react vigorously and to determine the array of rewards and punishments. Conformity to a "patriotic agenda," in contrast, imposes no such costs. Charges against official enemies barely require substantiation; they are, furthermore, protected from correction, which can be dismissed as apologetics for the criminals or as missing the forest for the trees. The system protects itself with indignation against a challenge to the right of deceit in the service of power, and the very idea of subjecting the ideological system to rational inquiry elicits incomprehension or outrage, though it is often masked in other terms.[21] One who attributes the best intentions to the U.S. government, while perhaps deploring failure and ineptitude, requires no evidence for this stance, as when we ask why "success has continued to elude us" in the Middle East and Central America, why "a nation of such vast wealth, power and good intentions [cannot] accomplish its purposes more promptly and more effectively" (Landrum Bolling).[22] Standards are radically different when we observe that "good intentions" are not properties of states, and that the United States, like every other state past and present, pursues policies that reflect the interests of those who control the state by virtue of their domestic power, truisms that are hardly expressible in the mainstream, surprising as this fact may be.

One needs no evidence to condemn the Soviet Union for aggression in Afghanistan and support for repression in Poland; it is quite a different matter when one turns to U.S. aggression in Indochina or its efforts to prevent a political settlement of the Arab-Israeli conflict over many years, readily documented, but unwelcome and therefore a non-fact. No argument is demanded for a condemnation of Iran or Libya for state-supported terrorism; discussion of the prominent— arguably dominant—role of the United States and its clients in organizing and conducting this plague of the modern era elicits only horror and contempt for this view point; supporting evidence, however compelling, is dismissed as irrelevant. As a matter of course, the media and intellectual journals either praise the U.S. government for dedicating itself to the struggle for democracy in Nicaragua or criticize it for the means it has employed to pursue this laudable objective, offering no evidence that this is indeed the goal of policy. A challenge to the underlying patriotic assumption is virtually unthinkable within the mainstream and, if permitted expression, would be dismissed as a variety of ideological fanaticism, an absurdity, even if backed by overwhelming evidence—not a difficult task in this case.

Case by case, we find that conformity is the easy way, and the path to privilege and prestige; dissidence carries personal costs that may be severe, even in a society that lacks such means of control as death squads, psychiatric prisons, or extermination camps. The very structure of the media is designed to induce conformity to established doctrine. In a three-minute stretch between commercials, or in seven hundred words, it is impossible to present unfamiliar thoughts or surprising conclusions with the argument and evidence required to afford them some credibility. Regurgitation of welcome pieties faces no such problem.

It is a natural expectation, on uncontroversial assumptions, that the major media and other ideological institutions will generally reflect the perspectives and interests of established power. That this expectation is fulfilled has been argued by a number of analysts. Edward Herman and I have published extensive documentation, separately and jointly, to support a conception of how the media function that differs sharply from the standard version.[23] According to this "propaganda model"—which has prior plausibility for such reasons as those just briefly reviewed—the media serve the interests of state and corporate power, which are closely interlinked, framing their reporting and analysis in a manner supportive of established privilege and limiting debate and discussion accordingly. We have studied a wide range of examples, including those that provide the most severe test for a propaganda model, namely, the cases that critics of alleged anti-establishment excesses of the media offer as their strongest ground: the coverage of the Indochina wars, the Watergate affair, and others drawn from the period when the media are said to have overcome the conformism of the past and taken on a crusading role. To subject the model to a fair test, we have systematically selected examples that are as closely paired as history allows: crimes attributable to official enemies versus those for which the United States and its clients bear responsibility; good deeds, specifically elections conducted by official enemies versus those in U.S. client states. Other methods have also been pursued, yielding further confirmation.

There are, by now, thousands of pages of documentation supporting the conclusions of the propaganda model. By the standards of the social sciences, it is very well confirmed, and its predictions are often considerably surpassed. If there is a serious challenge to this conclusion, I am unaware of it. The nature of the arguments presented against it, on the rare occasions when the topic can even be addressed in the mainstream, suggest that the model is indeed robust. The highly regarded Freedom House study, which is held to have provided the conclusive demonstration of the adversarial character of the media and its threat to democracy, collapses upon analysis, and when innumerable errors and misrepresentations are corrected, amounts to little more than a complaint that the media were too pessimistic in their pursuit of a righteous cause; I know of no other studies that fare better.[24]

There are, to be sure, other factors that influence the performance of social institutions as complex as the media, and one can find exceptions to the general pattern that the propaganda model predicts. Nevertheless, it has, I believe, been shown to provide a reasonably close first approximation, which captures essential properties of the media and the dominant intellectual culture more generally.

One prediction of the model is that it will be effectively excluded from discussion, for it questions a factual assumption that is most serviceable to the interests of established power: namely, that the media are adversarial and cantankerous, perhaps excessively so. However well-confirmed the model may be, then, it is inadmissible, and, the model predicts, should remain outside the spectrum of debate over the media. This conclusion too is empirically well-confirmed. Note that the model has a rather disconcerting feature. Plainly, it is either valid or invalid. If invalid, it may be dismissed; if valid, it *will* be dismissed. As in the case of eighteenth-century doctrine on seditious libel, truth is no defense; rather, it heightens the enormity of the crime of calling authority into disrepute.

If the conclusions drawn in the propaganda model are correct, then the criticisms of the media for their adversarial stance can only be understood as a demand that the media should not even reflect the range of debate over tactical questions among dominant elites, but should serve only those segments that happen to manage the state at a particular moment, and should do so with proper enthusiasm and optimism about the causes—noble by definition—in which state power is engaged. It would not have surprised George Orwell that this should be the import of the critique of the media by an organization that calls itself "Freedom House."[25]

Journalists often meet a high standard of professionalism in their work, exhibiting courage, integrity, and enterprise, including many of those who report for media that adhere closely to the predictions of the propaganda model. There is no contradiction here. What is at issue is not the honesty of the opinions expressed or the integrity of those who seek the facts but rather the choice of topics and highlighting of issues, the range of opinion permitted expression, the unquestioned premises that guide reporting and commentary, and the general framework imposed for the presentation of a certain view of the world. We need not, incidentally, tarry over such statements as the following, emblazoned on the cover of the *New Republic* during Israel's invasion of Lebanon: "Much of what you have read in the newspapers and newsmagazines about the war in Lebanon— and even more of what you have seen and heard on television—is simply not true."[26] Such performances can be consigned to the dismal archives of apologetics for the atrocities of other favored states.

I will present examples to illustrate the workings of the propaganda model, but will assume the basic case to have been credibly established by the extensive material already in print. This work has elicited much outrage and falsification (some of which Herman and I review in *Manufacturing Consent*, some elsewhere), and also puzzlement and misunderstanding. But, to my knowledge, there is no serious effort to respond to these and other similar critiques. Rather, they are simply dismissed, in conformity to the predictions of the propaganda model.[27] Typically, debate over media performance within the mainstream includes criticism of the adversarial stance of the media and response by their defenders, but no critique of the media for adhering to the predictions of the propaganda model, or recognition that this might be a conceivable position. In the case of the Indochina wars, for example, U.S. public television presented a retrospective series in 1985 followed by a denunciation produced by the right-wing media-monitoring organization Accuracy in Media and a discussion limited to critics of the alleged adversarial excesses of the series and its defenders. No one argued that the series conforms to the expectations of the propaganda model—as it does. The study of media coverage of conflicts in the Third World mentioned earlier follows a similar pattern, which is quite consistent, though the public regards the media as too conformist.[28]

The media cheerfully publish condemnations of their "breathtaking lack of balance or even the appearance of fair-mindedness" and "the ills and dangers of today's wayward press."[29] But only when, as in this case, the critic is condemning the "media elite" for being "in thrall to liberal views of politics and human nature" and for the "evident difficulty most liberals have in using the word dictatorship to describe even the most flagrant dictatorships of the left"; surely one would never find Fidel Castro described as a dictator in the mainstream press, always so soft on Communism and given to self-flagellation.[30] Such diatribes are not expected to meet even minimal standards of evidence; this one contains exactly one reference to what conceivably might be a fact, a vague allusion to alleged juggling of statistics by the *New York Times* "to obscure the decline of interest rates during Ronald Reagan's first term," as though the matter had not been fully reported. Charges of this nature are often not unwelcome, first, because response is simple or superfluous; and second, because debate over this issue helps entrench the belief that the media are either independent and objective, with high standards of professional integrity and openness to all reasonable views, or, alternatively, that they are biased towards stylishly leftish flouting of authority. Either conclusion is quite acceptable to established power and privilege—even to the media elites themselves, who are not averse to the charge that they may have gone too far in pursuing their cantankerous and obstreperous ways in defiance of orthodoxy and power. The spectrum of discussion reflects what a propaganda model would predict: condemnation of "liberal bias" and defense against this charge, but no recognition of the possibility that "liberal bias" might simply be an expression of one variant of the narrow state-corporate ideology—as, demonstrably, it is—and a particularly useful variant, bearing the implicit message: thus far, and no further.

Returning to the proposals of the Brazilian bishops, one reason they would appear superfluous or wrong-headed if raised in our political context is that the media are assumed to be dedicated to service to the public good, if not too extreme in their independence of authority. They are thus performing their proper social role, as explained by Supreme Court Justice Powell in words quoted by Anthony Lewis in his defense of freedom of the press: "No individual can obtain for himself the information needed for the intelligent discharge of his political responsibilities ... By enabling the public to assert meaningful control over the political process, the press performs a crucial function in effecting the societal purpose of the First Amendment."

An alternative view, which I believe is valid, is that the media indeed serve a "societal purpose," but quite a different one. It is the societal purpose served by state education as conceived by James Mill in the early days of the establishment of this system: to "train the minds of the people to a virtuous attachment to their government," and to the arrangements of the social, economic, and political order more generally.[31] Far from contributing to a "crisis of democracy" of the sort feared by the liberal establishment, the media are vigilant guardians protecting privilege from the threat of public understanding and participation. If these conclusions are correct, the first objection to democratizing the media is based on factual and analytic error.

A second basis for objection is more substantial, and not without warrant: the call for democratizing the media could mask highly unwelcome efforts to limit intellectual independence through popular pressures, a variant of concerns familiar in political theory. The problem is not easily dismissed, but it is not an inherent property of democratization of the media.[32]

The basic issue seems to me to be a different one. Our political culture has a conception of democracy that differs from that of the Brazilian bishops. For them, democracy means that citizens should have the opportunity to inform themselves, to take part in inquiry and discussion and policy formation, and to advance their programs through political action. For us, democracy is more narrowly conceived: the citizen is a consumer, an observer but not a participant. The public has the right to ratify policies that originate elsewhere, but if these limits are exceeded, we have not democracy, but a "crisis of democracy," which must somehow be resolved.

This concept is based on doctrines laid down by the Founding Fathers. The Federalists, historian Joyce Appleby writes, expected "that the new American political institutions would continue to function within the old assumptions about a politically active elite and a deferential, compliant electorate," and "George Washington had hoped that his enormous prestige would bring that great, sober, commonsensical citizenry politicians are always addressing to see the dangers of self-created societies."[33] Despite their electoral defeat, their conception prevailed, though in a different form as industrial capitalism took shape. It was expressed by John Jay, the president of the Continental Congress and the first chief justice of the U.S. Supreme Court, in what his biographer calls one of his favorite maxims: "The people who own the country ought to govern it." And they need not be too gentle in the mode of governance. Alluding to rising disaffection, Gouverneur Morris wrote in a dispatch to John Jay in 1783 that although "it is probable that much of Convulsion will ensue," there need be no real concern: "The People are well prepared" for the government to assume "that Power without which Government is but a Name ... Wearied with the War, their Acquiescence may be depended on with absolute Certainty, and you and I, my friend, know by Experience that when a few Men of sense and spirit get together and declare that they are the Authority, such few as are of a different opinion may easily be convinced of their Mistake by that powerful Argument the Halter." By "the People," constitutional historian Richard Morris observes, "he meant a small nationalist elite, whom he was too cautious to name"—the white propertied males for whom the constitutional order was established. The "vast exodus of Loyalists and blacks" to Canada and elsewhere reflected in part their insight into these realities.[34]

Elsewhere, Morris observes that in the post-revolutionary society, "what one had in effect was a political democracy manipulated by an elite," and in states where "egalitarian democracy" might appear to have prevailed (as in Virginia), in reality "dominance of the aristocracy was implicitly accepted." The same is true of the dominance of the rising business classes in later periods that are held to reflect the triumph of popular democracy.[35]

John Jay's maxim is, in fact, the principle on which the Republic was founded and maintained, and in its very nature capitalist democracy cannot stray far from this pattern for reasons that are readily perceived.[36]

At home, this principle requires that politics reduce, in effect, to interactions among groups of investors who compete for control of the state, in accordance with what Thomas Ferguson calls the "investment theory of politics," which, he argues plausibly, explains a large part of U.S. political history.[37] For our dependencies, the same basic principle entails that democracy is achieved when the society is under the control of local oligarchies, business-based elements linked to U.S. investors, the military under our control, and professionals who can be trusted to follow orders and serve the interests of U.S. power and privilege. If there is any popular challenge to their rule, the United States is entitled to resort to violence to "restore democracy"—to adopt the term conventionally used in reference to the Reagan Doctrine in Nicaragua. The media contrast the "democrats" with the "Communists," the former being those who serve the interests of U.S. power, the latter those afflicted with the disease called "ultranationalism" in secret planning documents, which explain, forthrightly, that the threat to our interests is "nationalistic regimes" that respond to domestic pressures for improvement of living standards and social reform, with insufficient regard for the needs of U.S. investors.

The media are only following the rules of the game when they contrast the "fledgling democracies" of Central America, under military and business control, with "Communist Nicaragua." And we can appreciate why they suppressed the 1987 polls in El Salvador that revealed that a mere 10 percent of the population "believe that there is a process of democracy and freedom in the country at present." The benighted Salvadorans doubtless fail to comprehend our concept of democracy. And the same must be true of the editors of Honduras's leading journal *El Tiempo*. They see in their country a "democracy" that offers "unemployment and repression" in a caricature of the democratic process, and write that there can be no democracy in a country under "occupation of North American troops and contras," where "vital national interests are abandoned in order to serve the objectives of foreigners," while repression and illegal arrests continue, and the death squads of the military lurk ominously in the background.[38]

In accordance with the prevailing conceptions in the U.S., there is no infringement on democracy if a few corporations control the information system: in fact, that is the essence of democracy. In the *Annals of the American Academy of Political and Social Science*, the leading figure of the public relations industry, Edward Bernays, explains that "the very essence of the democratic process" is "the freedom to persuade and suggest," what he calls "the engineering of consent." "A leader," he continues, "frequently cannot wait for the people to arrive at even general understanding ... Democratic leaders must play their part in ... engineering ... consent to socially constructive goals and values," applying "scientific principles and tried practices to the task of getting people to support ideas and programs"; and although it remains unsaid, it is evident enough that those who control resources will be in a position to judge what is "socially constructive," to engineer consent through the media, and to implement policy through the mechanisms of the state. If the freedom to persuade happens to be concentrated in a few hands, we must recognize that such is the nature of a free society. The public relations industry expends vast resources "educating the American people about the economic facts of life" to ensure a favorable climate for business. Its task is to control "the public mind," which is "the only serious danger confronting the company," an AT&T executive observed eighty years ago.[39]

Similar ideas are standard across the political spectrum. The dean of U.S. journalists, Walter Lippmann, described a "revolution" in "the practice of democracy" as "the manufacture of consent" has become "a self-conscious art and a regular organ of popular government." This is a natural development when "the common interests very largely elude public opinion entirely, and can be managed only by a specialized class whose personal interests reach beyond the locality." He was writing shortly after World War I, when the liberal intellectual community was much impressed with its success in serving as "the faithful and helpful interpreters of what seems to be one of the greatest enterprises ever undertaken by an American president" (*New Republic*). The enterprise was Woodrow Wilson's interpretation of his electoral mandate for "peace without victory" as the occasion for pursuing victory without peace, with the assistance of the liberal intellectuals, who later praised themselves for having "impose[d] their will upon a reluctant or indifferent majority," with the aid of propaganda fabrications about Hun atrocities and other such devices.

Fifteen years later, Harold Lasswell explained in the *Encyclopaedia of the Social Sciences* that we should not succumb to "democratic dogmatisms about men being the best judges of their own interests." They are not; the best judges are the elites, who must, therefore, be ensured the means to impose their will, for the common good. When social arrangements deny them the requisite force to compel obedience, it is necessary to turn to "a whole new technique of control, largely through propaganda" because of the "ignorance and superstition [of] ... the masses." In the same years, Reinhold Niebuhr argued that "rationality belongs to the cool observers," while "the proletarian" follows not reason but faith, based upon a crucial element of "necessary illusion." Without such illusion, the ordinary person will descend to "inertia." Then in his Marxist phase, Niebuhr urged that those he addressed—presumably, the cool observers—recognize "the stupidity of the average man" and provide the "emotionally potent oversimplifications" required to keep the proletarian on course to create a new society; the basic conceptions underwent little change as Niebuhr became "the official establishment theologian" (Richard Rovere), offering counsel to those who "face the responsibilities of power."[40]

After World War II, as the ignorant public reverted to their slothful pacifism at a time when elites understood the need to mobilize for renewed global conflict, historian Thomas Bailey observed that "because the masses are notoriously short-sighted and generally cannot see danger until it is at their throats, our statesmen are forced to deceive them into an awareness of their own long-run interests. Deception of the people may in fact become increasingly necessary,

unless we are willing to give our leaders in Washington a freer hand."
Commenting on the same problem as a renewed crusade was being
launched in 1981, Samuel Huntington made the point that "you may
have to sell [intervention or other military action] in such a way as to
create the misimpression that it is the Soviet Union that you are
fighting. That is what the United States has done ever since the
Truman Doctrine"—an acute observation, which explains one essential function of the Cold War.[41]

At another point on the spectrum, the conservative contempt
for democracy is succinctly articulated by Sir Lewis Namier, who
writes that "there is no free will in the thinking and actions of the
masses, any more than in the revolutions of planets, in the migrations
of birds, and in the plunging of hordes of lemmings into the sea."[42]
Only disaster would ensue if the masses were permitted to enter the
arena of decision-making in a meaningful way.

Some are admirably forthright in their defense of the doctrine:
for example, the Dutch Minister of Defense writes that "whoever
turns against manufacture of consent resists any form of effective
authority."[43] Any commissar would nod his head in appreciation and
understanding.

At its root, the logic is that of the Grand Inquisitor, who bitterly
assailed Christ for offering people freedom and thus condemning
them to misery. The Church must correct the evil work of Christ by
offering the miserable mass of humanity the gift they most desire and
need: absolute submission. It must "vanquish freedom" so as "to
make men happy" and provide the total "community of worship"
that they avidly seek. In the modern secular age, this means worship
of the state religion, which in the Western democracies incorporates
the doctrine of submission to the masters of the system of public
subsidy, private profit, called free enterprise. The people must be
kept in ignorance, reduced to jingoist incantations, for their own
good. And like the Grand Inquisitor, who employs the forces of
miracle, mystery, and authority "to conquer and hold captive for ever
the conscience of these impotent rebels for their happiness" and to
deny them the freedom of choice they so fear and despise, so the "cool
observers" must create the "necessary illusions" and "emotionally
potent oversimplifications" that keep the ignorant and stupid masses
disciplined and content.[44]

Despite the frank acknowledgment of the need to deceive the
public, it would be an error to suppose that practitioners of the art
are typically engaged in *conscious* deceit; few reach the level of

sophistication of the Grand Inquisitor or maintain such insights for long. On the contrary, as the intellectuals pursue their grim and demanding vocation, they readily adopt beliefs that serve institutional needs; those who do not will have to seek employment elsewhere. The chairman of the board may sincerely believe that his every waking moment is dedicated to serving human needs. Were he to act on these delusions instead of pursuing profit and market share, he would no longer be chairman of the board. It is probable that the most inhuman monsters, even the Himmlers and the Mengeles, convince themselves that they are engaged in noble and courageous acts. The psychology of leaders is a topic of little interest. The institutional factors that constrain their actions and beliefs are what merit attention.

Across a broad spectrum of articulate opinion, the fact that the voice of the people is heard in democratic societies is considered a problem to be overcome by ensuring that the public voice speaks the right words. The general conception is that leaders control us, not that we control them. If the population is out of control and propaganda doesn't work, then the state is forced underground, to clandestine operations and secret wars; the scale of covert operations is often a good measure of popular dissidence, as it was during the Reagan period. Among this group of self-styled "conservatives," the commitment to untrammeled executive power and the contempt for democracy reached unusual heights. Accordingly, so did the resort to propaganda campaigns targeting the media and the general population: for example, the establishment of the State Department Office of Latin American Public Diplomacy dedicated to such projects as Operation Truth, which one high government official described as "a huge psychological operation of the kind the military conducts to influence a population in denied or enemy territory."[45] The terms express lucidly the attitude towards the errant public: enemy territory, which must be conquered and subdued.

In its dependencies, the United States must often turn to violence to "restore democracy." At home, more subtle means are required: the manufacture of consent, deceiving the stupid masses with "necessary illusions," covert operations that the media and Congress pretend not to see until it all becomes too obvious to be suppressed. We then shift to the phase of damage control to ensure that public attention is diverted to overzealous patriots or to the personality defects of leaders who have strayed from our noble commitments, but not to the institutional factors that determine the persistent and substantive content of these commitments. The task of the Free Press, in such circumstances, is to take the proceedings seriously and to describe them as a tribute to the soundness of our self-correcting institutions, which they carefully protect from public scrutiny.

More generally, the media and the educated classes must fulfill their "societal purpose," carrying out their necessary tasks in accord with the prevailing conception of democracy.

2

Containing the Enemy

In the first chapter, I mentioned three models of media organization: (1) corporate oligopoly; (2) state-controlled; (3) a democratic communications policy as advanced by the Brazilian bishops. The first model reduces democratic participation in the media to zero, just as other corporations are, in principle, exempt from popular control by work force or community. In the case of state-controlled media, democratic participation might vary, depending on how the political system functions; in practice, the state media are generally kept in line by the forces that have the power to dominate the state, and by an apparatus of cultural managers who cannot stray far from the bounds these forces set. The third model is largely untried in practice, just as a sociopolitical system with significant popular engagement remains a concern for the future: a hope or a fear, depending on one's evaluation of the right of the public to shape its own affairs.

The model of media as corporate oligopoly is the natural system for capitalist democracy. It has, accordingly, reached its highest form in the most advanced of these societies, particularly the United States, where media concentration is high, public radio and television are limited in scope, and elements of the radical democratic model exist only at the margins, in such phenomena as listener-supported community radio and the alternative or local press, often with a noteworthy effect on the social and political culture and the sense of empowerment in the communities that benefit from these options.[1] In this respect, the United States represents the form towards which capitalist democracy is tending; related tendencies include the progressive elimination of unions and other popular organizations that interfere with private power, an electoral system that is increasingly stage-managed as a public relations exercise, avoidance of welfare measures such as national health insurance that also impinge on the prerogatives of the privileged, and so on. From this perspective, it is reasonable for Cyrus Vance and Henry Kissinger to describe the United States as "a model democracy," democracy being understood as a system of business control of political as well as other major institutions.

Other Western democracies are generally a few steps behind in these respects. Most have not yet achieved the U.S. system of one political party, with two factions controlled by shifting segments of the business community. They still retain parties based on working people and the poor which to some extent represent their interests. But these are declining, along with cultural institutions that sustain different values and concerns, and organizational forms that provide isolated individuals with the means to think and to act outside the framework imposed by private power.

This is the natural course of events under capitalist democracy, because of what Joshua Cohen and Joel Rogers call "the resource constraint" and "the demand constraint."[2] The former is straightforward: control over resources is narrowly concentrated, with predictable effects for every aspect of social and political life. The demand constraint is a more subtle means of control, one whose effects are rarely observed directly in a properly functioning capitalist democracy such as the United States, though they are evident, for example, in Latin America, where the political system sometimes permits a broader range of policy options, including programs of social reform. The consequences are well known: capital flight, loss of business and investor confidence, and general social decline as those who "own the country" lose the capacity to govern it—or simply a military coup, typically backed by the hemispheric guardian of order and good form. The more benign response to reform programs illustrates the demand constraint—the requirement that the interests of those with effective power be satisfied if the society is to function.

In brief, it is necessary to ensure that those who own the country are happy, or else all will suffer, for they control investment and determine what is produced and distributed and what benefits will trickle down to those who rent themselves to the owners when they can. For the homeless in the streets, then, the highest priority must be to ensure that the dwellers in the mansions are reasonably content. Given the options available within the system and the cultural values it reinforces, maximization of short-term individual gain appears to be the rational course, along with submissiveness, obedience, and abandonment of the public arena. The bounds on political action are correspondingly limited. Once the forms of capitalist democracy are in place, they remain very stable, whatever suffering ensues—a fact that has long been understood by U.S. planners.

One consequence of the distribution of resources and decision-making power in the society at large is that the political class and the cultural managers typically associate themselves with the sectors that dominate the private economy; they are either drawn directly from those sectors or expect to join them. The radical democrats of the seventeenth-century English revolution held that "it will never be a good world while knights and gentlemen make us laws, that are chosen for fear and do but oppress us, and do not know the people's sores. It will never be well with us till we have Parliaments of countrymen like ourselves, that know our wants." But Parliament and the preachers had a different vision: "when we mention the people, we do not mean the confused promiscuous body of the people," they held. With the resounding defeat of the democrats, the remaining question, in the words of a Leveller pamphlet, was "whose slaves the poor shall be," the King's or Parliament's.[3]

The same controversy arose in the early days of the American Revolution. "Framers of the state constitutions," Edward Countryman observes, "had insisted that the representative assemblies should closely reflect the people of the state itself"; they objected to a "separate caste" of political leaders insulated from the people. But the Federal Constitution guaranteed that "representatives, senators, and the president all would know that exceptional was just what they were." Under the Confederation, artisans, farmers, and others of the common people had demanded that they be represented by "men of their own kind," having learned from the revolutionary experience that they were "as capable as anyone of deciding what was wrong in their lives and of organizing themselves so they could do something about it." This was not to be. "The last gasp of the original spirit of the Revolution, with all its belief in community and cooperation, came from the Massachusetts farmers" during Shay's rebellion in 1786. "The resolutions and addresses of their county committees in the year or two before the rebellion said exactly what all sorts of people had been saying in 1776." Their failure taught the painful lesson that "the old ways no longer worked," and "they found themselves forced to grovel and beg forgiveness from rulers who claimed to be the people's servants." So it has remained. With the rarest of exceptions, the representatives of the people do not come from or return to the workplace; rather, law offices catering to business interests, executive suites, and other places of privilege.[4]

As for the media, in England a lively labor-oriented press reaching a broad public existed into the 1960s, when it was finally eliminated through the workings of the market. At the time of its demise in 1964, the *Daily Herald* had over five times as many readers as *The Times* and "almost double the readership of *The Times*, the *Financial Times* and the *Guardian* combined," James Curran observes, citing survey research showing that its readers "were also exceptionally devoted to their paper." But this journal, partially owned by the unions and reaching a largely working-class audience, "appealed to the wrong people," Curran continues. The same was true of other elements of the social democratic press that died at the same time, in large part because they were "deprived of the same level of subsidy" through advertising and private capital as sustained "the quality press," which "not only reflects the values and interests of its middle-class readers" but also "gives them force, clarity and coherence" and "plays an important ideological role in amplifying and renewing the dominant political consensus."[5]

The consequences are significant. For the media, Curran concludes, there is "a remarkable growth in advertising-related editorial features" and a "growing convergence between editorial and advertising content" reflecting "the increasing accommodation of national newspaper managements to the selective needs of advertisers" and the business community generally; the same is likely true of news coverage and interpretation. For society at large, Curran continues, "the loss of the only social democratic papers with a large readership which devoted serious attention to current affairs," including sectors of the working class that had remained "remarkably radical in their attitudes to a wide range of economic and political issues," contributed to "the progressive erosion in post-war Britain of a popular radical tradition" and to the disintegration of "the cultural base that has sustained active participation within the Labour movement," which "has ceased to exist as a mass movement in most parts of the country." The effects are readily apparent. With the elimination of the "selection and treatment of news" and "relatively detailed political commentary and analysis [that] helped daily to sustain a social democratic sub-culture within the working class," there is no longer an articulate alternative to the picture of "a world where the subordination of working people [is] accepted as natural and inevitable," and no continuing expression of the view that working people are "morally entitled to a greater share of the wealth they created and a greater say in its allocation." The same tendencies are evident elsewhere in the industrial capitalist societies.

There are, then, natural processes at work to facilitate the control of "enemy territory" at home. Similarly, the global planning undertaken by U.S. elites during and after World War II assumed that principles of liberal internationalism would generally serve to satisfy what had been described as the "requirement of the United States in a world in which it proposes to hold unquestioned power."[6] The global policy goes under the name "containment." The manufacture of consent at home is its domestic counterpart. The two policies are, in fact, closely intertwined, since the domestic population must be mobilized to pay the costs of "containment," which may be severe—both material and moral costs.

The rhetoric of containment is designed to give a defensive cast to the project of global management, and it thus serves as part of the domestic system of thought control. It is remarkable that the terminology is so easily adopted, given the questions that it begs. Looking more closely, we find that the concept conceals a good deal.[7]

The underlying assumption is that there is a stable international order that the United States must defend. The general contours of this international order were developed by U.S. planners during and after World War II. Recognizing the extraordinary scale of U.S. power, they proposed to construct a global system that the United States would dominate and within which U.S. business interests would thrive. As much of the world as possible would constitute a Grand Area, as it was called, which would be subordinated to the needs of the U.S. economy. Within the Grand Area, other capitalist societies would be encouraged to develop, but without protective devices that would interfere with U.S. prerogatives.[8] In particular, only the United States would be permitted to dominate regional systems. The United States moved to take effective control of world energy production and to organize a world system in which its various components would fulfill their functions as industrial centers, as markets and sources of raw materials, or as dependent states pursuing their "regional interests" within the "overall framework of order" managed by the United States (as Henry Kissinger was later to explain).

The Soviet Union has been considered the major threat to the planned international order, for good reason. In part this follows from its very existence as a great power controlling an imperial system that could not be incorporated within the Grand Area; in part from its occasional efforts to expand the domains of its power, as in Afghanistan, and the alleged threat of invasion of Western Europe, if not world conquest, a prospect regularly discounted by more serious analysts in public and in internal documents. But it is necessary to understand how broadly the concept of "defense" is construed if we wish to evaluate the assessment of Soviet crimes. Thus the Soviet Union is a threat to world order if it supports people opposing U.S. designs, for example, the South Vietnamese engaging in "internal aggression" against their selfless American defenders (as explained by the Kennedy liberals), or Nicaraguans illegimately combating the depredations of the U.S.-run "democratic resistance." Such actions prove that Soviet leaders are not serious about détente and cannot be trusted, statesmen and commentators soberly observe. Thus, "Nicaragua will be a prime place to test the sanguine forecast that [Gorbachev] is now turning down the heat in the Third World," the *Washington Post* editors explain, placing the onus for the U.S. attack against Nicaragua on the Russians while warning of the threat of this Soviet outpost to "overwhelm and terrorize" its neighbors.[9] The United States will have "won the Cold War," from this point of view, when it is free to exercise its will in the rest of the world without Soviet interference.

Though "containing the Soviet Union" has been the dominant theme of U.S. foreign policy only since the United States became a truly global power after World War II, the Soviet Union had been considered an intolerable threat to order since the Bolshevik revolution. Accordingly, it has been the main enemy of the independent media.

In 1920 Walter Lippmann and Charles Merz produced a critical study of *New York Times* coverage of the Bolshevik revolution, describing it as "nothing short of a disaster ... from the point of view of professional journalism." Editorial policy, deeply hostile, "profoundly and crassly influenced their news columns." "For subjective reasons," the *Times* staff "accepted and believed most of what they were told" by the U.S. government and "the agents and adherents of the old regime." They dismissed Soviet peace offers as merely a tactic to enable the Bolsheviks to "concentrate their energies for a renewed drive toward world-wide revolution" and the imminent "Red invasion of Europe." The Bolsheviks, Lippmann and Merz wrote, were portrayed as "simultaneously ... both cadaver and world-wide menace," and the Red Peril "appeared at every turn to obstruct the restoration of peace in Eastern Europe and Asia and to frustrate the resumption of economic life." When President Wilson called for intervention, the *New York Times* responded by urging that we drive "the Bolsheviki out of Petrograd and Moscow."[10]

Change a few names and dates, and we have a rather fair appraisal of the treatment of Indochina yesterday and Central America today by the national media. Similar assumptions about the Soviet Union are reiterated by contemporary diplomatic historians who regard the development of an alternative social model as in itself an intolerable form of intervention in the affairs of others, against which the West has been fully entitled to defend itself by forceful action in retaliation, including the defense of the West by military intervention in the Soviet Union after the Bolshevik revolution.[11] Under these assumptions, widely held and respected, aggression easily becomes self-defense.

Returning to post-World War II policy and ideology, it is, of course, unnecessary to *contrive* reasons to oppose the brutality of the Soviet leaders in dominating their internal empire and their dependencies while cheerfully assisting such contemporary monsters as the Ethiopian military junta or the neo-Nazi generals in Argentina. But an honest review will show that the primary enemies have been the indigenous populations within the Grand Area, who fall prey to the wrong ideas. It then becomes necessary to overcome these deviations by economic, ideological, or military warfare, or by terror and subversion. The domestic population must be rallied to the cause, in defense against "Communism."

These are the basic elements of containment in practice abroad, and of its domestic counterpart within. With regard to the Soviet Union, the concept has had two variants over the years. The doves were reconciled to a form of containment in which the Soviet Union would dominate roughly the areas occupied by the Red Army in the war against Hitler. The hawks had much broader aspirations, as expressed in the "rollback strategy" outlined in NSC 68 of April 1950, shortly before the Korean war. This crucial document, made public in 1975, interpreted containment as intended to "foster the seeds of destruction within the Soviet system" and make it possible to "negotiate a settlement with the Soviet Union (or a successor state or states)." In the early postwar years, the United States supported armies established by Hitler in the Ukraine and Eastern Europe, with the assistance of such figures as Reinhard Gehlen, who headed Nazi military intelligence on the Eastern front and was placed in charge of the espionage service of West Germany under close CIA supervision, assigned the task of developing a "secret army" of thousands of SS men to assist the forces fighting within the Soviet Union. So remote are these facts from conventional understanding that a highly knowledgeable foreign affairs specialist at the liberal *Boston Globe* could condemn tacit U.S. support for the Khmer Rouge by offering the following analogy, as the ultimate absurdity: "It is as if the United States had winked at the presence of a Nazi guerrilla movement to harass the Soviets in 1945"—exactly what the United States was doing into the early 1950s, and not just winking.[12]

It is also considered entirely natural that the Soviet Union should be surrounded by hostile powers, facing with equanimity major NATO bases with missiles on alert status as in Turkey, while if Nicaragua obtains jet planes to defend its airspace against regular U.S. penetration, this is considered by doves and hawks alike to warrant U.S. military action to protect ourselves from this grave threat to our security, in accordance with the doctrine of "containment."

Establishment of Grand Area principles abroad and necessary illusions at home does not simply await the hidden hand of the market. Liberal internationalism must be supplemented by the periodic resort to forceful intervention.[13] At home, the state has often employed force to curb dissent, and there have been been regular and quite self-conscious campaigns by business to control "the public mind" and suppress challenges to private power when implicit controls do not suffice. The ideology of "anti-Communism" has served this purpose since World War I, with intermittent exceptions. In earlier years, the United States was defending itself from other evil forces: the Huns, the British, the Spanish, the Mexicans, the Canadian Papists, and the "merciless Indian savages" of the Declaration of Independence. But since the Bolshevik revolution, and particularly in the era of bipolar world power that emerged from the ashes of World War II, a more credible enemy has been the "monolithic and ruthless conspiracy" that seeks to subvert our noble endeavors, in John F. Kennedy's phrase: Ronald Reagan's "Evil Empire."

In the early Cold War years, Dean Acheson and Paul Nitze planned to "bludgeon the mass mind of 'top government'," as Acheson put it with reference to NSC 68. They presented "a frightening portrayal of the Communist threat, in order to overcome public, business, and congressional desires for peace, low taxes, and 'sound' fiscal policies" and to mobilize popular support for the full-scale rearmament that they felt was necessary "to overcome Communist ideology and Western economic vulnerability," William Borden observes in a study of postwar planning. The Korean War served these purposes admirably. The ambiguous and complex interactions that led to the war were ignored in favor of the more useful image of a Kremlin campaign of world conquest. Dean Acheson, meanwhile, remarked that in the Korean hostilities "an excellent opportunity is here offered to disrupt the Soviet peace offensive, which ... is assuming serious proportions and having a certain effect on public opinion." The structure of much of the subsequent era was determined by these manipulations, which also provided a standard for later practice.[14]

In earlier years, Woodrow Wilson's Red Scare demolished unions and other dissident elements. A prominent feature was the suppression of independent politics and free speech, on the principle that the state is entitled to prevent improper thought and its expression. Wilson's Creel Commission, dedicated to creating war fever among the generally pacifist population, had demonstrated the efficacy of organized propaganda with the cooperation of the loyal media and the intellectuals, who devoted themselves to such tasks as "historical engineering," the term devised by historian Frederic Paxson, one of the founders of the National Board for Historical Service established by U.S. historians to serve the state by "explaining the issues of the war that we might the better win it." The lesson was learned by those in a position to employ it. Two lasting institutional consequences were the rise of the public relations industry, one of whose leading figures, Edward Bernays, had served on the wartime propaganda commission, and the establishment of the FBI as, in effect, a national political police. This is a primary function it has continued to serve as illustrated, for example, by its criminal acts to undermine the rising "crisis of democracy" in the 1960s and the surveillance and disruption of popular opposition to U.S. intervention in Central America twenty years later.[15]

The effectiveness of the state-corporate propaganda system is illustrated by the fate of May Day, a workers' holiday throughout the world that originated in response to the judicial murder of several anarchists after the Haymarket affair of May 1886, in a campaign of international solidarity with U.S. workers struggling for an eight-hour day. In the United States, all has been forgotten. May Day has become "Law Day," a jingoist celebration of our "200-year-old partnership between law and liberty" as Ronald Reagan declared while designating May 1 as Law Day 1984, adding that without law there can be only "chaos and disorder." The day before, he had announced that the United States would disregard the proceedings of the International Court of Justice that later condemned the U.S. government for its "unlawful use of force" and violation of treaties in its attack against Nicaragua. "Law Day" also served as the occasion for Reagan's declaration of May 1, 1985, announcing an embargo against Nicaragua "in response to the emergency situation created by the Nicaraguan Government's aggressive activities in Central America," actually declaring a "national emergency," since renewed annually, because "the policies and actions of the Government of Nicaragua constitute an unusual and extraordinary threat to the national security and foreign policy of the United States"—all with the approbation of Congress, the media, and the intellectual community generally; or, in some circles, embarrassed silence.

The submissiveness of the society to business dominance, secured by Wilson's Red Scare, began to erode during the Great Depression. In 1938 the board of directors of the National Association of Manufacturers, adopting the Marxist rhetoric that is common in the internal records of business and government documents, described the "hazard facing industrialists" in "the newly realized political power of the masses"; "Unless their thinking is directed," it warned, "we are definitely headed for adversity." No less threatening was the rise of labor organization, in part with the support of industrialists who perceived it as a means to regularize labor markets. But too much is too much, and business soon rallied to overcome the threat by the device of "employer mobilization of the public" to crush strikes, as an academic study of the 1937 Johnstown steel strike observed. This "formula," the business community exulted, was one that "business has hoped for, dreamed of, and prayed for." Combined with strongarm methods, propaganda campaigns were used effectively to subdue the labor movement in subsequent years. These campaigns spent millions of dollars "to tell the public that nothing was wrong and that grave dangers lurked in the proposed remedies" of the unions, the La Follette Committee of the Senate observed in its study of business propaganda.[16]

In the postwar period the public relations campaign intensified, employing the media and other devices to identify so-called free enterprise—meaning state-subsidized private profit with no infringement on managerial prerogatives—as "the American way," threatened by dangerous subversives. In 1954, Daniel Bell, then an editor of *Fortune* magazine, wrote that

> It has been industry's prime concern, in the post war years, to change the climate of opinion ushered in by ... the depression. This 'free enterprise' campaign has two essential aims: to rewin

the loyalty of the worker which now goes to the union and to
halt creeping socialism,

that is, the mildly reformist capitalism of the New Deal. The scale of
business public relations campaigns, Bell continued, was "staggering," through advertising in press and radio and other means.[17] The
effects were seen in legislation to constrain union activity, the attack
on independent thought often mislabeled McCarthyism, and the
elimination of any articulate challenge to business domination. The
media and intellectual community cooperated with enthusiasm. The
universities, in particular, were purged, and remained so until the
"crisis of democracy" dawned and students and younger faculty
began to ask the wrong kinds of questions. That elicited a renewed
though less effective purge, while in a further resort to "necessary
illusion," it was claimed, and still is, that the universities were virtually taken over by left-wing totalitarians—meaning that the grip of
orthodoxy was somewhat relaxed.[18]

As early as 1947 a State Department public relations officer
remarked that "smart public relations [has] paid off as it has before
and will again." Public opinion "is not moving to the right, it has been
moved—cleverly—to the right." "While the rest of the world has
moved to the left, has admitted labor into government, has passed
liberalized legislation, the United States has become anti-social
change, anti-economic change, anti-labor."[19]

By that time, "the rest of the world" was being subjected to
similar pressures, as the Truman administration, reflecting the concerns of the business community, acted vigorously to arrest such
tendencies in Europe, Japan, and elsewhere, through means ranging
from extreme violence to control of desperately needed food, diplomatic pressures, and a wide range of other devices.[20]

All of this is much too little understood, but I cannot pursue it
properly here. Throughout the modern period, measures to control
"the public mind" have been employed to enhance the natural pressures of the "free market," the domestic counterpart to intervention
in the global system.

It is worthy of note that with all the talk of liberal free trade
policies, the two major sectors of the U.S. economy that remain
competitive in world trade—high-technology industry and capital-
intensive agriculture—both rely heavily on state subsidy and a state-
guaranteed market.[21] As in other industrial societies, the U.S.
economy had developed in earlier years through protectionist mea-

sures. In the postwar period, the United States grandly proclaimed liberal principles on the assumption that U.S. investors would prevail in any competition, a plausible expectation in the light of the economic realities of the time, and one that was fulfilled for many years. For similar reasons, Great Britain had been a passionate advocate of free trade during the period of its hegemony, abandoning these doctrines and the lofty rhetoric that accompanied them in the interwar period, when it could not withstand competition from Japan. The United States is pursuing much the same course today in the face of similar challenges, which were quite unexpected forty years ago, indeed until the Vietnam War. Its unanticipated costs weakened the U.S. economy while strengthening its industrial rivals, who enriched themselves through their participation in the destruction of Indochina. South Korea owes its economic take-off to these opportunities, which also provided an important stimulus to the Japanese economy, just as the Korean War launched Japan's economic recovery and made a major contribution to Europe's. Another example is Canada, which became the world's largest per capita exporter of war materiel during the Vietnam years, while deploring the immorality of the U.S. war to which it was enthusiastically contributing.

Operations of domestic thought control are commonly undertaken in the wake of wars and other crises. Such turmoil tends to encourage the "crisis of democracy" that is the persistent fear of privileged elites, requiring measures to reverse the thrust of popular democracy that threatens established power. Wilson's Red Scare served the purpose after World War I, and the pattern was re-enacted when World War II ended. It was necessary not only to overcome the popular mobilization that took place during the Great Depression but also "to bring people up to [the] realization that the war isn't over by any means," as presidential adviser Clark Clifford observed when the Truman Doctrine was announced in 1947, "the opening gun in [this] campaign."

The Vietnam war and the popular movements of the 1960s elicited similar concerns. The inhabitants of "enemy territory" at home had to be controlled and suppressed, so as to restore the ability of U.S. corporations to compete in the more diverse world market by reducing real wages and welfare benefits and weakening working-class organization. Young people in particular had to be convinced that they must be concerned only for themselves, in a "culture of narcissism"; every person may know, in private, that the assumptions are not true for them, but at a time of life when one is insecure about personal identity and social place, it is all too tempting to adapt to what the propaganda system asserts to be the norm. Other newly mobilized sectors of the "special interests" also had to be restrained or dissolved, tasks that sometimes required a degree of force, as in the programs of the FBI to undermine the ethnic movements and other elements of the rising dissident culture by instigating violence or its direct exercise, and by other means of intimidation and harassment. Another task was to overcome the dread "Vietnam syndrome," which impeded the resort to forceful means to control the dependencies; as explained by *Commentary* editor Norman Podhoretz, the task was to overcome "the sickly inhibitions against the use of military force" that developed in revulsion against the Indochina wars,[22] a problem that was resolved, he hoped, in the glorious conquest of Grenada, when 6,000 elite troops succeeded in overcoming the resistance of several dozen Cubans and some Grenadan militiamen, winning 8,000 medals of honor for their prowess.

To overcome the Vietnam syndrome, it was necessary to present the United States as the aggrieved party and the Vietnamese as the aggressors—a difficult task, it might be thought by those unfamiliar with the measures available for controlling the public mind, or at least those elements of it that count. By the late stages of the war, the general population was out of control, with a large majority regarding the war as "fundamentally wrong and immoral" and not "a mistake," as polls reveal up to the present. Educated elites, in contrast, posed no serious problem. Contrary to the retrospective necessary illusion fostered by those who now declare themselves "early opponents of the war," in reality there was only the most scattered opposition to the war among these circles, apart from concern over the prospects for success and the rising costs. Even the harshest critics of the war within the mainstream rarely went beyond agonizing over good intentions gone awry, reaching even that level of dissent well after corporate America had determined that the enterprise was proving too costly and should be liquidated, a fact that I have documented elsewhere.

The mechanisms by which a more satisfactory version of history was established have also been reviewed elsewhere,[23] but a few words are in order as to their remarkable success. By 1977 President Carter was able to explain in a news conference that Americans have no need "to apologize or to castigate ourselves or to assume the status of culpability" and do not "owe a debt," because our intentions were "to defend the freedom of the South Vietnamese" (by destroying their

country and massacring the population), and because "the destruction was mutual"—a pronouncement that, to my knowledge, passed
without comment, apparently being considered quite reasonable.[24]
Such balanced judgments are, incidentally, not limited to soulful
advocates of human rights. They are produced regularly, evoking no
comment. To take a recent case, after the U.S. warship *Vincennes* shot
down an Iranian civilian airliner over Iranian territorial waters, the
Boston Globe ran a column by political scientist Jerry Hough of Duke
University and the Brookings Institute in which he explained:

> If the disaster in the downing of the Iranian airliner leads this
> country to move away from its obsession with symbolic nuclear-
> arms control and to concentrate on the problems of war-fighting,
> command-and-control of the military and limitations on conven-
> tional weapons (certainly including the fleet), then 290 people
> will not have died in vain

—an assessment that differs slightly from the media barrage after the
downing of KAL 007. A few months later, the *Vincennes* returned to
its home port to "a boisterous flag-waving welcome ... complete with
balloons and a Navy band playing upbeat songs" while the ship's
"loudspeaker blared the theme from the movie 'Chariots of Fire' and
nearby Navy ships saluted with gunfire." Navy officials did not want
the ship "to sneak into port," a public affairs officer said.[25] So much
for the 290 Iranians.

A *New York Times* editorial obliquely took exception to President Carter's interesting moral judgment. Under the heading "The
Indochina Debt that Lingers," the editors observed that "no debate
over who owes whom how much can be allowed to obscure the worst
horrors [of] ... our involvement in Southeast Asia," referring to the
"horrors experienced by many of those in flight" from the Communist monsters—at the time, a small fraction of the many hundreds of
thousands fleeing their homes in Asia, including over 100,000 boat
people from the Philippines in 1977 and thousands fleeing U.S.-
backed terror in Timor, not to speak of tens of thousands more
escaping the U.S.-backed terror states of Latin America, none of
whom merited such concern or even more than cursory notice in the
news columns, if that.[26] Other horrors in the wreckage of Indochina
are unmentioned, and surely impose no lingering debt.

A few years later, concerns mounted that "The Debt to the
Indochinese Is Becoming a Fiscal Drain," in the words of a *Times*
headline, referring to the "moral debt" incurred through our "in-

volvement on the losing side in Indochina"; by the same logic, had the Russians won the war in Afghanistan, they would owe no debt at all. But now our debt is fully "paid," a State Department official explained. We had settled the moral account by taking in Vietnamese refugees fleeing the lands we ravaged, "one of the largest, most dramatic humanitarian efforts in history," according to Roger Winter, director of the U.S. Committee for Refugees. But "despite the pride," *Times* diplomatic correspondent Bernard Gwertzman continues, "some voices in the Reagan Administration and in Congress are once again asking whether the war debt has now been paid."[27]

It is beyond imagining in responsible circles that we might have some culpability for mass slaughter and destruction, or owe some debt to the millions of maimed and orphaned, or to the peasants who still die from exploding ordnance left from the U.S. assault, while the Pentagon, when asked whether there is any way to remove the hundreds of thousands of anti-personnel bomblets that kill children today in such areas as the Plain of Jars in Laos, comments helpfully that "people should not live in those areas. They know the problem." The United States has refused even to give its mine maps of Indochina to civilian mine-deactivation teams. Ex-marines who visited Vietnam in 1989 to help remove mines they had laid report that many remain in areas were people try to farm and plant trees, and were informed that many people are still being injured and killed as of January 1989.[28] None of this merits comment or concern.

The situation is of course quite different when we turn to Afghanistan—where, incidentally, the Soviet-installed regime *has* released its mine maps. In this case, headlines read: "Soviets Leave Deadly Legacy for Afghans," "Mines Put Afghans in Peril on Return," "U.S. Rebukes Soviets on Afghan Mine Clearing," "U.S. to Help Train Refugees To Destroy Afghan Mines," "Mines Left by Departing Soviets Are Maiming Afghans," and so on. The difference is that these are Soviet mines, so it is only natural for the United States to call for "an international effort to provide the refugees with training and equipment to destroy or dismantle" them and to denounce the Russians for their lack of cooperation in this worthy endeavor. "The Soviets will not acknowledge the problem they have created or help solve it," Assistant Secretary of State Richard Williamson observed sadly; "We are disappointed." The press responds with the usual selective humanitarian zeal.[29]

The media are not satisfied with "mutual destruction" that effaces all responsibility for major war crimes. Rather, the burden of guilt must be shifted to the victims. Under the heading "Vietnam, Trying to be Nicer, Still has a Long Way to Go," *Times* Asia correspondent Barbara Crossette quotes Charles Printz of Human Rights Advocates International, who said that "It's about time the Vietnamese demonstrated some good will." Printz was referring to negotiations about the Amerasian children who constitute a tiny fraction of the victims of U.S. aggression in Indochina. Crossette adds that the Vietnamese have also not been sufficiently forthcoming on the matter of remains of American soldiers, though their behavior may be improving: "There has been progress, albeit slow, on the missing Americans." But the Vietnamese have not yet paid their debt to us, so humanitarian concerns left by the war remain unresolved.[30]

Returning to the same matter, Crossette explains that the Vietnamese do not comprehend their "irrelevance" to Americans, apart from the moral issues that are still outstanding—specifically, Vietnamese recalcitrance "on the issue of American servicemen missing since the end of the war." Dismissing Vietnamese "laments" about U.S. unwillingness to improve relations, Crossette quotes an "Asian official" who said that "if Hanoi's leaders are serious about building their country, the Vietnamese will have to deal fairly with the United States." She also quotes a Pentagon statement expressing the hope that Hanoi will take action "to resolve this long-standing humanitarian issue" of the remains of U.S. servicemen shot down over North Vietnam by the evil Communists—the only humanitarian issue that comes to mind, apparently, when we consider the legacy of a war that left many millions of dead and wounded in Indochina and three countries in utter ruins. Another report deplores Vietnamese refusal to cooperate "in key humanitarian areas," quoting liberal congressmen on Hanoi's "horrible and cruel" behavior and Hanoi's responsibility for lack of progress on humanitarian issues, namely, the matter of U.S. servicemen "still missing from the Vietnam war." Hanoi's recalcitrance "brought back the bitter memories that Vietnam can still evoke" among the suffering Americans.[31]

The nature of the concern "to resolve this long-standing humanitarian issue" of the American servicemen missing in action (MIAs) is illuminated by some statistics cited by historian (and Vietnam veteran) Terry Anderson:

> The French still have 20,000 MIAs from their war in Indochina, and the Vietnamese list over 200,000. Furthermore, the United States still has 80,000 MIAs from World War II and 8,000 from the Korean War, figures that represent 20 and 15 percent, respec-

tively, of the confirmed dead in those conflicts; the percentage is 4 percent for the Vietnam War.[32]

The French have established diplomatic relations with Vietnam, as the Americans did with Germany and Japan, Anderson observes, adding: "We won in 1945, of course, so it seems that MIAs only are important when the United States loses the war. The real 'noble cause' for [the Reagan] administration is not the former war but its emotional and impossible crusade to retrieve 'all recoverable remains'." More precisely, the "noble cause" is to exploit personal tragedy for political ends: to overcome the Vietnam syndrome at home, and to "bleed Vietnam."

The influential House Democrat Lee Hamilton writes that "almost 15 years after the Vietnam war, Southeast Asia remains a region of major humanitarian, strategic, and economic concern to the United States." The humanitarian concern includes two cases: (1) "Nearly 2,400 American servicemen are unaccounted for in Indochina"; (2) "More than 1 million Cambodians died under Pol Pot's ruthless Khmer Rouge regime." The far greater numbers of Indochinese who died under Washington's ruthless attack, and who still do die, fall below the threshold. We should, Hamilton continues, "reassess our relations with Vietnam" and seek a "new relationship," though not abandoning our humanitarian concerns: "This may be an opportune time for policies that mix continued pressure with rewards for progress on missing US servicemen and diplomatic concessions in Cambodia." At the left-liberal end of the spectrum, in the journal of the Center for International Policy, a project of the Fund for Peace, a senior associate of the Carnegie Foundation for International Peace calls for reconciliation with Vietnam, urging that we put aside "the agony of the Vietnam experience" and "the injuries of the past, " and overcome the "hatred, anger, and frustration" caused us by the Vietnamese, though we must not forget "the humanitarian issues left over from the war": the MIAs, those qualified to emigrate to the United States, and the remaining inmates of reeducation camps. So profound are the humanitarian impulses that guide this deeply moral society that even the right-wing Senator John McCain is now calling for diplomatic relations with Vietnam. He says that he holds "no hatred" for the Vietnamese even though he is "a former Navy pilot who spent 5 1/2 years as an unwilling guest in the Hanoi Hilton," editor David Greenway of the *Boston Globe* comments, adding that "If McCain can put aside his bitterness, so can we all."[33] Greenway knows Vietnam well, having compiled an outstanding record as a war correspondent there. But in the prevailing moral climate, the educated community he addresses would not find it odd to urge that we overcome our natural bitterness against the Vietnamese for what they did to us.

"In history," Francis Jennings observes, "the man in the ruffled shirt and gold-laced waistcoat somehow levitates above the blood he has ordered to be spilled by dirty-handed underlings."[34]

These examples illustrate the power of the system that manufactures necessary illusions, at least among the educated elites who are the prime targets of propaganda, and its purveyors. It would be difficult to conjure up an achievement that might lie beyond the reach of mechanisms of indoctrination that can portray the United States as an innocent victim of Vietnam, while at the same time pondering the nation's excesses of self-flagellation.

Journalists not subject to the same influences and requirements see a somewhat different picture. In an Israeli mass-circulation daily, Amnon Kapeliouk published a series of thoughtful and sympathetic articles on a 1988 visit to Vietnam. One is headlined "Thousands of Vietnamese still die from the effects of American chemical warfare." He reports estimates of one-quarter of a million victims in South Vietnam in addition to the thousands killed by unexploded ordnance—3,700 since 1975 in the Danang area alone. Kapeliouk describes the "terrifying" scenes in hospitals in the south with children dying of cancer and hideous birth deformities; it was South Vietnam, of course, that was targeted for chemical warfare, not the North, where these consequences are not found, he reports. There is little hope for amelioration in the coming years, Vietnamese doctors fear, as the effects linger on in the devastated southern region of this "bereaved country," with its millions of dead and millions more widows and orphans, and where one hears "hair-raising stories that remind me of what we heard during the trials of Eichmann and Demjanjuk" from victims who, remarkably, "express no hatred against the American people." In this case, of course, the perpetrators are not tried, but are honored for their crimes in the civilized Western world.[35]

Here too, some have been concerned over the effects of the chemical warfare that sprayed millions of gallons of Agent Orange and other poisonous chemicals over an area the size of Massachusetts in South Vietnam, more in Laos and Cambodia. Dr. Grace Ziem, a specialist on chemical exposure and disease who teaches at the

University of Maryland Medical School, addressed the topic after a two-week visit to Vietnam, where she had worked as a doctor in the 1960s. She too described visits to hospitals in the south, where she inspected the sealed transparent containers with hideously mal-formed babies and the many patients from heavily sprayed areas, women with extremely rare malignant tumors and children with deformities found far beyond the norm. But her account appeared far from the mainstream, where the story, when reported at all, has quite a different cast and focus. Thus, in an article on how the Japanese are attempting to conceal their World War II crimes, we read that one Japanese apologist referred to U.S. troops who scattered poisons by helicopter; "presumably," the reporter explains, he was referring to "Agent Orange, a defoliant suspected to have caused birth defects among Vietnamese and the children of American servicemen." No further reflections are suggested, in this context. And we can read about "the $180 million in chemical companies' compensation to Agent Orange victims"—U.S. soldiers, that is, not the Vietnamese civilians whose suffering is vastly greater. And somehow, these matters scarcely arose as indignation swelled in 1988 over alleged plans by Libya to develop chemical weapons.[36]

The right turn among elites took political shape during the latter years of the Carter administration and in the Reagan years, when the proposed policies were implemented and extended with a bipartisan consensus. But, as the Reaganite state managers discovered, the "Vietnam syndrome" proved to be a tough nut to crack; hence the vast increase in clandestine operations as the state was driven under-ground by the domestic enemy.

As it became necessary by the mid-1980s to face the costs of Reaganite military Keynesian policies, including the huge budget and trade deficits and foreign debt, it was predictable, and predicted, that the "Evil Empire" would become less threatening and the plague of international terrorism would subside, not so much because the world was all that different, but because of the new problems faced by the state management. Several years later, the results are apparent. Among the very ideologues who were ranting about the ineradicable evil of the Soviet barbarians and their minions, the statesmanlike approach is now mandatory, along with summitry and arms negoti-ations. But the basic long-term problems remain, and will have to be addressed.

Throughout this period of U.S. global hegemony, exalted rhet-oric aside, there has been no hesitation to resort to force if the welfare of U.S. elites is threatened by what secret documents describe as the threat of "nationalistic regimes" that are responsive to popular demands for "improvement in the low living standards of the masses" and production for domestic needs, and that seek to control their own resources. To counter such threats, high-level planning documents explain, the United States must encourage "a political and economic climate conducive to private investment of both foreign and domestic capital," including the "opportunity to earn and in the case of foreign capital to repatriate a reasonable return."[37] The means, it is frankly explained, must ultimately be force, since such policies somehow fail to gain much popular support and are constantly threatened by the subversive elements called "Communist."

In the Third World, we must ensure "the protection of our raw materials" (as George Kennan put it) and encourage export-oriented production, maintaining a framework of liberal internationalism—at least insofar as it serves the needs of U.S. investors. Internationally, as at home, the free market is an ideal to be lauded if its outcome accords with the perceived needs of domestic power and privilege; if not, the market must be guided by efficient use of state power.

If the media, and the respectable intellectual community generally, are to serve their "societal purpose," such matters as these must be kept beyond the pale, remote from public awareness, and the massive evidence provided by the documentary record and evolving history must be consigned to dusty archives or marginal publications. We may speak in retrospect of blunders, misinterpretation, exaggeration of the Communist threat, faulty assessments of national security, personal failings, even corruption and deceit on the part of leaders gone astray; but the study of institutions and how they function must be scrupulously ignored, apart from fringe elements or a relatively obscure scholarly literature. These results have been quite satisfactorily achieved.

In capitalist democracies of the Third World, the situation is often much the same. Costa Rica, for example, is rightly regarded as the model democracy of Latin America. The press is firmly in the hands of the ultra-right, so there need be no concern over freedom of the press in Costa Rica, and none is expressed. In this case, the result was achieved not by force but rather by the free market assisted by legal measures to control "Communists," and, it appears, by an influx of North American capital in the 1960s.

Where such means have not sufficed to enforce the approved version of democracy and freedom of the press, others are readily available and are apparently considered right and proper, so long as they succeed. El Salvador in the past decade provides a dramatic illustration. In the 1970s there was a proliferation of "popular organizations," many sponsored by the Church, including peasant associations, self-help groups, unions, and so on. The reaction was a violent outburst of state terror, organized by the United States with bipartisan backing and general media support as well. Any residual qualms dissolved after "demonstration elections" had been conducted for the benefit of the home front,[38] while the Reagan administration ordered a reduction in the more visible atrocities when the population was judged to be sufficiently traumatized and it was feared that reports of torture, murder, mutilation, and disappearance might endanger funding and support for the lower levels of state terror still deemed necessary.

There had been an independent press in El Salvador: two small newspapers, *La Crónica del Pueblo* and *El Independiente*. Both were destroyed in 1980-81 by the security forces. After a series of bombings, an editor of *La Crónica* and a photographer were taken from a San Salvador coffee shop and hacked to pieces with machetes; the offices were raided, bombed, and burned down by death squads, and the publisher fled to the United States. The publisher of *El Independiente*, Jorge Pinto, fled to Mexico when his paper's premises were attacked and equipment smashed by troops. Concern over these matters was so high in the United States that there was not one word in the *New York Times* news columns and not one editorial comment on the destruction of the journals, and no word in the years since, though Pinto was permitted a statement on the opinion page, in which he condemned the "Duarte junta" for having "succeeded in extinguishing the expression of any dissident opinion" and expressed his belief that the so-called death squads are "nothing more nor less than the military itself"—a conclusion endorsed by the Church and international human rights monitors.

In the year before the final destruction of *El Independiente*, the offices were bombed twice, an office boy was killed when the plant was machine-gunned, Pinto's car was sprayed with machine-gun fire, there were two other attempts on his life, and army troops in tanks and armored trucks arrived at his offices to search for him two days before the paper was finally destroyed. These events received no mention. Shortly before it was finally destroyed, there had been four bombings of *La Crónica* in six months; one of these, the last, received forty words in the *New York Times*.[39]

It is not that the U.S. media are unconcerned with freedom of the press in Central America. Contrasting sharply with the silence over the two Salvadoran newspapers is the case of the opposition journal *La Prensa* in Nicaragua. Media critic Francisco Goldman counted 263 references to its tribulations in the *New York Times* in four years.[40] The distinguishing criterion is not obscure: the Salvadoran newspapers were independent voices stilled by the murderous violence of U.S. clients; *La Prensa* is an agency of the U.S. campaign to overthrow the government of Nicaragua, therefore a "worthy victim," whose harassment calls forth anguish and outrage. We return to further evidence that this is indeed the operative criterion.

Several months before his paper was destroyed, Dr. Jorge Napoleón Gonzales, the publisher of *La Crónica,* visited New York to plead for international pressure to "deter terrorists from destroying his paper." He cited right-wing threats and "what [his paper] calls Government repression," the *Times* noted judiciously. He reported that he had received threats from a death squad "that undoubtedly enjoys the support of the military," that two bombs had been found in his house, that the paper's offices were machine-gunned and set afire and his home surrounded by soldiers. These problems began, he said, when his paper "began to demand reforms in landholdings," angering "the dominant classes." No international pressure developed, and the security forces completed their work.[41]

In the same years, the Church radio station in El Salvador was repeatedly bombed and troops occupied the Archdiocese building, destroying the radio station and ransacking the newspaper offices. Again, this elicited no media reaction.

These matters did not arise in the enthusiastic reporting of El Salvador's "free elections" in 1982 and 1984. Later we were regularly informed by *Times* Central America correspondent James LeMoyne that the country enjoyed greater freedom than enemy Nicaragua, where nothing remotely comparable to the Salvadoran atrocities had taken place, and opposition leaders and media that are funded by the U.S. government and openly support its attack against Nicaragua complain of harassment, but not terror and assassination. Nor would the *Times* Central America correspondents report that leading Church figures who fled from El Salvador (including a close associate of the assassinated Archbishop Romero), well-known Salvadoran writers, and others who are by no stretch of the imagination political activists, and who are well-known to *Times* correspondents, cannot return to the death squad democracy they praise and protect, for fear of assassination. *Times* editors call upon the Reagan administration to use "its pressure on behalf of peace and pluralism in Nicaragua," where the government had a "dreadful record" of "harassing those who dare to exercise ... free speech," and where there had never been "a free, contested election."[42] No such strictures apply to El Salvador.

In such ways, the Free Press labors to implant the illusions that are necessary to contain the domestic enemy.

3

The Bounds of the Expressible

While recognizing that there is rarely anything strictly new under the sun, still we can identify some moments when traditional ideas are reshaped, a new consciousness crystallizes, and the opportunities that lie ahead appear in a new light. Fabrication of necessary illusions for social management is as old as history, but the year 1917 might be seen as a transition point in the modern period. The Bolshevik revolution gave concrete expression to the Leninist conception of the radical intelligentsia as the vanguard of social progress, exploiting popular struggles to gain state power and to impose the rule of the "Red bureaucracy" of Bakunin's forebodings. This they proceeded at once to do, dismantling factory councils, Soviets, and other forms of popular organization so that the population could be effectively mobilized into a "labor army" under the control of far-sighted leaders who would drive the society forward—with the best intentions, of course. To this end, the mechanisms of Agitprop are fundamental; even a totalitarian state of the Hitler or Stalin variety relies on mass mobilization and voluntary submission.

One notable doctrine of Soviet propaganda is that the elimination by Lenin and Trotsky of any vestige of control over production by producers and of popular involvement in determining social policy constitutes a triumph of socialism. The purpose of this exercise in Newspeak is to exploit the moral appeal of the ideals that were being successfully demolished. Western propaganda leaped to the same opportunity, identifying the dismantling of socialist forms as the establishment of socialism, so as to undermine left-libertarian ideals by associating them with the practices of the grim Red bureaucracy. To this day, both systems of propaganda adopt the terminology, for their different purposes. When both major world systems of propaganda are in accord, it is unusually difficult for the individual to escape their tentacles. The blow to freedom and democracy throughout the world has been immense.

In the same year, 1917, John Dewey's circle of liberal pragmatists took credit for guiding a pacifist population to war "under the influence of a moral verdict reached after the utmost deliberation by the more thoughtful members of the community, ... a class which must be comprehensively but loosely described as the 'intellectuals'," who, they held, had "accomplished ... the effective and decisive work on behalf of the war."[1] This achievement, or at least the self-perception articulated, had broad consequences. Dewey, the intellectual mentor, explained that this "psychological and educational lesson" had proven "that it is possible for human beings to take hold of human affairs and manage them." The "human beings" who had learned the lesson were "the intelligent men of the community," Lippmann's "specialized class," Niebuhr's "cool observers." They must now apply their talents and understanding "to bring about a better reorganized social order," by planning, persuasion, or force where necessary; but, Dewey insisted, only the "refined, subtle and indirect use of force," not the "coarse, obvious and direct methods" employed prior to the "advance of knowledge." The sophisticated resort to force is justified if it satisfies the requirement of "comparative efficiency and economy in its use." The newly articulated doctrines of "manufacture of consent" were a natural concomitant, and in later years we were to hear much of "technocratic and policy-oriented intellectuals" who transcend ideology and will solve the remaining social problems by rational application of scientific principles.[2]

Since that time, the main body of articulate intellectuals have tended towards one or the other of these poles, avoiding "democratic dogmatisms" about people understanding their own interests and remaining cognizant of the "stupidity of the average man" and his need to be led to the better world that his superiors plan for him. A move from one to the other pole can be quite rapid and painless, since no fundamental change of doctrine or value is at stake, only an assessment of the opportunities for attaining power and privilege: riding a wave of popular struggle, or serving established authority as social or ideological manager. The conventional "God that failed" transition from Leninist enthusiasms to service to state capitalism can, I believe, be explained in substantial measure in these terms. Though there were authentic elements in the early stages, it has long since degenerated to ritualistic farce. Particularly welcome, and a sure ticket to success, is the fabrication of an evil past. Thus, the confessed sinner might describe how he cheered the tanks in the streets of Prague, supported Kim Il Sung, denounced Martin Luther King as a sellout, and so on, so that those who have not seen the light are implicitly tarred with the brush.[3] With the transition accomplished, the path to prestige and privilege is open, for the system values highly those who have seen the error of their ways and can now condemn independent minds as Stalinist-style apologists, on the basis of the superior insight gained from their misspent youth. Some may choose to become "experts" in the style candidly articulated by Henry Kissinger, who defined the "expert" as a person skilled in "elaborating and defining [the] … consensus [of] … his constituency," those who "have a vested interest in commonly held opinions: elaborating and defining its consensus at a high level has, after all, made him an expert."[4]

A generation later, the United States and the Soviet Union had become the superpowers of the first truly global system, realizing the expectations of Alexander Herzen and others a century before, though the dimensions of their power were never comparable and both have been declining in their capacity to influence and coerce for some years. The two models of the role of the intellectuals persist, similar at their root, adapted to the two prevailing systems of hierarchy and domination. Correspondingly, systems of indoctrination vary, depending on the capacity of the state to coerce and the modalities of effective control. The more interesting system is that of capitalist democracy, relying on the free market—guided by direct intervention where necessary—to establish conformity and marginalize the "special interests."

The primary targets of the manufacture of consent are those who regard themselves as "the more thoughtful members of the community," the "intellectuals," the "opinion leaders." An official of the Truman administration remarked that "It doesn't make too much difference to the general public what the details of a program are. What counts is how the plan is viewed by the leaders of the community"; he "who mobilizes the elite, mobilizes the public," one scholarly study of public opinion concludes. The "'public opinion' that Truman and his advisers took seriously, and diligently sought to cultivate," was that of the elite of "opinion leaders," the "foreign policy public," diplomatic historian Thomas Paterson observes[5]; and the same is true consistently, apart from moments when a "crisis of democracy" must be overcome and more vigorous measures are required to relegate the general public to its proper place. At other times they can be satisfied, it is hoped, with diversions and a regular dose of patriotic propaganda, and fulminations against assorted enemies who endanger their lives and homes unless their leaders stand fast against the threat.

In the democratic system, the necessary illusions cannot be imposed by force. Rather, they must be instilled in the public mind by more subtle means. A totalitarian state can be satisfied with lesser degrees of allegiance to required truths. It is sufficient that people obey; what they think is a secondary concern. But in a democratic political order, there is always the danger that independent thought might be translated into political action, so it is important to eliminate the threat at its root.

Debate cannot be stilled, and indeed, in a properly functioning system of propaganda, it should not be, because it has a system-reinforcing character if constrained within proper bounds. What is essential is to set the bounds firmly. Controversy may rage as long as it adheres to the presuppositions that define the consensus of elites, and it should furthermore be encouraged within these bounds, thus helping to establish these doctrines as the very condition of thinkable thought while reinforcing the belief that freedom reigns.

In short, what is essential is the power to set the agenda. If controversy over the Cold War can be focused on containment of the Soviet Union—the proper mix of force, diplomacy, and other measures—then the propaganda system has already won its victory, whatever conclusions are reached. The basic assumption has already been established: the Cold War is a confrontation between two superpowers, one aggressive and expansionist, the other defending the status quo and civilized values. Off the agenda is the problem of containing the United States, and the question whether the issue has been properly formulated at all, whether the Cold War does not rather derive from the efforts of the superpowers to secure for themselves international systems that they can dominate and control—systems that differ greatly in scale, reflecting enormous differences in wealth and power. Soviet violations of the Yalta and Potsdam agreements are the topic of a large literature and are well established in the general consciousness; we then proceed to debate their scale and importance. But it would require a careful search to find discussion of U.S. violations of the wartime agreements and their consequences, though the judgment of the best current scholarship, years later, is that "In fact, the Soviet pattern of adherence [to Yalta, Potsdam, and other wartime agreements] was not qualitatively different from the American pattern."[6] If the agenda can be restricted to the ambiguities of Arafat, the abuses and failures of the Sandinistas, the terrorism of Iran and Libya, and other properly framed issues, then the game is basically over; excluded from discussion is the unambiguous rejectionism of the United States and Israel, and the terrorism and other crimes of the United States and its clients, not only far greater in scale but also incomparably more significant on any moral dimension for American citizens, who are in a position to mitigate or terminate these crimes. The same considerations hold whatever questions we address.

One crucial doctrine, standard throughout history, is that the state is adopting a defensive stance, resisting challenges to order and to its noble principles. Thus, the United States is invariably resisting aggression, sometimes "internal aggression." Leading scholars assure us that the war in Vietnam was "undertaken in defense of a free people resisting communist aggression" as the United States attacked South Vietnam in the early 1960s to defend the client dictatorship against the South Vietnamese aggressors who were about to overthrow it; no justification need be offered to establish such an obvious truth, and none is. Some even refer blandly to "the Eisenhower administration's strategy of deterring aggression by threatening the use of nuclear weapons" in Indochina in 1954, "where French forces found themselves facing defeat" at Dienbienphu "at the hands of the Communist Viet Minh," the aggressors who attacked our French ally defending Indochina (from its population).[7] Cultivated opinion generally has internalized this stance. Accordingly, it is a logical impossibility that one should oppose U.S. aggression, a category that cannot exist. Whatever pretense they adopt, the critics must be "partisans of Hanoi" or "apologists for Communism" elsewhere, defending the "aggressors," perhaps attempting to conceal their "hidden agendas."[8]

A related doctrine is that "the yearning to see American-style democracy duplicated throughout the world has been a persistent theme in American foreign policy," as a *New York Times* diplomatic correspondent proclaimed after the U.S.-backed military government suppressed the Haitian elections by violence, widely predicted to be the likely consequence of U.S. support for the junta. These sad events, he observed, are "the latest reminder of the difficulty American policy-makers face in trying to work their will, no matter how benevolent, on other nations."[9] These doctrines require no argument and resist mountains of counter-evidence. On occasion, the pretense collapses under its manifest absurdity. It is then permissible to recognize that we were not always so benevolent and so profoundly dedicated to democracy as we are today. The regular appeal to this convenient technique of "change of course" over many years elicits not ridicule, but odes to our unfailing benevolence, as we set forth on some new campaign to "defend democracy."

We have no problem in perceiving the Soviet invasion of Afghanistan as brutal aggression, though many would balk at describing the Afghan guerrillas as "democratic resistance forces" (*New Republic* editor Andrew Sullivan).[10] But the U.S. invasion of South Vietnam in the early 1960s, when the Latin American-style terror state imposed by U.S. force could no longer control the domestic population by violence, cannot be perceived as what it was. True, U.S. forces were directly engaged in large-scale bombing and defoliation in an effort to drive the population into concentration camps where they could be "protected" from the enemy whom, it was conceded, they willingly supported. True, a huge U.S. expeditionary force later invaded and ravaged the country, and its neighbors, with the explicit aim of destroying what was clearly recognized to be the only mass-based political force and eliminating the danger of political settlement that was sought on all sides. But throughout, the United States was resisting aggression in its yearning for democracy. When the United States established the murderous Diem dictatorship as part of its effort to undermine the Geneva accords and to block the promised elections because the wrong side was expected to win, it was defending democracy. "The country is divided into the Communist regime in the north and a democratic government in the south," the *New York Times* reported, commenting on the allegation that "the Communist Vietminh was importing guns and soldiers from Red China 'in the most blatant fashion,' " threatening "free Vietnam" after having "sold their country to Peiping."[11] In later years, as the "defense of democracy" went awry, there was vigorous debate between the hawks, who felt that with sufficient dedication the enemy could be demolished, and the doves, who feared that the resort to violence to attain our noble ends might prove too costly; some preferred to be owls, distancing themselves from the two extremes.

Throughout the war, it was taken for granted within the mainstream that the United States was defending South Vietnam; unwisely, the doves came to believe. Years later, the doctrine remains beyond challenge. This is not only true of those who parodied the most disgraceful commissars as atrocities mounted, seeing nothing more in saturation bombing of densely populated areas than the "unfortunate loss of life incurred by the efforts of American military forces to help the South Vietnamese repel the incursion of North Vietnam and its partisans"—for example, in the Mekong Delta, where there were no North Vietnamese troops even long after the United States had expanded its aggression to North Vietnam, and where local people resisting the U.S. invaders and their clients evidently do not qualify as "South Vietnamese." It is perhaps not surprising that from such sources we should still read today, with all that is now known, that "the people of South Vietnam desired their freedom from domination by the communist country on their northern border" and that "the United States intervened in Vietnam ... to establish the principle that changes in Asia were not to be precipitated by outside force."[12] Far more interesting is the fact that, even though many would be repelled by the vulgarity of the apologetics for large-scale atrocities, a great many educated people would find little surprising in this assessment of the history, a most remarkable demonstration of the effectiveness of democratic systems of thought control.

Similarly, in Central America today, the United States is dedicated to the defense of freedom in the "fledgling democracies" and to "restoring democracy" to Nicaragua—a reference to the Somoza period, if words have meaning. At the extreme of expressible dissent, in a bitter condemnation of the U.S. attack on Nicaragua that went so far as to invoke the judgment of Nuremberg, *Atlantic Monthly* editor Jack Beatty wrote that "Democracy has been our goal in Nicaragua, and to reach it we have sponsored the killing of thousands of Nicaraguans. But killing for democracy—even killing by proxy for democracy—is not a good enough reason to prosecute a war."[13] One could hardly find a more consistent critic of the U.S. war in the corporate media than columnist Tom Wicker of the *New York Times*, who condemned the application of the Reagan Doctrine to Nicaragua because "the United States has no historic or God-given right to bring democracy to other nations."[14] Critics adopt without a second thought the assumption that our traditional "yearning for democracy" has indeed guided U.S. policy towards Nicaragua since July 19, 1979, when the U.S. client Somoza was overthrown, though admittedly not before the miraculous and curiously timed transformation took place, by some mysterious process. A diligent search through all the media would unearth an occasional exception to this pattern, but such exceptions are rare, another tribute to the effectiveness of indoctrination.[15]

"Central America has an evident self-interest in hounding" the Sandinistas "to honor their pledges to democratize"; and "those Americans who have repeatedly urged others 'to give peace a chance' now have an obligation to turn their attention and their passion to ensuring democracy a chance as well," the editors of the *Washington Post* admonished, directly below the masthead that proudly labels theirs "an Independent Newspaper."[16] There is no problem of "ensuring democracy" in the U.S.-backed terror states, firmly under military rule behind a thin civilian façade.

The same editorial warned that "from the incursions into Honduras [in March 1988], it is plain what Nicaragua's threats to Honduras are." The reference was to military operations in northern Nicaragua near an unmarked border, in which Nicaraguan forces in hot pursuit of contra invaders penetrated a few kilometers into areas of Honduras that had long been ceded to the U.S. "proxy force"—as they are described by contra lobbyists in internal documents circulated in the White House, and by their own official spokesman.[17] In the United States, these actions elicited renewed outrage over the threat of the Sandinistas to overrun their neighbors in the service of their Soviet master.

This heartfelt concern over the sanctity of borders is most impressive—even if somewhat tainted by the curious conception of a border as a kind of one-way mirror, so that its sanctity is not violated by CIA supply flights to the proxy forces who invade Nicaragua from their Honduran bases, or by U.S. surveillance flights over Nicaraguan territory to guide and direct them, among other crimes. Putting aside these matters, we can assess the seriousness of the concern by turning to the results of a controlled experiment that history obligingly constructed. Just at the time that the Free Press was consumed with rage over this latest proof of the aggressiveness of the violent Communist totalitarians, with major stories and angry commentary, the U.S. client state of Israel launched another series of its periodic operations in Lebanon. These operations were north of the sector of southern Lebanon that Israel has "virtually annexed" as a "security zone," integrating the area with Israel's economy and "compelling" its 200,000 Lebanese inhabitants "to provide soldiers for the South Lebanon army," an Israeli mercenary force, by means of an array of punishments and inducements.[18] The Israeli operations included bombing of Palestinian refugee camps and Lebanese towns and villages with large-scale destruction, dozens killed and many wounded, including many civilians. These operations were barely reported, and there was no noticeable reaction.

The only rational conclusion is that the outrage over the vastly less serious and far more justified Nicaraguan incursion was entirely unprincipled, mere fraud.

The U.S. government is happy to explain why it supports Israeli violence deep inside Lebanon: the grounds are the sacred inherent right of self-defense, which may legitimately be invoked by the United States and its clients, under quite a broad interpretation— though not, of course, by others, in particular, by victims of U.S. terror. In December 1988, just as Yasser Arafat's every gesture was being closely scrutinized to determine whether he had met the exacting U.S. standards on terrorism, to which we return, Israel launched its twenty-sixth raid of the year on Lebanon, attacking a base of the Popular Front for the Liberation of Palestine near Beirut. As is common, there was no attempt to provide a plausible pretext. "The Israelis were not in hot pursuit of terrorists," the London *Guardian* observed, "nor did they have their usual excuse of instant vengeance: they just went ahead and staged a demo" to prove that "the iron fist is in full working order." "The motive for the demonstration was obviously a show of strength." This "spectacular display," complete with "paratroops, helicopters, and gunboats," was "a militarily unjustifiable (and therefore politically motivated) combined operation." The timing explains the political motivation: the raid was carried out on the first anniversary of the outbreak of the Palestinian uprising in the occupied territories, where Israel imposed "a massive military presence, a curfew and strict censorship" to block "a commemorative general strike." In addition to this obvious political motivation, "one may also discern a calculated attempt to undermine Mr Arafat" and his unwelcome moves towards political accommodation, by strengthening the hand of militants within the PLO.[19]

The Israeli attack was brought to the U.N. Security Council, which voted 14 to 1, with no abstentions, for a resolution that "strongly deplored" it. Ambassador Patricia Byrne justified the U.S. veto on the grounds that the "resolution would deny to Israel its inherent right to defend itself" from "attacks and reprisals that have originated on the other side" of the border. *A fortiori*, Nicaragua is entitled to carry out massive and regular attacks deep inside Honduras, and indeed to set off bombs in Washington. Note that such actions would be far more justified than those that the United States defends in the case of its client, as is obvious from comparison of the level of the provocation. Needless to say, this truth is inexpressible, indeed unthinkable. We therefore conclude that media commentary concerning Nicaragua is just as hypocritical as the pretense of the state authorities, from whom one expects nothing else.[20]

The absence of comment on the Israeli actions or even serious reporting is perhaps understandable. These operations were, after all, rather muted by Israeli standards. Thus, they did not compare with the murderous "Iron Fist" operations in Lebanon in 1985; or the bombing of villages in the Bekaa valley in January 1984, with 100 killed and 400 wounded in one raid, mostly civilians, including 150 children in a bombed-out schoolhouse; or the attack on an UNRWA school in Damour in May 1979 by an Israeli F-16 that dropped cluster bombs, leaving forty-one children dead or wounded. These were reported, but without affecting the elevated status of "this tiny nation, symbol of human decency," as the editors of the *New York Times* described Israel during a peak period of the repression of the Palestinian uprising with beatings, killings, gassing, and collective punishment, "a country that cares for human life," in the admiring words of the *Washington Post* editors in the wake of the Iron Fist atrocities.[21] The fact that Israel maintains a "security zone" in southern Lebanon controlled by a terrorist mercenary army backed by Israeli might also passes without notice, as does Israel's regular hijacking of ships in international waters and other actions that are rarely even reported, and might perhaps arouse a whisper of protest in the case of "worthy victims."[22] If Soviet Jews were to suffer the treatment meted out regularly to Arabs, or if some official enemy such as Nicaragua were to impose repressive measures approaching those that are standard in this "symbol of human decency," the outcry would be deafening.

I will return to some further observations on the extraordinary protection the media have provided Israel while depicting its enemies, particularly the PLO, as evil incarnate, committed only to terror and destruction; and to the remarkable feats of "historical engineering" that have been performed, year by year, to maintain the required image.[23]

During Israel's March 1988 operations, there was no question of hot pursuit, and Israel is not an impoverished country attempting to survive the terrorist attack of a superpower and its lethal economic warfare. But Israel is a U.S. client, and therefore inherits the right of aggression. Nicaragua, in contrast, is denied the right even to drive attacking forces out of its own territory, on the tacit assumption that no state has the right to defend itself from U.S. attack, another crucial doctrine that underlies responsible debate.

It is remarkable to see how deeply the latter doctrine is entrenched. Thus, nothing arouses greater hysteria in the United States than reports that Nicaragua is planning to obtain MiG fighters. When the Reaganites floated such reports as part of the campaign to eliminate the minimal danger of honest reporting of the unwanted Nicaraguan elections in November 1984, even outspoken doves warned that the U.S. would have to bomb Nicaragua to destroy the invented MiGs, because "they're also capable against the United States," a dire threat to our security (Massachusetts Senator Paul Tsongas).[24] In another propaganda coup of December 1987, a Sandinista defector was produced with elaborate accompanying fanfare in the media on his "revelations" about Sandinista intentions, the most stunning of which was that Nicaragua was hoping to obtain jet planes to defend its territory from U.S. attack, an intolerable outrage. It is, of course, well understood that Nicaragua had no other way to prevent the CIA from supplying the forces it directs within Nicaragua, or to interfere with the U.S. surveillance flights to provide these forces with up-to-the-minute intelligence on Nicaraguan troop deployments so that they could safely attack "soft targets" (i.e., barely defended civilian targets) in accordance with Pentagon and State Department directives. But no such reflections disturbed the display of indignation over this latest proof of Communist aggressiveness.[25]

The logic is clear: Nicaragua has no right of self-defense. It is intolerable, tantamount to aggression, for Nicaragua to interfere with U.S. violence and terror by presuming to protect its airspace, or by defending the population against the U.S. proxy forces, "the democratic resistance" of public rhetoric. For the same reason, the report by the Sandinista defector that Nicaragua intended to reduce its military forces while providing light arms to the population for defense against possible U.S. invasion elicited further outrage as it was transmuted by the Free Press into a threat to conquer the hemisphere.

This doctrine of the elite consensus is, again, highly revealing, as is the fact that its meaning cannot be perceived. We might imagine the reaction if the Soviet Union were to respond in a similar way to the far more serious threat to its security posed by Denmark or Luxembourg.

It is interesting that, in the midst of the furor over the Sandinista plans to obtain means to defend themselves, the United States began shipping advanced F-5 jet planes to Honduras on December 15, 1987, unreported by the *New York Times*.[26] Since only the United States and its allies have security concerns, obviously Nicaragua could have no legitimate objection to this development, and it would be superfluous, surely, to report the protests in the Honduran press over the "debts unfairly imposed upon us by pressure from the United States" that force us to "pay the bill for the F-5 fighters that do nothing to feed our hungry people," though they please the military rulers.[27]

One might ask why Nicaragua was so intent on obtaining *Soviet* planes. Why not French Mirage jets instead? In fact, the Sandinistas would have been quite happy to obtain jet interceptors from France, and openly say so. They could not, because U.S. pressure had blocked supply from any non-Communist source. All of this is unreportable, because it would give the game away. Thus Stephen Kinzer and James LeMoyne of the *New York Times* would never disturb their efforts to fan hysteria over the Sandinista threat by reporting such facts, nor would they dwell on the reasons why the Sandinistas might be attempting to obtain jet interceptors.[28] Such inquiry escapes the bounds of propriety, for it would undermine the campaign to portray U.S. aggression and terror as legitimate defense.

The point is more general. Attack against those designated "Communists" will normally compel them to rely on the Soviet Union for defense, particularly when the United States pressures its allies and international lending institutions to refrain from offering assistance, as in the case of contemporary Nicaragua, where it was clear enough in early 1981 that "Nicaragua will sooner or later become another Soviet client, as the U.S. imposes a stranglehold on its reconstruction and development, rebuffs efforts to maintain decent relations, and supports harassment and intervention—the pattern of China, Cuba, Guatemala's Arbenz, Allende's Chile, Vietnam in the 1940s and the post-1975 period, etc."[29] This predictable consequence of policy can then be taken as retrospective proof that we are, indeed, simply engaged in defense against the Kremlin design for world conquest, and well-behaved journalists may refer to the "Soviet-supplied Sandinistas" in properly ominous tones, as they regularly do, carefully avoiding the reasons. An additional benefit is that we now test the sincerity of the Soviet Union in their professions about détente, asking whether they will withhold aid from Nicaragua if we reduce aid to the contras. The idea that U.S. sincerity could be tested by withholding aid from Turkey or El Salvador is too outlandish to merit discussion.

A corollary to the principle that official enemies do not have the right of self-defense is that if Nicaragua attacks contra forces within its territory after they break off negotiations, the United States plainly has the right to provide further military aid to its proxies. The Byrd Amendment on "Assistance for the Nicaraguan Resistance," passed in August 1988 with the effusive support of leading senatorial doves, permitted military aid to the proxy forces within Nicaragua upon "Sandinista initiation of an unprovoked military attack and any other hostile action directed against the forces of the Nicaraguan Resistance" or "a continued unacceptable level of military assistance by Soviet-bloc countries, including Cuba" (all other sources having been barred, and U.S. authorities being accorded the right to determine what is "acceptable").[30] The media had taken for granted throughout that it would be outrageous, another display of Communist intransigence, if the army of Nicaragua were to attack terrorist forces within their own country. Months earlier, the press had reported a letter by House Democrats to President Ortega expressing their "grave concern" over the possibility of a military offensive against the contras, which would lead to consideration of "a renewal of military aid to the resistance forces."[31] The prohibition against self-defense remained in force after the U.S. clients had undermined negotiations with last-minute demands contrived to this end, to which we return.

The media reaction is understandable, on the conventional assumption that the "resistance" and the political opposition that supports it within Nicaragua are the more legitimate of the "two Nicaraguan factions," as the *Times* described the contras and the government.[32] The bipartisan consensus on these matters, including outspoken congressional doves, reflects the understanding that Nicaragua has no right to resist U.S. terrorist forces implanted in its territory or attacking it from abroad; U.S. clients are immune from such constraints, and may even hijack ships, bomb civilian targets in other countries, and so on, in "legitimate self-defense."

The August 5 Senate debate on the Byrd amendment gains heightened significance from its timing. Three days earlier, the "resistance," after allowing an army patrol boat to pass by, had attacked the crowded passenger vessel *Mission of Peace*, killing two people and wounding twenty-seven, including a Baptist minister from New Jersey, Rev. Lucius Walker, who headed a U.S. religious delegation. All the victims were civilians. Senators Byrd and Dodd, and other doves, who bitterly condemned the Sandinistas while praising the "courageous leadership" of the "Democratic Presidents" of Guate-

mala, El Salvador, and Honduras, made no mention of this event;
perhaps they had missed the tiny notice it received the day before in
the *New York Times*, tacked on to a column reporting their delibera-
tions.[33] There was no subsequent commentary. The logic is again
clear. If the Sandinistas seek to root out the U.S.-run terrorists who
carried out the attack, that proves they are Communist totalitarians,
and the United States is entitled to send military as well as "humanitarian" aid to the "resistance" so that it can pursue such tasks more
effectively. Given the enthusiastic support for the Senate proceedings
by the Senate's leading liberal voices—Harkin, Kennedy, Kerry,
Mitchell, Pell, and others—we may assume that they accept these
principles.

It is frankly recognized that the principal argument for U.S.
violence is that "a longer war of attrition will so weaken the regime,
provoke such a radical hardening of repression, and win sufficient
support from Nicaragua's discontented population that sooner or
later the regime will be overthrown by popular revolt, self-destruct
by means of internal coups or leadership splits, or simply capitulate
to salvage what it can." This formulation by Viron Vaky, Assistant
Secretary of State for Interamerican Affairs under the Carter administration, merely reiterates the thrust of the 1981 CIA program outlined by CIA analyst David MacMichael in World Court testimony.
As a dove, Vaky regards the scenario as "flawed" and the strategy
unworkable, the contras having been unable to gain military successes despite the extraordinary advantages conferred upon them by
their sponsor, or "to elicit significant political support within Nicaragua." "However reasonable or idealistic" the U.S. demand that the
Sandinistas "turn over power" to U.S. favorites lacking political
support, he continues, the goal is beyond our reach. He therefore
urges "positive containment" instead of "rollback" to prevent "Nicaragua from posing a military threat to the United States" and to
induce it to observe human rights and move towards a "less virulent
... internal system." Since force is not feasible, the United States
should seek "other strategies" to pursue "the objective of promoting
Nicaraguan self-determination" that it has so idealistically pursued.
It should seek a diplomatic settlement with "border inspections,
neutral observers," and other devices that Nicaragua had been requesting for seven years (a fact unmentioned), though "the United
States frankly will have to bear the major share of enforcement." The
United States must be prepared to use force if it detects a violation,

while assisting "the Central American democracies" that are threatened by Nicaraguan subversion and aggression.[34]

Recall that these are the thoughts of a leading dove, and that they seem unremarkable to liberal American opinion, important facts about the political culture. These thoughts fall squarely within the conception of U.S. policy outlined by another Carter administration Latin American specialist, Robert Pastor, at the dovish extreme of the political and ideological spectrum—by now, perhaps well beyond it. Defending U.S. policy over many years, Pastor writes that "the United States did not want to control Nicaragua or other nations in the region, but it also did not want to allow developments to get out of control. It wanted Nicaraguans to act independently, *except* when doing so would affect U.S. interests adversely."[35] In short, Nicaragua and other countries should be free—to do what we want them to do—and should choose their course independently, as long as their choice conforms to our interests. If they use the freedom we accord them unwisely, then naturally we are entitled to respond in self-defense. Note that these ideas are a close counterpart to the domestic conception of democracy as a form of population control.

The basic presuppositions of discourse include those just reviewed: U.S. foreign policy is guided by a "yearning for democracy" and general benevolent intent; history and the secret planning record may tell a rather different story, but they are off the media agenda. It follows that the use of force can only be an exercise in self-defense and that those who try to resist must be aggressors, even in their own lands. What is more, no country has the right of self-defense against U.S. attack, and the United States has the natural right to impose its will, by force if necessary and feasible. These doctrines need not be expressed, apart from periodic odes to our awesome nobility of purpose. Rather, they are simply presupposed, setting the bounds of discourse, and among the properly educated, the bounds of thinkable thought.

In the first chapter, I mentioned some of the ways of approaching the study of the media and evaluating models of media performance. One appropriate method is to consider the spectrum of opinion allowed expression. According to the propaganda model, one would expect the spectrum to be bounded by the consensus of powerful elites while encouraging tactical debate within it. Again, the model is well confirmed.

Consider U.S. policy with regard to Nicaragua, a topic that has probably elicited more controversy and impassioned rhetoric than any other during the past several years. There is debate between the hawks and the doves. The position of the hawks is expressed by a joint declaration of the State and Defense Departments on International Human Rights Day in December 1986: "in the American continent, there is no regime more barbaric and bloody, no regime that violates human rights in a manner more constant and permanent, than the Sandinista regime." Similar sentiments are voiced in the media and political system, and it follows that we should support the "democratic resistance" to Communist terror. At the other extreme, the doves generally agree that we should dismiss the World Court, the United Nations, and other "hostile forums" that pander to Communists and pathological Third World anti-Americanism. They offer their support for the "noble objective" of the Reagan administration—"to somehow 'democratize' Nicaragua"—but they feel that the contras "are not the instrument that will achieve that objective" (Representative Michael Barnes, one of the most outspoken critics of the contra option).[36] A leading Senate dove, Alan Cranston, recognizes that "the Contra effort is woefully inadequate to achieve ... democracy in Nicaragua," so we should find other means to "isolate" the "reprehensible" government in Managua and "leave it to fester in its own juices" while blocking Sandinista efforts "to export violent revolution."[37]

Media doves observe that "Mr. Reagan's policy of supporting [the contras] is a clear failure," so we should "acquiesce in some negotiated regional arrangement that would be enforced by Nicaragua's neighbors" (Tom Wicker).[38] Expressing the same thought, the editors of the *Washington Post* see the contras as "an imperfect instrument," so we must find other means to "fit Nicaragua back into a Central American mode" and impose "reasonable conduct by a regional standard." We must also recognize that "the Sandinistas are communists of the Cuban or Soviet school" and "a serious menace—to civil peace and democracy in Nicaragua and the stability and security of the region." We must "contain ... the Sandinistas' aggressive thrust" and demand "credible evidence of reduced Sandinista support for El Salvador's guerrillas."[39] None of this is debatable: it "is a given; it is true," the editors proclaim. It is therefore irrelevant, for example, that Reagan administration efforts to provide evidence for their charges of Nicaraguan support for El Salvador's guerrillas were dismissed as without merit by the World Court, and in fact barely merit derision. At the outer limits of dissent, *Nation* columnist Jefferson Morley wrote in the *New York Times* that we should recognize that Nicaragua may be "beyond the reach of our good intentions."[40]

Other doves feel that we should not too quickly reject the State Department argument that agricultural cooperatives are legitimate targets for contra attacks, because "in a Marxist society geared up for war, there are no clear lines separating officials, soldiers and civilians"; what is required is careful "cost-benefit analysis," a determination of "the amount of blood and misery that will be poured in, and the likelihood that democracy will emerge at the other end" (*New Republic* editor Michael Kinsley).[41] Neither Kinsley nor the State Department explain why similar arguments do not justify attacks by Abu Nidal on Israeli kibbutzim, far better defended against an incomparably lesser threat. And it is naturally taken to be our right, as rulers of the world, to carry out the cost-benefit analysis and to pour in blood and misery if we determine that the likelihood of "democracy" is sufficiently high.

Notice that for the doves it is obvious without comment that there is no need to impose "regional arrangements" on our Salvadoran and Guatemalan friends, who have slaughtered perhaps 150,000 people during this period, or our clients in Honduras, who kill fewer outright but have left hundreds of thousands to starve to death while the country exports food for the profit of agribusiness. We need not "isolate" these admirable figures or "leave them to fester in their own juices." Their countries already conform to the "Central American mode" of repression, exploitation, and rule by privileged elements that accede to the demands of U.S. power ("democracy"), so even hideous atrocities are of no account; and they merit aid and enthusiastic backing, accompanied by occasional sighs of regret over the violent tendencies in these backward societies if the terror, torture, and mutilation that we organize and support become too visible to ignore or attack the wrong targets (Christian Democrat political figures rather than union and peasant organizers, for example).

By 1986, the contra option was opposed by 80 percent of "leaders," polls report.[42] The propaganda model would therefore predict debate over contra aid but near unanimity in opposition to the Sandinistas. To test the hypothesis, consider the period of maximum intensity of debate over Nicaragua policy, the first three months of 1986, when attention was focused on the issue of contra aid. During these months, the *New York Times* and the *Washington Post* ran no fewer than eighty-five opinion columns on the matter (including regular columnists). As expected, they were divided over contra aid.

But of the eighty-five columns, eighty-five were critical of the Sandinistas, the overwhelming majority harshly so; thus close to 100 percent conformity was achieved on the major issue.

It is not that more sympathetic voices are lacking in the mainstream. There are many who would easily qualify for admission to the forum if they had the right things to say,[43] including Latin American scholars whose opinion pieces are regularly rejected, or the charitable development agency Oxfam, with long experience in the region, which found Nicaragua's record to be "exceptional" among the seventy-six developing countries in which it works in the commitment of the political leadership "to improving the condition of the people and encouraging their active participation in the development process."

Or consider the founder of Costa Rican democracy, José Figueres, who, just at that time, described himself in an interview as "pro-Sandinista" and "quite friendly toward the Sandinistas," though Costa Rica generally is not, because public opinion is "heavily influenced" by "the Costa Rican oligarchy" which "owns the newspapers and the radio stations." He added that the 2-to-1 margin in favor of the Sandinistas in the 1984 elections, which he witnessed as an observer, "certainly seemed to reflect what you find in the streets." Figueres condemned "Washington's incredible policies of persecuting the Sandinistas" and its efforts "to undo Costa Rica's social institutions" and to "turn our whole economy over to the businesspeople, ... to the local oligarchy or to U.S. or European companies," though as a dedicated supporter of the United States, he found these efforts "no doubt well-intentioned." The United States is "turning most Central Americans into mercenaries" for its attack against Nicaragua, he continued. "I've been familiar with Nicaragua all my life," "and never before have I seen as I do now a Nicaraguan government that cares for its people." In another interview, he reiterated that "for the first time, Nicaragua has a government that cares for its people." Commenting on a recent visit, he said that he found "a surprising amount of support for the government" in this "invaded country," adding that the United States should allow the Sandinistas "to finish what they started in peace; they deserve it."[44]

Such comments lack ideological serviceability, as does Figueres's statement that he "understands why" La Prensa was closed, having censored the press himself when Costa Rica was under attack by Somoza. Hence, Central America's leading democratic figure must be censored out of the media, though his name may still be invoked for the anti-Sandinista crusade. Thus *New York Times* Central America correspondent James LeMoyne, in one of his anti-Sandinista diatribes, refers to Figueres as "the man who is widely considered the father of Costa Rican democracy," but does not tell us, nor would he or his colleagues ever tell us, what Figueres has to say about the Sandinistas.[45]

The front pages of the *New York Times* present a picture of Nicaragua as seen through the eyes of James LeMoyne as he passed through: a brutal and repressive state under "one-party rule" with "crowds of pot-bellied urchins in the streets," state security agents "ubiquitous" and the army "everywhere," growing support for the "peasant army" struggling against Sandinista oppression and the population reduced to "bitterness and apathy," though somehow resisting a foreign attack under which any other state in the region, and most elsewhere, would have quickly crumbled. They do not present the picture seen by Figueres, or by the CIA-appointed press spokesman for the contras, Edgar Chamorro, on a three-week visit just before LeMoyne's. Speaking to "dozens of people" in the streets after a Sandinista rally, Chamorro found them "very aware, very politically educated, very committed. They thought for themselves; they were there because they wanted to be there." "The days are gone when a dictator can get up and harangue people." "What I have seen here is very, very positive, people are walking on their own two feet," regaining the "dignity and nationalism" they had lost under Somoza. The contras are "like the Gurkhas in India," with the "colonial mentality" of those "fighting for the empire." He spoke on radio and television in Managua, saying "whatever I thought," criticizing Marxism-Leninism. He saw "very little militarization" and "a deep sense of equality," "one of the accomplishments of the revolution." "I didn't see people hungry"; "most people look very healthy, strong, alive," and he saw few beggars, unlike Honduras "or even in city streets in the US." The opposition are the old oligarchy, "reliant on the United States." The war has led to a sense of "nationalism, patriotism" on the part of the youth who are drafted. The Sandinistas continue to be a "people's party," with commitments and goals "that inspire so many people." They are "Nicaraguan nationalists, revolutionaries," who "want a more egalitarian model, to improve the lives of the majority." The elections were "good," the government is "legitimate," and we should "try and change from inside." After leaving the contras, Chamorro adds elsewhere, he lost the easy media access of his contra days.[46]

Readers of the *New York Times* do not receive a range of perceptions such as these, but only one: the one that accords with the needs of the state.

A year after these visits, severe malnutrition began to appear in Managua and parts of the countryside, as U.S. terror and economic warfare continued to take their bitter toll in a pathetically poor country, which, for obvious historical and geopolitical reasons, is utterly dependent on economic relations with the United States. George Shultz, Elliott Abrams, and their cohorts may not have overthrown the government, but they can take pride in having vanquished the programs of development, preventive medical care, and welfare that had offered hope to the poor majority for the first time. Their achievements can be measured by the significant increase in dying infants, epidemics, and other normal features of the "Central American mode" to which Nicaragua is to be "restored" by U.S. benevolence.[47] The propaganda system may cover their tracks today, but history will render a different judgment.

Returning to the eighty-five opinion columns in the *Times* and the *Post,* even more interesting than the uniform hostility to the Sandinistas was the choice of topics. There are two very striking differences between the Sandinistas and the U.S. favorites who adhere to "regional standards." The first is that the Sandinistas, whatever their sins, had not conducted campaigns of mass slaughter, torture, mutilation, and general terror to traumatize the population. In the eighty-five columns, there is not a single phrase referring to this matter, an illustration of its importance in American political culture. The second major difference is that the Sandinistas diverted resources to the poor majority and attempted measures of meaningful social reform—quite successfully, in fact, until U.S. economic and military warfare succeeded in reversing the unwelcome improvement in health and welfare standards, literacy, and development. These facts merit two passing phrases in eighty-five columns, one in a bitter condemnation of the "generally appalling leadership" in this "repressive society." There is no word on the fact that, unlike U.S. clients, the Sandinistas had protected the poor from starvation, eliciting much scorn about their economic mismanagement—scorn that is withheld from Honduras, which permits peasants to starve en masse while exporting specialty crops and beef to the United States, and from U.S. policymakers, who imposed development policies on Central America that produced statistical growth (eliciting much self-congratulation) and starvation (about which we hear much less).

There is also no mention of Sandinista efforts to maintain a neutralist posture—for example, of the trade figures at the time of the U.S. embargo that virtually wiped out private business and helped reduce the economy to bare survival: Nicaraguan trade with the Soviet bloc was then at the same level as U.S. trade with these countries and well below that of Europe and most of the Third World.[48]

Such matters are unhelpful for required doctrine, thus better ignored.

More generally, all of the eighty-five columns stay safely within the approved bounds. Even the few contributors who elsewhere have taken an independent stance do not do so here.[49]

A reader brought the published study of the spectrum of expressible opinion to the attention of *Times* dove Tom Wicker, who devoted part of a column to denouncing it.[50] He gave two reasons for dismissing the study. First, he saw "no reason why I have to praise the Sandinistas," which is quite true, and entirely irrelevant. As was clear and explicit, the individual contributions were not at issue but rather the range of permitted views; the question is not whether Wicker should be granted the opportunity to express his opinion that a "regional arrangement" must be imposed on Nicaragua alone and enforced by the U.S. terror states, but whether, in a free press, the spectrum of opinion should be bounded by this position, as the extreme of permissible dissent from government policy. Wicker's second reason was that "criticism by foot-rule and calculator is often as simplistic as the reportage it purports to measure." Curious to learn whether Wicker had some methodological or other critique to support this judgment, I wrote him a series of letters of inquiry, eliciting no response, from which I can only conclude that his objection is to the very idea of conducting a rational inquiry into the functioning of the media. Note that his reaction, and the general dismissal of the extensive documentation supporting the propaganda model, is quite in accord with its predictions.[51]

Perhaps, nevertheless, this sample of the major journals at the peak period of debate is misleading. Let us turn then to another sample a year later. In the first six months of 1987, the same two journals ran sixty-one columns and editorials relevant to U.S. policy in Nicaragua. Of these, thirteen favored diplomatic measures over contra aid, saying nothing about the Sandinistas. Of the forty-eight that expressed an opinion, forty-six were anti-Sandinista, again, most of them bitterly so. Of these, eighteen were pro-contra and twenty-eight anti-contra, primarily on the grounds that the contras were inept and could not win, or that the U.S. goal of "forc[ing] the Sandinista revolution into the American democratic mold" might not be worth "the risk" (John Oakes of the *New York Times*, at the dissident extreme[52]). Of the two columns that expressed some sympathy for the Sandinistas, one was by Nicaraguan ambassador Carlos Tunnerman, the other by Dr. Kevin Cahill, director of the tropical disease center at Lenox Hill Hospital in New York, the only non-Nicaraguan commentator who could draw upon personal experience in Nicaragua and elsewhere in the Third World[53]; his was also the only column that took note of the successful Nicaraguan health and literacy measures and the "struggle against oppression and corruption" waged under conditions of extreme adversity imposed by U.S. terror and economic warfare. Cahill's is one of the two contributions among sixty-one that mention the World Court decision and international law; two others, one by Tunnerman, refer to them obliquely. These facts reflect the attitude towards the rule of law in the dominant intellectual culture. We read that the United States "is working through the contras to restore democracy to Nicaragua and break the Sandinistas' Cuban and Soviet ties" and that Washington's role is "to help contain the spread of the Sandinista revolution beyond Nicaragua" (the editors of the *Washington Post*, who suggest that the United States test the Latin American consensus that "there is a better chance of reining in the Sandinistas by political envelopment than by military assault"). And we are treated to charges of "genocide" of the Miskito Indians (William Buckley, who concedes that the Sandinistas have not yet reached the level of Pol Pot, though they are plainly heading that way). But apart from Cahill, we read not a word about the constructive policies that were successfully pursued, and that, in the real world, elicited U.S. terror to "rein in the Sandinistas"—another inexpressible thought.[54]

Once again, not a single phrase refers to the fact that, unlike the U.S. clients in the "fledgling democracies," the Sandinistas had not launched a campaign of terror and slaughter to traumatize their populations. Rather, as a huge mass of generally ignored documentation demonstrates, this task had been assigned to the U.S. proxy forces; this inconvenient fact is placed in proper perspective by former *Times* executive editor A.M. Rosenthal, who writes that "James LeMoyne's carefully reported, sensitive accounts in the *Times* of rebel troops inside Nicaragua indicate growing self-confidence and skill." The totalitarian Sandinistas are contrasted with the "struggling democracies of Central America": the "imperfect but working" democracies of Guatemala and Honduras, and El Salvador, which, though "under communist guerrilla siege," is "an imperfect democracy but a democracy with an elected government" (*Post* columnist Stephen Rosenfeld), unlike Nicaragua, where there were no elections, so Washington has decreed.[55]

The assumptions revealed in these samples of expressible opinion are the very foundations of discourse, beyond challenge.

The effectiveness of the state doctrine that there were no elections in Nicaragua, in contrast to the U.S. terror states, provides useful lessons for future commissars. It confirms the judgment of Woodrow Wilson's Committee on Public Information (the Creel Commission) "that one of the best means of controlling news was flooding news channels with 'facts,' or what amounted to official information."[56] By dint of endless repetition, combined with media election coverage conforming to Washington dictates, the required doctrine has become established truth. Virtually no deviations are to be found. Even human rights groups that have made a real effort to steer an even course fall prey to these impressive achievements of state-media propaganda. Thus the Deputy Director of Human Rights Watch criticizes the Reaganites for inconsistency: they "have been loath to speak out [about] ... abuses under elected governments" (he mentions El Salvador and Guatemala), but they condemn "human rights abuses by the hemisphere's left-wing regimes—Cuba and Nicaragua." On the one hand, we have the "elected governments" of El Salvador and Guatemala, and on the other, Nicaragua, left-wing and therefore lacking an "elected government." At the outer reaches of dissidence in the media, the liberal *Boston Globe* contrasts El Salvador, Guatemala, and Honduras ("unstable democratic") with Cuba, Nicaragua, Guyana, and Suriname ("socialist"). The "democratic" governments have "civilian presidents" who were "elected," though they are "battling the army for political control"; but in Nicaragua, we have only a "socialist junta in power since 1979 revolution"—no elections, no "democracy" as in the U.S. clients.[57]

To escape the impact of a well-functioning system of propaganda that bars dissent and unwanted fact while fostering lively debate within the permitted bounds is remarkably difficult.

In recognition of the importance of preventing the free flow of ideas, the U.S. government has long sought to impress upon its clients the need to monitor and control travel and published materials. Thus, President Kennedy met with seven Central American presidents in San José, Costa Rica, in March 1963, where the seven agreed to an

April meeting in Somoza's Nicaragua "To develop and put into immediate effect common measures to restrict the movement of subversive nationals to and from Cuba, and the flow of materials, propaganda and funds from that country." In secret internal documents, the Kennedy liberals were concerned over the excessive liberalism of Latin American regimes, in particular, "the reluctance of governments to establish bilateral or multilateral arrangements for the control of travelers," such as exist and are extensively applied in the United States.[58] For similar reasons, there is no concern here when the independent media are destroyed by violence in U.S. dependencies or are securely in the hands of reliable right-wing elements, or when censorship is imposed by government terror, assassination, or imprisonment of journalists. At home, such measures are obviously inappropriate. More delicate ones are required, more sophisticated procedures of manufacture of consent.

The commitment to block the free flow of ideas reflects deeper concerns. For global planners, much of the Third World has been assigned the role of service to the industrial capitalist centers. Its various regions must "fulfill their functions" as sources of raw materials and markets, and must be "exploited" for the reconstruction and development of Western capitalism, as secret documents frankly explain. It is, of course, understood that such policies leave the United States "politically weak" though "militarily strong," the constant lament of government specialists and other commentators, and a fact recognized by the victims as well, in Latin America, Southeast Asia, and elsewhere. Although banning of improper thoughts, free travel, and "subversive nationals" can perhaps compensate in part for the political weakness of the United States and its clients, planners have clearly and explicitly recognized that the United States will ultimately have to rely on force, the local security forces if possible, to contain dissidence and popular movements. The basic commitments explain not only the regular reliance on military and state terror, but also the hostility to democracy (in the sense of popular participation in public affairs) that is such a striking feature of U.S. policy in the Third World—sometimes becoming a real passion, as under the Reagan administration.

For the same reasons, the Kennedy administration shifted the mission of the Latin American military from "hemispheric defense" to "internal security," and the United States lent support to the National Security States that spread throughout the region in subsequent years. Latin Americanist Lars Schoultz observes that these new forms of "military authoritarianism" developed in response to "increased popular political participation" and aimed "to destroy permanently a perceived threat to the existing structure of socioeconomic privilege by eliminating the political participation of the numerical majority, principally the working or (to use a broader, more accurate term) popular classes."[59] It is only when the threat of popular participation is overcome that democratic forms can be safely contemplated.

The same considerations explain why it is necessary to block dangerous ideas and "anti-U.S. subversion," indeed anything that might appeal to the "popular classes" who are to be excluded from the political system. This combination of political weakness and military strength underlies State Department concerns that the government of Guatemala in the early 1950s was too democratic, treating the Communist Party "as an authentic domestic political party and not as part of the world-wide Soviet Communist conspiracy."[60] It also explains why, in the early postwar period, the United States undertook a worldwide campaign to undermine the anti-fascist resistance, suppressing unions and other popular organizations and blocking democratic politics in Japan, Europe, and much of the Third World until proper outcomes were assured, while its junior partner in global management established its harsh rule in its own narrower domains.[61]

One of the bases for maintaining stability in client states of the Latin American variety is a symbiotic relationship between domestic liberalism and political figures in the dependencies who provide a façade for military rule. The conditions of the relationship are that the "democrats" in Central America pursue their task of preserving privilege and U.S. interests, while American liberals laud the encouraging growth of the tender plant of democracy while providing the means for the continuing terrorist assault against the population by the state security services and the death squads closely linked to them.

Well after the 1984 elections that established "democracy" in El Salvador to the applause of the Free Press, the human rights organization Socorro Juridico, operating under the protection of the Archdiocese of San Salvador, observed that the continuing terror is still conducted by

> the same members of the armed forces who enjoy official approval and are adequately trained to carry out these acts of collective suffering ... Salvadoran society, affected by terror and

panic, a result of the persistent violation of basic human rights, shows the following traits: collective intimidation and generalized fear, on the one hand, and on the other the internalized acceptance of the terror because of the daily and frequent use of violent means. In general, society accepts the frequent appearance of tortured bodies, because basic rights, the right to life, has absolutely no overriding value for society.[62]

The last comment also applies to the supervisors of these operations, as underscored by George Shultz in one of his lamentations on terrorism, a talk delivered just as the United States was carrying out the terror bombing of Libya. In El Salvador, he declared, "the results are something all Americans can be proud of"—at least, all Americans who enjoy the sight of tortured bodies, starving children, terror and panic, and generalized fear. And James LeMoyne, in one of his "carefully reported, sensitive accounts," concludes that "American support for elected governments [in El Salvador, Guatemala, and Honduras] has been a relative success." No doubt true, by some standards.[63]

The observations of Socorro Juridico on Salvadoran society under "democracy" were presented at the First International Seminar on Torture in Latin America, held at Buenos Aires in December 1985, a conference devoted to "the repressive system" that "has at its disposal knowledge and a multinational technology of terror, developed in specialized centers whose purpose is to perfect methods of exploitation, oppression and dependence of individuals and entire peoples" by the use of "state terrorism inspired by the Doctrine of National Security." This doctrine can be traced to the historic decision of the Kennedy administration to shift the mission of the Latin American military to "internal security," with consequences that are—or should be—well known.

The conference passed without notice in the U.S. media. None of this falls within the canon of terrorism as conceived in the civilized world or has the slightest bearing on the noble efforts of the United States to defend the imperfect but advancing democracies and to "restore democracy" to Nicaragua. Similarly, no celebration of the passionate U.S. commitment to human rights would be sullied by mention of the striking correlation between U.S. aid and torture worldwide documented in several studies, particularly in Latin America, where the leading academic specialist on human rights in the region concludes that U.S. aid "has tended to flow disproportionately to Latin American governments which torture their citizens, ... to the hemisphere's relatively egregious violators of fundamental human rights." This was prior to the Reagan administration, with its dedicated commitment to terror and torture.[64]

In one of their commentaries during the period we have been reviewing, the *Times* editors declared that "the Sandinistas have to understand that their neighbors and Washington rightly see a connection between internal and external behavior."[65] It must be, then, that the behavior of "their neighbors and Washington" illustrates this deep commitment to human rights. The editors also asked whether the Reagan administration could "bring itself to take [the calculated risk of a political settlement] and tolerate a Marxist neighbor, if it is boxed in by treaties and commitments to rudimentary human rights," commitments unnecessary for the "fledgling democracies" or their sponsor. They urged that the United States test the possibility of "securing Sandinista agreement to keep Soviet and Cuban bases, advisers and missiles out of Nicaragua" and agree not to "export revolution across Nicaragua's borders." The missiles and Soviet and Cuban bases are presumably added for dramatic effect, and Nicaragua's repeated offers to eliminate foreign advisers and installations are unmentioned, and are regularly unreported, just as no notice is merited when Cuba's foreign minister in early 1988 "reiterated his country's offer to withdraw its military advisers from Nicaragua once the U.S.-backed contra campaign against the Sandinista government ends."[66] The perceived problem throughout has been to find some way to "rein in the Sandinistas" and "contain their aggressive thrust" (*Washington Post*), to compel Nicaragua to "rein in its revolutionary army," as Democratic Senator Terry Sanford demands, an army that is illegitimately rampaging in Nicaragua when it seeks to defend the country from U.S. attack.[67] That Nicaragua might face some security problem remains beyond imagining.

Apart from regular unsupported allegations of Sandinista aid to the Salvadoran guerrillas, to which I return, the proclaimed basis for these fears concerning the Sandinista threat to the hemisphere is another coup of the State Department's Operation Truth, based upon a speech by commandante Tomás Borge. In it, he expressed his hopes that Nicaragua would be an example that others would follow, explaining that Nicaragua cannot "export our revolution" but can only "export our example" while "the people themselves of these countries ... must make their revolutions"; in this sense, he said, the Nicaraguan revolution "transcends national boundaries." In a conscious and purposeful fraud, State Department Psychological Operations converted these words into the threat of military conquest in pursuit of a "revolution without borders." The phrase was used as the title of the pathetic September 1985 State Department White Paper on alleged Nicaraguan subversion,[68] and repeatedly since, sometimes accompanied by the claim that this is a Sandinista *Mein Kampf*, as George Shultz warned Congress. The same fabrication served as the climax for Reagan's successful effort to obtain $100 million from Congress for the proxy army just as the World Court called upon the United States to terminate its aggression, and it remains a media staple in news columns and commentary, as I have reviewed elsewhere. The hoax was exposed at once by the Council on Hemispheric Affairs, and even received marginal notice in a review of State Department "public diplomacy" in the *Washington Post*. But none of this deterred media Agitprop in service of the worthy project "to demonize the Sandinista government" and "to turn it into a real enemy and threat in the minds of the American people," as a Reagan administration official phrased the goal.[69] Nor are these exercises of "perception management" deterred by the evident absurdity of the idea that Nicaragua *could* pose a threat of aggression while the U.S. stands by in helpless impotence. Again, a most impressive demonstration of what can be achieved by a mobilized independent press.

There was, to be sure, a basis for the perception that Nicaragua posed a threat. The real fear was that Borge's hopes might be realized. As Oxfam observed, Nicaragua posed "the threat of a good example." Like Arévalo and Arbenz in Guatemala, Allende in Chile, and many others, Nicaragua was perceived as a "rotten apple" that might "infect the barrel," a "virus" that might infect others, a "cancer" that might spread, in the terminology constantly used by planners when they contemplate the dread prospect of independent development geared to domestic needs. The real fear was expressed by Secretary of State Shultz in March 1986, when he warned that if the Sandinistas "succeed in consolidating their power," then *"all* the countries in Latin America, who *all* face serious internal economic problems, will see radical forces emboldened to exploit these problems."[70] It is therefore necessary to destroy the virus and inoculate the surrounding regions by terror, a persistent feature of U.S. foreign policy, based on the same concerns that animated Metternich and the Czar with regard to the threat to civilized order posed by American democracy. But these truths too lie far beyond the bounds of what can be expressed or imagined.

Returning to the range of expressible opinion, the second sample of opinion columns, like the first, confirms the expectations of the propaganda model, as do others. News reporting satisfies the same conditions, as has been documented in many investigations, ensuring that public opinion will not stray from proper bounds, at least among those segments of the population that count.

4

Adjuncts of Government

"It is very interesting," Senator William Fulbright observed in Senate hearings on government and the media in 1966, "that so many of our prominent newspapers have become almost agents or adjuncts of the government; that they do not contest or even raise questions about government policy."[1] These remarks are not precisely accurate: the media do contest and raise questions about government policy, but they do so almost exclusively within the framework determined by the essentially shared interests of state-corporate power. Divisions among elites are reflected in media debate,[2] but departure from their narrow consensus is rare. It is true that the incumbent state managers commonly set the media agenda. But if policy fails, or is perceived to be harmful to powerful interests, the media will often "contest government policy" and urge different means to achieve goals that remain beyond challenge or, quite often, even awareness.

To illustrate, I have reviewed a few samples of the media's contributions to the government project of "demonizing the Sandinistas" while praising the violent terror states backed or directly installed by the United States in the region. With all the skepticism I have personally developed through studying media performance over many years, I had not expected that they would rise to this challenge. When writing in 1985 about the Reaganite disinformation programs concerning Central America, I did not compare Nicaragua to El Salvador and Guatemala to demonstrate the hypocrisy of the charges (where they were not outright lies); that seemed an insult to the reader's intelligence. Instead, I compared the allegations concerning Nicaragua with the behavior of the "model democracy" of Israel during the same period and that of the United States itself in wartime conditions, showing that the Sandinista record was respectable by these—admittedly, not very impressive— standards.[3] But my assessment of the media was naive. Within a year they had succeeded in portraying the murderous U.S. clients as progressive if flawed democracies, while the Sandinistas, guilty of no crime that even begins to approach those of Washington's favorites, had become the very embodiment of evil.

The review in the last chapter of two periods of intense debate over U.S. policy towards Nicaragua kept to the spectrum of expressible opinion. News reporting conforms to the same implicit premises. The dichotomous treatment of the elections in El Salvador and Nicaragua provides one example, studied in detail elsewhere. The periods reviewed in the last chapter provide another. Political scientist Jack Spence studied 181 *New York Times* articles on Nicaragua during the first six months of 1986; the conclusions are similar to those drawn from the editorial and opinion columns.[4]

Spence observes that Central America was virtually ignored until U.S. control faced a challenge in 1978. From 1969 through 1977, the TV networks devoted a total of one hour to Nicaragua, all on the 1972 earthquake. They ignored the 1972 election in El Salvador, when the apparent victory of the Duarte-Ungo reformist ticket was overturned by blatant fraud and intervention by the U.S. clients in Nicaragua and Guatemala, guaranteeing the military rule that continues until the present. There being no challenge to U.S. domination, the problem of establishing "democracy" did not arise, just as it did not arise in 1984 in Panama when the notorious drug dealer General Noriega, then still a U.S. favorite, ran a fraudulent election legitimized by the attendance of George Shultz at the inauguration, where he "praised the vote as a triumph for democracy, taunting Nicaragua to do the same," after having been briefed by the CIA and the U.S. ambassador "that Noriega had stolen upwards of 50,000 ballots in order to ensure the election" of his candidates.[5]

Through the 1970s, the media ignored the growing crisis of access to land in Central America that lies at the roots of the current turmoil.[6] In the first six months of 1986, Spence observes, the "crucial issue" of "access to land and land ownership patterns" in Nicaragua received one sentence in the 181 articles, and agrarian policy was also virtually ignored in coverage of El Salvador, except for occasional mention of El Salvador's "progressive" reforms without serious analysis. Similarly, "Nicaraguan issues such as the effects of the war on Nicaragua, Sandinista programs, popularity, and support were not part of the news agenda." Most of the stories "emanated from Washington" and presented Reagan administration doctrine without challenge or analysis, including the laments about freedom fighters forced to fight with only "boots and bandages" against advanced Soviet armaments and Cuban-piloted helicopters, brutal repression in this "cancer, right here on our land mass" (George Shultz), guns to Colombian terrorists and subversion from Chile to Guatemala, Cuban troops "swarming the streets of Managua by the scores" in this terrorism sanctuary two days' drive from Texas, a second Libya, and so on through the familiar litany. In its news columns, Spence observes, "the *Times* tacitly accepted [the Reaganite] views, seeking out no others, thus contributing to a drastic narrowing for public debate." "Regarding the charges leveled against the Sandinistas, almost no contrary view could be found in the *Times* [and] ... supporting evidence was never present." "Four times the Nicaraguan Embassy was given a buried line or two," and in a few stories "the reporter added a background balance line": "it was as if the *Times* had a software program that, at rare and odd intervals, automatically kicked in a boilerplate 'balancing' graf beyond that story's halfway point." Critics of Reaganite *tactics* were cited, but virtually nothing beyond these limits.

As is well known, choice of sources can shield extreme bias behind a façade of objectivity. A study organized by media specialist Lance Bennett of the University of Washington investigated the distribution of attributed news sources for the month of September 1985 in the *New York Times* and the Seattle press. In *Times* coverage of El Salvador, over 80 percent of the sources were supportive of the government of El Salvador; 10 percent were drawn from the opposition. In *Times* coverage of Nicaragua, the pattern was reversed: more than two-thirds of sources selected were hostile to the government of Nicaragua, under 20 percent were from that government. The local media were similar. In fact, despite the apparent difference, the two patterns reflect the same criterion of source selection: in both cases, the primary sources were the U.S. government and its allies and clients (the government of El Salvador, the Nicaraguan political opposition and the contras). The study observes that in both countries, "the vast majority of Central Americans, the ordinary peasants, urban dwellers, workers and merchants, are virtually mute in U.S. news coverage of their lives." They account for 9 percent of attributed news sources, of which one-third are "U.S. individuals."

The study suggests that the reasons for these discrepancies may lie in the tendency to rely on "easily available 'official' sources" and other such "institutional factors." That is plausible, but one should not be misled. Opposition sources are, of course, easy to find in Nicaragua, where they operate freely and openly despite government harassment, while in El Salvador and Guatemala, most were murdered by the U.S.-backed security forces or fled; a nontrivial distinction that the media manage to suppress, indeed to reverse. In coverage of Afghanistan, the Kremlin is a more "easily available" source than guerrillas in the hills, but coverage is radically biased in the other direction (as it should be). Similarly, great efforts have been made to report the war in Nicaragua from the point of view of the contras. Reporting from the point of view of the Salvadoran or Guatemalan guerrillas, or the Viet Cong, has been next to nonexistent, and important sources that exist are often simply suppressed.[7] The same is true of publication of refugee studies, which typically reflects political priorities, not ease of access.[8] The "institutional factors" are doubtless real, but throughout there are conscious choices that flow from doctrinal needs.[9]

Spence found the same tendencies in his study of news reporting on Nicaragua in early 1986. Top priority was given to the U.S. government. Ranking second were the U.S. proxy forces. The contras received 727 column inches as compared to 417 for the Nicaraguan government, a discrepancy that was increased by 109 inches devoted to the U.S.-backed internal opposition in Nicaragua, overwhelmingly those who had refused to participate in the 1984 elections as the U.S. government had demanded. There were extensive reports of the concerns of the businessmen's association COSEP, harassment of the U.S.-funded journal La Prensa, one of whose owners was issuing thinly veiled calls for contra aid in Washington at the time, and other abuses. Coverage of the U.S. clients was largely favorable; only one of thirty-three stories on the contras focused on human rights abuses, and there were a few other references to atrocities that were by then reaching a remarkable scale. Like the State Department and Congress, the media preferred what human rights investigators described as "intentional ignorance."[10]

Turning to El Salvador, we find that the pattern is sharply reversed. Here, the guerrillas were castigated as Marxist terrorists, and the official line, as laid forth in New York Times editorials, was that things were improving under the democratic government of "the honorable Mr. Duarte," "the honest, reform-minded Christian Democrat," who is desperately trying to lead his people to a better life while "beset by implacable extremes," though he may have been "less than rigorous in bringing death squad operatives to judicial account" (in translation: he has done nothing to curb the security forces he praises for their "valiant service alongside the people against subversion" while conceding quietly that "the masses were with the guerrillas" when he assumed the role of front man for the war against the population). News reporting was similar in style. Duarte was portrayed in the major media as a victim, not as the willing agent whose role was to ensure adequate congressional funding for the state terrorists whom he protected. Analyzing over 800 articles in the major dailies from March 1984 through October 1985, journalist Marc Cooper found a consistent pattern of suppressing massive atrocities and "singing the praise of Administration policy." There were hundreds of column inches lauding Duarte's *promises* to end the rampant state terror conducted under his aegis, but virtually nothing on his actual record of apologetics for state terror and service to it, and not a single article "analyzing the nature of Duarte's alliance with the military establishment," the effective rulers.[11]

In the editorials reviewed over six and a half years, the *Times* never mentioned such matters as the assassination of Archbishop Romero or the raid by the security forces on the legal aid office of the archbishopric to destroy evidence implicating them in the assassination; the destruction and closure of the university by the army, with many killed; the physical destruction of the independent media and the murder and expulsion of their editors and publishers; or the Salvadoran state of siege from March 1980 when Duarte joined the junta, under which the atrocities were conducted with his backing and constant apologetics. In contrast, when Nicaragua declared a state of siege on October 15, 1985, the *Times* bitterly condemned this demonstration of Nicaragua's lack of "respect for democracy and human rights," dismissing with contempt "President Ortega's claim that the crackdown is the fault of 'the brutal aggression by North America and its internal allies' "; the *renewal* of El Salvador's far more draconian state of siege two days later received no mention. The events ignored in the editorials were also largely suppressed or falsified in the news columns.

There was no hint or concern in the editorials, and little (if any) reporting, about the fact that "since 1981 the Salvadoran press has either supported the government or criticized it from a right-wing perspective," avoiding "stories critical of government forces from a human rights standpoint," as observed in an Americas Watch review of freedom of the press. The political opposition had been murdered by Duarte's security forces or had fled the country, so there was no need to report or comment on their problems.[12] Similarly, no second thoughts were aroused by the fact that one of the leading murderers was selected to be Duarte's Minister of Defense, having completed his service as director of the National Guard. Earlier, he had coolly explained that "the armed forces are prepared to kill 200,000-300,000, if that's what it takes to stop a Communist takeover," and he had acted accordingly as the Guard under his command administered its "pedagogy of terror." When he was named Defense Minister, this mass murderer and torturer was described by the *New York Times* as "a soft-spoken, amiable man who has a reputation as an excellent administrator." Conceding that the Guard under his command had been responsible for horrible atrocities, including the rape and murder of four American churchwomen and the assassination of two U.S. labor advisors, the *Times* adds that "in his defense, others contend that under his command the National Guard's reputation has improved to the point where it is no longer considered the most abusive of Salvador's three security forces"—an impressive achievement, doubtless.[13]

With regard to Nicaragua, in contrast, the typical pattern was for the state propaganda services to concoct some charge that the media would then prominently and uncritically relay. Occasionally, when the charges were recognized to be too outlandish, a mild disclaimer might appear on the inside pages. Often the charges persisted even when they were acknowledged to be groundless or even sheer fabrication, a pattern that has also been well documented in the case of other official enemies.[14]

To fully appreciate the dichotomous treatment, we must bear in mind what had been happening in Nicaragua and El Salvador during these years, facts that I presume are familiar and so will not review here.[15] The disgrace of the Free Press could hardly be more dramatic.

It is worth stressing that far more is at issue here than dereliction of duty, incompetence, or service to power. The protection afforded to state terrorists in the "fledgling democracies" provides a veil behind which they can pursue their atrocities with crucial U.S. support, while the indignant focus on far lesser abuses in Nicaragua has facilitated the Reagan programs of terror and economic warfare that reversed social and economic progress in Nicaragua and reduced the economy to ruins, permitting regular media gloating over "Sandinista incompetence" and malevolence. The media were willing accomplices in an extraordinary outburst of violence and repression.

The point is more general. The U.S. government has been able to provide crucial support for mass slaughter by its Indonesian client in Timor (with the help of other Western powers) because the media simply refused to investigate the facts or report what they knew. The same was true of the destruction of the peasant societies of northern Laos, Cambodia, and South Vietnam, among many other cases. To mention only one current example, Israel has been emboldened to conduct its pogroms in the occupied territories by the same indulgence, knowing that all would be explained away as regrettable exceptions by its U.S. apologists: the editorial staff of the *New York Times,* the U.S. labor bureaucracy, or Elie Wiesel, the noted apostle of the obligation of silence in the face of atrocities by the state one loves, among many others.[16]

To raise the level of public understanding of Central American affairs during the critical early 1986 period, the *Times* devoted the cover story in the Sunday Magazine to an analysis by James LeMoyne of the deeper issues behind the rise of the "guerrilla network."[17] LeMoyne observes that "virtually every study of the region ... has concluded that the revolutions of Central America primarily have been caused by decades of poverty, bloody repression and frustrated efforts at bringing about political reform." Furthermore, every serious study has concluded that the United States bears a certain responsibility for these conditions, hence for the rise of "the guerrilla network," but no hint of that will be discovered in LeMoyne's discussion. He considers the role of Cuba, the Soviet Union, North Korea, the PLO, Vietnam, and so on, but one participant in the drama is missing, except for the statement that in El Salvador, "the United States bolstered the Salvadoran Army, insisted on elections and called for some reforms." Also missing is the fact that the army we "bolstered" conducted a program of slaughter and torture to destroy "the people's organizations fighting to defend their most fundamental human rights," to borrow the words of Archbishop Romero shortly before his assassination as he vainly pleaded with President Carter not to "bolster" these forces, which "know only how to repress the people and defend the interests of the Salvadorean oligarchy."

This combination of convenient historical ignorance and praise for the benevolence of our intentions is typical of media and other commentary. To cite only one more example, in an earlier *Times Magazine* cover story, Tad Szulc discussed the "radical winds of the Caribbean," noting that "the roots of the Caribbean problems are not entirely Cuban"; the "Soviet offensive" is also to blame along with the consequences of "colonial greed and mismanagement" by European powers. The United States is blamed only for "indifference" to the brewing problems. Few seem willing to comprehend the observation by former Costa Rican president Daniel Oduber that the "thugs" who threaten "the lives of Central Americans and their families ... are not the Leninist commissars but the armed sergeants trained in the United States."[18]

Spence observes that "the obviously relevant pending World Court decision was not mentioned in the 171 [news] stories that preceded the World Court decision itself" on June 27, 1986. In this decision, the court condemned the United States for its support for the contras and illegal economic warfare and ordered it to desist from its violations of international law and valid treaties and to pay reparations. The decision was reported, but dismissed as a minor annoyance. Its contents were suppressed or falsified, the World Court—not the United States—was portrayed as the criminal, and the rule of law was held inapplicable to the United States.

In its editorial response on July 1, the *Times* dismissed the court as a "hostile forum"; the editors had voiced no criticism when this same "hostile forum" ruled in favor of the United States in the matter of the Iran hostage crisis. They stated that "even the majority [of the court] acknowledged that prior attacks against El Salvador from Nicaragua made 'collective defense' a possible justification for America's retaliation." The editors assumed without comment that the United States was "retaliating" against Nicaraguan aggression and failed to mention that the court had explicitly *rejected* the claim of "collective self-defense" as a justification, even if the United States could establish the charges against Nicaragua that the court rejected as groundless after examining the evidence in official U.S. government documents; the court also noted, rather sardonically, that El Salvador had not even charged "armed attack" until August 1984, four months after Nicaragua had brought its claim to the court. In a July 17 op-ed, Thomas Franck of New York University Law School, a noted advocate of world order, argued that the United States should dismiss the World Court ruling because "America—acting alone or with its allies—still needs the freedom to protect freedom"; as in Nicaragua, for example.[19]

The U.S. government and the media are surpassed by none in their appeals to the august rule of law and the call for diplomacy rather than violence—when the derelictions of official enemies are at issue. Hence the events of summer 1986 called for some careful "perception management." Until June, Nicaragua's failure to accept the Contadora treaty draft was a major story. In May, the *New York*

Times published a lengthy report by Stephen Kinzer headlined "Nicaragua Balks at Latin Peace Accord," criticizing Ortega for his unwillingness to sign the agreement without some commitment from the United States. "Nicaragua appears to be the only Central American nation reluctant to sign the draft agreement," Kinzer wrote.[20] A few weeks later, Contadora was off the agenda. In mid-June the U.S. client states rejected the treaty draft under U.S. pressure. This fact was excluded from the national press, though reported abroad. Nicaragua declared its readiness to sign the treaty on June 21. The *Washington Post* ignored the unwelcome fact, but it received oblique mention in two tiny items in the *New York Times* under the headings "Nicaragua Makes Offer to Limit Some Weapons" and "U.S. Condemns Offer by Nicaragua on Treaty" (June 22, 23), focusing on the Reagan administration rejection of the move as "propagandistic." Both items appeared in the "Around the World" roundup of marginal news.

For adjuncts of government, news value is determined by utility for ideological warfare.

A few days after Nicaragua's acceptance of the treaty draft blocked by the United States and its clients, the World Court condemned the United States for its "unlawful use of force" and called for termination of U.S. aid to the contras. Congress responded by voting $100 million of military aid to implement the unlawful use of force, while government officials commented happily, "This is for real. This is a real war."[21]

Still pursuing the peaceful means that all states are obliged to follow under international (and U.S.) law, Nicaragua brought the matter to the U.N. Security Council, where the United States vetoed a resolution (11 to 1, 3 abstentions) calling on all states to observe international law. Nicaragua then turned to the General Assembly, which passed a resolution 94 to 3 calling for compliance with the World Court ruling. Two client states, Israel and El Salvador, joined the United States in opposition. The Security Council vote merited a brief note in the Newspaper of Record, but the General Assembly endorsement passed unmentioned; the *Times* U.N. correspondent preferred a story that day on overly high U.N. salaries. At the same session, Nicaragua called upon the U.N. to send an independent fact-finding mission to the border after a conflict there; the proposal was rejected by Honduras with U.S. backing, and was unreported, the general fate of Nicaraguan efforts to secure international monitoring of the borders—which would, of course, curb the Sandinista aggression that so terrifies U.S. leaders and ideological managers. A year later, on November 12, 1987, the General Assembly again called for "full and immediate compliance" with the World Court decision. This time only Israel joined the United States in opposing adherence to international law, another blow to the Central American accords, which had been signed in August much to the discomfiture of Washington. The vote was not reported by the *New York Times*, the *Washington Post*, or the three TV networks. Subsequent World Court proceedings on the matter of reparations to Nicaragua for U.S. crimes have also rarely reached the threshold; thus the August 1988 World Court announcement that the United States had failed to meet the court's deadline on determining war reparations passed virtually without notice.[22]

Not all U.N. resolutions are ignored. The day before the unreported 1987 General Assembly resolution again calling on the United States to comply with international law, the *Times* ran a substantial story headlined "U.N. Urges Soviet to Pull Forces from Afghanistan," reporting that the General Assembly voted "overwhelmingly today for the immediate withdrawal of Soviet forces from Afghanistan, brushing aside Moscow's first concerted attempt to deflect such criticism from the United Nations" in this "annual resolution." A *Times* review of the General Assembly session on December 26 is headlined "General Assembly delivers setbacks to U.S. and Soviet," subheaded "Washington Loses on Budget, Moscow on Afghanistan and Cambodia issues." The report mentioned nothing about the 94-to-2 vote on the World Court decision, in which the majority included U.S. allies Australia, Canada, Denmark, Iceland, the Netherlands, New Zealand, Norway, and Spain, as well as major Latin American countries (Argentina, Brazil, Colombia, Ecuador, Mexico, Peru, Uruguay, Venezuela), along with Sweden, Finland, and others.[23]

The reaction of the U.S. government and the media to world opinion as expressed through international institutions deserves closer attention. The same U.N. session provides a number of interesting examples. While all eyes were focused on the Washington summit, the INF treaty, and Reagan's achievements as a peacemaker,[24] the U.N. voted on a series of disarmament resolutions. The General Assembly voted 154 to 1, with no abstentions, opposing the buildup of weapons in outer space, a resolution clearly aimed at Reagan's Strategic Defense Initiative (Star Wars). It voted 135 to 1 against developing new weapons of mass destruction. In both cases, the United States was alone in opposition. The United States was joined by France in opposing a resolution, passed 143 to 2, calling for a comprehensive test ban treaty. Another vote calling for a halt to all nuclear test explosions passed by a vote of 137 to 3, with the United States joined by France and Britain in opposition. A week later, the *New York Times Magazine* published a review of the Star Wars program by its correspondent William Broad, observing that "since the dawn of the space age, many people have felt that man's final frontier, the edge of the universe, should be a preserve used exclusively for peaceful purposes" and raising the question of whether space "should be armed." But the expression of opinion on the matter by the world community merited no comment. All of these votes were unreported, and unmentioned in the review of "Setbacks to U.S. and Soviet" at the United Nations.[25]

Other *New York Times* reports on the same U.N. session provide further insight into the style of coverage of world opinion. Two days after the overwhelming U.N. votes in favor of the unreported disarmament resolutions that the United States opposed virtually alone, a *Times* story reported a vote on a resolution that "reaffirms the United Nations' previous strong condemnation of international terrorism in all its forms," calls "on all countries to cooperate in eradicating terrorism," and "invites the Secretary General to seek the views of member states on terrorism and on 'the ways and means' of combating it." The resolution passed 128 to 1, Israel alone in opposition, with the United States abstaining and "the other 128 members present vot[ing] in favor." The headline reads: "Syria, Isolated at U.N., Drops Terrorism Plan."[26]

Five days later, the General Assembly passed a resolution condemning "Terrorism Wherever and by Whomever Committed." The vote was 153 to 2, with Israel and the United States opposed and Honduras alone abstaining. In particular, all NATO countries voted for it. This vote was unreported, and unmentioned in the December 26 review of the session. The U.S.-Israeli objection was presumably based on the statement that "nothing in the resolution would prejudice the right of peoples, particularly those under colonial or racist regimes, or under foreign occupation or other forms of domination, to struggle for self-determination, freedom and independence, or to seek and receive support for that end."[27]

Media refusal to report the isolation of the United States and Israel on these matters is of no small importance, as was illustrated a year later, when the Palestine National Council met in Algiers in November 1988 and passed an important political resolution which centered upon a declaration of Palestinian independence, issued on November 15. The resolution opened by stating that "This session [of the PNC] was crowned by the declaration of a Palestinian state on our Palestinian territory." This, however, was not to the taste of U.S. policymakers so that the matter quickly moved to the margins of media discussion. The PNC resolution went on to suggest modalities for implementing a political settlement that would include an independent national state for the Palestinians and "arrangements of security and peace for all the states of the region." Here we enter into areas that the U.S. government is willing to consider, so these issues quickly became the focus of media attention.[28]

The PNC resolution called for an international conference "on the basis of United Nations Security Council Resolutions 242 and 338 and the assurance of the legitimate national rights of the Palestinian people and, first and foremost, their right to self-determination." In its statement the PNC "again declares its rejection of terror in all its forms, including state terror," and "renews its commitment to the United Nations resolutions that affirm the right of peoples to resist foreign occupation, colonialism and racial discrimination and their right to struggle for their independence." The latter phrases reiterate the content and wording of the unreported General Assembly resolution on terrorism. The rejection and denunciation of terrorism was nothing new. Thus, the PLO journal *Shu'un Filastiniyya*, May-June 1986, presents the text of a PLO proposal which calls for an international conference including "the Israeli government" and aimed at reaching "a peaceful settlement of the Palestinian problem on the basis of the pertinent United Nations resolutions including Security Council resolutions 242 and 338." The text continues: "The PLO declares its rejection and denunciation of terrorism, which had been assured in the Cairo Declaration of November, 1985."[29]

The U.S. government declared the PNC declaration unacceptable. The "crowning" achievement was of course dismissed. Turning to matters that Washington was willing to take seriously, first, the PNC acceptance of U.N. 242 was too "ambiguous," because it was accompanied by a call for recognition of the rights of the Palestinians alongside of those of Israel, and therefore failed to meet the demands of U.S.-Israeli rejectionism, in which the two countries are largely isolated.[30] Second, the PNC did not meet U.S. conditions on renunciation of terror; that is, the PNC adopted the position of the international community, which the United States and Israel alone reject.

One can imagine two ways in which these events might be presented in the media. One would be to report that the highest Palestinian authority has issued a declaration of independence, officially accepting the principle of partition. Furthermore, the PNC has, even more clearly than before, expressed PLO support for the broad international consensus in favor of a political settlement that recognizes the rights of Israel and the Palestinians to self-determination and security, and has officially reaffirmed its support for the stand of the international community, including the NATO powers, on the matter of terrorism. Meanwhile, the United States and Israel remain largely isolated on the first issue, keeping to their rejectionist position and again barring the peace process, and are entirely isolated in their opposition to the right of people to struggle for freedom and self-determination against racist and colonial regimes and foreign occupation. And Israel alone refuses to accept U.N. 242; see below.

A second alternative would be to dismiss the declaration of independence as an irrelevance, to ignore completely the isolation of the United States and Israel on the other issues, and to accept the U.S. position as by definition correct, as the "moderate stance" and the basis for any further discussion. Then we conduct a debate over whether the Palestinians should be encouraged to progress further towards moderation now that, under our tutelage, they have taken these halting steps, or whether their stern mentor should simply dismiss these moves and demand that the PLO begin to be serious, or disappear.

The first version, which would have the merit of truth, is not to be found in the U.S. media. The second alternative not only prevailed, but was close to exceptionless. In the *New York Times*, the editors quoted the statement on terrorism, describing it as "the old Arafat hedge" and failing to note that it reiterates the U.N. resolutions that the United States and Israel alone reject. Anthony Lewis, who is virtually alone in the mainstream in his efforts to escape the bounds of dogma on these issues, deplored the failure to reward the PLO for its progress towards the U.S. stand, adding that it still must become more "clear" in its political pronouncements and that "the United States says correctly that the PLO must unambiguously renounce all terrorism before it can take part in negotiations." He raises no question about the "clarity" of the rejectionist U.S. stance, and holds that the United States is right not to be fooled by "the old Arafat hedge," that is, the position accepted by the entire world community apart from the United States and Israel (and, of course, South Africa). If

Arafat does not join us off the spectrum of world opinion, plainly he cannot be taken seriously. Elsewhere, the same bounds were observed, often even more narrowly.[31]

In short, the world does not agree with us, so it follows, by simple logic, that the world is wrong; that is all there is to the matter. No alternative possibility can be discussed, even conceived. Still more strikingly, even the fact that the world does not agree with us cannot be acknowledged. Since it fails to see the light, the world outside our borders does not exist (Israel aside). We see here the grip of doctrine in a form that would have deeply impressed the medieval Church, or the mullahs in Qum today.

Once again, the consequences should not be disregarded. Media self-censorship over many years has enabled the United States and Israel to block what has long been a possible political settlement of one of the world's most explosive and threatening issues. That continued to be the case as the United States changed its increasingly untenable position on discussions with the PLO under a fraudulent pretext while maintaining its commitment to obstruct the peace process.[32] Senator Fulbright's observation is both pertinent and of much significance.

Returning to coverage of the United Nations, a March 1988 story, headlined "U.N. to Study Rights in Cuba: U.S. Sees Diplomatic Victory," reported Cuba's invitation to the U.N. Human Rights Commission for an on-the-scene investigation, undercutting a U.S. campaign for a resolution condemning Cuba. The first thirteen paragraphs present Washington's point of view, turning the failure into a great triumph of U.S. diplomacy; the last paragraph quotes a Cuban official stating that "the outcome shows our continent's growing political unity" in rejecting the U.S. effort. Another *Times* article reports a visit of American human rights specialists to Cuban prisons, with a line in the final paragraph noting, with no comment, that the State Department has denied visas to Cuban officials for a reciprocal visit to U.S. prisons, just as Reagan launched his human rights drive in Moscow.[33]

Unreported is a resolution on the Middle East passed by the Human Rights Commission on the same day as its rejection of the U.S. initiative on Cuba. The resolution, passed 26 to 1 with the United States alone in opposition, expressed grave concern at "the continuation of acts of aggression and the arbitrary practices of the Israeli occupation forces in southern Lebanon which constitute a flagrant violation" of international law, and called upon Israel's allies to pressure it to end "its aggressive and expansionist policy in southern Lebanon."[34]

World opinion must pass through the same filters that set the bounds of respectability at home. Failing to meet these standards, it is ignored, or subjected to puzzled inquiry as to just why the world is out of step. The pattern, again, is pervasive.[35]

The government-media campaign to "demonize the Sandinistas" faced a new challenge when the Central American presidents reached a peace agreement in August 1987. The Reagan administration had long sought to undercut diplomatic initiatives. After bitterly condemning the Sandinistas for refusing to sign the Contadora draft of 1984, the administration quickly changed its tune when Nicaragua unexpectedly announced that it would sign, at which point the draft became a deception and a fraud and the United States proceeded to undermine it with further denunciations of the treacherous Sandinistas. "Washington tried by all means available to block the signing of the Contadora Peace Act," Costa Rican vice-for-eign affairs minister Gerardo Trejos Salas observed in an unreported interview, reviewing how the United States "strongly pressured" Costa Rica and its client states during 1985-86 when he was "a first-hand witness."[36] Events followed the same course in June 1986, as we have seen.

The Arias initiatives of 1987 were also most unwelcome to the Reagan administration. In June its "peace emissary," Philip Habib, informed "high ranking Senators" that "if the administration felt its views and interests were not reflected in the regional arrangements it would continue to fund the Nicaraguan contra rebels despite agreements reached by the [Central American] leaders," an advance notice that elicited little attention. In the same month, the adminis-tration pressured President Duarte to block a scheduled meeting of Central American presidents in Guatemala. A Guatemalan official reported that Duarte "personally told Guatemala's president the reason he asked for the postponement was because of US pressure," applied by Habib.[37] The Guatemalan and Honduran press published the dialogue between Habib and Duarte, as reported by Salvadoran officials to the Guatemalan government (then to the Guatemalan Congress). In the talks, Habib pressed Duarte to reject the Arias peace plan, informing him that the requirement that El Salvador negotiate with the unarmed opposition would destroy "democracy in El Sal-vador." Duarte acceded and insisted upon postponement of the June meeting.[38]

The U.S. media were uninterested. Habib is regularly depicted as a forthright advocate of diplomacy and peace.

In a last-ditch effort to undermine the peace agreement, Washington put forth the Reagan-Wright plan on August 5, calling for dismantling the political system in Nicaragua, an end to arms aid to Nicaragua, and demobilization of Sandinista forces. In return the United States would *pledge* to halt shipments of arms to the contras. This proposal received wide media acclaim as fair and just; the Iran-contra hearings that had concluded two days earlier had passed into ancient history, along with their suggestion that a U.S. pledge might be worth less than gold. Nevertheless, to the surprise and annoyance of the administration, the Central American presidents reached an agreement on August 7.

Government propaganda then shifted, predictably, to the demolition of the unacceptable accords. The media followed faithfully along. I have reviewed the details elsewhere, so I will only summarize this most remarkable campaign.[39]

The problem to be addressed was a familiar one: a great power has been unable to impose its will and finds itself confronted with conditions and circumstances that it refuses to accept. A state that commands unusual power, such as the United States, has a variety of ways to deal with the problem. One is to pretend that the adversary has capitulated, accepting the U.S. stand. This option can be pursued only if the information system can be trusted to fall into line, presenting the U.S. government version as if it were true, however outlandish the pretense. If the media meet their responsibilities in this way, then the adversary must indeed accept U.S. terms, or else suffer retribution for violating the alleged solemn commitment to adhere to them.

One striking example of this technique was the treatment of the Paris peace treaty of January 1973, which the United States was compelled to sign after the failure of its attempt to bludgeon North Vietnam into submission by the Christmas B-52 bombings of populated areas. The U.S. government at once offered a version of the treaty that was diametrically opposed to its terms on every crucial point. This version was uniformly accepted and promulgated by the media, so that the actual terms of the peace treaty had been dismissed to the memory hole literally within a few days. The United States and its South Vietnamese client then proceeded with massive violations of the actual treaty in an effort to attain their long-sought goals by violence, and when the Vietnamese adversaries finally responded in kind, they were universally denounced for the breakdown of the agreements and compelled to suffer for their crime.[40] The case of the Central America peace accords was similar. It was necessary to refashion them to conform to U.S. dictates, a task that was accomplished with the anticipated cooperation of the media, though it took a little longer than the overnight victory at the time of the Paris peace accords—perhaps an indication that the media really have become more "adversarial" than in the past.

The first requirement of the demolition campaign was to establish that it was U.S. support for the contras that had forced the Sandinistas to negotiate. This is always an important doctrine, since it can be exploited to justify subsequent resort to armed force and terror. The thesis hardly withstands the evidence of history: Nicaragua's effort to pursue the peaceful means required by international law through the World Court, the United Nations, and the Contadora process, and Washington's success in "trumping" these initiatives.[41] Such problems were readily overcome by dismissal of the facts to the memory hole. The required doctrinal truth then became the merest cliché. The *New York Times* editors could therefore criticize Michael Dukakis during the 1988 election campaign because he "undervalues the role of force in bringing the Sandinistas to the bargaining table."[42] It would be unreasonable to expect troublesome facts to stand in the way of a principle that authorizes continued reliance on violence as the necessary means for bringing peace. More generally, what is useful is True. Period.

The first task was accomplished with dispatch. The next problem was to dismantle the accords themselves. Their first phase ran from the signing in August 1987 to January 1988, when the Central American presidents were to receive the report of the International Verification Commission (CIVS), which was charged with monitoring the accords. The goal of the Reagan administration was to focus all attention on the Sandinistas, thus ensuring that the United States could maintain the attack by its proxy forces and exclude the U.S. client states from the provisions of the accords. The media at once dedicated themselves to these further tasks, and by January the last shreds of the original accords disappeared, replaced by the initial U.S. terms. Henceforth, the irrelevant facts become of interest only to archivists. It is the necessary illusions that prevail.

The peace plan specified one "indispensable element" for peace, namely, a termination of open or covert aid of any form ("military, logistical, financial, propagandistic") to "irregular forces" (the contras) or "insurrectionist movements" (indigenous guerrillas). In response, the United States at once stepped up its illegal CIA supply flights, which had already reached the phenomenal level of one a day in an effort to keep the proxy forces in the field. These doubled in September and virtually tripled in the months that followed. Surveillance flights also increased. Successes were immediately evident as contra attacks on civilians doubled in intensity, including ambushes, murders, attacks on farm cooperatives, and kidnappings.[43] The CIA also offered bribes to Miskito leaders to prevent them from joining the peace process.

The peace agreements were thus effectively dead from the first moment. These were, by far, the most significant developments during the August-January phase of the accords.

The media responded to these unacceptable facts by suppressing them. The United States was of course not a signatory, so technically speaking it could not "violate" the accords. An honest accounting, however, would have noted—indeed, emphasized—that the United States acted at once to render the accords nugatory. Nothing of the sort is to be found. Apart from marginal groups with access to alternative media, not subject to the code of discipline, even the most assiduous media addict could hardly have been more than minimally aware of these crucial facts. The behavior of the *New York Times* was particularly remarkable, including outright falsification along with scrupulous suppression.

Suppression of evidence concerning U.S. supply flights persisted after the accords were finally demolished in January 1988. Nicaraguan reports, which had been accurate and ignored in the past, continued to be ignored by the media, as inconsistent with the images they seek to convey. In December 1988, Defense Minister Humberto Ortega alleged that the Reagan administration was continuing supply flights to contras inside Nicaragua in violation of the congressional ban (not to speak of the forgotten peace accords and the even more profoundly irrelevant terms of international law). He claimed that Nicaraguan radar detected ten clandestine supply flights into Nicaragua from Ilopango air base near San Salvador in November—the "Hasenfus route"—adding that "We are talking about CIA flights; we do not know if they have the approval of the Salvadoran government." Apart from faith in the doctrine of miraculous "change of course," there was little reason to doubt that the report might be true. It was as usual ignored, and no investigation, commentary, or conclusions followed. These quite significant reports from Nicaragua were available to readers of the English language *Barricada Internacional* (Managua), but not those of the *New York Times*, or elsewhere to my knowledge. Attacks by the U.S.-run terrorist forces on civilians also continued, unreported, in accordance with the general pattern for years.[44]

The accords called for "justice, freedom and democracy" and guarantees for "the inviolability of all forms of life and liberty" and "the safety of the people," for "an authentic pluralistic and participatory democratic process to promote social justice" and "respect for human rights." These provisions were also unacceptable to the United States, because they plainly could not be met or even approached in the U.S. client states without the dismantling of the governmental structure, dominated by the armed forces and security services. Having eliminated the provisions applying to the United States, the media therefore faced a second task: to remove the practices of the client states from the agenda. This problem was readily overcome by the same means: simple refusal to report the facts, or marginalization and distortion when they were too visible to ignore entirely. State terror in the U.S. client states escalated, but no matter. The laser-like focus of the media was on Nicaragua, which received far more coverage than the other countries combined—virtually all of it concentrating on departures from the accords as interpreted in Washington.

Another unacceptable feature of the accords was the role given to international monitors, the CIVS. The United States brooks no interference in its domains; hence the longstanding U.S. opposition to the peace efforts of the Latin American democracies, and now to the CIVS as well. Furthermore, the CIVS presence would inhibit violation of the accords, thus interfering with U.S. intentions. The first phase of the accords ended in January with a report by the CIVS, which had the bad taste to condemn the United States and its clients while praising steps taken by Nicaragua. Obviously it had to go. The *Times* cooperated by virtually suppressing the CIVS report, and under U.S. pressure the monitoring commission was abolished.

The victory was complete: not a shred of the original agreements remained. Nicaragua responded by announcing that it would satisfy the terms of the former accords unilaterally, requesting international supervision to monitor its agreement alone. The loyal media responded by announcing that finally Nicaragua had agreed to comply with the peace accords, though of course Communists cannot be trusted.

Meanwhile state terror escalated in the client states, without, however, influencing the judgment that Nicaragua bore prime responsibility for violating the accords; the correct response, given that the United States and its clients were now exempt, by Washington-media edict. In the *Times,* the terror was barely noted, apart from *guerrilla* terror in El Salvador, to which the government sometimes "responded," James LeMoyne commented with regret. In October 1988, Amnesty International released a report on the sharp increase in death squad killings, abduction, torture, and mutilation, tracing the terror to the government security forces. The *Times* ignored the story, while the Senate passed a resolution warning Nicaragua that new military aid would be sent to the contras if the *Sandinistas* continued to violate the peace accords.[45]

Returning to January 1988, with the accords now restricted to the question of Nicaraguan compliance with Washington's dictates, the crucial issue became the willingness of the Sandinistas to negotiate with the CIA-established civilian front for Washington's proxy forces. The accords themselves required no such negotiations, as was occasionally noted in the small print, but they had long since been dismissed to oblivion. In early 1988, Nicaragua did agree to this U.S. condition, reaching an unexpected cease-fire agreement with the contras. Meanwhile the indigenous guerrillas in El Salvador and Guatemala were consistently rebuffed in their efforts to negotiate, but these facts were suppressed as irrelevant, in conformity with the Washington-media version of the accords. Where not suppressed, the facts were simply denied, as when Jeane Kirkpatrick wrote in June that "Duarte has seen his generous offers of amnesty and negotiations rejected by the FMLN [guerrillas], one by one." This pronouncement followed Duarte's rejection of a series of efforts by the FMLN, the political opposition, and the Church to arrange negotiations; the generous offer of amnesty, as Kirkpatrick fully understands, would be an offer to be slaughtered by the death squads, quite apart from the fact that the Duarte government—unlike the Sandinistas—was refusing amnesty for guerrilla leaders.[46]

The Nicaraguan cease-fire was signed on March 23. The agreement stated that "only humanitarian aid will be negotiated and accepted in accordance with article 5" of the August 1987 accords, to "be channeled through neutral organizations." Organization of American States (OAS) secretary general João Clemente Baena Soares was entrusted with ensuring compliance with the agreement. Congress responded by voting overwhelmingly to violate the terms of the cease-fire, approving $47.9 million in aid to the contras, to be administered by the State Department through the U.S. Agency for International Development (AID). The aid would be delivered in Honduras and within Nicaragua by a "private company," James LeMoyne reported, quoting contra leader Alfredo César; the phrase "private company" is a euphemism for the CIA, for which AID has admittedly served as a front in the past. Contra leader Aldolfo Calero stated that the cease-fire agreement allowed for delivery of aid to the Nicaraguan border by the CIA, and Democratic Congressperson David Bonior added that the rebels would select "the private carrier." By no stretch of the imagination can AID be considered a "neutral organization."[47]

The congressional legislation stipulated that all aid must be administered in a manner consistent with the March 23 cease-fire agreement and in accord with the decisions of the Verification Commission established by that agreement, for which Secretary General Soares was the responsible authority. In a letter to George Shultz on April 25, Soares drew his attention to this passage of the congressional legislation and stated that reliance on AID was in clear violation of the cease-fire agreement, expressing his "deep concern about this whole situation." He emphasized further that article 5 of the peace accords, which determines how aid shall be delivered under the cease-fire agreement, quite explicitly rules out any assistance whatsoever to the contras except for repatriation or resettlement. Aid can be sent to contras within Nicaragua by means agreed by both sides, as a means towards their "reintegration into normal life," but for no other end. The objections of the official in charge of monitoring the agreement were disregarded—in fact unreported to my knowledge—and the illegal operations continued.[48]

It would be interesting to learn whether any reference appeared in the U.S. media to the decision of the World Court concerning "humanitarian aid" (paragraph 243). If such aid is "to escape condemnation" as illegal intervention, the court declared, "not only must it be limited to the purposes hallowed in the practice of the Red Cross, namely, 'to prevent and alleviate human suffering', and 'to protect life and health and to ensure respect for the human being'; it must also, and above all, be given without discrimination to all in need in Nicaragua, not merely to the *contras* and their dependents." "An essential feature of truly humanitarian aid is that it is given 'without discrimination' of any kind." Even the most imaginative commentator would have some difficulty rendering that judgment compatible with the congressional legislation. Best, then, to suppress the matter, an easy matter in an intellectual culture that disdains the rule of law as a childish absurdity (when it applies to us) and that conforms to the requirements of the powerful virtually as a reflex.

The *Times* report on the decision of Congress to fund the contras in violation of the cease-fire agreement, the peace accords, and international law cited views ranging from hawks who condemned the sellout of the contras "as a low point in United States history" (Senator John McCain), to Senator Brock Adams, who voted against the aid proposal on the grounds that "the United States attempt to create a government through the contras is a historic mistake, similar to our trying to create a government in Southeast Asia. We are in a position again of supporting military force without victory." These two quotes also appeared in "Quotations of the Day."[49] Appropriately, the highlighted opinion falls well within the acceptable bounds of mere tactical disagreement.

AID head Alan Woods said that the aid would have to be delivered by "private American aircraft" and that there was no assurance that the Sandinistas would permit such airdrops to the contras within Nicaragua—in violation of the cease-fire agreement, as Secretary General Soares had determined. The *Times* article reporting this is headed "Official Sees Problems on Contra Aid: The big hurdle is Sandinista mistrust." AID then began delivering supplies to contras in Honduras, violating the congressional legislation that stipulated that the aid was to be delivered "in cease-fire zones," all of which are in Nicaragua, and violating the cease-fire agreement for the reasons already spelled out; for one, because "AID, a U.S. agency, clearly is not ... [a] neutral organization," the Council on Hemispheric Affairs pointed out, noting the protest by Soares, and the Nicaraguan complaint "that weapons originating from the CIA base at Swan Island, Honduras, had been concealed in the banned shipments." Wire services reported that Nicaragua had offered to have supplies sent to the contras through the Red Cross or other neutral agencies and that representatives of rebel Indian groups "agreed with the government that the International Red Cross should handle distribution of humanitarian aid to them," offers rejected or ignored by the U.S. government and its proxies.[50]

The Democratic Study Group of Congress issued a report condemning the administration for numerous violations of the cease-fire agreement and the congressional legislation. It noted that the Sandinistas had proposed the Red Cross, UNICEF, and other recognized relief agencies as delivery agents, but that all but one of them had been rejected by AID, which proposed several organizations with right-wing political ties and no experience in Latin America. The Study Group reported also that the Sandinistas had "invited the contras to propose another agency," receiving no response from the contras—not surprisingly, since they were being supplied in violation of the cease-fire agreement. The report also noted that while sending aid illegally to the contras, the administration had refused to provide assistance to the families of Indian rebels and would only supply fighters based in Honduras, using a company that had carried supplies to the contras.[51]

The facts were largely ignored by the *Times*, which offered a different version. James LeMoyne reported that "because the Sandinistas have managed to obstruct efforts to resupply the rebels, as called for under the cease-fire terms, they may attack them at a moment of maximum weakness when the cease-fire ends." Robert Pear alleged that President Ortega "has blocked deliveries" of the aid authorized by Congress on grounds "that the deliveries would violate the cease-fire agreement." Unmentioned was the fact that this was also the conclusion of the official in charge of monitoring the agreement; his name did appear in the article, but only in the context of the Reagan administration decision that he had not met their financial "accountability standards," so they had not disbursed the $10 million provided by Congress for the commission to verify compliance with the cease-fire agreement—an understandable reaction to verification mechanisms when the U.S. government is intent on violating agreements and international law with the protection of the media.[52]

In further violation of both the cease-fire agreement and the congressional legislation, the Reagan administration sent funds to the contras to spend as they wished, a method "regarded by AID as sufficient accounting," congressperson Tony Coelho commented sardonically. AID officials announced that in addition to food aid, "more than $1 million in materiel—military equipment and supplies—also was delivered," though not weapons and ammunition, the *Washington Times* reported. Congress had legislated the delivery of aid to Nicaraguan children, stipulating, however, that "no assistance may be provided to or through the government of Nicaragua," which operates most medical facilities and hospitals. AID predictably gave the condition the narrowest interpretation, thus effectively restricting this rather cynical gesture on the part of those funding the "unlawful use of force" against Nicaragua. AID also rejected offers by nonpartisan humanitarian organizations to deliver aid to Nicaraguan children. A letter from Brown University Medical School offering to submit a detailed proposal to distribute this aid was not even acknowledged. The Nicaraguan government later refused all such aid as long as the United States supports the contras, on grounds that "it makes no sense to receive aid for children from the same body that is responsible for their injuries," the Embassy press officer said. "It's like someone giving you a beating and then, to relieve his conscience, he gives you a Band-Aid. Then he gives you another beating."[53]

The national media remained unperturbed throughout, in accordance with the doctrine that the United States stands above any law or international agreement—and needless to say, above any moral principle.

Meanwhile, the U.S. Treasury Department announced a new ruling that barred import of Nicaraguan coffee processed in a third country, which "will not be considered sufficiently transformed to lose its Nicaraguan identity." It suffices to replace "Nicaraguan" with "Jewish" to know to which phase of history this edict belongs. "The language echoes definitions of ethnic purity in the Third Reich," the *Boston Globe* observed.[54]

During the same months, negotiations on a political settlement broke down through the device of demand escalation by the contras, no doubt following the State Department script. Each new government agreement, going far beyond the terms of the long-forgotten peace accords, simply led to new demands. In their final effort to prevent an agreement, the contras submitted a new list of demands on June 9, 1988, including: immediate freeing of all people imprisoned for political or related common crimes; the right of draftees to leave the army as they choose; forced resignation of the Supreme Court Justices (to be replaced by decision of the contras, the opposition, and the government, thus ensuring Washington's clients a 2-to-1 majority); restoration of or compensation for seized contra property distributed to smallholders and cooperatives (benefiting mainly Somoza supporters); suspension of government military recruitment; opening of contra offices in Managua and licensing of "independent" television stations (which means, in effect, stations run by the United States, which will quickly dominate the airwaves for obvious reasons of resource access). All of these actions, some unconstitutional, were to be taken by the government while the contra forces remain armed and in the field. Reviewing the record, the

Center for International Policy observed that the goal could only have been "to torpedo the negotiations and throw the issue back once more to a divided U.S. Congress." Julia Preston commented that "the contras' six-page proposal appeared to be a farewell gesture rather than a negotiating document," with its "sweeping new demands" followed by their quick departure from Managua before negotiations were possible.[55]

The government of Nicaragua urged resumption of the talks, receiving no response from Washington or the contras, who added new demands. Even Cardinal Obando, who barely conceals his sympathy for the contras, urged them to return to the talks, to no avail. There followed what the Council on Hemispheric Affairs described as "a CIA-managed campaign of provocation and internal disruption inside Nicaragua," which "established a false crisis atmosphere" in which Congress could turn to new aid for the contras. Congressional doves implemented legislation providing renewed aid, while warning the Sandinistas that military aid would follow if Nicaragua continued to stand alone in the way of peace and democracy or attacked the contra forces, who reject negotiations and carry out atrocities in Nicaragua.[56] The media trailed happily along.

As the Reagan administration drew to a close, it was becoming less realistic, and less necessary, to rely on contra terror as an instrument to punish Nicaragua for its efforts to direct resources to the poor majority, to improve health and welfare standards, and to pursue the path of independent development and neutralism. Despite levels and forms of military support unheard of in authentic insurgencies and domination of large areas of Nicaragua by U.S. propaganda, the United States had failed to create a viable guerrilla force, quite a remarkable fact. A new administration, less intent on punishing disobedience by sheer terror, would be likely to join the elite consensus of the preceding years, which recognized that there are more cost-effective ways to strangle and destroy a small country in a region so dependent on relations with the United States for survival. They are capable of understanding the assessment of a World Bank Mission in October 1980, which concluded that economic disaster might ensue if Nicaragua did not receive extensive foreign assistance to overcome the effects of the destruction and robbery of the last Somoza years: "Per capita income levels of 1977 will not be attained, in the best of circumstances, until the 1990s.[57] With private enterprise wrecked and the economy ruined probably beyond repair by U.S. economic warfare, the resort to violence—costly to the United States in world opinion and disruptive at home—had lost much of its appeal for those who do not see inflicting pain and suffering as ends in themselves. There are, surely, other and more efficient ways to eliminate the danger of successful independent development in a weak and tiny country.

We can, then, become a "kinder, gentler nation" pursuing more "pragmatic" policies to attain our ends.

Furthermore, although the government-media campaign succeeded in wrecking the peace accords of 1987 and their promise, nevertheless forces were set in motion that the administration could not control. Illegal clandestine support for the contras became more difficult after the partial exposures during the Iran-contra affair, and it was no longer possible to organize overt congressional support for the contras at the extraordinary level required to keep them in the field. As the level of supply flights reduced in early 1988 along with prospects for renewed official aid, the proxy forces fled to Honduras and might well have been wiped out had it not been for the dispatch of elite U.S. military units—the "invasion" of Honduras by the United States, as the mainstream media there described it, the defense of Honduras from Sandinista aggression in the terms of U.S. discourse.

Elements of the contras can and presumably will be maintained within Nicaragua as a terrorist force, to ensure that Nicaragua cannot demobilize and divert its pitifully limited resources to reconstruction from the ruins left by Somoza and Reagan. A persistent U.S. threat of invasion can also be maintained to guarantee that Nicaragua must keep up its guard, at great cost, while commentators ridicule Sandinista paranoia, Jeane Kirkpatrick-style. But it will no longer be necessary to depict the contras as the people, united, rising against their tormentors, sturdy peasants struggling against Soviet "hegemonism," as the media's favorite experts had soberly explained. By early 1989, we read that "Sandinista claims that the contras were merely U.S. mercenaries gained new credence among Nicaraguans ... The contras are viewed as an army of Nicaraguans who thought they would get well-paid, secure jobs from the United States but guessed wrong."[58] Low-level terror, "perception management," and "containment" will compel the Nicaraguan government to maintain a high level of military preparation and internal controls, and along with economic and ideological warfare, should suffice to secure the achievements of Reaganite violence, even if the further goal of restoring Nicaragua to the "Central American mode" must be ruefully abandoned. That is what the future holds, if the domestic population of the United States permits it. The task of the media is to ensure that they do.

The devastating hurricane of October 1988, with its welcome prospects of mass starvation and vast long-term ecological damage, reinforced this understanding. The United States naturally refused any aid. Even the inhabitants of the demolished town of Bluefields on the Atlantic Coast, with longstanding links to the United States and deep resentment over Sandinista methods of extending Nicaraguan sovereignty over the region, must be deprived of sustenance or building materials; they must starve without roofs to shield them from the rain, to punish the Sandinistas. At the outer reaches of mainstream criticism of Reagan administration policies, the *Boston Globe* explained in a Christmas message why the United States is sending no assistance after the hurricane. Under a picture of Daniel Ortega, the caption reads: "Nicaragua has received little US humanitarian aid because of policies of President Daniel Ortega."[59] The U.S. allies, intimidated by the global enforcer and far more subject to U.S. propaganda than they like to believe, also refused to send more than very limited aid. Some professed distaste for Sandinista repression, pure hypocrisy, as we see at once from the fact that the far more brutal regimes of El Salvador and Guatemala do not offend their sensibilities.

Under these circumstances, the task for the media is clear. First, they must apply the standard technique of historical amnesia and "change of course," which obliterates all memory of U.S. policies and their effects. Virtually a reflex, this device can be applied instantaneously. With the record and effects of U.S. violence removed from consciousness, along with the nature and consequences of U.S. economic warfare that have always been downplayed, we turn to the next phase. All suffering, discontent, and disruption are now plainly attributable to the evil Sandinistas. It is also useful to imply that Nicaraguans see the matter the same way, by careful selection of sources or misinterpretation of polls, for example.[60] A fine model is presented in a three-part series on Nicaragua by Edward Sheehan in the liberal *Boston Globe*, headlined "A country still in agony." The three lengthy articles, bitterly denouncing the Sandinistas throughout, contain exactly *one phrase* that notes in passing that "the United States is partially to blame for Nicaragua's sorrow and the wrecked economy."[61] For Nicaragua's agony, the Sandinistas are responsible. Apart from all else, the moral cowardice remains astonishing, however often the record is replayed.

For intelligent U.S. planners, it would be sensible to avoid the total destruction of Nicaragua or even its reincorporation within the "Central American mode," as liberal opinion prefers. It can then serve as "an object lesson" to poor countries that might be tempted to "[go] berserk with fanatical nationalism," as the *New York Times* editors thundered when the CIA successfully overthrew the parliamentary regime in Iran.[62] In a conflict with a Third World country, a violent superpower with only limited internal constraints can hardly fail to achieve the goal of destroying any hope.

The U.S. achievements in Central America in the past decade are a major tragedy, not only because of the appalling human cost, but because a decade ago there were incipient and promising steps throughout the region towards popular organization and confronting basic human needs, with early successes that might have taught useful lessons to others plagued with similar problems—exactly the fear of U.S. planners. These steps have been successfully aborted, and may never be attempted again.

The achievements of the Reagan administration in Nicaragua, revealed in the cold statistics of corpses, malnutrition, childhood epidemics, and the like, take on a more human cast in the occasional glimpse at the lives of the victims. Julia Preston provides one of the rare examples in the mainstream media under the headline: "In Jalapa, War-Induced Hardships Are Bolstering the Sandinista Cause." Jalapa, Preston writes, is a tiny town in "a vulnerable finger of land poking into hostile Honduras," an area readily accessible to the "Sons of Reagan" in their Honduran bases and largely dominated by hostile propaganda from powerful U.S.-run radio stations in Honduras. Here, if anywhere, the contras could apply the lessons imparted to them by their CIA trainers and exhibit the "growing self-confidence and skill" that so impressed A.M. Rosenthal as he read "James LeMoyne's carefully reported, sensitive accounts."[63]

In Jalapa, the contras are an object of contempt, Preston writes, mercenaries who "guessed wrong" about the "well-paid, secure jobs" they would get from the United States (see above). But "the contra war has left Jalapans enduring penury far worse than any they have ever known before." Severe hunger is rampant. The hospital, built in 1982 as "a symbol of the Sandinistas' commitment to improving social conditions" is nearly empty because people doubt it "will have the means to take care of them," thanks to the diversion of resources to the war and "away from this kind of social project"—an achievement of which U.S. citizens can feel proud. Nevertheless, "the immense hardship has not turned Jalapa against the Sandinista revolution." Even anti-Sandinista townspeople "view the war as a new stage in a history of U.S. bullying of everyday Nicaraguans, of which the Somoza family dynasty was an indelible example." The literacy campaigns and "educational explosion," sharply curtailed by U.S. violence, "attract abiding loyalty" in Jalapa, if not in the United States, where they have been much derided as an instrument of totalitarianism. Many residents of the town see "a more informal, egalitarian society today." Peasants are no longer "servile" and landowners "superior," as under the Somoza regime and the U.S. model generally. "The Sandinistas made bank credit available for the first time to small farmers," and today, "everyone shares the same poverty," though with "a cry of frustration" over Reagan's success in having "delayed the revolution," a "gaunt peasant farmer says."

The long-term goals of the Reagan administration for Central America were clear from the outset. While Shultz, Abrams, Kirkpatrick, and company occupy an extreme position on the political spectrum in their enthusiasm for terror and violence, the general policy goals are conventional and deeply rooted in U.S. tradition, policy planning, and institutions, which is why they have received little attention or criticism within the mainstream. For the same reasons, they can be expected to persist. It is necessary to demolish "the people's organizations fighting to defend their most fundamental human rights" (Archbishop Romero) and to eliminate any threat of "ultranationalism" in the "fledgling democracies." As for Nicaragua, if it cannot be restored by violence to the "Central American mode" of repression and exploitation, then at least the United States must implement the reported boast of a State Department insider in 1981: to " 'turn Nicaragua into the Albania of Central America,' that is, poor, isolated, and radical." The U.S. government must ensure that Nicaragua will "become a sort of Latin American Albania," so that "the Sandinista dream of creating a new, more exemplary political model for Latin America would be in ruins" (British journalist John Carlin).[64]

The goals have for the most part been achieved. The independent media deserve a large share of the credit, serving as adjuncts of government.

5

The Utility of Interpretations

Hypocrisy, Milton wrote, is "the only evil that walks Invisible, except to God alone." To ensure that "neither Man nor Angel can discern" the evil is, nonetheless, a demanding vocation. Pascal had discussed it a few years earlier while recording "how the casuists reconcile the contrarieties between their opinions and the decisions of the popes, the councils, and the Scripture." "One of the methods in which we reconcile these contradictions," his casuist interlocutor explains, "is by the interpretation of some phrase." Thus, if the Gospel says, "Give alms of your superfluity," and the task is "to discharge the wealthiest from the obligation of alms-giving," "the matter is easily put to rights by giving such an interpretation to the word *superfluity* that it will seldom or never happen that any one is troubled with such an article." Learned scholars demonstrate that "what men of the world lay up to improve their circumstances, or those of their relatives, cannot be termed *superfluity*; and accordingly, such a thing as superfluity is seldom to be found among men of the world, not even excepting kings"—nowadays, we call it tax reform. We may, then, adhere faithfully to the preachings of the Gospel that "the rich are bound to give alms of their superfluity, ... [though] it will seldom or never happen to be obligatory in practice." "There you see the utility of interpretations," he concludes.[1]

In our own times, the device, thanks to Orwell, is called Newspeak; the casuists are no less accomplished, though less forthcoming about the practice than Pascal's monk.

In the last two chapters, noting the recommendation of the liberal intellectuals that with the "advance of knowledge" we should keep to "subtle" and "refined" methods of social control, avoiding "coarse, obvious and direct methods," I discussed some of the modalities of thought control developed in democratic societies. The most effective device is the bounding of the thinkable, achieved by tolerating debate, even encouraging it, though only within proper limits. But democratic systems also resort to cruder means, the method of "interpretation of some phrase" being a notable instrument. Thus aggression and state terror in the Third World become "defense of democracy and human rights"; and "democracy" is successfully achieved when the government is safely in the hands of "the rich men dwelling at peace within their habitations," as in Winston Churchill's prescription for world order.[2] At home the rule of the privileged must be guaranteed and the population reduced to the status of passive observers, while in the dependencies stern measures may be needed to eliminate any challenge to the natural rulers. Under the proper interpretation of the phrase, it is indeed true that "the yearning to see American-style democracy duplicated throughout the world has been a persistent theme in American foreign policy," as *Times* correspondent Neil Lewis declared.[3]

There is, accordingly, no "contrariety" when we yearn for democracy and independence for South Vietnam while demolishing the country to eradicate the National Liberation Front (NLF), then turning to the destruction of the politically organized Buddhists before permitting stage-managed "elections." Casuistry even permits us to proceed on this course while recognizing that until compelled by U.S. terror "to use counter-force to survive," the indigenous enemy insisted that its contest with the United States and its clients "should be fought out at the political level and that the use of massed military might was in itself illegitimate." Our rejection of politics in favor of military might is natural, because we also recognized that the NLF was the only "truly mass-based political party in South Vietnam," and no one, "with the possible exception of the Buddhists, thought themselves equal in size and power to risk entering a coalition, fearing that if they did the whale would swallow the minnow."[4] With the same reasoning, it was only proper to subvert the first and last free election in the history of Laos, because the wrong people won; to organize or support the overthrow of elected governments in Guatemala, Brazil, the Dominican Republic, the Philippines, Chile, and Nicaragua; to support or directly organize large-scale terror to bar the threat of democracy, social reform, and independence in Central America in the 1980s; to take strong measures to ensure that the postwar world would return to proper hands; and much else—all in our "yearning for democracy."

From the same perspective, we can understand why, in December 1965, the *New York Times* editors should praise Washington for having "wisely stayed in the background during the recent upheavals" in Indonesia. In these "recent upheavals," the Indonesian military had "de-fused the country's political time-bomb, the powerful

Indonesian Communist party (P.K.I.)" by eliminating "virtually all the top- and second-level leaders of the P.K.I." in one or another manner—and, incidentally, slaughtering hundreds of thousands of people, mostly landless peasants, while Washington "wisely" observed in silence, the editors choose to believe.[5] This concomitant of a welcome victory for freedom was not mentioned, though the editors did warn that the social conditions that enabled the PKI to organize 14 million people persisted. They urged Washington to remain cautious about providing aid to the perpetrators of the slaughter, for fear that the nationalist leader Sukarno and the remnants of the PKI might yet benefit, despite the encouraging achievements of the friends and allies of the United States in conducting the largest slaughter since the Holocaust.

Similarly, it is natural that the *New York Times* should praise the government of the Shah of Iran, restored to power by the CIA, for its "highly successful campaign against subversive elements" and its "long record of success in defeating subversion without suppressing democracy." The subversives, now thankfully suppressed without suppressing democracy, include the "pro-Soviet Tudeh party," formerly "a real menace" but "considered now to have been completely liquidated," and the "extreme nationalists" who had been almost as subversive as the Communists.[6] And few, apparently, find it jarring to read an upbeat report on "the return of full democracy" in the Philippines under the headline "Aquino's decree bans Communist Party," with a lead paragraph explaining that a presidential decree stipulated penalties of imprisonment for membership in the party, which had been legalized under the Marcos dictatorship.[7] Not long before, Marcos himself had been a model democrat, a man "pledged to democracy," as Ronald Reagan explained; "we love your adherence to democratic principle and to the democratic processes" and your "service to freedom," his vice president, George Bush, proclaimed in Manila.[8] That, however, was before Marcos had lost control, and with it his credentials as a freedom-loving democrat.

On the same principles, we can recall with nostalgia the days of "democracy" under the Diem and Thieu-Ky dictatorships in South Vietnam (see chapter 3). And what is more natural than to observe proudly that "democracy is on the ideological march" because the experience of the last several decades shows that it leads to prosperity and development: "As an economic mechanism, democracy demonstrably works," James Markham writes in the lead article in the *Times Week in Review*. Economic growth has indeed occurred in the "newly industrializing countries," notably South Korea, Taiwan, Hong Kong, and Singapore. We are to understand, then, that "democracy" is a system that rejects democratic forms so as to facilitate reduced consumption and superexploitation, with state control over the economy in coordination with domestic conglomerates and international corporations, a pattern closer to traditional fascism than to democracy. All makes sense, however, when we take the term "democracy" to mean domination of the economy and social and political life by domestic elements that are properly sensitive to the needs of corporations and the U.S. government.[9]

These are constant themes in the media and political system, reflecting broader norms. There are no contrarieties here, as long as we understand the proper interpretation of the term "democracy."

All of this is quite in accord with the doctrine that other countries should control their own destinies, unless "developments ... get out of control" and "affect U.S. interests adversely" (see p. 59). The logic is similar when a National Intelligence Estimate of 1955 discusses the quandary the United States faced in Guatemala after the successful overthrow of the democratic capitalist regime. "Many Guatemalans are passionately attached to the democratic-nationalist ideals of the 1944 revolution," particularly to "the social and economic programs" of the regime overthrown in the CIA coup, the study observes with some distress; but few Guatemalans "understand the processes and responsibilities of democracy," so that "responsible democratic government is therefore difficult to achieve."[10] The apparent contradiction is dispelled when we give the proper interpretation to "democracy." It is the task of the media, and the specialized class generally, to ensure that the hypocrisy "walks Invisible, except to God alone."

As we see from these and many other examples, a solicitous concern for democracy and human rights may go hand in hand with tolerance for large-scale slaughter, or direct participation in it. The *Christian Science Monitor* observed approvingly—and accurately— that after General Suharto's impressive achievement in eliminating the political threat in Indonesia by mass murder, "many in the West were keen to cultivate Jakarta's new moderate leader, Suharto"; here the term "moderate" is used with an appropriate casuistic interpretation. Suharto's subsequent achievements include extraordinary human rights violations at home and slaughter in the course of aggression in East Timor that bears comparison to Pol Pot in the same years, backed enthusiastically by the United States, with the effective support of Canada, Britain, France, and other guardians of morality. The media cooperated by simply eliminating the issue; *New York Times* coverage, for example, declined as atrocities increased along with U.S. participation, reaching zero as the atrocities peaked in 1978; and the few comments by its noted Southeast Asia correspondent Henry Kamm assured us, on the authority of the Indonesian generals, that the army was protecting the people fleeing from the control of the guerrillas. Scrupulously excluded was the testimony of refugees, Church officials, and others who might have interfered with public acquiescence in what appears to be the largest massacre, relative to the population, since the Holocaust. In retrospect, the London *Economist*, in an ode to Indonesia under General Suharto's rule, describes him as "at heart benign," referring, perhaps, to his kindness to international corporations.[11]

In accord with the same principles, it is natural that vast outrage should be evoked by the terror of the Pol Pot regime, while reporters in Phnom Penh in 1973, when the U.S. bombing of populated areas of rural Cambodia had reached its peak, should ignore the testimony of the hundreds of thousands of refugees before their eyes.[12] Such selective perception guarantees that little is known about the scale and character of these U.S. atrocities, though enough to indicate that they may have been comparable to those attributable to the Khmer Rouge at the time when the chorus of indignation swept the West in 1977, and that they contributed significantly to the rise, and probably the brutality, of the Khmer Rouge.[13]

These achievements of "historical engineering" allow the editors of the *New York Times* to observe that "when America's eyes turned away from Indochina in 1975, Cambodia's misery had just begun," with "the infamous barbarities of the Khmer Rouge, then dreary occupation by Vietnam" (incidentally, expelling the Khmer Rouge). "After long indifference," they continue, "Washington can [now] play an important role as honest broker" and "heal a long-ignored wound in Cambodia." The misery began in 1975, not before, under "America's eyes," and the editors do not remind us that during the period of "indifference" Washington offered indirect support to the Khmer Rouge while backing the coalition in which it was the major element because of its "continuity" with the Pol Pot regime.[14]

U.S. relations with the Khmer Rouge require some careful maneuvering. The Khmer Rouge were, and remain, utterly evil insofar as they can be associated with the Communist threat, perhaps because of their origins in Jean-Paul Sartre's left-wing Paris circles. Even more evil, evidently, are the Vietnamese, who finally reacted to brutal and murderous border incidents by invading Cambodia and driving out the Khmer Rouge, terminating their slaughters. We therefore must back our Thai and Chinese allies who support Pol Pot. All of this requires commentators to step warily. The *New York Times* reports the "reluctance in Washington to push too hard" to pressure China to end its support for Pol Pot—with the goal of bleeding Vietnam, as our Chinese allies have forthrightly explained. The Assistant Secretary of State for East Asian Affairs rejected a congressional plea to call for a cutoff of aid to Pol Pot because the situation was "delicate." U.S. pressure on China "might irritate relations unnecessarily," the *Times* explained, and this consideration overcomes our passionate concern over the fate of Cambodians exposed to Khmer Rouge terror. The press explains further that while naturally the United States is "one of the nations most concerned about a Khmer Rouge return," nevertheless "the US and its allies have decided that without some sign of compromise by Vietnam toward a political settlement [on U.S. terms], the Khmer Rouge forces must be allowed to serve as military pressure on Vietnam, despite their past"—and despite what the population may think about "a Khmer Rouge return." Not only relations with China, but also the tasks of propagandists are "delicate" under these demanding conditions.[15]

An appropriate casuistic interpretation of the concept of democracy solves only half the problem; we also need a phrase for the enemies of democracy in some country where we yearn to establish or maintain it. The reflex device is to label the indigenous enemy "Communists," whatever their social commitments and political allegiances may be. They must be eliminated in favor of the "democrats" who are not "out of control." José Napoleón Duarte and his Defense Minister Vides Casanova are therefore "democrats," defending civilization against "Communists," such as the hundreds murdered by the security forces as they tried to flee to Honduras across the Rio Sumpul in May 1980. They were all "Communist guerrillas," Duarte explained, including, presumably, the infants sliced to pieces with machetes; the U.S. media took the simpler path of suppressing the massacre, one of the opening shots in the terrorist campaign for which Duarte provided legitimacy, to much acclaim.[16]

The U.S. attitude towards "American-style" democracies illustrates the prevailing conception in more subtle ways. Europe and Japan provide interesting examples, particularly in the early postwar years when it was necessary to restore traditional elites to power and undermine the anti-fascist resistance and its supporters, many of them imbued with unacceptable radical democratic commitments.[17]

The Third World provides a few similar illustrations, standing alongside the many cases where people with the wrong ideas are controlled by violence or liquidated "without suppressing democracy." Consider Costa Rica, the one functioning parliamentary democracy in Central America through the post-World War II period. It is sometimes argued, even by scholars who should know better, that U.S. support for Costa Rica undermines the thesis that a primary policy goal is to bar "nationalistic regimes" that do not adequately guarantee the rights of business,[18] a thesis well supported by the documentary and historical records. This argument reflects a serious misunderstanding. The United States has no principled opposition to democratic forms, as long as the climate for business operations is preserved. As accurately observed by Gordon Connell-Smith in his study of the inter-American system for the Royal Institute of International Affairs,[19] the U.S. "concept of democracy" is "closely identified with private, capitalistic enterprise," and it is only when this is threatened by what is regularly called "Communism" that action is taken to "restore democracy"; the "United States concern for representative democracy in Latin America [as elsewhere] is a facet of her anti-communist policy," or more accurately, the policy of opposing any threat to U.S. economic penetration and political control. And when these interests are safeguarded, democratic forms are not only tolerated, but approved, if only for public relations reasons. Costa Rica fits the model closely, and provides interesting insight into the "yearning for democracy" that is alleged to guide U.S. foreign policy.

In Costa Rica the system established under the leadership of José (Don Pepe) Figueres after the 1948 coup remains in place. It has always provided a warm welcome to foreign investment and has promoted a form of class collaboration that often "sacrificed the rights of labor," Don Pepe's biographer observes,[20] while establishing a welfare system that continues to function thanks to U.S. subsidies, with one of the highest per capita debts in the world. Don Pepe's 1949 constitution outlawed Communism. With the most militant unions suppressed, labor rights declined. "Minimum wage laws were not enforced," and workers "lost every collective-bargaining contract except one that covered a single group of banana workers," Walter LaFeber notes. By the 1960s "it was almost as if the entire labor movement had ceased to exist," an academic study concludes. The United Fruit Company prospered, nearly tripling its profits and facing no threat of expropriation. Meanwhile, Figueres declared in 1953 that "we consider the United States as the standard-bearer of our cause."[21] As the United States tried to line up Latin American states behind its planned overthrow of the Guatemalan government, Costa Rica and Bolivia were the only two elected governments to join the Latin American dictatorships in giving full support to the State Department draft resolution authorizing the United States to violate international law by detaining and inspecting "vessels, aircraft and other means of conveyance moving to and from the Republic of Guatemala" so as to block arms shipments for defense of Guatemala from the impending U.S. attack and "travel by agents of International Communism."[22]

By aligning itself unequivocally with the United States, fostering foreign investment, guaranteeing the domestic predominance of business interests, and maintaining a basis for repression of labor and political dissidence, the democratic government satisfied the basic conditions demanded by the United States. Correspondingly, it has received a measure of U.S. support. Thus in 1955, when a small force of Costa Ricans attacked border areas from Nicaragua, Figueres suspended individual rights and constitutional guarantees, and repelled the incursion with U.S. aid—thus not forfeiting his democratic credentials by the repressive measures he instituted, permitted for U.S clients.

Nevertheless, concerns over Costa Rica did not abate. State Department intelligence warned in 1953 that Figueres had turned his country into "a haven for exiles from the dictatorships" and was toying with ideas about "a broad program of economic development and firmer control over foreign investment." He hoped to finance development "preferably by domestic capital" and "does not look with favor upon capital organized beyond the individual or family level. Large private corporations, such as those in the United States, are an anathema in his opinion." He also sought "to increase the bargaining power of the small, undeveloped countries vis-à-vis the large manufacturing nations." He was dangerous, LaFeber comments, "because he hoped to use government powers to free Costa Rica's internal development as much as possible from foreign control," thus undermining "the Good Neighbor policy's assumption that Latin America could be kept in line merely through economic pressure."[23]

The U.S. government was particularly concerned that the Costa Rican constitution, while outlawing Communism, still provided civil libertarian guarantees that impeded the kind of persecution of dissidents that is mandatory in a well-functioning democracy. And despite Don Pepe's cooperation with U.S. corporations and the CIA, support for U.S. interventions in the region, and general loyalty to the United States over the years, he has continued to exhibit an unacceptable degree of independence, so much so that the leading representative of capitalist democracy in Central America must be excluded from the media, as we have seen.[24]

If the enemies of democracy are not "Communists," then they are "terrorists"; still better, "Communist terrorists," or terrorists supported by International Communism. The rise and decline of international terrorism in the 1980s provides much insight into "the utility of interpretations."[25]

What Ronald Reagan and George Shultz call "the evil scourge of terrorism," a plague spread by "depraved opponents of civilization itself" in "a return to barbarism in the modern age," was placed on the agenda of concern by the Reagan administration. From its first days, the administration proclaimed that "international terrorism" would replace Carter's human rights crusade as "the Soul of our foreign policy." The Reaganites would dedicate themselves to defense of the civilized world against the program of international terrorism outlined most prominently in Claire Sterling's influential book *The Terror Network*. Here, the Soviet Union was identified as the source of the plague, with the endorsement of a new scholarly discipline, whose practitioners were particularly impressed with Sterling's major insight, which provides an irrefutable proof of Soviet guilt. The clinching evidence, as Walter Laqueur phrased it in a review of Sterling's book, is that terrorism occurs "almost exclusively in democratic or relatively democratic countries." By 1985, terrorism in the Middle East/Mediterranean region was selected as the top story of the year in an Associated Press poll of editors and broadcasters, and concern reached fever pitch in subsequent months. The U.S. bombing of Libya in April 1986 largely tamed the monster, and in the following years the plague subsided to more manageable proportions as the Soviet Union and its clients retreated in the face of American courage and determination, according to the preferred account.

The rise and decline of the plague had little relation to anything happening in the world, with one exception: its rise coincided with the need to mobilize the U.S. population to support the Reaganite commitment to state power and violence, and its decline with rising concern over the need to face the costs of Reaganite military Keynesian excesses with their technique of writing "hot checks for $200 billion a year" to create the illusion of prosperity, as vice-presidential candidate Lloyd Bentsen phrased the perception of conservative business elements at the 1988 Democratic convention.

The public relations apparatus—surely the most sophisticated component of the Reagan administration—was faced with a dual problem in 1981: to frighten the domestic enemy (the general population at home) sufficiently so that they would bear the costs of programs to which they were opposed, while avoiding direct confrontations with the Evil Empire itself, as far too dangerous for us. The solution to the dilemma was to concoct an array of little Satans, tentacles of the Great Satan poised to destroy us, but weak and defenseless so that they could be attacked with impunity: in short, Kremlin-directed international terrorism. The farce proceeded perfectly, with the cooperation of the casuists, whose task was to give a proper interpretation to the term "terrorism," protecting the doctrine that its victims are primarily the democratic countries of the West.

To conduct this campaign of ideological warfare successfully, it was necessary to obscure the central role of the United States in organizing and directing state terror, and to conceal its extensive involvement in international terrorism in earlier years, as in the attack against Cuba, the prime example of "the evil scourge of terrorism" from the early 1960s. Some "historical engineering" was also required with regard to terrorism in the Middle East/Mediterranean region, the primary focus of concern within the propaganda operations. Here, it was necessary to suppress the role of the United States and its Israeli client.

These tasks have been well within the capacity of the media and the terrorologists.[26] The U.S. role is easily excised; after all, the phrase "U.S. terrorism" is an oxymoron, on a par with "thunderous silence" or "U.S. aggression." Israeli state terrorism escapes under the same literary convention, Israel being a client state, though it is recognized that there were Jewish terrorists in a distant and forgotten past. This fact can be placed in proper perspective by following the suggestion of the editor of a collection of scholarly essays, who invokes the plausible distinction between "morally unacceptable terrorist attacks" on civilians and more ambiguous attacks on agents of authority and persecution. "We would therefore distinguish sharply between the Irgun Zvai Leumi's attacks on British soldiers and the

Popular Front for the Liberation of Palestine's violence against airline passengers traveling to Israel."[27]

One can imagine a different formulation, for example, a sharp distinction between the attacks against Israeli and U.S. soldiers by Arabs who are termed "terrorists," and the many murderous attacks on Arab civilians by the Irgun Zvai Leumi, and the Israeli army in later years. But that would hardly create a proper image for a sound and sober analysis of "the consequences of political violence."

The great significance of international terrorism as an ideological instrument is illustrated by the reaction when someone breaks ranks and documents the part that the United States and its clients have played in conducting, organizing, and supporting international terrorism. If such work cannot simply be ignored, it elicits virtual frenzy—"deranged," "absurd," and "fantasies" are some phrases drawn from 1988 commentary, unaccompanied by even a semblance of an argument. Such reactions are not without interest, and merit some thought.

There are three positions that one might take with regard to terrorism: (1) We can attribute it to official enemies, whatever the facts. (2) We can dismiss the entire discussion of terrorism as ideologically motivated nonsense, not worthy of attention. (3) We can take the phenomenon seriously, agree that terrorism warrants concern and condemnation, investigate it, and let the chips fall where they may. On rational assumptions, we dismiss the first and accept the third. The second position is at least arguable, though in my judgment wrong; I think there is every reason to take terrorism seriously, and the concept is as clear as most that enter into political discourse.

But considerations of rationality are not pertinent. The first and wholly irrational position is the standard one in the media and the literature of terrorology, overwhelmingly dominant. The second position is regarded as more or less tolerable, since it absolves the United States and its clients from blame apart from their attempts at ideological manipulation. The third position, in contrast, is utterly beyond the pale, for when we pursue it, we quickly reach entirely unacceptable conclusions, discovering, for example, that Miami and Washington have been among the major world centers of international terrorism from the Kennedy period until today, under any definition of terrorism—whether that of the U.S. Code, international conventions, military manuals, or whatever.

A variant of the first position, still tolerable though less so than the pure form, is to argue that it is unfair to condemn Palestinians,

Lebanese kidnappers, etc., without considering the factors that led them to these crimes. This position has the merit of tacitly accepting—hence reinforcing—the approved premises as to the origins of the plague. The second position can be made still more palatable by restricting it to a psychocultural analysis of the Western obsession with terrorism, avoiding the institutional factors that led to the choice of this marvellously successful public relations device in the 1980s (an analysis of such institutional factors, readily discernible, can be dismissed with the label "conspiracy theory," another familiar reflex when it is necessary to prevent thought and protect institutions from scrutiny). The idea that talk of terrorism is mere confusion provides a useful fall-back position in case the role of the United States is exposed. One can, in short, adopt this device to dismiss those who pursue the unacceptable third option as hopeless fanatics and conspiracy theorists, and then return to the favored first position for the interpretation of ongoing events.

The first position, simple and unsubtle, completely dominates public discussion, the media, and what is regarded as the scholarly literature. Its dominance and utility are obvious at every turn. To select an example from late 1988, consider the refusal of the State Department to permit Yasser Arafat to address the United Nations in November. The official grounds were that his visit posed a threat to U.S. security, but no one pretended to take that seriously; even George Shultz did not believe that Arafat's bodyguards were going to hijack a taxi in New York or take over the Pentagon (it is, perhaps, of some interest that no one cared that the official rationale was unworthy even of refutation, but let us put that aside). What *was* taken seriously was the story that accompanied the spurious reasons offered: that Arafat was not permitted to set foot on U.S. soil because of the abhorrence for terrorism on the part of the organizers and supporters of the contra war, government-run death squads in El Salvador and Guatemala, the bombing of Tripoli, and other notable exercises in violence—all of which qualify as international terrorism, or worse, if we are willing to adopt the third position on the matter of terrorism, that is, the position that is honest, rational, and hence utterly unthinkable.

As the invitation to Arafat was being considered, Senator Christopher Dodd warned that if Arafat were permitted to address the General Assembly, Congress would cut off U.S. funding for the United Nations. "I think you can't underestimate the strong feeling in this country about terrorism," Dodd informed the press; a leading dove, Dodd has ample knowledge of Central America and the agency of terror there. Explaining "Shultz's 'No' to Arafat," the front-page *New York Times* headline reads: "Personal Disgust for Terrorism Is at Root of Secretary's Decision to Rebuff the P.L.O." The article goes on to describe Shultz's "visceral contempt for terrorism." *Times* Washington correspondent R.W. Apple added that Mr. Shultz "has waged something of a personal crusade against terrorism," which "has always mattered so intensely to Mr. Shultz."[28] The press, television, and radio either expressed their admiration for Shultz for taking such a forthright stand against the plague of terrorism, or criticized him for allowing his understandable and meritorious rage to overcome his statesmanlike reserve.

The news reports and commentary did not call upon witnesses from Nicaragua, El Salvador and Guatemala, Angola, southern Lebanon, Gaza, and elsewhere to share their insights into Shultz's "visceral contempt for terrorism" and the "strong feelings" in Congress about the resort to violence. Rather, the media warned soberly that "Yasser Arafat is not your ordinary politically controversial visa applicant: his group kills people."[29] Arafat is thus quite unlike Adolfo Calero, José Napoleón Duarte and his cohorts, or Yitzhak Shamir, among the many leaders whom we welcome from abroad because, one must assume, they do not "kill people."

Those who might have expected the media to take the occasion to review George Shultz's record of advocacy and support for terrorism, perhaps raising the question of whether there might be a note of hypocrisy in his "personal statement" or the media interpretation of it, would have been sorely disappointed. As in totalitarian states, however, cartoonists had greater latitude, and were able to depict the leaders who Shultz may have had in mind when he lamented that "people are forgetting what a threat international terrorism is": France's Mitterand, who "forgot when we sank the Greenpeace ship"; Britain's Thatcher, who "forgot when we had those IRA blokes shot at Gibraltar"; the USSR's Gorbachev, who "forgot how we mine bombed all those children in Afghanistan"; and the United States' Shultz, who "forgot about all the civilians our friends, the contras, murdered in Nicaragua."[30]

Other examples can readily be added. That Arafat and the PLO have engaged in terrorist acts is not in doubt; nor is it in doubt that they are minor actors in the arena of international terrorism.[31]

One of the acts of PLO terror that most outraged the Secretary of State and his admirers in Congress and the media was the hijacking of the *Achille Lauro* and the murder of Leon Klinghoffer, doubtless a vile terrorist act. Their sensibilities were not aroused, however, by the Israeli bombing of Tunis a week earlier, killing twenty Tunisians and fifty-five Palestinians with smart bombs that tore people to shreds beyond recognition, among other horrors described by Israeli journalist Amnon Kapeliouk on the scene. U.S. journals had little interest, the victims being Arabs and the killers U.S. clients. Secretary Shultz was definitely interested, however. The United States had cooperated in the massacre by refusing to warn its ally Tunisia that the bombers were on their way, and Shultz telephoned Israeli Foreign Minister Yitzhak Shamir, a noted terrorist himself from the early 1940s, to inform him that the U.S. administration "had considerable sympathy for the Israeli action," the press reported. Shultz drew back from this public approbation when the U.N. Security Council unanimously denounced the bombing as an "act of armed aggression" (the United States abstaining). Foreign Minister Shimon Peres was welcomed to Washington a few days later as a man of peace, while the press solemnly discussed his consultations with President Reagan on "the evil scourge of terrorism" and what can be done to counter it.[32]

The outrage over hijacking does not extend to *Israeli* hijackings that have been carried out in international waters for many years, including civilian ferries travelling from Cyprus to Lebanon, with large numbers of people kidnapped, over 100 kept in Israeli prisons without trial, and many killed, some by Israeli gunners while they tried to stay afloat after their ship was sunk, according to survivors interviewed in prison. The strong feelings of Congress and the media were also not aroused by the case of Na'il Amin Fatayir, deported from the West Bank in July 1987. After serving eighteen months in prison on the charge of membership in a banned organization, he was released and returned to his home in Nablus. Shortly after, the government ordered him deported. When he appealed to the courts, the prosecutor argued that the deportation was legitimate because he had entered the country illegally—having been kidnapped by the Israeli navy while travelling from Lebanon to Cyprus on the ship *Hamdallah* in July 1985. The High Court accepted this elegant reasoning as valid.[33]

The visceral outrage over terrorism is restricted to worthy victims, meeting a criterion that is all too obvious.

The hijacking of the *Achille Lauro* was in retaliation for the bombing of Tunis, but the West properly dismissed this justification for a terrorist act. The bombing of Tunis, in turn, was in retaliation for a terrorist murder of three Israelis in Cyprus by a group which, as Israel conceded, had probable connections to Damascus but none to Tunis, which was selected as a target rather than Damascus because it was defenseless; the Reagan administration selected Libyan cities as a bombing target a few months later in part for the same reason. The bombing of Tunis, with its many civilian casualties, was described by Secretary Shultz as a "a legitimate response" to "terrorist attacks," to general approbation. The terrorist murders in Cyprus were, in turn, justified by their perpetrators as retaliation for the Israeli hijackings over the preceding decade. Had this plea even been heard, it would have been dismissed with scorn. The term "retaliation" too must be given an appropriate interpretation, as any casuist would understand.

The same is true of other terms. Take, for example, the notion of "preventing" or "reducing" violence. A report headlined "Palestinian casualties nearly double" opens by quoting the Israeli army chief of staff, who says "that the number of Palestinians wounded in the occupied West Bank and Gaza Strip has almost doubled in recent weeks but that the army has failed to reduce violence in the occupied areas." The statement makes no sense, but a look at the background allows it to be decoded. Shortly before, Minister of Defense Yitzhak Rabin had authorized the use of plastic bullets, stating that "more casualties ... is precisely our aim": "our purpose is to increase the number of (wounded) among those who take part in violent activities." He also explained the notion of "violent activities": "We want to get rid of the illusion of some people in remote villages that they have liberated themselves," he said, explaining that army raids "make it clear to them where they live and within which framework." Palestinians must "understand that the solution can be achieved only by peaceful means," not by illusions of self-government. The army is therefore stepping up raids on remote villages that have declared themselves "liberated zones," with a resulting increase in injuries, the report continues. In a typical example, "Israeli troops raided more than a dozen West Bank villages and wounded 22 Palestinians yesterday"; an army spokeswoman explained that a strike had been called and the army wanted to "prevent violence" by an "increased presence and by making more arrests."[34]

We can now return to the original Newspeak: "the number of Palestinians wounded in the occupied West Bank and Gaza Strip has almost doubled in recent weeks but ... the army has failed to reduce violence in the occupied areas." Translating to intelligible English, the army has doubled the violence in the occupied territories by aggressive actions with the specific intent of increasing casualties, and by expanding its violent attacks to remote and peaceful villages that were attempting to run their own affairs. But it has so far failed to rid the people of illusions of self-government. For the Israeli authorities and the U.S. media, an attempt by villagers to run their own affairs is "violence," and a brutal attack to teach them who rules is "preventing violence." Orwell would have been impressed.

A report a few days later, headlined "Israelis kill three in West Bank, Gaza clashes," describes how soldiers shot and wounded three Palestinians in a "remote town rarely visited by soldiers" and "generally ignored by the military." "Defense Minister Yitzhak Rabin said two weeks ago the army would step up its actions in such villages to remind the inhabitants where they live and who is in control." This was one of thirty villages raided "in an offensive aimed at preventing violence," the report continues. And one can see the point; *after* the Israeli soldiers shot three Palestinians in the village in their "offensive aimed at preventing violence," "angry residents later stoned vehicles in the area." An accompanying story is devoted to the question of whether the PLO will really "renounce terror," quoting officials from Rabin's Labor Party and others in disbelief.[35]

With appropriate interpretations, then, we can rest content that the United States and its clients defend democracy, social reform, and self-determination against Communists, terrorists, and violent elements of all kinds. It is the responsibility of the media to laud the "democrats" and demonize the official enemy: the Sandinistas, the PLO, or whoever gets in the way. On occasion this requires some fancy footwork, but the challenge has generally been successfully met.[36]

Our "yearning for democracy" is accompanied by a no less profound yearning for peace, and the media also face the task of "historical engineering" to establish this required truth. We therefore have phenomena called "peace missions" and "the peace process," terms that apply to whatever the United States happens to be doing or advocating at some moment. In the media or responsible scholarship, one will therefore find no such statement as "the United States opposes the peace process" or "Washington has to be induced to join the peace process." The reason is that such statements would be logical contradictions. Through the years, when the United States was "trumping" the Contadora process, undermining the Central America peace accords, and deflecting the threat of peace in the

Middle East, it never opposed the peace process in acceptable commentary, but always supported the peace process and tried to advance it. One might imagine that even a great power that is sublime beyond imagination might sometimes be standing in the way of some peace process, perhaps because of misunderstanding or faulty judgment. Not so the United States, however—by definition.

A headline in the *Los Angeles Times* in late January 1988 reads: "Latin Peace Trip by Shultz Planned." The subheading describes the contents of the "peace trip": "Mission Would Be Last-Ditch Effort to Defuse Opposition on Contra Aid."[37] The article quotes administration officials who describe the "peace mission" as "the only way to save" contra aid in the face of "growing congressional opposition." In plain English, the "peace mission" was a last-ditch effort to block peace and mobilize Congress for the "unlawful use of force" now that Washington and its loyal media had succeeded in completely dismantling the unwanted Central American peace plan and Ortega had agreed that its provisions should apply to Nicaragua alone, foiling the hope that Nicaragua would reject these U.S. conditions so that they could be depicted as the spoilers.

A further goal of the "peace mission," the article continues, was to "relegate Nicaragua's four democratic neighbors to the sidelines in peace talks," with the United States taking command; the "democracies," though pliable, still show an annoying streak of independence. A few months later, the *New York Times* reported further efforts by the administration "to 'keep pressure' on the Sandinistas by continuing to provide support for the contras," including "more military aid," while urging U.S. allies to "join the United States in efforts to isolate Nicaragua diplomatically and revive the peace process ..."; George Shultz is quoted as reflecting that perhaps he might have become "involved in the peace process" still earlier. The *Los Angeles Times* described these renewed administration efforts "to build support for the resumption of U.S. military aid to Nicaragua's Contras" under the headline: "Shultz Will Try to Revive Latin Peace Process."[38]

In short, War is Peace.

The task of "historical engineering" has been accomplished with no less efficiency in the case of the Arab-Israeli conflict. The problem has been to present the United States and Israel as yearning for peace and pursuing the peace process while in fact, since the early 1970s, they have led the rejectionist camp and have been blocking peace initiatives that have had broad international and regional support. The technique has been the usual one: the "peace process" is, by definition, whatever the United States proposes. The desired conclusion now follows, whatever the facts. U.S. policy is also by definition "moderate," so that those who oppose it are "extremist" and "uncompromising." History has been stood on its head in a most intriguing manner, as I have documented elsewhere.[39]

There are actually two factors that operate to yield the remarkable distortion of the record concerning "peace," "terrorism," and related matters in the Middle East. One is the societal function of the media in serving U.S. elite interests; the other, the special protection afforded Israel since it became "the symbol of human decency" by virtue of the smashing military victory in 1967 that established it as a worthy strategic asset.

The interplay of these factors has led to some departure from the usual media pattern. Typically, as discussed throughout, the media encourage debate over tactical issues within the general framework of the elite consensus concerning goals and strategy. In the case of the Arab-Israeli conflict, however, the spectrum has been even narrower. Substantial segments of elite opinion, including major corporations with Middle East interests, have joined most of the world in favor of the political settlement that the United States and Israel have been able to block for many years. But their position has largely been excluded from the media, which have adhered to the consensus of Israel's two major political groupings, generally taking Labor Party rejectionism to represent the "peace option."

A problem develops when U.S. and Israeli positions diverge. One such case arose in October 1977, when a Soviet-American statement was issued calling for "termination of the state of war and establishment of normal peaceful relations" between Israel and its neighbors, as well as for internationally guaranteed borders and demilitarized zones. The statement was endorsed by the PLO but bitterly denounced by Israel and its domestic U.S. lobby. The media reaction was instructive. The media normally adopt the stand of their leader in the White House in the event of conflict with some foreign state. The administration is allowed to frame the issues and is given the most prominent coverage, with its adversaries sometimes permitted a line here and there in rebuttal, in the interest of objectivity and fairness. In this case, however, the pattern was reversed. As described in Montague Kern's detailed analysis of TV coverage, the media highlighted the Israeli position, treating the Carter administration in the manner of some official enemy. Israeli premises framed the issues, and Israeli sources generally dominated coverage and interpretation. Arab sources, in particular the PLO, were largely dismissed or treated with contempt. "Israel was able to make its case on television," Kern concludes, while "this was not so for the [U.S.] administration, which trailed the Israelis in terms of all the indicators" of media access and influence.[40] Carter soon backed down. With the threat of a peaceful settlement deflected, the "peace process" could resume on its rejectionist course.

Nevertheless, the media are bitterly condemned as "pro-PLO" and as imposing an unfair "double standard" on Israel. We then debate the sources of this strange malady. As in other cases, attack is the best defense, particularly when dominance over the media and exclusion of contrary views has reached a sufficient level so that any criticism, however outlandish, will be treated with respect.[41]

Reinhold Niebuhr once remarked that "perhaps the most significant moral characteristic of a nation is its hypocrisy."[42] The point is well taken. There is a simple measure of hypocrisy, which we properly apply to our enemies. When peace groups, government figures, media, and loyal intellectuals in the Soviet sphere deplore brutal and repressive acts of the United States and its clients, we test their sincerity by asking what they say about their own responsibilities. Upon ascertaining the answer, we dismiss their condemnations, however accurate, as the sheerest hypocrisy. Minimal honesty requires that we apply the same standards to ourselves.

Freedom of the press, for example, is a prime concern for the media and the intellectual community. The major issue of freedom of the press in the 1980s has surely been the harassment of *La Prensa* in Nicaragua. Coverage of its tribulations probably exceeds all other reporting and commentary on freedom of the press throughout the world combined, and is unique in the passion of rhetoric. No crime of the Sandinistas has elicited more outrage than their censorship of *La Prensa* and its suspension in 1986, immediately after the congressional vote of $100 million for the contras, a vote that amounted to a virtual declaration of war by the United States, as the Reaganites happily proclaimed, and a sharp rebuff to the World Court. *La Prensa* publisher Violeta Chamorro was at once given an award by the Nieman Journalism Foundation at Harvard for her courageous battle for freedom of speech. In the *New York Review of Books*, Murray Kempton appealed to all those committed to free expression to provide financial aid for the brave struggle of the owners and editors to maintain their staff and equipment; such gifts would supplement the funding provided by the U.S. government, which began shortly after the Sandinista victory, when President Carter authorized the CIA to support *La Prensa* and the anti-Sandinista opposition. Under the heading "A Newspaper of Valor," the *Washington Post* lauded Violeta Chamorro, commenting that she and her newspaper "deserve 10 awards." Other media commentary has been abundant and no less effusive, while the Sandinistas have been bitterly condemned for harassing or silencing this Tribune of the People.[43]

We now ask whether these sentiments reflect libertarian values or service to power, applying the standard test of sincerity. How, for example, did the same people and institutions react when the security forces of the Duarte government that we support eliminated the independent media in the U.S. client state of El Salvador—not by intermittent censorship and suspension, but by murder, mutilation, and physical destruction? We have already seen the answer. There was silence. The *New York Times* had nothing to say about these atrocities in its news columns or editorials, then or since, and others who profess their indignation over the treatment of *La Prensa* are no different. This extreme contempt for freedom of the press remains in force as we applaud our achievements in bringing "democracy" to El Salvador.

We conclude that, among the articulate intellectuals, those who believe in freedom of the press could easily fit in someone's living room, and would include few of those who proclaim libertarian values while assailing the enemy of the state.

To test this conclusion further, we may turn to Guatemala. No censorship was required in Guatemala while the United States was supporting the terror at its height; the murder of dozens of journalists sufficed. There was little notice in the United States. With the "democratic renewal" that we proudly hail, there were some halting efforts to explore the "political space" that perhaps had opened. In February 1988, two journalists who had returned from exile opened the center-left weekly *La Epoca*, testing Guatemalan "democracy." A communiqué of the Secret Anti-Communist Army (ESA) had warned returning journalists: "We will make sure they either leave the country or die inside it."[44] No notice was taken in the United States.

In April great indignation was aroused when *La Prensa* could not publish during a newsprint shortage. For the *Washington Post*, this was another "pointed lesson in arbitrary power ... by denying La Prensa the newsprint." There were renewed cries of outrage when *La Prensa* was suspended for two weeks in July after what the government alleged to be fabricated and inflammatory accounts of violence that had erupted at demonstrations.[45]

Meanwhile, on June 10, fifteen heavily armed men broke into the offices of *La Epoca*, stole valuable equipment, and firebombed the offices, destroying them. They also kidnapped the night watchman, releasing him later under threat of death if he were to speak about the attack. Eyewitness testimony and other sources left little doubt that it was an operation of the security forces. The editor held a press conference on June 14 to announce that the journal would shut down "because there are not conditions in the country to guarantee the exercise of free and independent journalism." After a circular appeared threatening "traitor journalists" including "communists and those who have returned from exile," warning them to flee the country or find themselves "dead within," he returned to exile, accompanied to the airport by a Western diplomat. Another journalist also left. The destruction of *La Epoca* "signalled not only the end of an independent media voice in Guatemala, but it served as a warning as well that future press independence would not be tolerated by the government or security forces," Americas Watch commented.[46]

These events elicited no public response from the guardians of free expression. The facts were not even reported in the *New York Times* or *Washington Post*, though not from ignorance, surely.[47] It is simply that the violent destruction of independent media is not important when it takes place in a "fledgling democracy" backed by the United States. There was, however, a congressional reaction, NACLA reported: "In Washington, liberal Democratic Senators responded by adding $4 million onto the Administration's request for military aid. With Sen. Inouye leading the way, these erstwhile freedom-of-the-press junkies have offered the brass $9 million plus some $137 million in economic aid, including $80 million cash, much of which goes to swell the army's coffers," while *La Epoca* editor Bryan Barrera "is back in Mexico" and "Guatemala's press is again confined to rightwing muckraking and army propaganda."[48] The vigilant guardians of freedom of the press observed in silence.

A few weeks later, Israeli security forces raided the offices of a leading Jerusalem daily, *Al-Fajr*, arresting its managing editor Hatem Abdel-Qader and jailing him for six months without trial on unspecified security grounds.[49] There were no ringing editorial denunciations or calls for retribution; in fact, these trivialities were not even reported in the *New York Times* or *Washington Post*. Unlike Violeta

Chamorro, to whom nothing of the sort has happened, Abdel-Qader does not "deserve 10 awards," or even one, or even a line.

Once again, the facts are clear: the alleged concern for freedom of the press in Nicaragua is sheer fraud.

Perhaps one might argue that censorship of *La Prensa* is more important than the murder of an editor by U.S.-backed security forces and the destruction of offices by the army or its terrorist squads, because *La Prensa* is a journal of such significance, having courageously opposed our ally Somoza under the leadership of Pedro Joaquín Chamorro, assassinated by the dictator in 1978. That would be a poor argument at best; freedom of the press means little if it only serves powerful institutions. But there are further flaws. One is that the post-1980 *La Prensa* bears virtually no relation to the journal that opposed Somoza. After the murder of Pedro Joaquín Chamorro, his brother Xavier became editor and remained so until the owners ousted him in 1980; 80 percent of the staff left with him and founded *El Nuevo Diario*, which is the successor to the old *La Prensa* if we consider a journal to be constituted of its editor and staff, not its owners and equipment. The new editor of *La Prensa*, son of the assassinated editor, had previously been selling advertising; later, he joined the CIA-run contra directorate, remaining co-editor of the journal, which publicly supports his stand.[50]

These facts are not be found in the media tributes to the brave tradition of *La Prensa*; they are either unmentioned in the course of lamentations over the fate of this "newspaper of valor," or treated in the style of Stephen Kinzer, who writes that *El Nuevo Diario* "was founded ... by a breakaway group of employees of La Prensa sympathetic to the Sandinista cause"—a "breakaway group" that included 80 percent of the staff and the editor, who opposed the new line of the CIA-supported journal.[51]

The extent of the hypocrisy becomes still more obvious when we consider the "newspaper of valor" more closely. The journal has quite openly supported the attack against Nicaragua. In April 1986, as the campaign to provide military aid to the contras was heating up, one of the owners, Jaime Chamorro, wrote an Op-Ed in the *Washington Post* calling for aid to "those Nicaraguans who are fighting for democracy" (the standard reference to the U.S. proxy forces). In the weeks preceding the summer congressional votes, "a host of articles by five different *La Prensa* staff members denounced the Sandinistas in major newspapers throughout the United States," John Spicer Nichols observes, including a series of Op-Eds signed by *La*

Prensa editors in the *Washington Post* as they traveled to the United States under the auspices of front organizations of the North contra-funding network. Under its new regime, *La Prensa* has barely pretended to be a newspaper; rather, it is a propaganda journal devoted to undermining the government and supporting the attack against Nicaragua by a foreign power. Since its reopening in October 1987 the commitments are quite open and transparent.[52] To my knowledge, there is no precedent for the survival and continued publication of such a journal during a period of crisis in any Western democracy, surely not the United States.[53]

Advocates of libertarian values should, nonetheless, insist that Nicaragua break precedent in this area, despite its dire straits, and deplore its failure to do so. As already mentioned, however, such advocates are not easy to discover, as the most elementary test of sincerity demonstrates.

It could be argued that comparison with the United States is inadequate, given the dismal U.S. record. We might take that to be the import of remarks by Supreme Court Justice William Brennan in a speech delivered at Hebrew University Law School in December 1987, where he observed that the United States "has a long history of failing to preserve civil liberties when it perceived its national security threatened"—as during World War I, when there was not even a remote threat. "It may well be Israel, not the United States, that provides the best hope for building a jurisprudence that can protect civil liberties against the demands of national security," Brennan said, adding that "the nations of the world, faced with sudden threats to their own security, will look to Israel's experience in handling its continuing security crisis, and may well find in that experience the expertise to reject the security claims that Israel has exposed as baseless and the courage to preserve the civil liberties that Israel has preserved without detriment to its security." If we can draw lessons from Israel's stellar record, "adversity may yet be the handmaiden of liberty."[54]

Following the precepts of this characteristic accolade to the "symbol of human decency"—and not coincidentally, loyal U.S. ally and client—we derive a further test of the sincerity of those who denounce the totalitarian Sandinistas for their treatment of *La Prensa* and the political opposition. Let us proceed to apply it.

Just at the time that *La Prensa* was suspended in 1986 after the virtual U.S. declaration of war against Nicaragua, Israel permanently closed two Jerusalem newspapers, *Al-Mithaq* and *Al-Ahd*, on the grounds that "although we offer them freedom of expression, ... it is forbidden to permit them to exploit this freedom in order to harm the State of Israel." The Interior Ministry declared that it was compelled to act "in the interest of state security and public welfare." We believe in freedom of the press, the Ministry asserted, but "one has to properly balance freedom of expression and the welfare of the state." The closure was upheld by the High Court on the grounds that "it is inconceivable that the State of Israel should allow terrorist organizations which seek to destroy it to set up businesses in its territory, legitimate as they may be"; the government had accused these two Arab newspapers of receiving support from hostile groups.[55] To my knowledge, the only mention of these facts in a U.S. newspaper was in a letter of mine to the *Boston Globe*.

As *La Prensa* was reopened in 1987, the Israeli press reported the closing of a Nazareth political journal (within Israel proper) on grounds of its "extreme nationalist editorial line" and an Arab-owned news office in Nablus was shut down for two years; its owner had by then been imprisoned for six months without trial on the charge of "membership in an illegal organization," and a military communiqué stated that his wife had maintained the ties of the office to the PLO. Such repressive actions are "legal" under the state of emergency that has been in force since the state was founded in 1948. The High Court upheld the closing of the Nazareth journal, alleging that the security services had provided evidence of a connection between the journal and "terrorist organizations" and dismissing as irrelevant the plea of its publisher that everything that had appeared in the journal had passed through Israeli censorship.[56] None of this appears to have been reported here; *New York Times* correspondent Thomas Friedman chose the day of the closing of the Nablus office to produce one of his regular odes to freedom of expression in Israel.[57] There was no outcry of protest among American civil libertarians, no denunciation or even comment on acts that far exceed the harassment and temporary suspension of the U.S.-funded journal in Nicaragua that openly supports the overthrow of the government, no call for organizing a terrorist army to enforce our high standards, so grievously offended. Silence continued to reign as the Nazareth weekly *Al-Raia* was closed by order of the Ministry of Interior, after its editor had been jailed for three months without trial.[58]

Once again, history has devised a controlled experiment to demonstrate the utter contempt for freedom of speech on the part of professed civil libertarians. Critics of Nicaraguan abuses of press freedom who pass the most elementary test of sincerity could fit into a very small living room indeed, perhaps even a telephone booth.[59]

As for the jurisprudence that so impressed Justice Brennan, the Hebrew press observes that "Israeli journalism lacks any guarantees, even the slightest, for its freedom. The state is armed with weapons that have no parallel in any democratic society in the world," deriving from colonial British regulations that were reinstituted by Israel as soon as the state was established. These draconian regulations include measures to forbid and punish publications that might encourage "disobedience or displeasure among the inhabitants of the country" or "unpleasantness to the authorities." The law authorizes the Interior Ministry "to terminate the appearance of a journal, for any period that he will deem appropriate, if it has published lies or false rumors that are likely, in his opinion, to enhance panic or despair." The measures are held in reserve, sometimes applied, and they contribute to fear and an "atmosphere of McCarthyism" that enhances the self-censorship normally practiced by editors. This voluntary self-censorship, Israeli legal analyst Moshe Negbi writes, adds substantially to the effects of the "rich and unusual array of tools for crushing press freedom" in the hands of the government. The censor has the legal authority to forbid any information "which might, in his view, harm the defense of the country, public safety or public order." The military censor is "immune to public scrutiny" and "the law forbids the press from publishing any hint that the censor ordered any changes, additions or deletions," though often the fact is obvious, as when the lead editorial is blanked out in Israel's most respected newspaper, *Ha'aretz*. The censor also has the authority to punish, without trial, any newspaper he deems to have violated his orders. The Declaration of Independence of 1948, which expressed Israel's obligations with regard to freedom and civil rights, "makes no mention of freedom of expression," Negbi continues, adding that it was not an accidental omission, but rather reflected the attitudes of Prime Minister David Ben-Gurion, who "vigorously opposed reference to these rights," adhering, along with his associates, to the "Leninist doctrine" that the state should suffer no criticism for actions it regards as right. The state is even authorized to refuse to register a journal (so that it cannot be published) or to terminate it, "without providing any motivation for its refusal."[60]

This authority is used: for example, in barring an Arabic-language social and political journal in Israel edited by an Israeli Arab lecturer at the Hebrew University in 1982, a decision approved by the

High Court for unstated "security reasons"; or the arrest of an Arab from Nazareth a few months later "for publishing a newspaper without permission," namely, four informational leaflets. The courts offer no protection when the state produces the magic word "security."[61]

While Arab citizens are the usual targets, Jews are not immune from these principles of jurisprudence. When the dovish Progressive List, one of whose leaders is General Matti Peled (retired), sought to broadcast a campaign advertisement showing an interview with Arafat announcing that he accepts U.N. resolutions 242 and 338, High Court Justice Goldberg ruled it illegal, stating: "From the time when the government declared that the PLO is a terrorist organization, television is permitted to produce only broadcasts that conform to this declaration and present the PLO in a negative manner as a terrorist organization. It is forbidden to broadcast anything that contradicts the declaration and presents the PLO as a political organization." Commenting, attorney Avigdor Feldman writes: "The logic is iron-clad. State television [there is no other] is not permitted to broadcast a reality inconsistent with government decision, and if the facts are not consistent with the government stand, then not in our school, please."[62]

In the United States, one will discover very little reference to the severe constraints on free expression in Israel over many years. It was not until the violent reaction to the Palestinian uprising from December 1987 that even cursory notice was taken of these practices. In the *New York Times* there has been virtually nothing; it requires considerable audacity for former chief editor A.M. Rosenthal to assert in May 1988 that censorship in Israel "deserves and gets Western criticism."[63] Furthermore, the rare exceptions[64] do not lead to condemnations for these departures from our high ideals or a call for some action on the part of Israel's leading patron.

The reaction of the U.S. media and the American intellectual community to Israeli law and practices provides further dramatic evidence that the show of concern for civil liberties and human rights in Nicaragua is cynical pretense, serving other ends.

The standard test of sincerity yields similar results wherever we turn. These conclusions are well enough documented by now, in such a wide range of cases, as to raise some serious questions among people willing to consider fact and reason. The answers to these questions will not be pleasant to face, so we can be confident that the questions will not be asked.

Discussing "our un-free press" half a century ago, John Dewey observed that criticism of "specific abuses" has only limited value:

> The only really fundamental approach to the problem is to inquire concerning the necessary effect of the present economic system upon the whole system of publicity; upon the judgment of what news is, upon the selection and elimination of matter that is published, upon the treatment of news in both editorial and news columns. The question, under this mode of approach, is not how many specific abuses there are and how they may be remedied, but how far genuine intellectual freedom and social responsibility are possible on any large scale under the existing economic regime.

Publishers and editors, with their commitments to "the public and social order" of which they are the beneficiaries, will often prove to be among the "chief enemies" of true "liberty of the press," Dewey continued. It is unreasonable to expect "the managers of this business enterprise to do otherwise than as the leaders and henchmen of big business," and to "select and treat *their* special wares from this standpoint." Insofar as the ideological managers are "giving the public what it 'wants'," that is because of "the effect of the present economic system in generating intellectual indifference and apathy, in creating a demand for distraction and diversion, and almost a love for crime provided it pays" among a public "debauched by the ideal of getting away with whatever it can."[65]

To these apt reflections we may add the intimate relations between private and state power, the institutionally determined need to accommodate to the interests of those who control basic social decisions, and the success of established power in steadily disintegrating any independent culture that fosters values other than greed, personal gain, and subordination to authority, and any popular structures that sustain independent thought and action. The importance of these factors is highlighted by the fact that even the formal right to freedom of speech was gained only by unremitting popular struggle that challenged existing social arrangements.[66]

Within the reigning social order, the general public must remain an object of manipulation, not a participant in thought, debate, and decision. As the privileged have long understood, it is necessary to ward off recurrent "crises of democracy." In earlier chapters, I have discussed some of the ways these principles have been expressed in the modern period, but the concerns are natural and have arisen from the very origins of the modern democratic thrust. Condemning the radical democrats who had threatened to "turn the world upside down" during the English revolution of the seventeenth century, historian Clement Walker, in 1661, complained:

> They have cast all the mysteries and secrets of government ... before the vulgar (like pearls before swine), and have taught both the soldiery and people to look so far into them as to ravel back all governments to the first principles of nature ... They have made the people thereby so curious and so arrogant that they will never find humility enough to submit to a civil rule.[67]

Walker's concerns were soon overcome, as an orderly world was restored and the "political defeat" of the democrats "was total and irreversible," Christopher Hill observes. By 1695 censorship could be abandoned, "not on the radicals' libertarian principles, but because censorship was no longer necessary," for "the opinion-formers" now "censored themselves" and "nothing got into print which frightened the men of property." In the same year, John Locke wrote that "day-labourers and tradesmen, the spinsters and dairymaids" must be told what to believe. "The greatest part cannot know and therefore they must believe." "But at least," Hill comments, "Locke did not intend that priests should do the telling: that was for God himself."[68] With the decline of religious authority in the modern period, the task has fallen to the "secular priesthood," who understand their responsibility with some clarity, as already discussed.

Despite these insights, some have continued to be seduced by the "democratic dogmatisms" that are derided by those dedicated to the art of manipulation. John Stuart Mill wrote: "Not the violent conflict between parts of the truth, but the quiet suppression of half of it, is the formidable evil. There is always hope when people are forced to listen to both sides." Coming to the present, the Code of Professional Conduct of the British National Union of Journalists enjoins the journalist to "eliminate distortion" and "strive to ensure that the information he/she disseminates is fair and accurate, avoid the expression of comment and conjecture as established fact and falsification by distortion, selection, or misrepresentation."[69] The manipulation of the public in the 1960s elicited the concerns expressed in 1966 by Senator Fulbright, quoted earlier. A year later, Jerome Barron proposed "an interpretation of the first amendment which focuses on the idea that restraining the hand of government is quite useless in assuring free speech if a restraint on access is effectively secured by private groups," that is, "the new media of communication": only they "can lay sentiments before the public, and it is they rather than government who can most effectively abridge expression by nullifying the opportunity for an idea to win acceptance. As a constitutional theory for the communication of ideas, laissez faire is manifestly irrelevant" when the media are narrowly controlled by private power.[70]

Many viewed such ideas with alarm. The editors of the *St. Louis Post-Dispatch*, for many years one of the more independent segments of the local quality press, agreed that the newspaper "has an obligation to the community in which it is published to present fairly unpopular as well as popular sides of a question," but "such a dictum" should not be enforced by law. "As a practical matter," they held, "a newspaper which consistently refuses to give expression to viewpoints with which it differs is not likely to succeed, and doesn't deserve to."[71]

The editors were wrong in their factual assessment, though their qualms about legal obligations cannot be lightly dismissed. In reality, only those media that consistently restrict "both sides" to the narrow consensus of the powerful will succeed in the guided free market.

It is particularly important to understand what stories not to seek, what sources of evidence to avoid. Refugees from Timor or from U.S. bombing in Laos and Cambodia have no useful tales to tell. It is important to stay away from camps on the Honduran border, where refugees report "without exception" that they were "all fleeing from the army that we are supporting" and "every person had a tale of atrocity by government forces, the same ones we are again outfitting with weapons" as they conduct "a systematic campaign of terrorism" with "a combination of murder, torture, rape, the burning of crops in order to create starvation conditions," and vicious atrocities; the report of the congressional delegation that reached these conclusions after their first-hand investigation in early 1981 was excluded from the media, which were avoiding this primary source of evidence on rural El Salvador.[72] It would be bad form to arouse public awareness of Nicaragua's "noteworthy progress in the social sector, which is laying a solid foundation for long-term socio-economic development," reported in 1983 by the Inter-American Development Bank, barred by U.S. pressure from contributing to these achievements.[73] Correspondingly, it is improper to set forth the achievements of the Reagan administration in reversing these early successes, to record the return of disease and malnutrition, illiteracy and dying infants, while the country is driven to the zero grade of life to pay for the sin of independent development. In contrast, it is responsible journalism for James LeMoyne to denounce the Sandinistas for the "bitterness and apathy" he finds in Managua.[74] Those who hope to enter the system must learn that terror traceable to the PLO, Qaddafi, or Khomeini leaves worthy victims who merit compassion and concern; but those targeted by the United States and its allies do not fall within this category. Responsible journalists must understand that a grenade attack on Israeli Army recruits and their families leaving one killed and many wounded deserves a front-page photograph of the victims and a substantial story, while a contra attack on a passenger bus the day before with two killed, two kidnapped, and many wounded merits no report at all.[75] Category by category, the same lessons hold.

There is, in fact, a ready algorithm for those who wish to attain respectability and privilege. It is only necessary to bear in mind the test for sincerity already discussed, and to make sure that you fail it at every turn. The same simple logic explains the characteristic performance of the independent media, and the educated classes generally, for reasons that are hardly obscure.

I have been discussing methods of thought control and the reasons why they gain such prominence in democratic societies in which the general population cannot be driven from the political arena by force. The discussion may leave the impression that the system is all-powerful, but that is far from true. People have the capacity to resist, and sometimes do, with great effect.

Take the case of the Western-backed slaughter in Timor. The media suppressed the terrible events and the complicity of their own governments, but the story nevertheless did finally break through, reaching segments of the public and Congress. This was the achievement of a few dedicated young people, whose names will not be known to history, as is generally true of those whose actions have improved the world. Their efforts did not bring an end to the Indonesian terror or the U.S. support for it, but they did mitigate the violence. Finally, as a result of their work, the Red Cross was allowed limited access. In this and other ways, tens of thousands of lives were saved. There are very few people who can claim to have achieved so much of human consequence. The same is true of many other cases. Internal constraints within a powerful state provide a margin of survivability for its victims, a fact that should never be forgotten.

The United States is a much more civilized place than it was twenty-five years ago. The crisis of democracy and the intellectual independence that so terrify elites have been real enough, and the effects on the society have been profound, and on balance generally healthy. The impact is readily discernible over a wide range of concerns, including racism, the environment, feminism, forceful intervention, and much else; and also in the media, which have allowed some opening to dissident opinion and critical reporting in recent years, considerably beyond what was imaginable even at the peak of the ferment of the sixties, let alone before. One illustration of the improvement in the moral and cultural level is that it has become possible, for the first time, to confront in a serious way what had been done to Native Americans during the conquest of the continent; and many other necessary illusions were questioned, and quickly crumbled upon inspection, as challenges were raised to orthodoxy and authority. Small wonder that the sixties appear as a period of horror, chaos, and destructive abandon in the reflections of privileged observers who are distressed, even appalled, by intellectual independence and moral integrity on the part of the young.

The same developments have had their impact on state policy. There was no protest when John F. Kennedy sent the U.S. Air Force to attack the rural society of South Vietnam. Twenty years later, the Reagan administration was driven underground, compelled to resort to clandestine terror in Central America. The climate of opinion and concern had changed, outside of elite circles, and the capacity of the state to exercise violence had been correspondingly reduced. The toll of Reaganite terror was awesome: tens of thousands of tortured and mutilated bodies, massive starvation, disease and destruction, hundreds of thousands of miserable refugees. It would have been a great deal worse without the constraints imposed by people who had found ways to escape the system of indoctrination, and the courage and honesty to act. These are no small achievements—again, on the part of people whose names will be lost to history.

There are ample opportunities to help create a more humane and decent world, if we choose to act upon them.

I began with the questions raised by the Brazilian bishops about the problems of democracy and the media. Perhaps I may close with my own conclusions on these matters. The professed concern for freedom of the press in the West is not very persuasive in the light of the easy dismissal of even extreme violations of the right of free expression in U.S. client states, and the actual performance of the media in serving the powerful and privileged as an agency of manipulation, indoctrination, and control. A "democratic communications policy," in contrast, would seek to develop means of expression and interaction that reflect the interests and concerns of the general population, and to encourage their self-education and their individual and collective action. A policy conceived in these terms would be a desideratum, though there are pitfalls and dangers that should not be overlooked. But the issue is largely academic, when viewed in isolation from the general social scene. The prospects for a democratic communications policy are inevitably constrained by the distribution of effective power to determine the course and functioning of major social institutions. Hence the goal can be approached only as an integral part of the further democratization of the social order. This process, in turn, requires a democratic communications policy as a central component, with an indispensable contribution to make. Serious steps towards more meaningful democracy would aim to dissolve the concentration of decision-making power, which in our societies resides primarily in a state-corporate nexus. Such a conception of democracy, though so familiar from earlier years that it might even merit the much-abused term "conservative," is remote from those that dominate public discourse—hardly a surprise, given its threat to established privilege.

Human beings are the only species with a history. Whether they also have a future is not so obvious. The answer will lie in the prospects for popular movements, with firm roots among all sectors of the population, dedicated to values that are suppressed or driven to the margins within the existing social and political order: community, solidarity, concern for a fragile environment that will have to sustain future generations, creative work under voluntary control, independent thought, and true democratic participation in varied aspects of life.

Appendix I

1. The Propaganda Model: Some Methodological Considerations[1]

Some methods for testing the propaganda model of the media were mentioned in chapter 1, including the study of paired examples of crimes and of meritorious actions, and the harshest test: the investigation of those cases selected as their strongest grounds by those who take the opposing stand, arguing that the media adopt an adversarial stance. The model stands up quite well under these and other challenges.[2]

The study of paired examples reveals a consistent pattern of radically dichotomous treatment, in the predicted direction. In the case of enemy crimes, we find outrage; allegations based on the flimsiest evidence, often simply invented, and uncorrectible, even when conceded to be fabrication; careful filtering of testimony to exclude contrary evidence while allowing what may be useful; reliance on official U.S. sources, unless they provide the wrong picture, in which case they are avoided (Cambodia under Pol Pot is a case in point); vivid detail; insistence that the crimes originate at the highest level of planning, even in the absence of evidence or credible argument; and so on. Where the locus of responsibility is at home, we find precisely the opposite: silence or apologetics; avoidance of personal testimony and specific detail; world-weary wisdom about the complexities of history and foreign cultures that we do not understand; narrowing of focus to the lowest level of planning or understandable error in confusing circumstances; and other forms of evasion.

The murder of one priest in Poland in 1984 by policemen who were quickly apprehended, tried, and jailed merited far more media coverage than the murder of 100 prominent Latin American religious martyrs, including the Archbishop of San Salvador and four raped American churchwomen, victims of the U.S.-backed security forces. Furthermore, the coverage was vastly different in style—gory details repeated prominently in the former case, evasion in the latter—as was the attribution of responsibility: to the highest level in Poland and even the Soviet Union in the former case, and in the latter, tempered allusions to the centrist government unable to constrain violence of left and right, in utter defiance of the factual record that was largely suppressed.

To take another case, the prison memoirs of released Cuban prisoner Armando Valladares quickly became a media sensation when they appeared in May 1986. Multiple reviews, interviews, and other commentary hailed this "definitive account of the vast system of torture and prison by which Castro punishes and obliterates political opposition," an "inspiring, and unforgettable account" of the "bestial prisons," "inhuman torture," and "record of state violence" under "yet another of this century's mass murderers" (*Washington Post*), who, we learn at last from this book, "has created a new despotism that has institutionalized torture as a mechanism of social control" in "the hell that was the Cuba [Valladares] lived in" (*New York Times*). There were many other vivid and angry denunciations of the "dictatorial goon" Fidel Castro (*Time*) and his atrocities, here revealed so conclusively that "only the most lightheaded and cold-blooded Western intellectual will come to the tyrant's defense" (*Washington Post*). Valladares was singled out for his courage in enduring "the horrors and sadism" of the bloody Cuban tyrant by Ronald Reagan at the White House ceremony marking Human Rights Day in December. Subsequent coverage was pitched at the same level.[3]

Just as Valladares' memoirs appeared in May 1986, arousing great horror, most of the members of the nongovernmental human rights commission of El Salvador (CDHES) were arrested and tortured, including its director Herbert Anaya. While in the "La Esperanza" (Hope) prison, they compiled a 160-page report of sworn testimony of 430 political prisoners, who gave precise and extensive details of their torture by the U.S.-backed security forces; in one case, electrical torture by a North American major in uniform, who is described in some detail. This unusually explicit and comprehensive report was smuggled out of the prison along with a videotape of testimony right in the midst of the furor aroused by Valladares's memoirs, and distributed to the U.S. media. They were not interested. This material was suppressed entirely, without a word, in the national media, where more than a few "lightheaded and cold-blooded Western intellectuals" sing the praises of José Napoleon Duarte and Ronald Reagan. Anaya was not the subject of tributes on Human Rights Day. Rather, he was released in a prisoner exchange, then assassinated, probably by the U.S.-backed security forces; much of the evidence about his assassination did not appear in the national

U.S. media, and few asked whether media exposure might have offered him some protection in the U.S. terror state.[4] Applying the standard test of sincerity already discussed, we know exactly how to evaluate the outraged commentary elicited by Valladares's memoirs.

No less remarkable than the extraordinary double standard is the inability to see it. In extreme cases, we read bitter condemnation of the "liberal media" for their unwillingness even to describe Castro as a dictator and for their "double standard" in focusing on human rights violations in El Salvador while ignoring the Cuban human rights violations exposed by Valladares.[5]

Numerous other cases that have been investigated reveal the same pattern. It is, of course, familiar elsewhere. The state-controlled media and human rights organizations of the Soviet bloc have rightly become an object of ridicule for their great indignation over enemy crimes while they manage to miss those closer to home. A minimal level of moral integrity suffices to show that the pattern should be reversed: one's own responsibilities should be the primary concern, and actions should be largely directed by an assessment of their actual impact on suffering people—again, typically leading to a focus on one's own responsibilities—while authentic human rights organizations undertake the charge of compiling a comprehensive factual record. Such elementary moral reasoning is well within the reach of our intellectual culture when it considers official enemies; extreme moral cowardice very efficiently bars the exercise at home.

Comparison of elections in enemy Nicaragua and the client states of El Salvador and Guatemala yields similar results, as has been shown by several studies. One approach has been to compare the U.S. coverage of the two cases; another, to compare U.S. and European coverage of the same case. The results provide a dramatic indication of the subordination of the U.S. media to the goals established by the state authorities.[6]

By any reasonable standard, the elections in Nicaragua were superior in circumstances, conditions, and procedure to those in El Salvador; the media overcame these facts by adopting the U.S. government agenda, which differed radically in the two cases. Freedom of speech, association, and organization, even massive state terror, were all off the agenda for the elections in client states, while attention was focused on long lines of patient voters (in elections where voting was obligatory, and the penalties for not participating could be severe), on alleged guerrilla threats (often fabricated), and so on. The very fact that elections were held at all under conditions of strife was considered a triumph of democracy. In the case of Nicaragua, the agenda was reversed: terrorist actions of the U.S.-run proxy forces to disrupt the elections were off the agenda, as were proper procedures, far less repression than in the client states, broad participation with no compulsion, and a wide range of choices constrained by no serious interference apart from U.S. pressures to induce its favored candidates to withdraw so as to discredit the election as "lacking any real choice." Any deviations from the performance of advanced industrial democracies under peacetime conditions were scrutinized and angrily deplored, and the only serious issue was the prospects for the U.S.-backed candidate for president, taken to be the measure of democracy. Apart from the U.S. government, the major news sources were the U.S.-backed opposition, who, along with the contra "civilian directorate" established and lavishly supported by the CIA, received extensive and favorable press; the fact that the U.S. candidates appeared to have little popular support, and little in the way of democratic credentials so far as was known, was also off the agenda.[7] In the client states, there was no need to report on any domestic opposition, since they had not been able to survive the conditions of democracy, U.S.-style. Close analysis of coverage reveals these and related patterns quite dramatically.

The 1984 elections in Nicaragua were dismissed with derision or ignored, while studies by highly qualified observers and analysts were, and remain, beyond the pale, because they consistently reached the wrong conclusions: for example, the detailed examination by a delegation of the professional association of Latin American scholars (LASA), probably the most careful study of any Third World election, and the supporting conclusions by an Irish Parliamentary delegation drawn primarily from the center-right, among many others, all passing without mention.

The media even permitted themselves to be duped by a transparent fraud, the well-timed "discovery" of a shipment of MiG fighter planes to Nicaragua, which predictably turned out to be fanciful and was later attributed to Oliver North's shenanigans, but which admirably served its purpose of helping to efface the unwanted Nicaraguan elections. When it had become obvious that no MiGs had arrived, a new phase of disinformation began, shifting attention to the leak of secret information (that is, to the planned release of intelligence fabrications, so it appears), condemned as "criminal" by Secretary Shultz. The press again went along, taking the issue to be the alleged leak and not the propaganda exercise in which they had participated, even claiming that the MiG pretense had harmed the U.S. and anti-Sandinista groups. In reality, the exercise had succeeded in every achievable aim, helping to bury the results of the election "under an avalanche of alarmist news reports," as the LASA report observed. The media never returned to the matter to provide a meaningful report or analysis of the elections. Cooperation in the MiG fraud was, of course, only one ancillary device employed to eliminate the unwanted elections from official history, but it played its useful role.[8]

In contrast, elections at the same time in the terror state of El Salvador were effusively lauded as a bold and courageous advance towards democracy, on the basis of reporting of shameful bias and superficiality reflecting the U.S. government agenda and reliance on official observers who made barely a pretense of inquiry. There was virtually no concern over the fact that the political opposition had been murdered and the independent media physically destroyed by the U.S.-organized security forces while the population was thoroughly traumatized by extraordinary terror, and surely no mention of the conclusion by observers from the British Parliamentary Human Rights Group that the elections were held in an "atmosphere of terror and despair, of macabre rumor and grisly reality," or the evidence that justifies this conclusion. The same was true in the case of the elections in Guatemala, where state terror had reached even more extreme heights with constant U.S. support. *New York Times* correspondent Stephen Kinzer even suggested that the Guatemalan election offered a model for Nicaragua.[9]

Subsequent commentary, virtually exceptionless in the mainstream, contrasts the "fledgling democracies" of the client states and their "elected presidents" with totalitarian Nicaragua, run by the dictator Ortega, placed in power in a sham election, hence unelected. The performance merits comparison with the official media of totalitarian states.

Coverage of the 1982 Salvadoran elections was comparable. The three U.S. TV networks devoted over two hours to upbeat and enthusiastic coverage (the Nicaraguan elections of 1984, in contrast, merited fifteen minutes of skepticism or derision). The British networks had eighty minutes of coverage, but the character was radically different. The U.S. networks reported with much fanfare the conclusions of the official U.S. government observers, who, after a cursory look, reported in a press conference their amazement at this thrilling exercise in democracy. In contrast, BBC's Martin Bell in his summary report commented that a fair election under the circumstances of state terror that BBC had reviewed was completely out of the question, while the commercial TV channel ITN featured Lord Chitnis of the British Parliamentary Human Rights Group, speaking not in a plush hotel but in a Salvadoran slum, where he pointed out that what observers see under army guard is hardly worth reporting under the prevailing conditions of hideous repression and trauma.[10]

More generally, the U.S. and European media gave radically different accounts of the Salvadoran elections. Analyzing the comparative coverage, Jennifer Schirmer concludes that the enthusiastic U.S. coverage was "remarkably different" from the reaction of the European press, which focused on the circumstances of terror that made an election meaningless, coerced voting, and other crucial factors suppressed in the euphoric U.S. commentary. She observes that "the major difference is that while the European press consistently emphasized the political context of fear and the climate of official terror in which the elections took place, the U.S. press predominantly focused on electoral mechanics and theatre, echoing U.S. and Salvadoran officials in labelling those who were legally and physically excluded from the contest as marxist, anti-democratic and violent." *New York Times* Paris Bureau Chief John Vinocur added to the deception by falsifying the European reaction to bring it into line with the upbeat U.S. response. Schirmer's conclusion is that the picture provided by the European media, apart from being accurate, was virtually barred in the United States, where "the 'reality' created and assumed by the U.S. press is so one-sided and partisan that the U.S. government shall not need to censor its press in future coverage of the Third World."[11]

As for the media and Indochina, the facts are quite different from what is commonly alleged. Throughout the war, there were individual journalists who reported honestly and courageously, and made serious and sometimes successful efforts to escape the conventional reliance on government handouts and official premises, but the general picture presented by the media conformed with great precision to the official version.

In the early stages, several young journalists (David Halberstam and others) turned to officers in the field, whose accounts did not substantiate Washington rhetoric. Col. John Paul Vann was the major example, as is now regularly acknowledged. For this, they were bitterly attacked for undermining the U.S. effort. These facts helped create the picture of an adversarial press, but quite falsely. Reporters who turned to Vann for assessment of the military realities did not inform their readers of his conclusion that the government lacked any political base and that the rural population supported the NLF.[12] Their reporting remained within the patriotic agenda; the South Vietnamese guerrillas were "trying to subvert this country" and it was only proper for the United States to defend its people against "Communist aggression" and to offer the peasants "protection against the Communists" by driving them "as humanely as possible" into strategic hamlets (David Halberstam, E.W. Kenworthy, Homer Bigart).[13] The only issue was whether corruption and dishonesty were harming the prospects for a victory of U.S. arms, taken to be right and just. Contrary to what is often believed, there was little departure from this stand, and gross distortion and suppression in the interest of U.S. power remained a major feature of news reporting as of admissible commentary until the end, and indeed since. Reporters did not attempt to cover the war and the background social and political conflicts from the standpoint of the indigenous population, or the guerrillas; the Afghan resistance to the Soviet invasion, in contrast was invariably and properly covered from this perspective. The media supported the U.S. attack with enthusiasm or at most skepticism about prospects, and within the approved assumptions of "defense of South Vietnam." It was well after elite circles had determined that the enterprise was too costly to pursue that criticisms were heard of these "blundering efforts to do good" (Anthony Lewis, at the outer limits of expressible dissent). Furthermore, again contrary to common belief, "the often-gory pictorial reportage by television" to which Landrum Bolling and others refer is largely mythical. Television played down such images, and the public impact of the media, particularly television, was if anything to increase public support for the war; this is true, in particular, of the coverage of the Tet offensive.

With regard to the Freedom House study of the Tet offensive that is widely assumed to have proven the case for the media's irresponsibility and adversarial stance, the massive evidence presented collapses under scrutiny. When dozens of crucial errors, misrepresentations, and outright falsehoods are cleared away, we find that the media performed very much in the manner predicted by the propaganda model: with professional competence in the narrow sense, but without any challenge to the doctrine that the U.S. forces demolishing South Vietnam were "defending" the country from the indigenous guerrillas.

The Freedom House critique reduces to the accusation that the media were overly pessimistic—though in fact they were less pessimistic than internal assessments of U.S. intelligence, government officials, and high-level advisers. It is tacitly assumed by Freedom House that the responsibility of a free press is to cheer for the home team. Complaints of the Freedom House variety were voiced by the Soviet military command and Party ideologues with regard to Afghanistan. The Soviet Defense Minister "sharply critized the Soviet press for undermining public respect for the Soviet army" by its negative commentary. The mass circulation weekly *Ogonyok* was subjected to particularly sharp criticism because it had presented a "bleak picture" of the war in Afghanistan, describing "poor morale and desertion" among Afghan units, the inability of the Soviet forces to control territory, and drug use among Soviet troops, and publishing excerpts from a helicopter pilot's journal that describe "the sight and smell of colleagues' charred bodies" and imply that "helicopter losses are high." In December 1987, the *Moscow News* published a letter by Andrei Sakharov calling for the immediate withdrawal of Soviet troops; similar statements in the U.S. press regarding Vietnam were rare to nonexistent until well after the Tet offensive had convinced U.S. elites that the game was not worth the candle. There was even the remarkable example of Moscow news correspondent Vladimir Danchev, who, in radio broadcasts extending over five days in May 1983, denounced the Soviet invasion of Afghanistan and called on the rebels to resist, eliciting justified praise in the West and outrage when he was sent to a psychiatric hospital, then returned to his position. There was no Vladimir Danchev in the United States during the American wars in Indochina—or since.[14]

In a review of media coverage of the United States and Indochina from 1950 until the present, Herman and I show that these conclusions hold throughout, sometimes in a most astonishing way.[15] To the best of my knowledge, the same is true in other cases that provide a test of the competing conceptions of the media.

As noted in the text, one of the predictions of the propaganda model, quite well confirmed, is that it must be effectively excluded from ongoing debate over the media despite its initial plausibility and its conformity to the needs of propaganda as articulated by the substantial segment of elite opinion who advocate "the manufacture of consent." While initial plausibility and elite advocacy do not, of course, prove the model to be correct, they might suggest that it be a candidate for discussion. But neither this thought nor the substantial empirical support for the model allows it to achieve such status.

By and large, the possibility of studying the functioning of the media in terms of a propaganda model is simply ignored. Within the mainstream, discussion of the media keeps to the narrow conserva-tive-liberal spectrum, with its assumption that the media have either gone too far in their defiance of authority or that they are truly independent and undaunted by authority, committed to "the scrappy spirit of open controversy" that typifies American intellec-tual life (Walter Goodman), with no holds barred.[16] On the rare occasions when the possibility of another position is addressed, the failure of comprehension and level of reasoning again indicate that the conception advanced is too remote from the doctrinal framework of the elite intellectual culture to be intelligible.

One example, already noted, is the reaction of *Times* columnist Tom Wicker to a study of the range of opinion permitted expression in the national press. As in this case, the reactions commonly reflect an inability even to perceive what is being said. Thus, a discussion of how media access might be diversified through listener-supported radio and other local initiatives can be understood by the national correspondent of the *Atlantic Monthly*, Nicolas Lemann, only as a call for state control over the media; the idea of diversified public access in local communities offers a "frightening" prospect of "a politicized press," he continues, as where the press is "controlled by a left-wing political order," Stalinist-style—unlike the current system of corpo-rate oligopoly, where the press is thankfully not "politicized." Or, to take another case, the executive editor of *Harper's Magazine* criticizes Michael Parenti's analysis of the media on the grounds that he "overlooks a key feature of American journalism," namely, that "the press generally defines the news as what politicians say." Parenti's thesis is that the same groups—the "corporate class"—control the state and the media, so the criticism amounts to the charge that the thesis is valid.[17]

Willingness to recognize the bare possibility of analysis of the media in terms of a propaganda model, as in work of the past years cited earlier, is so uncommon that the few existing cases perhaps merit a word of comment. Lemann's critique of our *Manufacturing Consent* is, in fact, one of the rare examples. His review contains several allusions to the book, few of which even approach accuracy; the example just cited is typical. We may dispense with further discussion of the falsehoods,[18] the stream of abuse, or the occasional apparent disagreement over facts, for which his evidence reduces to "the literature" or common knowledge, which allegedly does not confirm what he claims that we assert.

Consider, rather, Lemann's criticisms of our presentation of the propaganda model. His main point is: "in no instance do they prove" the claim that the press "knowingly prints falsehoods and suppresses inconvenient truths." He is quite right. In empirical inquiry, nothing is ever literally *proven*; one presents evidence and tries to show that it can be explained on the basis of the hypotheses advanced. A critic could then rationally argue that the evidence is mistaken, poorly chosen, or otherwise inadequate, or that there is a better theory to explain the facts. Lemann suggests no inadequacy of the evidence (when we eliminate false allegations), but does appear to suggest an alternative theory. It is that "the big-time press does operate within a fairly narrow range of assumptions" and "concentrates intensely on a small number of subjects at a time," shifting attention "unpredictably from country to country" and reflecting "what Herman and Chomsky, meaning to be withering, call 'patriotic premises'." He does not, however, proceed to say how this conception of the media explains the facts we discuss, or others, if he regards these as poorly chosen for unstated reasons. Thus, to take virtually the only reference to the book that is accurate, he notes with much derision that we give actual figures (worse yet, in "tabular lingo") concerning the relative attention given to the murdered Polish priest and 100 Latin American religious martyrs.[19] Clearly, the case confirms our hypothesis ("which, of course, turns out to be correct," he writes with further derision). Does the case support Lemann's alternative theory? Insofar as his proposals differ from ours, they plainly have nothing whatsoever to say about these facts, or about others that might be relevant.

In response to a letter by Edward Herman raising this point, Lemann elaborates: "As for Father Popieluszko, he was killed when the U.S. press was most focused on Poland. Archbishop Romero was killed before the press had really focused on El Salvador. Popieluszko's murder wasn't more important; the discrepancy can be explained by saying the press tends to focus on only a few things at a time." This, then, is the explanation of why the media gave far more coverage to the murder of Father Popieluszko than to the murder of 100 religious martyrs in Latin America, including archbishop Romero and the four U.S. religious women raped and murdered, and why the coverage was so radically different in character, as shown in detail. Let us ask only the simplest question: how much coverage were the media giving to El Salvador and to Poland when Archbishop Romero and Father Popieluszko were murdered? We find that the coverage was almost identical, eliminating this proposed explanation without any further consideration of its quite obvious flaws.[19]

Once again, the only plausible conclusion is that it is the very idea of subjecting the media to rational inquiry that is outrageous, when it yields conclusions that one would prefer not to believe.

Confirming further that this is precisely what is at stake, Lemann condemns us for "devot[ing] their greatest specific scorn to liberal journalists ... in the time-honored tradition of the left," particularly Stephen Kinzer, Sydney Schanberg, and William Shawcross. He does not, however, explain how one can investigate the coverage of Central America and Cambodia by the *New York Times* while avoiding the work of its correspondents there; or how one can explore the remarkable success of the idea that the left imposed "silence" on media and governments during the Pol Pot years—by publications that went to press after the overthrow of Pol Pot, no less—without reference to its creator. Quite evidently, it is the topics addressed that Lemann finds unacceptable, for reasons that can readily be discerned. These observations apart, Lemann appears not to understand the elementary point that discussion of the most dissident and critical elements of the media is of particular significance, for obvious reasons, in exploring the bounds that are set on thinkable thought.

Throughout, Lemann is particularly incensed by attention to fact, as his derisive comments about "tabular lingo" indicate. Thus he writes that we "dismiss the standard sources on the countries they write about," as in discussing coverage of the Nicaragua election, making use instead of such absurd sources as the report of the Irish Parliamentary Delegation of largely center-right parties and the detailed study of the professional association of Latin American scholars (whom we call "independent observers," he adds derisively, apparently regarding Latin American scholars as not "independent" if their research does not conform to his prejudices). Asked by Herman to explain why he finds our use of sources inadequate in this or any other case, he writes: "By standard sources, I mean the American press, which usually weighs the government handouts against other sources." What he is saying, then, is that in investigating how the media dealt with the Nicaraguan election, we must rely on the media that are under investigation and not make use of independent material to assess their performance. Following this ingenious procedure, we will naturally conclude that the media are performing superbly: what they produce corresponds exactly to what they produce. Quite apart from this, Lemann does not seem to comprehend that our account of how the media radically shifted the agenda in the case of El Salvador and Nicaragua in no way depended on the sources he finds unacceptable and exotic.

The same is true throughout. It is difficult to believe that such performances are intended seriously. A more plausible interpretation is that the questions raised are so intolerable that even a semblance of seriousness cannot be maintained.

It is sometimes argued that the propaganda model is undermined by the fact that some escape the impact of the system. This is an "anomaly" that the model leaves unexplained, Walter LaFeber alleges. Thus, a "weakness" of the model is "its inability to explain the anti-contra movement that has—so far—blunted Administration policy." LaFeber argues further that proponents of the model want "to have it both ways: to claim that leading American journals 'mobilize bias,' but object when I cite crucial examples that weaken" their thesis; the only example cited, the "key exception," is the case of the nonexistent MiGs. He also puts forth a third argument against the model, as it is presented in our book *Manufacturing Consent*: "If the news media are so unqualifiedly bad, the book should at least explain why so many publications (including my own) can cite their stories to attack President Reagan's Central American policy."

This is one of the very rare attempts to evaluate a propaganda model with actual argument instead of mere invective, and is furthermore the reasoning of an outstanding and independent-minded historian. It is therefore worth unravelling the logic of the three arguments.

Consider the first argument: the model is undermined by the fact that efforts to "mobilize bias" sometimes fail. By the same logic, an account of how *Pravda* works to "mobilize bias" would be undermined by the existence of dissidents. Plainly, the thesis that *Pravda* serves as an organ of state propaganda is not disconfirmed by the fact that there are many dissidents in the Soviet Union. Nor would the thesis be confirmed if every word printed by *Pravda* were accepted uncritically by the entire Soviet population. The thesis says nothing about the degree of success of propaganda. LaFeber's first argument is not relevant; it does not address the model we present.

Turning to the different question of actual media impact on opinion, comprehensive and systematic studies are lacking, but there is little doubt that the impact is substantial, surely among the educated classes.[20] Analysis of a kind not as yet undertaken would be required to determine more closely just how much impact to attribute to media distortion and filtering, and how much to narrowly conceived self-interest and other causes, in establishing the remarkable illusions that prevail on critical issues. It is also true that, with great effort, some are able to find ways to think for themselves, even to act effectively in the political arena, thus bringing about a "crisis of democracy." But that neither confirms nor refutes an account of how the media function.

Let us put aside for a moment the matter of "the anti-contra movement," and turn to the second argument, based on the "key exception." This we have already discussed. It is no exception, but conforms to the propaganda model (see note 8). This fact eliminates the second argument. But suppose that real cases had been presented of media failure to conform to the government line. Proponents of the model would not "object," as LaFeber believes; this is exactly what the model predicts, as we see when a persistent misinterpretation is overcome.

The propaganda model does not assert that the media parrot the line of the current state managers in the manner of a totalitarian regime; rather, that the media reflect the consensus of powerful elites of the state-corporate nexus generally, including those who object to some aspect of government policy, typically on tactical grounds. The model argues, from its foundations, that the media will protect the interests of the powerful, not that it will protect state managers from their criticisms; the persistent failure to see this point may reflect more general illusions about our democratic systems. In the present case, a propaganda model is not refuted if the media provide a platform for powerful domestic elites that came to oppose the contra option for destroying Nicaragua; rather it is suppported by this fact. As noted earlier, by 1986 80 percent of "leaders" (executives, etc.) objected to the contra policy—as flawed, too costly, and unnecessary to achieve shared goals, to judge by public discussion. A propaganda model therefore predicts that these views should be reflected in the media, thus conflicting with the government line. In fact, the model arguably does fail in the case of the contras, though in a manner *opposite* to what LaFeber believes: as we have seen, the media not only adopted without thought or question the basic doctrines of the narrow (and quite remarkable) elite consensus on Central America policy, but even kept largely to the extremist position of the incumbent state managers, thus showing a degree of subordination to state authorities beyond what the model expects.

Having clarified this point, let us return to the "anti-contra movement that has ... blunted Administration policy." Here some care is necessary. There are two very different anti-contra movements, just as there were two very different movements against the Vietnam war. One opposed administration policy on tactical grounds, the other on grounds of principle. After the Tet offensive, much of the corporate elite came to oppose the war as unwise or unnecessary. The same has been true of the contras, as just noted. The popular and principled opposition to the U.S. attacks against Vietnam and Nicaragua did "blunt administration policies," but not through the media. These movements raised the costs to the perpetrators, and in this way were in large part responsible for the ultimate emergence of the narrowly based and self-interested elite critique. But however important these matters, we need not explore them more closely here. The point is that there were two very different kinds of "anti-contra movement"; the media reflected the narrow tactical objections in conformity with their societal function, but never offered more than the most marginal opening to the principled critique, as illustrated by the samples reviewed earlier. Again, the predictions of a propaganda model are confirmed.

What is more, a propaganda model is not weakened by the discovery that with a careful and critical reading, material could be unearthed in the media that could be used by those who objected to "President Reagan's Central American policy" on grounds of principle, opposing not its failures but its successes: the near destruction of Nicaragua and the blunting of the popular forces that threatened to bring democracy and social reform to El Salvador, among other achievements. Analogously, the assertion that the Soviet press transmits government propaganda and tries to "mobilize bias" is in no way refuted when we find in it—as of course we do—material undermining the claim that the heroic Soviet military is marching from success to success in defending Afghanistan from bandits dispatched by the CIA. The point is obvious in the latter case; equally so in the former. The third argument thus collapses as well.

Note finally LaFeber's belief that administration policy was unsuccessful. True, in the terms of official propaganda, the policies failed: the United States did not "restore democracy" to Nicaragua or establish "democracy" fully in El Salvador and Guatemala. As the propaganda model predicts, the media with virtual unanimity describe the policy as a failure, adopting official pretenses without skepticism or inquiry. If we permit ourselves a measure of critical detachment, thus granting the right to analyze the U.S. ideological system in the manner of other societies, then the conclusions are rather different. Administration policies met with substantial success in achieving the basic goals, though maximal objectives were not attained and the partial failures were costly to the interests represented by the planners—not exactly an unknown event in history, the Indochina wars being another case.

Perhaps it is worth stressing a point that should be obvious. If the media function as predicted by a propaganda model, then they must present a picture of the world that is tolerably close to reality, even if only a selective version. Investors have to make judgments based on the facts of the real world, and the same is true of state managers. Privileged and politically active elites, who rely on the media, must have some awareness of basic realities if they are to serve their own interests effectively and play their social roles. Often, these realities demonstrate the ineptness, incompetence, corruption, and other failings of the state managers and their policies. These realities are detectable, even emphasized, in the media, and would be even if their sole function were to provide services to the powerful. To appeal to these facts to show that the media do not attempt to "mobilize bias" is to betray a serious misunderstanding of social realities.

It is rare to discover in the mainstream any recognition of the existence or possibility of analysis of the ideological system in terms of a propaganda model, let alone to try to confront it on rational grounds. The failure of argument in the few examples that can be found again suggests that the model is indeed robust.

One of the most appropriate ways to test the propaganda model, or any other conception of how the media function, is by close comparison of paired examples. Of course, history does not provide perfect experiments, but there are many cases that are close enough to permit an instructive test. A number of examples are discussed in the text and appendices, many more elsewhere. To my knowledge, they confirm the propaganda model with a degree of consistency that is surprising in a complex social world and in a manner that is often dramatic.

Some care has to be taken in selecting such examples. Thus, suppose we were to argue that the *Boston Globe* applies a double standard to the city of Boston, subjecting it to unfair criticism. To prove the point, we take paired examples: say, corruption in the city government in Boston and Seattle, or a murder traceable to the police in Boston and in Karachi. Doubtless we would find that coverage of the Boston cases is far greater, thus proving the point: the editors and staff are "self-hating Bostonians."

The argument is plainly absurd. Obviously, comparison must begin by setting as a baseline the ordinary level of coverage of affairs in Boston, Seattle, and Karachi in the *Globe*, and the reasons for the general selection. It must also consider such factors as the level of *favorable* coverage of the three cities. Correcting for the obvious errors, the theory of self-hating Bostonians quickly collapses.

These points are so trivial that it is rather startling to discover that they are commonly ignored. Thus, a familiar condemnation of the media—very probably the most common, as measured by letters to the editor, impassioned commentary, etc. — is that they are unfair to Israel and apply a "double standard" to it, perhaps because of anti-Semitism, or because the journalists are self-hating Jews or in love with left-wing fascists or Third World terrorists. The proof typically offered for the thesis is that Israeli crimes receive more coverage than comparable or worse crimes in Syria, South Yemen, and other Arab and Third World states.[21]

The fallacy is transparent; it is exactly the one just discussed. The level of media coverage of Israel is vastly beyond that of the examples cited to prove a "double standard," and is totally different in character. One would have to search a long time to find a favorable word about Syria, South Yemen, etc., or any word at all. Such coverage as there is is uniformly negative, generally harshly so, with no mitigating elements.

Coverage of Israel is radically different in scale and in character. The Israeli elections of 1988, for example, received extensive and prominent coverage in the national media, second only to the United States itself.[22] The same is true of other cases one might select. Furthermore, coverage of Israel is extremely favorable, even obsequious, as illustrated by examples cited earlier and below; overwhelmingly, events are reported and interpreted from an Israeli point of view. Of course, it also follows that when Israeli atrocities become too extreme to overlook, the coverage will be more substantial than in the case of countries that are generally reviled or ignored, much as in the case of Boston and Karachi. Furthermore, if any country that approached Israel in the scale and laudatory character of coverage (none exists, to my knowledge) were to carry out atrocities of the kinds in which

Israel has regularly engaged, or if Jews in the Soviet Union or elsewhere were subject to the kind of treatment regularly meted out to Arabs, there is little doubt what the media reaction would be. I return to some examples, and there is extensive literature demonstrating the protectiveness of the media towards Israel, which will be obvious to anyone familiar with them. My point here, however, is to clarify the methodological point. Once we understand it, this large literature can be dismissed, with scarcely an exception.

A fair number of examples that I think are properly selected have been discussed in the literature, in the references cited, and again here. There are enough complexities so that a challenge to any particular choice is always in order. No serious ones have been raised, to my knowledge. There are, however, some methodological issues that are worth thinking through carefully if the analysis of ideological systems is to be pursued in a serious way. Let us consider some of these.

A propaganda model makes predictions at various levels. There are first-order predictions about how the media function. The model also makes second-order predictions about how media performance will be discussed and evaluated. And it makes third-order predictions about the reactions to studies of media performance. The general prediction, at each level, is that what enters the mainstream will support the needs of established power. The first-order predictions are those we have been concerned with throughout. The second-order prediction is that media debate will be bounded in a manner that satisfies these external needs, thus limited to the question of the alleged adversarial stance of the media; the point has been discussed in chapter 1, and I will return to it in the next section. But suppose that some study of the media escapes these bounds, and reaches unwanted conclusions. The model yields third-order predictions about this case as well: specifically, it predicts that such inquiry will be ignored or bitterly condemned, for it conflicts with the needs of the powerful and privileged. A few examples have already been mentioned,[23] but a closer look is in order, because the matter is of some significance for inquiry into the ideological system. It is worth understanding the devices that are used to prevent such inquiry.

Since the matter can become intricate, let us take a concrete example. Consider the examination in *Political Economy of Human Rights* of three categories of atrocities: what we called there "constructive," "benign," and "nefarious" bloodbaths. "Constructive bloodbaths" are those that serve the interests of U.S. power; "benign bloodbaths" are largely irrelevant to these concerns; and "nefarious bloodbaths" are those that can be charged to the account of official enemies and are thus useful for mobilizing the public.

The first-order prediction of a propaganda model is that constructive bloodbaths will be welcomed (with perhaps some clucking of tongues and thoughts about the barbarity of backward peoples), benign bloodbaths ignored, and nefarious bloodbaths passionately condemned, on the basis of a version of the facts that need have little credibility and that may adopt standards that would merely elicit contempt if applied in the study of alleged abuses of the United States or friendly states. We presented a series of examples to show that these consequences are exactly what we discover.

The second-order prediction of the model is that within mainstream circles, studies of this kind will not be found, and that is quite correct. But now we have an example that escapes these bounds. We therefore turn to the third-order predictions: what will the reactions be?

At this level, the model predicts that exposure of the facts would be rather unwelcome. In fact, one might draw an even sharper conclusion: exposure will be ignored in the case of constructive bloodbaths; it may be occasionally noted without interest in the case of benign bloodbaths; and it will lead to great indignation in the case of nefarious bloodbaths. The reasons are clear: the welcome afforded constructive bloodbaths cannot be acknowledged, if only because it exposes the hypocrisy of the furor over nefarious bloodbaths and enemy abuses generally; exposure of the lack of attention to benign bloodbaths is not too damaging, at least if the U.S. role in implementing these atrocities is suppressed; and exposure of the treatment of and reaction to nefarious bloodbaths not only again reveals the hypocrisy and the social role of the "specialized class" of privileged intellectuals, but also interferes with a valuable device for mobilizing the public in fear and hatred of a threatening enemy.

The first-order predictions of the model are systematically confirmed. The constructive bloodbaths were welcomed and approved, the benign bloodbaths were ignored, and the nefarious bloodbaths were angrily condemned on the basis of evidence and charges of a kind that would be dismissed with ridicule if offered against the U.S. or its allies. Turning to the second-order predictions, as the propaganda model predicts, such inquiry is regarded as completely out of bounds and is not to be found within the mainstream.[24] Turning finally to the third-level predictions, these too are confirmed. Our discussion of constructive bloodbaths has been entirely ignored, the discussion of benign bloodbaths has merited an occasional phrase in a context that exculpates the United States, and our exposure of the handling of nefarious bloodbaths has elicited a huge literature of denunciation.

These reactions are worth exploring; they have definite implications for the study of ideological institutions. To see why, let us look at the two cases that we investigated in most detail: the U.S.-backed Indonesian invasion of East Timor (benign) and the terror in Cambodia under the Khmer Rouge (nefarious).

These two cases are well chosen for the purpose of testing the propaganda model. In both cases it was clear that there were horrendous massacres. Furthermore, they took place in the same part of the world, and in the very same years—though the Indonesian violence and repression in Timor continue, with the support of the United States and other industrial democracies. The evidence in the two cases was comparable in accessibility, credibility, and character. This evidence also indicated that the atrocities were comparable in absolute scale for the time period under review, though larger in Timor relative to the population.[25] The crucial difference was that the slaughter in Timor was carried out by a U.S. client with critical U.S. diplomatic and military support that mounted along with escalating atrocities, while the slaughter in Cambodia was conducted by an official enemy and was, furthermore, highly functional at that time in helping to overcome the "Vietnam syndrome" and to restore popular support for U.S. intervention and violence in the Third World "in defense against the Pol Pots." In fact, a few months after we wrote about this prospect, the deepening engagement of the U.S. government in Pol Pot-style state terror in El Salvador was being justified as necessary to save the population from the "Pol Pot left."

In our comparative study of the response to the Cambodia and Timor massacres, we drew no specific conclusions about the actual facts. As we reiterated to the point of boredom, an attempt to assess the actual facts is a different topic, not pertinent to our specific inquiry. That is a simple point of logic. The question we addressed was how the evidence available was transmuted as it passed through the filters of the ideological system. Plainly, that inquiry into the propaganda system at work is not affected, one way or another, by whatever may be discovered about the actual facts. We did tentatively suggest that in the case of Timor, the church sources and refugee studies we cited were plausible, and that in the case of

Cambodia, State Department specialists were probably presenting the most credible accounts. Both suggestions are well confirmed in retrospect, but the accuracy of our suspicions as to the facts is not pertinent to the question we addressed, as is evident on a moment's thought, and as we repeatedly stressed.

Our goal, then, was to consider the relation between the evidence available and the picture presented by the media and journals of opinion; to determine the actual facts is a different task. The latter task, we emphasized, was well worth undertaking (it simply wasn't ours). Thus we took issue with the assertion of Jean Lacouture in the *New York Review of Books* that facts do not matter; we did not accept his contention that it is of no consequence whether killings under Pol Pot were in the thousands or millions (he had originally claimed that the Khmer Rouge boasted in 1976 of killing 2 million people, but in corrections a few weeks later stated that deaths might be only in the thousands, adding that the reduction of his estimate by perhaps a factor of 1,000 was of no significance).[26] We pointed out that this position, while widely praised and respected in this case, would be rejected with scorn if applied by others to the U.S. or its clients and allies; imagine the reaction if some critic of Israel were to allege that Israel boasted of killing several million people during its invasion of Lebanon in 1982, then conceding that perhaps the number was in the thousands, but that the difference is of no consequence.

Turning to the first-order predictions of the propaganda model, in the case of Cambodia under the Khmer Rouge[27] there were denunciations of genocide from the first moment, a huge outcry of protest, fabrication of evidence on a grand scale, suppression of some of the most reliable sources (including State Department Cambodia watchers, the most knowledgeable source at the time) because they did not support the preferred picture, reiteration of extraordinary fabrications even after they were openly conceded to have been invented, and so on. In the case of Timor, coverage declined from a substantial level before the U.S.-backed Indonesian invasion to flat zero as the atrocities reached their peak with increasing U.S. support.

The importance of this suppression cannot be too strongly stressed. Because of it, few knew what was happening, or paid sufficient attention to the little that did seep through. As should be obvious, this is a criticism of great severity. I do not exempt myself from it, I must say with regret. The atrocities in Timor and Cambodia under Pol Pot began at about the same time, but I published my first word about the former nineteen months after writing about Khmer

Rouge atrocities, though the Timor massacres were far more important by any moral criterion for the simple and sufficient reason that
something could be done to terminate them. Thanks to media self-
censorship, there were no substantial efforts to organize the kind of
opposition that might have compelled the United States to desist
from its active participation in the slaughter and thus quite possibly
to bring it to an end. In the case of Cambodia, in contrast, no one
proposed measures that could be taken to mitigate the atrocities.
When George McGovern suggested military intervention to save the
victims in late 1978, he was ridiculed by the right wing and government advisers. And when Vietnam invaded and brought the slaughter to an end, that aroused new horror about "the Prussians of Asia"
who overthrew Pol Pot and must be punished for the crime.

The first-order predictions, then, are well confirmed. The second-order predictions were not only confirmed, but far surpassed;
the doctrine that was concocted and quickly became standard, utterly
inconsistent with readily documented facts, is that there was "silence" in the West over the Khmer Rouge atrocities.[28] This fantasy is
highly serviceable, not only in suppressing the subordination of
educated elites to external power, but also in suggesting that in the
future we must focus attention still more intensely and narrowly on
enemy crimes. The third-order predictions are also confirmed. Our
discussion of Cambodia under Pol Pot aroused a storm of protest.[29]
The condemnation is, to my knowledge, completely lacking in substance, a fact that has not passed without notice in the scholarly
literature,[30] and I am aware of no error or misleading statement that
has been found in anything that we wrote. Much of the criticism is
absurd, even comical; there was also an impressive flow of falsehoods, often surely conscious. But I will not pursue these topics here.[31]
Much more interesting was a different reaction: that the entire enterprise is illegitimate. It is improper, many felt, perhaps even inhuman,
to urge that we keep to the truth about the Pol Pot atrocities as best
we can, or to expose the ways in which the fate of the miserable
victims was being crudely exploited for propaganda purposes.

Very strikingly, the second term of the comparison—our discussion of the media reaction to the U.S.-backed atrocities in Timor—
was virtually ignored, apart from apologetics for the atrocities and
for the behavior of the media, or a few words of casual mention.
Again this confirms the third-order predictions, in close detail.

In short, the model is confirmed at every level.

Let us now examine the logic of the reaction that alleges it to be improper, inhuman, to expose the fabrications of the ideological system in the case of the Pol Pot atrocities. Evidently, it either is or is not legitimate to study the U.S. ideological system. Assume that it is legitimate. Then it is legitimate to formulate the propaganda model as a hypothesis, and to test it by investigating paired examples: media treatment of Cambodia and Timor, for example. But, the critics allege, the study of media treatment of Cambodia is illegitimate. Therefore, unless there is something special about this case that has yet to be pointed out, their position must be that it is *not* legitimate to study the U.S. ideological system. The fact that the reaction has been marked by such extraordinary dishonesty, as repeatedly exposed, merely underscores the obvious: the right to serve the state must be protected; the ideological system cannot be subjected to inquiry based on the hypothesis that its societal function is to serve external power. The logic is very clear.

To establish this conclusion even more firmly, we may take note of the fact that no objection is raised to exposure of false or misleading accounts of atrocities by the United States and its clients, whether in retrospect or when they are in progress. It is only exposure of fabrications about official enemies that is subject to general opprobrium. Thus, none of those who are scandalized by exposure of the vast flood of deceit concerning Cambodia raise a peep of protest over exposure of false charges against Israel; that is considered an entirely legitimate and praiseworthy effort. Or take a case involving Cambodia itself. Our 1977 review-article, mentioned above, included a review of François Ponchaud's French study of Cambodia under the Khmer Rouge, the first review that attended to the text, to my knowledge. We praised the book as "serious and worth reading" with its "grisly account" of the "barbarity" of the Khmer Rouge. We also raised several questions about it. We noted that some of the quotes Ponchaud attributed to the Khmer Rouge seemed dubious, since he had given them in radically different wording elsewhere and had attributed them to a variety of conflicting sources; it was later shown that his alleged quotes, widely and prominently repeated throughout the world, were either gross mistranslations or had no source at all. We also pointed out that Ponchaud had apparently misread figures and considerably exaggerated the scale of U.S. atrocities in Cambodia in the early 1970s. Our questioning of his quotes has elicited much outrage, but not a word has appeared on our questioning of his charges about U.S. atrocities; to challenge misrepresentation on this matter is taken to be quite obviously legitimate. The proper conclusion seems equally obvious: it is all a matter of whose ox is being gored.

To reinforce the conclusion still further, we can turn to other examples. I doubt that the *New York Times Book Review* has ever published a longer and more detailed study than Neil Sheehan's analysis in 1970 of Mark Lane's *Conversations With Americans*,[32] a book that presented testimony of American soldiers on war crimes in which they said they had participated. Sheehan denounced this "wretched book" as based on unevaluated evidence, statements contradicted by Pentagon sources, conflicting accounts, failure to distinguish "understandable brutalities of war, such as killing prisoners in the passion of battle" from far graver atrocities, and other flaws that undermine its credibility. He went on to condemn the "new McCarthyism, this time from the left," that permits "any accusation, any innuendo, any rumor" to be "repeated and published as truth," while "the accused, whether an institution or an individual, has no right to reply because whatever the accused says will ipso facto be a lie." He bitterly denounced Lane for allegedly claiming that the details didn't matter, only the general picture of atrocities—exactly the position that Lacouture and others were later to endorse, to much approval and acclaim, with regard to the Khmer Rouge.

Sheehan's detailed exposure appeared at the height of U.S. atrocities in Vietnam, at a time when such atrocities were being vigorously denied (as they still are). No objection was raised to his exposure, or his condemnation of those who claim that facts do not matter in a worthy cause.

Another relevant case is that of Bertrand Russell. Then well into his eighties, Russell had the courage and integrity to condemn the Vietnam war and its mounting atrocities when this was unfashionable, and to warn of what lay ahead.[33] In retrospect, his commentary stands up well, certainly as compared to the falsehoods, evasions, and apologetics of the time, and it is a model of probity and restraint in comparison to standard condemnations of official enemies, as has been documented beyond serious question. Some of Russell's comments, however, were unjust, exaggerated, and incorrect. To criticize these statements would have been appropriate. What happened, however, was different. Russell became an object of contempt and obloquy; one would be hard put to find a word in his defense against the venom of the commissars. The denunciations were only heightened by Russell's willingness to engage in nonviolent civil disobedience in protest against the nuclear arms race, unlike others who shared his perceptions about the threat but contented themselves with occasional sage comments, then retreated to their work and personal lives. The attacks are not, of course, a reaction to Russell's errors and excesses. Rather, to the fact that he stood virtually alone against the herd and dared to tell truths that were then, and remain now, unacceptable, exposing by his example the behavior of those who chose the normal path of submissiveness to the state and support for its violence.

Putting aside the vulgar hypocrisy, we note again that no objection is raised to exposure of false or exaggerated charges against the United States, at the moment when it is perpetrating awesome crimes with near immunity from comment or critique. Nor should an objection be raised. Truth is worth the effort to uphold.

For such reasons as these, it is hard to take seriously the show of indignation over the exposure of fabrications concerning enemy atrocities. If some error can be found in such exposures, that is a different matter, though one not relevant here, for no such errors have been found. But let us look further. If, indeed, such exposures are deemed illegitimate, then comparative study of paired examples is also illegitimate, and one promising avenue of study of the U.S. ideological system is barred. We see again the real issue lurking behind the barrage of rhetoric: it is the need to protect the ideological institutions and those who participate in them from analysis of their service to power. That intellectuals should adopt this stance will hardly come as a surprise to anyone familiar with the lessons of history and the nature of contemporary social institutions.

2. On Critical Balance[34]

As just discussed, a propaganda model makes predictions about the performance of the media, but it also yields second-order predictions about debate over how they perform: these too would be expected to be bounded in a manner that fits the needs of established power. We should expect, then, that debate over the media will turn on the question of their alleged anti-establishment zeal: critics of these adversarial excesses will be pitted against those who defend the media as balanced and without bias.[35] The possibility that the media conform to the propaganda model—a natural expectation based on uncontroversial assumptions and widely believed by the public, as discussed earlier—should, according to the model, be excluded from the debate, as offensive to the interests of the privileged. This is exactly what we discover.

As always, a complex social order permits a certain range of variation. There is, in fact, one notable circumstance in which critics of the media for their submissiveness to power are welcomed. Generally, the media tolerate or even welcome denunciation of their hostility to authority, for obvious self-serving reasons. But there are times when such attacks can become a real threat. To defend themselves, the media may then turn—briefly—to critics of their conformity. If they are accused of being unpatriotic, or too harsh towards creations of the public relations industry of the Reagan variety, they may request—even feature—critiques of their subordination to the state and awe of powerful figures. Media spokespersons can then observe that they are being criticized from both sides, so it must be that they are right in the middle, doing their work properly. The argument might have some force if the "criticism from both sides" were actually evaluated. Such is not the case, however; to serve the purpose at hand, it is enough that criticism of media subordination exist.

Even this departure from the norm has its limits. The critics of media conformity must keep to matters of personality and secondary issues, steering clear of the nature and functioning of dominant institutions or such eternal verities as U.S. benevolence and yearning for democracy.

There are some interesting examples of these minor effects, but I will put them aside and keep to the main predictions of the propaganda model with regard to tolerable controversy over media performance.

A number of examples have already been noted. A report of the Institute for the Study of Diplomacy of Georgetown University on media coverage of conflicts in the Third World, summarizing a series of seminars, is one of the most natural choices for a more careful test of these second-order predictions.[36] The published report focuses on coverage of the Israeli invasion of Lebanon in 1982 and conflicts in Central America. The contributions offer little evidence to sustain the critiques that are offered, but the study does provide an enlightening view of how these matters are perceived by people in and close to the media.

The agenda is set throughout by those who condemn the media for their alleged anti-U.S. and anti-Israel bias. The colloquy and documents[37] debate the validity of these charges, with virtually no recognition that the opposite criticism is at least a logical possibility.

The basic assumptions are laid down by editor Landrum Bolling in his introductory remarks. He states that

> whatever else may be said about them, American media reports on international affairs cannot be counted on to echo the pronouncements of official spokesmen, our own or others ... the official version of things has no monopoly in the public print ... On matters of controversy, contrary opinions are avidly sought and may, indeed, on occasion be given an attention they do not merit. The media thrives on the reporting of debate and more strenuous forms of conflict.

Bolling notes the contention that "the failure to win in Southeast Asia ... was directly related to the broad, unrelenting and detailed coverage of that war by the U.S. mass media," and "particularly the often-gory pictorial reportage by television," which "produced in time a popular revulsion." Then comes the basic question: "Can a 'free-press', democratic society defend itself and its friends and allies, in a dangerous world, against the totalitarian adversaries that do not have to contend with a free press and uncontrolled television?"

The framework for the discussion of the media, then, is that predicted by the propaganda model. The same is true of the assumptions concerning the U.S. government and its international relations, presented as truths so obvious that no evidence, questions, or qualifications are in order. Bolling holds that in the Third World, "success has continued to elude us—until Grenada ... What is wrong? Why cannot a nation of such vast wealth, power *and good intentions* accomplish its purposes more promptly and more effectively? ... why haven't we been more successful in the carrying out of our foreign policies *in support of freedom* ...?" (my emphasis). Examples of our disturbing failures are cited, specifically Cuba, a "particularly painful [story] to the people and government of the United States. How could these dreadful things happen to and through a warm-hearted people only 90 miles off the Florida coast?" That Cubans generally share this assessment of Castro's Cuba as compared with the good old days under U.S. dominance is perhaps less than obvious, just as one might question whether those affected by policies carried out "through Cuba" agree that the consequences have been "dreadful."[38] One also wonders whether other "dreadful things" may have happened to warm-hearted people not far away in the Caribbean-Central American region, including stories that might be painful to the people of the United States, were they to learn something about the role their government has played, guided by its unfailing "good intentions." No such questions trouble the proceedings.

The question that *is* raised is whether the free press is to blame for the frustration of American benevolence. Is it true that "sentimental and naive media representatives have been slanting their reports in favor of underdog revolutions" and "are taken in by the humanitarian rhetoric of terrorists"? Bolling believes that "there may be some validity to these complaints," though being on the liberal side of the spectrum, he is skeptical.

I have argued throughout that the basic assumptions set forth as the premises for the debate have little merit. Thus contrary opinions are indeed "avidly sought," but only when they conform to doctrinal presuppositions. There has been no avid search for the opinion that the United States was attacking South Vietnam and that it has sought to undermine freedom, independence, democracy, and social reform in Central America in the past decade; or that Nicaraguan elections were at least as valid as those in El Salvador; or that the United States succeeded (with the aid of the free press) in demolishing the Central American peace accords, much as it had undermined the 1973 Paris peace treaty concerning Vietnam (again with critical media assistance); or that the United States has stood in the way of the peace process in the Middle East for close to twenty years; or other positions that are not at all difficult to support with ample evidence but that depart from the narrowly limited bounds set by the requirements of established privilege and power. Media coverage of the Indochina wars was far from "unrelenting"; pictorial reportage by TV was consciously subdued, and the effect of TV on public opinion, if any, was probably to increase hawkish sentiment, so public opinion studies reveal; the media were highly supportive of the war until well after the corporate elite had turned against the enterprise as too costly, and even then departures from the framework of the propaganda model were so marginal as to count as statistical error.[39] Contrary to much "necessary illusion" fostered in later years, the media were almost entirely closed to principled critics of the war and representatives of the mass popular movements that spontaneously developed, considerably more closed, in fact, than they have been in the 1980s.[40] I know this from personal experience, and others who have been part of the dissident culture will, I presume, confirm this judgment.

The other doctrines set forth as the basis for the discussion, however conventional they may be, are also hardly tenable. But my point here is not that these doctrines are false; rather, that they are beyond question or controversy, not subject to doubt. There is no need to sustain them because they are simply given truths that establish the framework within which discussion can proceed.

The report adheres closely to this framework. The twenty-two-page discussion of media coverage of Central America is introduced by Daniel James, an extreme hawk, who condemns the media for having "departed considerably from the traditional principles of journalism—which is to say, of objectivity and fairness"; "the prestige media's coverage of Central America has been very biased [against the U.S. government and its allies], leading one to conclude that it comes under the heading of tendentious or advocacy journalism." Thus, "there is a distinct overplaying on this issue of human rights" in the coverage of El Salvador, James holds; recall that these discussions took place after an extraordinary outburst of atrocities backed and organized by the U.S. government and generally ignored by the media. And there is a corresponding failure, James continues, to face "the overriding" issue: "whether freedom or dictatorship will rule El Salvador," freedom being the goal of the United States, dictatorship that of its adversaries (by definition, evidence being irrelevant). But the situation is not entirely bleak. "Happily, the media have shown a capacity for self-criticism. In the case of El Salvador, and to some extent Nicaragua, a fair number of pieces have appeared, notably in the *Washington Post*, that criticized their own performance in the former country"—meaning, their excessive concern for human rights and failure to adopt the U.S. government perspective. This is a "very healthy trend" that offers hope that the media will desist from their antagonism to Washington and support for its enemies.

Eighteen pages of colloquy follow, ranging from defense of media coverage of Central America as not "biased and tendentious" (Latin America scholar William LeoGrande) to support for James's contentions. Contra lobbyist Robert Leiken states that "It is U.S. policy to defend and help preserve democracy in Central America." No one hints at a different analysis. There is not a word suggesting that the media might be biased *in favor of* the U.S. government perspective. There is no discussion of the scandalous refusal of the media to cover massive atrocities in the U.S. client states during these years, their pretense that the killings were chargeable to the left and the extreme right but not to the security forces of the U.S.-backed regimes, and their apologetics for the political figures assigned the task of denying government atrocities and presenting a moderate image to Congress so that the killings could continue—all well documented, but excluded from these proceedings.

My point here, once again, is not that the assumptions about U.S. policy and the media that bound discussion are false (though they are), but rather that the possibility that they are false cannot be raised; it lies beyond the conceivable.

Following the colloquy, there are twenty-three pages of documents, introduced by a condemnation of "The Foregone Conclusions of the Fourth Estate" by Shirley Christian. Concentrating on the war against Somoza, she claims that the *Washington Post* and the *New York Times* perceived it "through a romantic haze. This romantic view of the Sandinistas is by now acknowledged publicly or privately by virtually every American journalist who was in Nicaragua during the two big Sandinista offensives. Probably not since Spain has there been a more open love affair between the foreign press and one of the belligerents in a civil war." There follow responses by Karen DeYoung, who wrote most of the stories on Nicaragua in the *Washington Post*, and Alan Riding of the *New York Times*, whose reports had come under particular attack. DeYoung says she has "never met nor spoken to Ms. Christian" and refutes her specific claims point by point, and Riding also takes issue with her charges. Neither accepts what Christian claims virtually everyone reporting from Managua acknowledges.

Apart from some brief remarks on "the resiliency of Caribbean democracies in the face of economic hardship" and other matters not pertinent here, the only other selection is by Allen Weinstein. He condemns the failure of reporters to show concern over "the status of the press in Nicaragua," "the total repression of the free press" there, and "the many threats to the physical safety of journalists in that country." "Sandinista chic," he writes, "remains infectious in Western countries." "The Nicaraguan tragedy deserves at least as much attention from the press—and the U.S. Congress—as the question of American involvement in El Salvador," including the "state of emergency" (in Nicaragua, that is; the earlier and far more onerous state of emergency in El Salvador is not mentioned, just as it was ignored by the media), and the threat to "independent journalists," such as those of "the independent daily newspaper, La Prensa, ... a beacon of free expression throughout Central America."

As discussed in the text, the physical destruction of the independent media in El Salvador by government terror was ignored by the media, literally not mentioned in news reports or editorials in the *Times*. The "censorship" exercised by government-backed death squads in the U.S. dependencies also received little notice. Nothing remotely comparable happened in Nicaragua, which has, throughout, been the prime focus of charges of government repression. The tribulations of *La Prensa* have been virtually the sole concern of alleged defenders of freedom of the press in Central America, and have received very extensive coverage. It is a considerable understatement to say that Weinstein's contentions are false. Whatever his motives may be, plainly concern for freedom of the press is not among them, and truth is not his business.

But again, falsehood—even sheer absurdity—is not the issue here. Rather, the point is that the documents collected, like the colloquy, remain entirely within the bounds predicted by the propaganda model: condemnation of the media for their adversarial stance and anti-U.S. bias, defense of the media as fair and balanced. This case of literally 100 percent conformity is particularly remarkable in the light of the overwhelming evidence of media submissiveness to the basic doctrines of the Reaganite propaganda system on the matter of Central America (with at most tactical debate), and of their suppression of the mounting atrocities as the Carter administration drew to its close.

The second subject investigated is what the editors of the *New York Times* hailed as the "liberation" of the Lebanese from the yoke of Syria and the PLO; or, to use the words introducing the discussion here, "the incursion of Israeli forces into South Lebanon" followed by the bombing and siege of Beirut. The discussion is opened by Ben Wattenberg—like Daniel James, an extreme hawk—who denounces the media for their "double standard" as they defamed Israel. The media, he continues, had "inflicted" the same double standard upon ourselves in Vietnam, and are doing so again in Central America, where they have turned "American public opinion, in terms of further Congressional aid and so on, against what I regarded as a relatively moderate and moral response on the part of the United States." Wattenberg's "relatively moderate and moral response" is what even Daniel James concedes to be a record of "unheard-of brutality" in El Salvador by the forces organized, trained, and supplied by the United States. Furthermore, contrary to what Wattenberg appears to believe, the unheard-of brutality for which he voices his approval proceeded with no lapse in congressional aid and aroused only limited public concern. This concern developed despite the apologetics and evasion of the media, relying on other channels of information: human rights groups, church sources, the alternative media, and so on. It is worthy of note that these apologetics for hideous atrocities are treated with respect on all sides, a fact that tells us a good deal about the prevailing moral climate and intellectual culture.

Milton Viorst, a dove, responds to Wattenberg's allegations about coverage of the Lebanon war, largely in agreement. One reason for the anti-Israel double standard, he suggests, is that "the Israelis have a reputation of not manipulating the press either as effectively or as deliberately as other nations"—a perception that will surprise journalists and others familiar with the sophisticated operations of the Israeli *hasbara* ("explanation") apparatus, which easily surpasses any competitors.[41] Viorst does not indicate which "other nations" are more effective in press manipulation. Presumably, he does not mean the Arab states. The double standard, he continues, also results from our higher expectations with regard to Israel. He does not explain how this accounts for the immense outrage over PLO terrorism and the muted response, or total silence, in the face of vastly greater terror by the state that remains "the symbol of human decency."

The twenty-three pages of colloquy that follow keep to the same terms: condemnation of the media for their alleged double standard, and responses to the charge of anti-Israel bias. The division is roughly fifty-fifty, with virtually nothing to suggest that the opposite charge is far more to the point, or even that it is conceivable.

The spectrum of discussion extends from Wattenberg and *New Republic* editor Morton Kondracke at the jingoist extreme to Viorst and Nick Thimmesch of the American Enterprise Institute at the outer reaches of dissidence. Kondracke condemns the "adversarial relationships which we are used to applying to our own govern- ment—by which we rip our own society to shreds as best we can, believing it our professional duty," an attitude now applied to Israel as well. To illustrate, he offers two examples: "the Bulgarian/KGB involvement in the shooting of the Pope," which, he claims, "received very little attention in the American press" apart from NBC news; and the State Department "yellow rain" charges, which the press sought to undermine. These are interesting choices. The "yellow rain" charges, widely relayed by the media when they were produced by the State Department, are now generally conceded to have little merit. As for the Bulgarian/KGB connection, it received extensive and largely uncritical media coverage, far beyond the Marvin Kalb NBC documentary that Kondracke presumably has in mind. Furthermore, the line put forth by Claire Sterling, former CIA official Paul Henze, and Marvin Kalb has been thoroughly undermined, after having dominated coverage in a most effective government-media operation.[42] That Kondracke should offer these two examples to illustrate the anti-establishment bias of the media reveals clearly the intellectual bankruptcy of the position he represents.

At the opposite end of the spectrum, Nick Thimmesch questions Kondracke's judgment that "the American press somehow succeeded in ripping this country apart." He believes that

> we've now come through a long metamorphosis from one-sided coverage to two-sided coverage. We now have a very honest and legitimate debate of crucial issues in an enlightened manner. For that we can be thankful for the more aggressive and more intelligent press.

In the colloquy, there is one limited departure from this spectrum. William Ringle of Gannett Newspapers agrees that "some people are accepting everything unquestioningly that comes from Arafat"; it would be intriguing to know just whom he had in mind. But, he adds, in the past there were "a number of reporters who accepted unquestioningly and ingenuously everything that Israel put out, or what they had been shown on government-sponsored tours of Israel." Apart from this last sentence, there is no suggestion in the colloquy that an alternative perspective might be considered.

There is, in fact, a great body of evidence showing that the media continued to adopt the basic U.S.-Israeli premises throughout the Lebanon war, and beyond, quite uncritically.[43] But the relevant point here, once again, is that the possibility of pro-Israel bias in the media (hence pro-U.S. bias, since the U.S. government gave strong backing to the invasion until the last moment) is virtually not raised, even to be dismissed, and is clearly unthinkable.

Bolling does observe that "we had very little representation [in the meetings] of Arabs and pro-Arabs who feel, and have long felt, that U.S. media coverage of the Middle East is, basically, blatantly pro-Israeli and that Arabs and their interests and viewpoints are consistently denigrated—and who see no reason to change their opinions on the basis of the coverage of the war in Lebanon." He does not explain why only "Arabs and pro-Arabs" could draw such conclusions from investigation of the media. The tacit assumption is that people have only passions, no thoughts. This assumption is not only remarkable, but also manifestly untrue; the contention that the U.S. media are heavily biased in favor of Israel is familiar among American, European, and Israeli commentators who are neither Arab nor pro-Arab and who are in many cases extremely critical of the Arab states and the PLO. Bolling also does not indicate what efforts were made to obtain views that depart from the framework of the seminars, but the selection is probably a fair sample of intellectual opinion in the United States.

Forty-eight pages of documents follow, keeping closely to the same framework. The initial essay, by Roger Morris, defends the media for highly professional reporting of the events of the war (a largely accurate judgment, in my personal view) and for "providing balanced comment" (which is another matter). To illustrate this proper balance, he cites a *New York Times* editorial of early August, which says: "Blame the P.L.O. for the torment of West Beirut and blame Israel no less." Recall that these words were written during the days when Israeli artillery and aircraft were killing thousands of people, overwhelmingly civilians, destroying hospitals and demolishing residential areas in the defenseless city, holding the population hostage under harsh siege and terror to coerce them to demand the evacuation of the PLO. Morris also observes that the journalists "showed genuine empathy for the suffering city, and dismay at the destruction wrought by the encircling army, *however understandable its presence might have been*" (my emphasis). Again, proper balance.

Throughout the documents, the media are bitterly assailed as anti-Israel, or defended for maintaining a high standard of objectivity under difficult conditions. Of the forty-eight pages, approximately thirty-two are devoted to denunciation of the media for their unfairness to Israel, twelve to responses to these charges, and the remainder to a media analysis by Middle East scholar Eric Hooglund, published by the American-Arab Anti-Discrimination Committee, arguing that the coverage of the Israeli invasion "reveals a consistent pro-Israeli bias." Hooglund's analysis elicited no reaction.[44] At one point, Roger Morris observes, quite accurately, that the media "continued to credit the Israeli justification for the invasion—right up to the gates of Beirut"; and indeed beyond. Milton Viorst writes that "until recently, Israel hardly knew critical reporting." This exhausts the recognition that an alternative perspective on the performance of the media might be considered.

Of the total in the colloquy and documents, over 60 percent is devoted to charges against the media for unfairness to Israel, about one-third to defense of the media against these charges, and 5 percent to (unanswered) charges of a pro-Israel bias. The balance is slightly better than the 100 percent devoted to charges of anti-U.S. bias and defense against these charges in the Central America section, but once again, we find strong confirmation of the propaganda model.

The specific issues discussed are no less instructive. Several contributions refer to the charge—one of the staples in the barrage of media criticism—that the press and TV were irresponsible in reporting figures on casualties and refugees in southern Lebanon. An Anti-Defamation League (ADL) study charges that "no network reported" the Red Cross conclusion that the original figure of 600,000 refugees was an exaggeration, and that the correct figure was 300,000. Two sentences later, the ADL study cites the report of the revised 300,000 figure by John Chancellor of NBC; the example provides a fair indication of the quality of this critique, and the utter contempt of the ADL for its audience, as for elementary rationality and fact.[45] Norman Podhoretz repeats the claim circulated by Israeli *hasbara* that the total population of the area was just over 500,000, so that the refugee figures are plainly absurd. Edward Alexander writes that the refugee figures are "a patent absurdity," since "the entire population" of the area "is under 500,000." Within a year, the Israeli army had revised the population figures that had received wide publicity from Israeli propagandists in the United States, estimating the population at close to a million[46]; but these facts are nowhere mentioned.

Alexander is also contemptuous of reporters who cite the International Committee of the Red Cross, because it works "with the Palestinian Red Crescent Society (which happens to be headed by Yasser Arafat's brother)." He does not, however, conclude that we must also reject reports from any organization that works with Israelis, not to speak of Israeli sources. Suppose that someone were to make such a proposal, with a similar sneer. The cries of anti-Semitism would be deafening. But these remarks, published in the *Washington Post* and reprinted here, passed without notice, a reflection of the easy acceptance of virulent anti-Arab racism.[47]

As for the early casualty figures reported for southern Lebanon, provided by the Lebanese police and other sources, they appear to be plausible in retrospect. And there seems little reason to doubt the final estimates of close to 20,000 killed, overwhelmingly civilian, provided by the police, relief agencies, and the Lebanese Maronite government that Israel backed and helped install. Furthermore, as the Israeli army and others observed, these figures are probably an underestimate, possibly a serious underestimate, since they are based on actual counts in hospitals, clinics, and civil defense centers and do not include people buried in mass graves or in the wreckage of bombing.[48]

In their effort to prove anti-Israel bias, several commentators refer to inadequate coverage of the atrocities of the civil war in Lebanon, specifically, the destruction of the Christian town of Damour by the PLO in 1976, mentioned several times. Charles Krauthammer denounces the media for their failure "to recount the history of the killings by the PLO and their allies of the Christian villagers they drove from their homes." Kondracke recalls "no coverage until after the fact of what happened in Damour where the Palestinians virtually destroyed a Christian town." Wattenberg adds that "those things like Damour, that show the PLO's atrocities, did not get into the media loop as big items." Jim Hoagland of the *Washington Post* replies that Damour "was a page one story." No one brings up the Muslim Karantina slum, overrun by Christian forces shortly before the Damour attack, then burned and razed with bulldozers, with large numbers massacred—not a page one story, or a story at all, and forgotten—or the atrocities of Israel's Phalangist allies against Palestinians and Lebanese Muslims, which brought the PLO into the civil conflict.[49] No one brings up the cluster-bomb attack on a U.N. school in Damour by Israeli jet fighters, leaving forty-one children dead or wounded (see p. 54). Again, partisans of the United States and its Israeli ally set the agenda; others respond, within the framework set by the critics.

PLO atrocities at Damour are a staple of Israeli propaganda, regularly presented in isolation from the background. The scale of the atrocities during the civil war is unknown, and all estimates must be taken with caution. Yale University political scientist Naomi Weinberger, in a scholarly study, gives the figure of 1,000 Muslim and Palestinian deaths in the Karantina massacre, citing standard sources, and no figure for Damour. Israeli Lt. Col. Dov Yermiya, reporting from Damour with the occupying Israeli forces and (Christian) Phalangist military in June 1982, estimates 250 massacred at Damour, and notes that the town was "partly destroyed by the Syrians and the terrorists [the PLO], and partly by our air force and artillery" in 1976 and 1982 respectively. Others invent figures to suit their fancy. Thus Walter Laqueur states that 600 civilians were killed at Damour, citing no source and avoiding the background; and journalist Eric Silver, citing "reliable Israeli sources," speaks of "the murder of thousands of Lebanese Christians" at Damour. An honest reference appears in a study of Israel's war in Lebanon by Israeli military specialist Ze'ev Schiff and Arabist Ehud Ya'ari, who describe the town of Damour as "the site of one of the many tit-for-tat massacres of that savage conflict" of 1975-76.[50]

Kondracke also complains about the limited coverage of "the 50,000 people who were killed in Lebanon before the Israelis invaded." Wattenberg asserts that "five to ten times as many people were killed in Lebanon" from 1975 to 1982 "as were killed during the 1982 Israeli action"; that would be a toll of 100,000-200,000 people killed from 1975 to 1982 given the conservative estimate of 20,000 killed during the "Israeli action." Israel's leading specialist on the topic, Itamar Rabinovich, writes that the death toll for the Lebanese civil war prior to 1982 was "well over 10,000, according to some estimates"; that is, about half the 20,000 or more deaths attributable to the Israeli invasion.[51]

While allegations of Arab atrocities are bandied about without analysis or comment, there is no mention of the death toll from the Israeli scorched-earth operations in southern Lebanon from the early 1970s. These were scarcely reported in the media, which were uninterested, and the usual skepticism about figures must therefore be even more pronounced. The meager evidence suggests that the toll was many thousands killed and hundreds of thousands driven from their homes.[52] Also unmentioned is the failure of the media to cite Lebanese opinion—in particular, published opinion—during the Israeli "incursion," another illustration of what can only be called racist bias. It was, after all, their country that was being "liberated," though anyone who bothered to check would have discovered that they were not too delighted about their good fortune, over a remarkably broad range. The *New York Times* hailed the "liberation of Lebanon," but managed to avoid the bitter denunciations of the liberation of his country by U.N. Ambassador Ghassan Tueni, the conservative Christian owner of Lebanon's leading newspaper who was speaking a few blocks away from their editorial offices; his name does not appear in the *Times* index for those months. And opinion within Lebanon, easily accessible in Western languages or by interview, was notably absent from media reporting, as it is in subsequent literature on the war.[53] One can hardly imagine that if Israel were invaded by Syria and Tel Aviv were bombarded and under siege, the media would fail to cite Israel's U.N. Ambassador and would avoid Israeli sources.

Bolling remarks that the media made "no effort to compare the suffering caused by Israeli fighters with the even greater destruction and loss of life caused by the Arabs fighting among themselves in the Lebanese civil war of 1975-6" and the Syrian massacre in Hamma. Even if this were true, the relevance to the reporting of Israel's invasion is less than obvious, for reasons discussed in the preceding section. Media coverage of Syria and Arabs generally, slim at best, is extremely negative, apart from a few U.S. favorites. Syria and the contending elements within Lebanon are never depicted as "symbols of human decency" with exalted moral standards, who "care for human life," nor were they conducting their slaughters with U.S. material, diplomatic, and ideological support. Journalists covering the Soviet invasion of Afghanistan are not enjoined to temper their accounts of the suffering caused by the Soviet army by referring to the millions killed in the U.S. wars in Indochina or to Muslim atrocities—except, perhaps, in *Pravda*. The logic of Bolling's statement seems to be that any criticism of what Israel does to Arabs must be balanced by some condemnation of what Arabs do to each other, though I doubt that he would suggest that every criticism of Arabs must be balanced by a condemnation of Israel; no such principle is suggested here, or anywhere—nor, of course, should it be. This kind of argument sometimes reaches an astonishing level, as when Wolf Blitzer of the *Jerusalem Post* endorses Wattenberg's "double standard" charge on the grounds that the *Washington Post* sent no one to cover an earthquake in North Yemen. Blitzer's point about the "negative racism at work by which we tend to discount Third World people who are being killed" is well-taken, however, and—though he does not appear to see this—applies very well to the media reaction to Israeli violence for many decades. (For more on these standard fallacies, see Appendix I, section 1.)

A related charge, also repeated by several commentators, is that the media failed to depict "the terror of six years of living under the PLO" (Edward Alexander, who believes that major media were "depicting Israel as the devil's experiment station, with its capital neither in Jerusalem nor in Tel Aviv, but in Sodom and Gomorrah," a fair indication of the hysteria induced among apologists for Israeli violence by the temporary breakdown of the usual norms on which they rely). The truth is very different. PLO oppression and atrocities in Lebanon were emphasized.[54] But I found no reference in the U.S. media to the conclusions of Israeli journalists who toured Lebanon to inquire into these well-publicized allegations, finding much evi-

dence of Israeli and Christian terror, but far less that could be charged
to the PLO. Particularly revealing was the report in Israel's leading
journal *Ha'aretz* by Attallah Mansour, a Christian Maronite and
respected Israeli journalist who was well placed to give an accurate
critical assessment. His account of atrocities by Israel's Christian
allies as contrasted with much less repressive behavior by the "left-
Muslim-Palestinian camp" drew entirely the wrong conclusions, and
was ignored. The same was true of accounts by leading Israeli Jewish
journalists, published in English and readily available, but with the
wrong conclusions.[55]

Alexander denounces *Newsweek* for reporting that Israel's war
against the PLO "sorely weakened its more moderate elements,"
another proof that the media were waging a "propaganda battle
against Israel." He does not, however, remind us that respected
Israeli scholars argued from the outset that a primary motive for the
invasion was precisely to weaken more moderate elements in the
PLO. PLO moderation was regarded "as a veritable catastrophe in
the eyes of the Israeli government" because it posed the threat of a
political settlement; the hope was that the PLO would be driven to
terrorism, undercutting the danger of "future political accommoda-
tions" (Yehoshua Porath, Israel's leading academic specialist on Palestinian nationalism and a political centrist). "Dealing a major blow
to the PLO as a political force was the raison d'être of the entire
operation," Israeli strategic analyst Avner Yaniv concludes (approvingly). It was necessary to apply "the fiercest military pressures [to]
... undermine the position of the moderates within [the PLO] ranks,"
to block "the PLO 'peace offensive' " and prevent Arafat from gain-
ing PLO support for qualified acceptance of U.N. Resolution 242, and
"to halt [the PLO's] rise to political respectability." The perceived
problem was that "a moderate—political rather than terrorist—PLO
... could become far more dangerous than the violent PLO of the
previous years." Military action served "the purpose of weakening
PLO moderates and strengthening their radical rivals." Yehoshafat
Harkabi (ex-director of Israeli military intelligence, former Begin
adviser, professor of International Relations and Middle East Studies
at Hebrew University, and one of Israel's most highly-regarded
specialists on these issues) writes that "Begin's principal motive in
launching the war was his fear of the momentum of the peace
process"; the 1982 war should be called "The War to Safeguard the
Occupation of the West Bank," an occupation threatened by Palestinian moderation, not Palestinian terrorism, as understood on all sides,

and a threat particularly grave with Israel's failure to elicit a violent response to its provocations in Lebanon through mid-1982. Chief of Staff Rafael ("Raful") Eitan states frankly that the action was a success: "we destroyed the PLO as a candidate for negotiations with us about the Land of Israel."[56] Anti-Semitism reaches deep into mainstream Israeli circles, by Alexander's intriguing standards.

It is unnecessary to comment on the contributions of Martin Peretz and Norman Podhoretz, reprinted from the journals they edit (*New Republic, Commentary*).[57]

The point, again, is that the agenda is set by advocates of U.S. and Israeli violence, who condemn the media for their alleged anti-establishment bias. The most extraordinary charges against the media are voiced with wild abandon, and sometimes refuted. But there is little attempt at serious analysis of the events discussed or of media performance, and the idea of investigating a possible pro-Israel, pro-U.S. bias is off the agenda, apart from Hooglund's careful analysis.

The final chapter, "Reflections on Media Coverage of the Third World," is opened by Ambassador David Newsom, who says that "there is today in the press a strong tendency towards skepticism regarding official U.S. policy and those foreign officials abroad who are identified with it." He asks, "what is the effect in the public mind of the contrast between the ragged and open-shirted revolutionary and the well-dressed oligarch in contrasting scenes transmitted by television from Central America?" He would have us believe, then, that television presents a sympathetic portrait of the guerrillas in El Salvador and Guatemala. A response by David Lichtenstein of the right-wing media monitoring organization Accuracy in Media (AIM) condemns the media for their "instantaneous moral condemnation" of U.S. policy in Vietnam and El Salvador, and of Israel during "the Lebanon incursion." Much of the criticism of the press, he feels, "arises from this sort of ... pro-Arab or pro-Israel bias—sentiments in favor of Ho Chi Minh or in favor of the Communist guerrillas." He mentions no examples of critics of the press who favor Ho or Communist guerrillas, and does not explain why they are not represented in these seminars if they are so influential and numerous. He concludes that "You have within the media ideological conflicts which run all the way across the political spectrum," a position that can be sustained if we take the political spectrum to be determined by the needs of powerful elites. With regard to El Salvador, he says that "the whole uproar over human rights, for example, is often the shrill cry of the not-very-well-informed journalistic visitor who lacks historical perspective, who is not familiar with Latin American culture, or how an entirely different culture developed out of entirely different social conditions." Putting aside his judgment about the "uproar" in media that regularly suppressed U.S.-backed atrocities in El Salvador while praising the "moderate" Duarte regime that carried them out, he does not indicate whether similar considerations apply to the atrocities carried out by official enemies. The remaining discussion stays within the predicted bounds, without exception.

In summary, of the 155 pages, fewer than four fall beyond the bounds predicted by the propaganda model: the ADC contribution on pro-Israel bias, and a few scattered sentences. Naturally, there are matters of judgment, but I doubt that other standards would lead to a materially different evaluation. The conclusion is that the propaganda model is again very well confirmed in its second-order predictions. I will comment no further on the startling remarks by some of the participants, such as those sampled here, or what they indicate, except to note that justification for massive atrocities is considered quite normal and respectable.

Recall that the basic question raised in the seminar was the problem faced by "a 'free-press', democratic society" that allows "open coverage of all the wartime events" (Bolling). There is no allusion to the fact that allowing "open coverage" is relatively cost-free when the media can be trusted to adopt the basic principles (if not, always, the tactical judgments) of state propaganda and keep closely within its bounds in what they transmit and how they interpret it, and to report from the standpoint of approved elements: the client governments of South Vietnam and El Salvador, but not the indigenous guerrillas; the guerrillas in Afghanistan, but not the Soviet client regime; the U.S.-supported opposition and the CIA-run civilian front for the contras in Nicaragua but not the elected government (described by Washington edict as unelected); and so on.

Bolling discusses one major exception to this policy of allowing "open coverage," one that the media generally found offensive: the barring of correspondents during the first days of the invasion of Grenada, the first occasion on which success in our noble endeavors did not "elude us," in his judgment. Bolling evidently regards "the overthrow of the callous and unpopular little Marxist dictatorship and the expulsion of the Cuban advisors, workers and soldiers" as meritorious, though the censorship raises serious questions. We may put aside his characterization of these events and turn to a matter more pertinent here. True, the media were briefly excluded, and condemned this infringement on their prerogatives. But more to the point, they exercised self-censorship so severe as to render the events unintelligible and to protect the U.S. government stance, a fact not mentioned in the volume under discussion, and rarely elsewhere.

U.S. actions in earlier years to undermine the government of Maurice Bishop were barely reported.[58] The large-scale military operations simulating an invasion of "Amber and the Amberdines," clearly intended to intimidate the government of Grenada and the Grenadines, passed without mention in the *New York Times*. The only hint was a tiny item noting Grenada's charge that it was the target of "an imminent attack" by the United States, dismissed by the State Department as "ridiculous," with no further details or inquiry.[59] There was no report of the refusal of the Carter administration to provide aid when 40 percent of Grenada's banana crop was destroyed by a hurricane in August 1980, and Carter's further condition that Grenada be excluded from rehabilitation aid provided to affected countries through the West Indian Banana Exporting Association (the Association refused the condition, and no U.S. aid was forthcoming).[60] There was also no report of the termination of U.S. aid and pressures on the Common Market to terminate aid in early 1981. Also unreported were the other measures pursued to abort progress and development under a government now conceded to have been popular and relatively successful in early efforts. The media thus ensured that few would comprehend what took place in October 1983, when Bishop was assassinated and the invasion was launched, and the significant U.S. background role.

Turning to the invasion itself, the government role in censorship was the least of the story. Far more important is the fact that the most crucial information about the invasion was largely suppressed by media choice, even while the media were denouncing government censorship.

The invasion of Grenada took place on the morning of October 25. Various conflicting justifications were offered that we need not review. The tale on which the government finally settled was that U.S. troops on a "rescue mission" were fighting a bitter battle against Cuban military forces struggling to maintain this outpost of Soviet imperialism. The media gave enormous coverage to the events, basically keeping to this version while raising questions about the motives for the invasion and deploring the censorship. Prominent reports featured battles with Cuban forces, efforts to put down Cuban resistance, the exploits of the U.S. military, and so on. But there is more to the story.

As the U.S. invaded, Cuba released a series of official documents to the press. According to these documents, when the murder of Maurice Bishop was reported on October 20, the government of Cuba declared that it was "deeply embittered" by the murder and rendered "deep tribute" to the assassinated leader. The same official statement reported instructions to Cubans in Grenada that "they should abstain absolutely from any involvement in the internal affairs of the Party and of Grenada," while attempting to maintain the "technical and economic collaboration that could affect essential services and vital economic assistance for the Grenadian people." On October 22, Castro sent a message to Cuban representatives in Grenada, stressing that they should take no action in the event of a U.S. invasion unless they are "directly attacked." If U.S. forces "land on the runway section [of the airport that Cubans were constructing with British assistance] near the university or on its surroundings to evacuate their citizens," Cubans were ordered "to fully refrain from interfering." The military rulers of Grenada were informed that "sending reinforcements is impossible and unthinkable" because of the actions in Grenada that Cuba and the Grenadan people deplore, and Cuba urged them to provide "total guarantees and facilities for the security and evacuation of U.S., English and other nationals." The message was repeated on October 23, stating that reinforcement would be politically wrong and "morally impossible before our people and the world" after the Bishop assassination. On October 24, Cuba again informed the Grenadan regime that Cubans would only defend themselves if attacked, and advised that the airport runway be cleared of military personnel.

Surely Washington was aware of these communications, barring colossal incompetence. But we need not speculate on this matter. On October 22, Cuba sent a message to Washington explaining its policy "of not interfering in the internal affairs" of Grenada and suggesting that the U.S. and Cuba "keep in touch on this matter, so as to contribute to a favorable solution of any difficulty that may arise or action that may be taken relating to the security of [U.S. or other foreign nationals in Grenada], without violence or intervention in that country." There was no response to this message until October 25, well *after* the United States had invaded and attacked Cuban personnel. At that point, the United States stated that it "agrees to the Cuban proposal of October 22 to maintain contact concerning the safety of the personnel of each side." Several hours later, the U.S. delivered a message to Cuba stating its "regret" for the armed clashes and attributing them to "confusion and accidents." Cuba responded at once, calling again for cooperation to resolve the problems "without violence or intervention."[61]

These facts were known to the media at once, and even received some mention, though they were relegated to obscurity and did not interfere with pursuit of the patriotic agenda. Knight-Ridder news service reported Castro's October 26 statement that Cuba had rejected Grenada's request for reinforcements and had offered "Cuban cooperation to guarantee the safety of 1000 Americans on the island," though Washington had not responded until "90 minutes after U.S. troops had invaded Grenada and had begun fighting against Cubans on the island." On October 26, Alma Guillermoprieto reported in the *Washington Post* that at a "post-midnight news conference" with "almost 100 foreign and local journalists," Castro "released texts of what he said were diplomatic communications among Cuba, Grenada and the United States," giving the essential facts. U.S. sources "confirmed the exchange of messages," she added, but said they could not respond to Cuba at once because the telephone lines of the U.S. interest section in Havana were down from the evening of October 23 to late at night on October 24; how unfortunate that the U.S. government, so lacking in technical facilities, could not find some way to respond to the message of October 22, perhaps by carrier pigeon, thus rendering the invasion unnecessary (according to the government-media justification for it) and ensuring that there would be no clash with Cubans. White House spokesman Larry Speakes, she reported, said that "the U.S. disregarded Cuban and Grenadan assurances that U.S. citizens in Grenada would be safe because, 'it was a floating crap game and we didn't know who was in charge'." The readers of the *New York Times* could learn the facts from an advertisement of the government of Cuba on November 20, placed, no doubt, in a vain effort to overcome media self-censorship. The facts were accurately reported by Alan Berger in the *Boston Globe* on the same day.[62]

In short, the story of Cuban resistance to the U.S. "rescue mission" was mere deception, and this fact was known from the start. The media, however, kept to the official line, with only bare recognition of the actual facts, which was quickly shelved. Cuban officials were sometimes cited accusing the United States of "manipulating information," but without reference to these crucial facts (Jo Thomas,

New York Times). Editorials raised various questions about the "Orwellian arguments" offered by the Reagan administration, avoiding, however, the revelations that exposed the entire operation as a public relations fraud.[63] The pattern was pervasive.

There are hardly serious grounds for accusing the U.S. government of censorship when the media themselves proved so adept in the process, without instruction or pressure—as in other examples, so common as to be fairly called the norm.

Appendix II

1. The Containment Doctrine[1]

The project of containing the Soviet Union and its allies is a predominant theme of contemporary history, which merits some comment.

The fact that the rhetoric of "containment" carries with it some rather significant presuppositions has of course been recognized in the scholarly literature. In one of the leading studies of containment, John Lewis Gaddis observes that "the term 'containment' poses certain problems, implying as it does a consistently defensive orientation in American policy." He nevertheless finds the term appropriate, because "American leaders consistently *perceived* themselves as responding to rather than initiating challenges to the existing international order" and were in fact concerned with "maintaining a global balance of power with the perceived Muscovite challenge to that equilibrium" in Western Europe.[2] Leaders of other powers have similar perceptions, but we do not permit this fact to guide our interpretation of history.

What was "the existing international order" that had to be "defended"? U.S. planners intended to construct what they called a Grand Area, a global order subordinated to the needs of the U.S. economy and subject to U.S. political control. Regional systems, particularly the British, were to be eliminated, while those under U.S. control were to be extended, on the principle, expressed by Abe Fortas in internal discussion, that these steps were "part of our obligation to the security of the world ... what was good for us was good for the world."[3] This altruistic concern was unappreciated by the British Foreign Office. Their perception was that "the economic imperialism of American business interests, which is quite active under the cloak of a benevolent and avuncular internationalism," is "attempting to elbow us out." The Minister of State at the British Foreign Office, Richard Law, commented to his Cabinet colleagues that Americans believe "that the United States stands for something in the world—something of which the world has need, something which the world is going to like, something, in the final analysis, which the world is going to take, whether it likes it or not."[4] Not an inaccurate perception.

181

Against which enemies was it necessary to defend the Grand Area, apart from the British and other commercial rivals? At the rhetorical level, the enemy was the Soviet Union, and there is little reason to doubt that the sentiment was genuine, though, as the scholarly literature recognizes, it was exaggerated. But the sincerity of the concern is not very relevant; it is easy to persuade oneself of what it is convenient to believe, and state managers readily accept the reality of the threats they concoct for quite different reasons.

The Soviet Union is indeed a threat to the Grand Area because it has refused to be incorporated within it and assists others equally recalcitrant. But the Soviet threat is regarded as far more profound, justifying stern measures in defense. Woodrow Wilson "and his allies saw their actions in a defensive rather than in an offensive context" when they invaded the Soviet Union after the Bolshevik revolution, John Lewis Gaddis observes approvingly. Wilson was "determined above all else to secure self-determination in Russia," by invading the country and installing what we determine to be its proper rulers. By the same logic, the United States has been devoted to self-determination for Vietnam, Guatemala, Nicaragua, and other beneficiaries of our concern, and the U.S.S.R. is dedicated to self-determination in Czechoslovakia and Afghanistan. But more deeply, Gaddis continues, "Intervention in Russia took place in response to a profound and potentially far-reaching intervention by the new Soviet government in the internal affairs, not just of the West, but of virtually every country in the world." This Soviet "intervention" in the internal affairs of others was "the Revolution's challenge—which could hardly have been more categorical—to the very survival of the capitalist order." "The security of the United States" was therefore "in danger" in 1917, so defensive actions were entirely warranted; perhaps even the first use ever of gas bombs from aircraft that was considered by the British GHQ to be the primary factor in their early military successes in 1919, the same year when "poisoned gas" was recommended by Secretary of State Winston Churchill for use "against uncivilised tribes" in Mesopotamia (Iraq) and Afghanistan.[5]

The Soviet Union's "self-proclaimed intention to seek the overthrow of capitalist governments throughout the world," Gaddis explains further, justified invasion of the U.S.S.R. in defense against this announced intention, and after World War II "the increasing success of communist parties in Western Europe, the Eastern Mediterranean, and China" justifiably aroused renewed "suspicion about the Soviet Union's behavior," even though their popularity "grew primarily out of their effectiveness as resistance fighters against the Axis."

Gaddis criticizes Soviet historians who see the Western intervention after the revolution as "shocking, unnatural, and even a violation of the legal norms that should exist between nations." "One cannot have it both ways," he responds, complaining about a Western invasion while "the most profound revolutionary challenge of the century was mounted against the West": by changing the social order in Russia and proclaiming revolutionary intentions.[6]

With such an expansive conception of "defense," here expressed by a highly-regarded diplomatic historian, one could readily construct a justification for Hitler's actions in the late 1930s to "defend" Germany against what the Nazi ideologists called the terror and aggression of the Czechs and Poles and the attempted strangulation of Germany by hostile powers. And by the same logic, it would be legitimate for the U.S.S.R. (or Cuba, etc.) to invade the United States "to secure self-determination" there in defense against the clearly stated U.S. challenge "to the very survival of the Soviet and Cuban sociopolitical order."

U.S. policy towards the Soviet Union has fluctuated over the years between two concepts of "containment": rollback and détente. To a considerable extent, the fluctuations reflect the problem of controlling the far-flung domains "defended" by American power, and the need for a credible threat to induce the public to provide a subsidy to advanced industry through the military system.[7] The latter issue was recognized in NSC 68. The document estimated the economic power of the Soviet bloc as approximately the same as Western Europe, with Soviet GNP about one quarter that of the United States and its military expenditures about half as great.[8] Nevertheless, it called for a great expansion of military spending, warning that the West would face "a decline in economic activity of serious proportions" without this Keynesian stimulus; the military budget was almost quadrupled shortly after, with the Korean war as a pretext. The document obscures the significance of the figures scattered through it, but it was apparently anticipated that some bureaucrat might perform the calculations and draw the obvious conclusions. The author, Paul Nitze, parried this potential insight by observing that the figures mean nothing because, as a poor and underdeveloped society, "the Soviet world can do more with less"—their weakness is their strength, a constant refrain in other cases too as we defend the Free World from "internal aggression." One can see how dire is the threat to our existence when the enemy is so wicked as to exploit the advantage of weakness to overwhelm us.

Over the years, fear of Soviet weakness has been almost as intense as concerns over awesome Soviet power. The task assigned to the responsible strategic analyst, after all, is to establish the conclusion that the United States is facing a threat to its existence, so that it is necessary to keep up our guard—and incidentally, to guarantee that the Pentagon system will continue to perform its crucial domestic and international roles. When it is difficult to conjure up bomber gaps, missile gaps, windows of vulnerability, threats to our survival from superpowers such as Grenada, and the like, other means must suffice, such as the idea that the Soviet world can do more with less.

The problem arose again in late 1988, as analysts sought a way to detect a threat to our survival in Gorbachev's unilateral arms reduction initiatives. A U.S. Air Force intelligence conference on Soviet affairs in Washington may have found the key. Commenting on the conference, strategic analyst William V. Kennedy of the U.S. Army War College warns of a terrible discovery revealing that intelligence assessments for the past thirty-five years were far from the mark and severely underestimated the Soviet threat. U.S. intelligence had believed all along that the Soviet Union had "the most elaborate, best organized and equipped civil defense system on earth—so elaborate that it might provide the Soviet Union with a major, perhaps decisive advantage in a nuclear conflict." But the Armenia earthquake showed that that assessment was wrong. It revealed "inefficiency on so vast a scale that any US state governor or federal official who presided over such chaos would have been lucky to escape lynching by now"—a great surprise to U.S. intelligence, apparently, though hardly to anyone with a minimal familiarity with the Soviet Union. This discovery, Kennedy continues, "is staggering in its implications." A paper presented at the intelligence conference, six weeks before the earthquake, had warned that "internal Soviet mismanagement and reemergent nationalism may be a greater threat to world peace than the threat of calculated Soviet aggression as it has been portrayed for the past 40 years." The danger is "that a Soviet leadership that saw carefully laid plans going awry and the fires of nationalism spreading throughout the realm could panic into a desperate international venture"—the "wounded bear" theory, some call it. The Armenia earthquake confirmed our worst fears: the Soviet Union has no civil defense capacity at all, hence no capacity for a first strike with relative impunity as the hawks had been ominously warning for years. Now we are in real danger: the wounded bear may strike. Surely at this moment of grave national crisis we should not succumb to absurd ideas about weakening our "defensive" capacities.[9]

Such arguments are premature at a moment when the immediate task is to face the costs of military Keynesian excesses. Their time will come when it is necessary to undertake more militant foreign adventures to preserve the domains of U.S. power or to provide a shot in the arm to high tech industry. It would be naive to assume, however, that strategic theory is incapable of coming up with arguments to support the conclusion that may be required at the moment, whatever the objective facts may be.

Gaddis observes that "To a remarkable degree, containment has been the product, not so much of what the Russians have done, or of what has happened elsewhere in the world, but of internal forces operating within the United States." "What is surprising," he continues, "is the *primacy* that has been accorded economic considerations [namely, state economic management] in shaping strategies of containment, *to the exclusion of other considerations.*"[10] In fact, throughout this period, the policies of military Keynesianism, justified in terms of the Soviet threat, have been instrumental in the growth of high-technology industry and have served as a mechanism of state industrial management, once again in the early Reagan years, with accompanying inflammatory rhetoric about the "Evil Empire" that is "the focus of evil in our time" and the source of all problems in the world. These crucial matters barely enter public discussion. They will not fade away easily, despite much careless talk about the end of the Cold War.

2. The Red Scare[11]

Woodrow Wilson's Red Scare was the earliest and most extreme resort to state power in twentieth-century America to suppress labor, political dissidence, and independent thought. It provided a model for later efforts, and left as one crucial institutional residue the national political police, which has cast a long shadow in the years that followed.

FBI director J. Edgar Hoover rose to national prominence when he was appointed chief of the General Intelligence division of the Justice Department in August 1919. This was just before the "Palmer raids" of January 1920, when thousands of alleged radicals were rounded up in many parts of the country (hundreds of aliens were subsequently deported). Meanwhile, the *Washington Post* editorialized that "there is no time to waste on hairsplitting over infringement of liberty" in the face of the Bolshevik menace, and a *New York Times* editorial declared that "If some or any of us, impatient for the swift confusion of the Reds, have ever questioned the alacrity, resolute will and fruitful, intelligent vigor of the Department of Justice in hunting down these enemies of the United States, the questioners have now cause to approve and applaud ... This raid is only the beginning ... [The Department's] further activities should be far-reaching and beneficial." "These Communists," the *Times* noted the same day, "are a pernicious gang" who "in many languages ... are denouncing the blockade of Russia" as well as calling for better wages and working conditions. The *Times* report of the raids was headlined "Reds Plotted Country-Wide Strike."

The *Washington Post* lauded the House of Representatives for its expulsion of socialist congressman Victor Berger, observing that it could not have given a "finer or more impressive demonstration of Americanism." Reporting the deportation of Emma Goldman, the *Post* praised Hoover's "most painstaking" brief against Goldman, with its proof that she was "instrumental in helping to form the unnatural ideas" of the assassin of President McKinley in 1901. The *Times* described the expulsion of socialist assemblymen as "an American vote altogether, a patriotic and conservative vote" which "an immense majority of the American people will approve and sanction," whatever the benighted electorate may believe. The editors went on to say that the expulsion "was as clearly and demonstrably a measure of national defense as the declaration of war against Germany," invoking the familiar concept of "defense" in an editorial of January 7, 1920, long after the war had ended. A month earlier the *Times* had endorsed the sedition bill proposed by Attorney General Palmer and his aide Hoover, which called for prosecution of those guilty of aiding or abetting "the making, displaying, writing, printing, or circulating, of any sign, word, speech, picture, design, argument, or teaching, which advises, advocates, teaches, or justifies any act of sedition," "or any act which tends to indicate sedition." Also subject to prosecution were those affiliated in any way with any organization, "whether the same be formally organized or not, which has for its object, in whole or in part, the advising, advocating, teaching or justifying any act of sedition," the latter term defined so broadly as to satisfy many a totalitarian.[12]

These ideas have precedents, among them the Alien and Sedition Acts of 1798 by which "the Federalists sought to suppress political opposition and to stamp out lingering sympathy for the principles of the French Revolution," and the judicial murder of four anarchists for having advocated doctrines that allegedly lay behind the explosion of a bomb in Chicago's Haymarket Square after a striker had been killed by police in May 1886. For the authorities, the "seditious utterances" of the Haymarket anarchists sufficed to attribute "moral responsibility" for the bombing in which they had no part and to justify their prosecution and hanging.[13]

During Wilson's Red Scare, Attorney General Palmer proceeded, as he explained, "to clean up the country almost unaided by any virile legislation." He justified repressive actions on grounds of the failure of Congress "to stamp out these seditious societies in their open defiance of law by various forms of propaganda." He explained that "Upon these two basic certainties, first that the 'Reds' were criminal aliens, and secondly that the American Government must prevent crime, it was decided that there could be no nice distinctions drawn between the theoretical ideals of the radicals and their actual violations of our national laws." Palmer went on to say that his "information showed that communism in this country was an organization of thousands of aliens, who were direct allies of [Trotsky]." Thus, "the Government is now sweeping the nation clean of such alien filth." All of this had the overwhelming support of the press, until they perceived that their own interests might be threatened.[14]

To suppress these criminals was surely just, for reasons that Palmer outlined in congressional testimony prepared by Hoover. The leaders of these pernicious movements, he explained, included "idealists with distorted minds, many even insane; many are professional agitators who are plainly self-seekers and a large number are potential or actual criminals whose baseness of character leads them to espouse the unrestrained and gross theories and tactics of these organizations." Any doubt of their criminality will quickly be dispelled by "an examination of their photographs": "Out of the sly and crafty eyes of many of them leap cupidity, cruelty, insanity, and crime; from their lopsided faces, sloping brows, and misshapen features may be recognized the unmistakable criminal type." And they are dangerous. "Like a prairie fire the blaze of revolution was sweeping over every American institution of law and order," Palmer wrote, subverting workers, the churches and schools, even "crawling into the sacred corners of American homes seeking to replace marriage vows with libertine laws, burning up the foundations of society."[15]

Just think what fun the Office of Public Diplomacy and a host of apparatchiks in government, journalism, and the larger intellectual community could have if only the Sandinistas would oblige with statements remotely similar to those of the U.S. Justice Department and the press at a time of expansive U.S. power, 140 years after the American revolution, and a century after the last credible security threat.

Palmer was a liberal and progressive. His intention was "to tear out the radical seeds that have entangled American ideas in their poisonous theories." He was particularly impressed that "the result of the arrests of January 2, 1920, was that there was a marked cessation of radical activities in the United States. For many weeks following the arrests the radical press had nearly gone out of existence in so far as its communistic tendencies were concerned"; and, in general, the organizations "had been completely broken."[16] Among the notable achievements of the period was the sentencing in March 1919 of presidential candidate Eugene Debs to ten years in prison for opposing the draft and "savage sentences for private expressions of criticism" of the war along with "suppression of public debate of the issues of the war and peace," as the ACLU was later to record.[17]

Palmer's belief that the state has the authority to prevent these seeds from germinating is within the general American tradition. The mass media, the schools, and the universities defend ideological orthodoxy in their own, generally successful, ways. When a threat to reigning doctrine is perceived, the state is entitled to act.

After World War I, labor militancy menaced established privilege. J. Edgar Hoover portrayed the 1919 steel strike as a "Red conspiracy." A subsequent miners' strike was described by President Wilson as "one of the gravest steps ever proposed in this country," "a grave moral and legal wrong." Meanwhile the press warned that the miners, "red-soaked in the doctrines of Bolshevism," were "starting a general revolution in America."[18] The Red Scare, Murray Levin observes, "was promoted, in large part, by major business groups which feared their power was threatened by a leftward trend in the labor movement"; and they had "reason to rejoice" at its substantial success, namely, "to weaken and conservatize the labor movement, to dismantle radical parties, and to intimidate liberals." It "was an attempt—largely successful—to reaffirm the legitimacy of the power elites of capitalism and to further weaken workers' class consciousness." The Red Scare was strongly backed by the press and elites generally until they came to see that their own interests would be harmed as the right-wing frenzy got out of hand—in particular, the anti-immigrant hysteria, which threatened the reserve of cheap labor.

The Red Scare also served to buttress an interventionist foreign policy. Diplomatic historian Foster Rhea Dulles observed that "governmental agencies made most of these fears and kept up a barrage of anti-Bolshevik propaganda throughout 1919 which was at least partially inspired by the need to justify the policy of intervention in both Archangel and Siberia." In line with his concept of self-defense, already discussed, John Lewis Gaddis puts the point a bit differently: "the Red Scare, with its suggestion that even the United States might not be immune from the bacillus of revolution," was one of the factors that engendered "American hostility toward Communism." The reasoning is instructive.[19]

The pattern then established has persisted in many ways, until today. In the 1960s, as the effect of post-World War II repression waned and a wide range of popular movements began to develop, the FBI launched one of its major programs of repression (COINTELPRO) to disrupt them by instigating violence in the ghetto, direct participation in the police assassination of a Black Panther organizer, burglaries and harassment of the Socialist Workers Party over many years, and other methods of defamation and disruption.[20]

These programs were exposed just at the time when the nation was scandalized by Nixon's Watergate capers and the press was hailed, or denounced, for its aggressiveness in pursuing his misdeeds, barely a tea party in comparison with the programs of the nation's leading subversive organization under the direction of the Kennedy, Johnson, and Nixon administrations. Once again, history was kind enough to contrive a controlled experiment to allow us to evaluate the reaction to Watergate. The conclusions are unequivocal. Attention was limited to the relatively minor infringement of the rights of people and organizations with power and influence; the far more serious crimes against the powerless were scantily reported, and never entered the congressional proceedings.[21]

The lesson of Watergate is stark and clear: the powerful are capable of defending themselves, and the press may offer them some assistance, to the applause of some, the dismay of others, depending on the degree of their commitment to the goverment's right to control the public. The decision to focus attention on Watergate, hailed by the media as their proudest moment, was yet another cynical exercise in the service of power.

Appendix III

1. The Sanctity of Borders[1]

When the army of Nicaragua attempts to drive U.S. proxy forces from the national territory, sometimes crossing over an unmarked border into the areas of Honduras that have long been ceded to the contras under American dictates, the chorus of abuse over this violation of the sanctity of borders is dramatic in its intensity. We may ask the usual question: is this common refrain based upon a firm commitment to law and the sanctity of borders, or on the doctrine that no country has the right to defend itself from a U.S. assault? The latter is clearly the operative principle. That this is so is demonstrated by the reaction to Nicaragua's efforts since 1981 to pursue the peaceful means required by law to reconcile differences, settle conflicts, and arrange for international supervision of the borders. Other tests yield the same conclusion.

After one such border incident in March 1988, the editors of the Toronto *Globe and Mail* observed that when Nicaraguan forces cross "the border in hot pursuit of the contras," "the United States responds only selectively to this supposed outrage, the deciding factor apparently being whether a contra vote is imminent," as in this case, when "Mr. Reagan was revving up to ask Congress for renewed aid to the rebels." They add that the peace agreement signed by Honduras "forbids Honduras or any other country to give aid to foreign insurgents such as the contras," and it is far from clear that Nicaragua is in violation of international law in "crossing the border in hot pursuit of contras," apparently penetrating a few kilometers into southern Honduras where the contras had established their bases after expelling thousands of Honduran peasants. It is U.S. policy, not Nicaraguan defense of its territory, that "exhausts outrage," or would, the editors continue, "if it were not for the extraordinary suffering U.S. policy causes in the region."[2] An insight foreign to the Free Press south of the Canadian border, which also cannot permit itself to perceive that what is clearly in violation of international law is the U.S. support for the contra forces attacking Nicaragua from foreign bases. The reigning dogma holds that the United States stands above the law, free to use violence as it pleases, and that this is just and right. Correspondingly, the media avoid repeated Nicaraguan offers to

191

have the border monitored by international authorities, always dismissed by the United States for the obvious reasons; and little notice can be given to the World Court's demand that the United States cease its aggression and observe its treaty obligations, or its endorsement of Nicaragua's call for reparations from the world's most pious advocate of the rule of law.

The response to the Nicaraguan incursions has been considerably more selective than the *Globe and Mail* indicates, as revealed by Israeli operations in southern Lebanon at exactly the same time (see pp. 52-3). The reaction to these events can be gauged by a review of *New York Times* reports.

On March 12, Israeli planes bombed Palestinian refugee camps near Sidon, unreported. On March 18, a sentence in an article on another topic noted that "Israeli warplanes struck targets in Lebanon southeast of Beirut, ... apparently in reprisal for a small-scale rocket attack on northern Israel." A few days later, Israeli troops joined South Lebanon Army mercenaries in attacks north of the "security zone," also unreported. On March 24, the *Times* carried a brief notice of another attack, reporting that fifteen people were killed or wounded according to Lebanese police. Others were "feared buried under the rubble," some killed when "the planes returned and dropped more bombs ... while relief workers were digging through the debris" of the first wave of attacks, a standard device to augment casualties. The March 24 report also gave the first passing mention to the March 12 bombing. An Israeli attack the following day near Sidon with five casualties merited twelve lines. On March 31, a brief notice reported five killed and several houses set ablaze in an Israeli attack on another village north of the security zone under cover of a heavy artillery barrage, as Lebanese Muslims were observing a general strike in support of Arabs commemorating Land Day in Israel.[3]

Wire services added a few details to this casual record, reporting that victims of the March 23 attack included four children aged seven to ten who were hospitalized with "critical wounds," and that most casualties were attributed to the third round of bombing, during relief operations. They described the "smoke and dust" that "engulfed" four villages after the raids the following day and reported nine killed, bringing the total killed for the year in Israeli air strikes to forty-seven. In the March 30 attack, at least seven more were killed, including two Egyptians and three Lebanese civilians. "Dozens of mortar shells and rockets crashed in and around the market town of Nabatiyeh" and four nearby villages, badly damaging at least fifteen houses, while "Israeli helicopters strafed the rugged territory with machine guns during the withdrawal."[4]

Nothing remotely comparable happened in Honduras. Israeli forces were not engaged in hot pursuit, but were moving beyond the "security zone" that Israel has virtually annexed in southern Lebanon, controlled by Israeli forces and a terrorist mercenary army. The right of annexation, and of destruction and killing beyond its borders as well, is granted to Israel by virtue of its status as a leading U.S. client state. The significance of the alleged concern over the sanctity of borders is dramatically revealed.

Subsequent developments merely confirmed the point, as have the Israeli bombings in Lebanon since the early 1970s. In October 1988 Israeli bombing attacks killed fifteen and wounded thirty-five, police reported. According to police, most of the twenty wounded in the Bekaa valley town of Mashgara were civilians in a clinic, including Lebanese physicians and nurses. "Wailing women beat their chests while workers pulled victims from the rubble of Hezbollah's clinic." "The raids were apparently to avenge seven Israeli soldiers killed in a suicide car bombing earlier this week" by a Lebanese Shi'ite—a bombing *inside Lebanon,* where soldiers of the occupying army were providing support for the mercenary force employed to control the so-called security zone. The State Department spokesman "called for an end to violence *between Israel and Lebanon,*" a balanced and judicious assessment.[5]

A few days later, with no pretext, Israeli planes bombed the Mieh Mieh refugee camp near Sidon, wounding forty-one people, according to police; "a family of six and three other persons were missing and feared dead under the rubble." The raid hit a "battered Palestinian shantytown." In the attack on Mieh Mieh and two villages, seventeen were reported killed. Meshgara was again hit by "heavy barrages of shellfire, from artillery batteries stationed inside Israel." The same villages and others were attacked a few days later, killing four and wounding twenty-two. Palestinian refugee camps and other targets were attacked by Israeli helicopter gunships shortly after, including the shop of a boat dealer who was "thought to have rented two motorboats to Palestinian guerrillas and suspected of selling spare parts to the guerrillas." Israeli bombing of the Ein el-Hilweh refugee camp later in November, unreported to my knowledge, killed six Palestinians, including a woman and her four-year-old daughter who were buried in the rubble. "Police said smoke billowed from the teeming camp as ambulances raced from Sidon to evacuate casualties" from this bombing "as the country marked the 45th anniversary of its independence from France." Other raids near Sidon killed five and wounded fifteen, including nine civilians. The last of these, on November 25, was the twenty-third Israeli air strike on Lebanon through November, bringing the toll for 1988 to 119 killed and 333 wounded.[6]

The final police count for the year was 128 killed and 356 wounded in Israeli air attacks on Lebanon in 1988, continuing right through the period when Arafat's every gesture and phrase was being scrutinized to determine whether he really meant to renounce terrorism.[7]

During the same period, Israel stepped up its terrorist activities within the "security zone" as well. Wire services reported that at least 76 people were deported from the region by Israel's terrorist mercenaries in January 1989, and that an "uproar" was caused in Israel when a Norwegian officer of the U.N. forces patrolling the region compared the Israeli practice of expulsion to the methods used by the Nazis in trying to expel Jews from Norway under occupation; no uproar was caused by the expulsions, either in Israel or in the country that funds the operations. Julie Flint reported in the *Guardian* (London) on the expulsion of dozens of old men, women, and children from the town of Shebaa, because of "their refusal to support the Israeli-controlled South Lebanon Army" (SLA), the victims said. Norwegian troops tried to prevent the expulsion by blocking the main street with a jeep, but it was "crushed" by an SLA armoured car. Israeli troops "stormed the town before dawn, seized 48 people from their beds, drove them out of the region and blockaded the town," informing villagers that "the siege will be lifted only when they agree to form a 'coordination bureau' and join the SLA." Israeli troops surrounded the town, "depriving its inhabitants of food for refusing to cooperate with the Israeli-sponsored local administration, a U.N. source said." Ten percent of Shebaa's 15,000 people have been "forced into exile" by such practices. Young men are informed that they "have to be soldiers with the SLA or we will cut off your town." Deportees report that the headmaster of a school was "bruised and beaten" while detained by the Israeli army for refusing to collaborate. Another victim reported electric torture on the fingers and testicles. A woman expelled with her eight children reports that "Israeli troops stormed the house at five in the morning. They took the children out in their night clothes, though it was bitterly cold. They put us in a jeep, covered us with a tarpaulin and drove off. Later, we were all put into a truck. My husband's father and mother were there. He is 90 years old." U.N. spokesman Timur Goksel reports that "Most of those expelled were women and children" and the Norwegian UNIFIL commander condemned the expulsions as "inhuman acts." Israel reacted to the protests only by continuing the expulsions. The director of political affairs at the Lebanese foreign ministry said that the Lebanese "fear that Israeli policy in the occupied south may aim at gradually emptying that area of all those who oppose Israel hegemony over that zone, and that it may turn into a sort of creeping Israeli colonization."[8]

These events, sometimes reported, elicited no response apart from occasional expressions of regret over the "violence between Israel and Lebanon." The reaction to PLO bombs in Israel, or Nicaraguan efforts to drive U.S. proxy forces from their territory, is slightly different.

Appendix IV

1. The Craft of "Historical Engineering"[1]

The vocation of "historical engineering" is as old as history, and was recognized as a professional responsibility as the United States entered World War I. Examples are given in the text and appendices, many others in the references cited. A closer look at particular cases sheds light on how the system works. Two cases will be examined here as illustrations, drawn from a major government-media project of the 1980s: "demonizing the Sandinistas" while defending Washington's terror states.

One of the proofs that Nicaragua is a cancer causing subversion to spread through the hemisphere, as plausible as others, is that the Sandinistas supplied arms for a terrorist attack on the Palace of Justice by M-19 guerrillas in Colombia in November 1985. On January 5 and 6, 1986, the *New York Times* published stories on the Colombian charge against Nicaragua and Nicaragua's denial. The next day, January 7, Colombia officially accepted the Nicaraguan denial. The Colombian foreign minister stated in a news conference that "Colombia accepts Nicaraguan Foreign Minister Miguel D'Escoto's explanation and considers the incident closed." This news made it to page 81 of the *Boston Globe,* in the sports section. The *Times* did not report the fact at all; rather, its editorial the following day asserted that "Colombia's patience has since been strained by evidence—which Nicaragua disputes—that the Sandinistas supplied guns to terrorists who staged" the November incident. On January 15, the *Times* reported that "American officials have linked Nicaragua to the Terrorism in Bogota—a charge denied by the Nicaraguan Government," and published an opinion column by Elliott Abrams repeating the charges that both Abrams and the editors knew to be without merit. These were repeated in a news column of February 26, again ignoring the fact that Colombia had officially rejected the charges and considered the incident closed. The *Washington Post* also failed to report Colombia's acceptance of Nicaragua's disclaimer of responsibility.[2]

On March 18, a *Times* editorial entitled "The Nicaragua Horror Show" discussed Reagan's "appeal for $100 million to help the 'contras' against Nicaragua's leftist tyrants." The editorial was critical of a Reagan speech so replete with falsehoods and unsupported allegations that it elicited some discomfort. The editors urged that "Mr. Reagan should have held to [the] undeniable transgressions" of the Sandinistas; he should have asked how they can be "contained and what can the United States do to promote democracy in Nicaragua," raising it to the standards of Washington's terror states. They present a list of "the hemisphere's real grievances," namely Nicaragua's "totalitarian" domestic policies and complication of "the region's security problems" by building the biggest military airfield in Central America and a deep-water port in the Caribbean, with Soviet-bloc aid, and its support for "guerrilla comrades in El Salvador." The list of "undeniable transgressions" concludes as follows: "more than piety explains why Tomás Borge, the Interior Minister, participated in a mass for the M-19 guerrillas who shot up the Palace of Justice in Bogota, Colombia," sure proof of Sandinista complicity in the terrorist attack.

Others too were impressed by this proof of Sandinista iniquity. William Beecher, diplomatic correspondent of the *Boston Globe*, highlighted the attendance of Borge at the "memorial service for the M-19 guerrillas" who used "arms allegedly supplied by Nicaragua"; this is the kind of "mistake" that "serious analysts" hope will be caused by "rising military pressure" against Nicaragua, he observed, apparently forgetting that, nine days earlier, his newspaper had reported Colombia's dismissal of the allegation.[3]

A reader in Arizona, Dr. James Hamilton, was curious to learn the basis for the renewed charge by the *Times* editors, which he knew had been denied by the Colombian government. He wrote a series of letters to *Times* editor Max Frankel, and after receiving a dismissive form letter from foreign editor Warren Hoge, to him as well. After many attempts to obtain a response to this simple question, he finally received a letter from Hoge in mid-July. "In answer to your question about Tomás Borge," Hoge wrote, "Mr. Borge attended a mass in Managua celebrated by the Rev. Uriel Molina commemorating the first anniversary of the death of Enrique Schmidt, the Minister of Communications, who had been killed in a battle with the contras. During the service, a member of the congregation shouted for prayers for the M-19 and unfurled their flag."[4] Hamilton writes: "Thus, did a memorial service for a former Sandinista cabinet member become, in the hands of an editorial writer, 'a mass for the M-19 guerrillas,' permitting the *Times* to misrepresent Borge and imply an affiliation between the Sandinistas and the M-19, using the behavior of one individual in the church on that day as support for this contention." Some tales are just too useful to abandon.[5]

The remainder of the "undeniable transgressions" on the *Times* list fare no better, and are, in fact, of some interest with regard to the hysteria evoked in establishment circles over Nicaragua's unwillingness to follow orders and its unconscionable efforts to survive a U.S. attack.

A more important requirement has been to establish a "symmetry" between the contras and the Salvadoran guerrillas. This "symmetry" was crucial for U.S. government propaganda, hence a media staple. It is readily established by ignoring the scale and character of U.S. aid to the contras and direct involvement in their terror, and by the insistent claim that although rebels in El Salvador deny receiving support from Nicaragua, "ample evidence shows it exists, and it is questionable how long they could survive without it," as James LeMoyne reported after the Central American peace accords were signed in August 1987.[6] LeMoyne presented no evidence, then or ever, to support this claim. He has yet to comment on the failure of the U.S. government, which is not entirely lacking in facilities, to provide any credible evidence since early 1981—and little enough then—as was noted by the World Court, which reviewed the public materials produced by the U.S. government to establish its case, dismissing them as lacking substantive basis.[7] The claim is a propaganda necessity; therefore it is true.

Times efforts to protect the required fact are illuminating. After LeMoyne's statement appeared, the media monitoring organization FAIR wrote the *Times* asking it to share LeMoyne's "ample evidence" with its readers. Their letter was not published, but they received a private communication from foreign editor Joseph Lelyveld acknowledging that LeMoyne had been "imprecise."[8]

After the September 1987 acknowledgement that the charges were "imprecise," the *Times* had many opportunities to correct the imprecision, and used them—to repeat the charges that are privately acknowledged to be without merit. Thus, in his contribution to the media barrage organized in December in connection with the Sandinista defector Roger Miranda, LeMoyne announced that in response to Miranda's charges, Defense Minister Ortega "seemed indirectly to confirm the existence of Sandinista assistance to Salvadoran rebels." This is LeMoyne's rendition of Ortega's statement that the Reagan administration had no right to produce such charges given its arming of the contras. What Ortega went on to say, unreported, is that "the Salvadoran guerrillas have some resources and ways to get weapons" and they "are basically armed through their own efforts," not depending "on outside sources; they are self-sufficient." Thus Ortega's denial of Nicaraguan support for Salvadoran guerrillas is neatly converted by LeMoyne and the *Times* into a "confirmation" of such support.[9]

LeMoyne's *Times* colleagues also joined in the fray. Stephen Engelberg wrote that the U.S. government charge "appears to have been confirmed" by Miranda, who "said the Sandinistas were shipping the weapons to El Salvador by sea," that is, via the Gulf of Fonseca.[10] The Gulf is thirty kilometers wide, heavily patrolled by U.S. naval vessels and SEAL teams and covered by a radar facility on Tiger Island in the Gulf that is able to locate and track boats not only in that area but far beyond, as discussed in World Court testimony by David MacMichael, the CIA specialist responsible for analyzing the relevant material during the period to which Engelberg refers. Despite these extensive efforts, no evidence could be produced, though Nicaragua, curiously, has no difficulty providing evidence of CIA supplies in the supposedly "symmetrical" situation. It takes a measure of self-control to refrain from ridicule at this point.

After the peace accords were finally dismantled in January 1988, George Volsky wrote that the provision of the accords calling "for all countries to deny the use of their territories to insurgents in neighboring nations ... applies mainly to Nicaragua, which is said to be helping rebels in El Salvador, and to Honduras, whose territory is reportedly an important part of the United States-directed contra supply effort."[11] Surely a fair summary of the available evidence on the support for irregular and insurrectionist forces outlawed by the accords.

Volsky did not explain why the same provision of the accords is inapplicable to El Salvador, which is also "reportedly" involved in the U.S. support structure for the contras, or to Costa Rica, which "has long been the base for the more liberal faction of the Nicaraguan rebels" and where "the Costa-Rican based contras" continue to operate, as we regularly learn when news reports cite a "contra source in Costa Rica," and as we would learn in greater detail if there were some interest in the facts.[12]

LeMoyne later warned that if in the future "the Sandinistas [are] found still to be aiding Salvadoran guerrillas," then the peace accords will collapse; he mentioned no similar problem elsewhere. As for Honduras, LeMoyne cautiously observed several months later that its support for the contras *"appears* to be a direct violation of the accord."[13] His colleague, *Times* military correspondent Bernard Trainor, observed that "To this date, the amount of support provided by the Sandinistas to the Salvadoran guerrillas has never been established conclusively"—*Times* jargon to express the fact that no credible evidence has been presented since a trickle of aid flowed for a few months seven years earlier, well after the U.S.-backed security forces had launched a "war of extermination and genocide against a defenseless civilian population" (Bishop Rivera y Damas, the successor of the assassinated Archbishop Romero).[14]

So required doctrine is established.

No less interesting is the fact that it is taken for granted by hawks and doves alike that it would have been a major crime to provide the defenseless civilian population with means to defend themselves against a war of extermination and genocide—at least, when the war is conducted by U.S. clients, with U.S. support and, as it reached its climax, direct organization and participation. To have provided victims of Pol Pot with arms to defend themselves, had this been possible, would have been considered a sign of true nobility. It is enlightening that such simple observations as these, and their obvious import, are next to unintelligible.

In late 1988, LeMoyne completed his four-year assignment as *New York Times* correspondent in El Salvador, and took the occasion to publish a comprehensive analysis of aid to the Salvadoran guerrillas.[15] Fifteen months had passed since he had written, shortly after the signing of the peace accords, of the "ample evidence" that Nicaraguan aid to the guerrillas in El Salvador was so extensive that "it is questionable how long they could survive without it." Fourteen months had passed since the foreign editor of the *Times* had agreed that the "ample evidence" did not exist, and nine months since he had instructed LeMoyne to devote an entire article to the actual evidence, such as it may be (see note 8). The results of this nine-month inquiry merit a careful look.

Gone completely is the "ample evidence" of the aid from Nicaragua on which the Salvadoran guerrillas relied for their very existence. LeMoyne makes no reference to his claims of the past, or to the request that he produce his "ample evidence," or to the contribution his unsubstantiated allegations made to the project of "demonizing the Sandinistas," protecting the murderous U.S. clients, and undercutting the peace accords.

It turns out now that the evidence is "largely circumstantial and is open to differing interpretations." It is not "ample," but is rather "limited evidence," of which nothing credible is provided. Furthermore, this "limited evidence" indicates that shipments "are small and probably sporadic," not the large-scale aid that kept the Salvadoran guerrillas alive according to the version of August 1987 and since— conclusions that will hardly surprise those who have been studying U.S. government propaganda on the matter during the past years. The "limited evidence" has to do with transshipments from the Soviet bloc, primarily Cuba, he asserts—again without evidence. Reading on, we find that there seems to be at least as much evidence of direct arms transfers from the contras to the Salvadoran guerrillas, and of Honduran army involvement in transshipment of arms to them. This also comes as no surprise to those who have taken the trouble to *read* government propaganda instead of simply reporting the press release; thus a State Department background paper of 1984 presented testimony of a Sandinista defector, who provided no credible evidence of Sandinista arms supply but did allege that arms were coming from Mexico and Guatemala[16] (it is also likely, but not investigated, that when the U.S. proxies broke for the border in February 1988 after their thrice-daily supply flights were curtailed, they began selling their arms to corrupt Honduran officers, who sell them in turn to Salvadoran guerrillas, a matter to which we return directly). The major Sandinista contribution to the Salvadoran guerrillas, LeMoyne now informs the reader, is a "safe haven" in Nicaragua for offices, logistics, and communications, and the opportunity to travel through Nicaragua to other countries. The same is true of many other countries outside of the United States or its dependencies; and all states of the region, including Costa Rica, have always afforded such support—indeed far more—to the U.S. proxy forces attacking Nicaragua.

The careful reader will therefore discover that the whole charade of many years has collapsed. As was always obvious, the tales of "symmetry" hardly merit ridicule. The fraud was successfully maintained as long as support for the contras was an important and viable policy option; then it was necessary to present the U.S. proxy forces as authentic guerrillas, thus to insist upon the "symmetry" between the contras attacking Nicaragua and the indigenous guerrillas in El Salvador, both dependent on outside aid for survival. By late 1988, the contra option was losing its residual appeal, in part because it was no longer needed as a means to achieve the goal of maximizing civilian suffering and discontent in Nicaragua and reducing the country to ruin, in part because it was proving impossible to keep the proxy forces in the field. The tale can therefore be allowed to fade—without, however, any acknowledgement of what came before. That is to be removed from history, and surely will be.

The rules of the game are that established power sets the terms of debate. The government-media system produces claims about Sandinista aid to the Salvadoran guerrillas and reiterates them insistently, in full knowledge that they are groundless, as long as they are needed for the cause. Occasionally a skeptic is allowed to intrude with the observation that the evidence is meager indeed. The question of Salvadoran aid to the U.S.-run contra forces, however, is off the agenda and is not investigated even though there is no doubt about the use of El Salvador to attack Nicaragua through 1986, and the same sources that told the truth then, but were ignored, allege that the process continues, and are ignored (see p. 92). As long as it was serviceable, the absurd "symmetry" thesis was maintained, and the doctrine of crucial outside sustenance now put aside can be resurrected whenever it may be needed, the basis having been laid in general consciousness despite the quiet retraction.[17] Mainstream discussion is closed to the thought that Nicaragua and other governments—and individuals, were this possible—*should* send aid to people trying to defend themselves from the rampaging armies and death squads of a military regime implanted by a foreign power. A closer look at the forbidden question would yield some interesting conclusions about the prevailing moral and intellectual climate, but it would stray so far from the consensus of power that it is unthinkable.

We may note finally that not all defectors enjoy the royal treatment accorded to the Sandinista defector Miranda, critically timed in the final phase of the government-media campaign to demolish the unwanted peace accords. In the use of Miranda, the media barrage began with two long front-page articles in the *Washington Post* (Dec. 13, 1987) and continued for weeks as the media relayed State Department propaganda based upon his testimony, with its ominous warning that Nicaragua might attempt to defend the national territory from CIA supply flights to the U.S. proxy forces; the allegation that Nicaragua was thumbing its nose at the impotent U.S. Navy by merrily sending arms to El Salvador, undetected, via the Gulf of Fonseca; and the report that the Sandinistas were planning to reduce their regular military forces and provide light arms to citizens for defense against a possible U.S. invasion, a report transmuted by the independent media into a threat to "overwhelm and terrorize" their neighbors.[18]

Compare, in contrast, the media reaction to the defection of Horacio Arce, Chief of Intelligence of the FDN (the main contra force) from 1985. After receiving asylum in the Mexican Embassy in Tegucigalpa, Arce left for Mexico City in November 1988, then for Managua under the government amnesty program. While in Mexico City, he was interviewed and had a number of interesting things to say.

The contra Chief of Intelligence provided details of support for the contras by the Pentagon in violation of congressional restrictions, including training by U.S. military instructors through 1986 at a U.S. air base in a southern state, a semi-secret base with 17 airstrips, which they reached in Hercules C-130 transports without passing through immigration or customs, of course. The trainers were from Fort Bragg. After the 1982 Falklands/Malvinas war, the contras in Honduras lost their Argentine trainers and advisers, but in the U.S. base where they were being illegally trained (including Arce himself), the instructors included a specialist in psychological warfare from Chile, so the links to the neo-fascist states of the U.S. orbit remained.

Arce was also among those trained at the Ilopango air base near San Salvador by Salvadoran and U.S. instructors. In Honduras, they were trained directly by the Honduran military, who had been providing the essential training and logistics from 1980 and also provided pilots for supply flights into Nicaragua. Honduran immigration authorities also assisted, helping the contras gain access to refugee camps for recruitment, sometimes by force. Miskito recruits were trained separately, by a Japanese officer. Most of the supervisors of training and aid were of Hispanic origin—Cubans, Dominicans, Puerto Ricans, South Americans, and some Spaniards. The arms were mainly from Israel, as "everyone knows," much of it captured in the 1982 Lebanon war. "Cubans in the CIA are all over the place," also deeply involved in the extensive corruption. Part of the contra financing came from drug trafficking.

The United States is a global power and is thus capable of constructing elaborate systems of terror and corruption, making use of its client and mercenary states and longstanding relations with international terrorism and criminal syndicates.

U.S. Embassy officials in Tegucigalpa, Arce continues, provided the contras with intelligence information and other aid. His contacts at the U.S. Embassy included "Robert McHorn of the CIA or Alexander Zunnerman who ostensibly is with AID but is CIA also." Arce was also in direct contact with the Tegucigalpa AID warehouse on the premises of the Electropura company. AID has admittedly served as a front for CIA terrorist operations in the past, particularly in Laos during the "clandestine war."

Arce himself had fled Nicaragua with his father, a major in Somoza's National Guard, on the day of the Sandinista victory, July 19, 1979. In 1980, he was recruited for the contras, adopting the *nom de guerre* "Mercenario" ("mercenary"). By January 1981, the operation had become "something serious and something big." He went on to reach the rank of *comandante*, becoming intelligence chief after the former chief, Ricardo Lau, was dismissed (and possibly murdered by the contras, Arce believes). Lau had become an embarrassment in early 1985 when former Salvadoran intelligence chief Roberto Santivañez implicated him in arranging the assassination of Archbishop Romero and in having played a "key role" in organizing and training death squads in El Salvador and Guatemala, as well as in political killings in Honduras. He was "a thief among thieves," Arce reports.

Not all the contras "are rented," *El Mercenario* continues; some have loyalties to their chiefs. They are, however, well paid by regional standards. Without a family, Arce's salary was about $500 a month.

The Honduran armed forces "participate in every operation that takes place close to the border," while also providing intelligence "on military and non-military targets in Nicaragua." The latter service is particularly important, Arce continues, because "We attack a lot of schools, health centers, and those sort of things. We have tried to make it so that the Nicaraguan government cannot provide social services for the peasants, cannot develop its project ... that's the idea." Evidently, their U.S. training was successful in getting the basic idea across.

Arce also discussed the vast corruption in the contra organization from commander Enrique Bermúdez on down, and their sales of U.S. arms and supplies, "much of it ... probably ending up in the hands of the guerrillas of El Salvador." In cooperation with Honduran officers, who take a cut for themselves, contras are selling assault rifles and radiocommunications equipment to the FMLN in El Salvador—who therefore may be receiving aid from Nicaraguans after all, James LeMoyne and the *Times* will be happy to hear.[19]

Arce had far more of significance to report than Miranda, and had a more important role within the contra organization than Miranda did in Nicaragua. Furthermore, as we have seen, the contras were favored with enormous publicity, generally receiving more than the government. But in this case, there was no way to deform the testimony into a weapon for the campaign of "demonizing the Sandinistas" and mobilizing support for the terror states; on the contrary, the message was all wrong. Editors made their choices accordingly.

2. The Obligation of Silence[20]

As discussed earlier, a doctrine commonly held is that "we tend to flagellate ourselves as Americans about various aspects of our own policies and actions we disapprove of." The reality is rather different.

The prevailing pattern is one of indignant outrage over enemy crimes with much self-congratulatory appeal to high principle, combined with a remarkable ability "not to see" in the case of crimes for which we bear responsibility. In the West, there is an ample literature—much of it fraudulent—scornfully denouncing apologists or alleged apologists for the Soviet Union and Third World victims of U.S. intervention, but little about the behavior that is the norm: silence and apologetics about the crimes of one's own state and its clients, when a willingness simply to face the facts might make a substantial difference in limiting or terminating these abuses. This is standard procedure elsewhere as well. In the Soviet sphere, dissidents are condemned as apologists for Western crimes that are bitterly denounced by right-thinking commissars, exactly the pattern mimicked here.

A number of examples have been mentioned, and many have been discussed elsewhere. For evaluating U.S. political culture and the media, the cases to which a serious analyst will immediately turn, apart from the crimes of the United States itself, are those of its major clients; in recent years, El Salvador and Israel. The latter case has been a particularly illuminating one ever since Israel's display of power in 1967 elicited the adulation and awe that has persisted among American intellectuals. The apologetic literature is often little more than a parody of the Stalinist period.[21]

The elaborate campaigns of defamation launched against those who do not satisfy the requirements of the faithful also strike a familiar chord. The effect, as elsewhere, has been to intimidate critics and to facilitate the exercise of violence; and also to erect barriers in the way of a political settlement that has long been feasible.[22]

Israel can be secure that as long as it is perceived as a "strategic asset," it will remain "the symbol of human decency," as the *New York Times* described it while Israeli atrocities in the occupied territories reached such a level that the media briefly took serious notice. Israel can rely upon the American labor movement bureaucracy to justify whatever it does, to explain that although "in their effort to maintain order, Israeli Defense Forces have on occasion resorted to unnecessary force, ... no doubt such incidents can be attributed to the inexperience of the Israeli army in riot control and other police functions, and to the frustrations of Israeli soldiers as they confront young Palestinians hurling stones and petrol bombs."[23] To fully appreciate this statement and what it means, one must bear in mind that it followed one of the rare periods when the media actually gave some picture of atrocities of the kind that had been taking place for many years in the occupied territories, at a lesser but still scandalous level. John Kifner's reports in the *New York Times* were particularly good examples of professional journalism, consistent with his outstanding record over many years.

Apologetics of the AFL-CIO variety have served for twenty years to authorize harsh repression and endless humiliation, finally reaching the level of regular pogroms in which soldiers break into houses, smash furniture, break bones, and beat teenagers to death after dragging them from their homes; settler violence conducted with virtual impunity; and collective punishments, deportation, and systematic terror on orders of the Defense Ministry. As fashions change, leading figures in the campaign to protect state violence from scrutiny will doubtless create for themselves a different past, but the record is there for those who choose to see.

There has always been an Elie Wiesel to assure the reader that there are only some "regrettable exceptions—immediately corrected by Israeli authorities," while he fulminates about the real crime: the condemnation of Israeli atrocities by public opinion. He tells us of the "dreamlike eyes" of the Israeli soldiers, perhaps those who had been described a few weeks earlier by reservists returning from service in the territories. They reported the "acts of humiliation and violence against Palestinian inhabitants that have become the norm, that almost no one seeks to prevent," including "shameful acts" that they personally witnessed, while the military authorities look the other way.[24] Or perhaps Wiesel has in mind the soldiers who caught a ten-year-old boy, and, when he did not respond to their demand that he identify children who had thrown stones, proceeded "to mash his head in," leaving him "looking like a steak," as soldiers put it, also beating the boy's mother when she tried to protect him, only then discovering that the child was deaf, dumb, and mentally retarded. It "didn't bother" the soldiers, one participant in the beating said, and the platoon commander ordered them on to the next chore because "we don't have time for games." Or perhaps Wiesel's point is that "a picture of an Israeli soldier kicking an old Arab woman is no longer news," as the Hebrew press bitterly comments, speaking of those who accept atrocities as readily as the author of *Against Silence*, whose words could actually mitigate suffering and abuse if he were not committed to silence as the proper course.[25] The fact that such consistent behavior over many years is treated with respect, even regarded as saintly, speaks volumes about Western culture.

Given these dispensations, Israel is free to use its phenomenal U.S. aid to send its military forces to conduct the regular operations described in the Israeli press (but rarely here) at the time when Wiesel's thoughts on "regrettable exceptions" appeared: To bar supplies from refugee camps where there is "a serious lack of food." To beat young prisoners so severely that a military doctor in the Ansar 2 detention camp refuses to admit them, one lying "battered and motionless for an hour and a half, surrounded by soldiers, without receiving any medical treatment," then "dumped" from a jeep on the way to the hospital and "brutally beaten" again "in front of dozens of soldiers" (one was allegedly censured). To break into a home and drag out a seven-year-old boy who had been hiding under his bed, then "beat him up savagely in front of his parents and the family," then to beat his father and brother too because they did not reveal the hiding place of the child, while the other children scream hysterically and "the mother cannot calm them because she is told not to move"; and to mercilessly beat children of age five and up, sometimes three or four soldiers with sticks "until his hands and legs are broken," or to spray gas directly into their eyes; these are among the horror stories that soldiers report from the miserable Jabaliya refugee camp, where the army has "succeeded in breaking them" so that "they are totally crushed, weak and tired." To rake a boy twelve to fifteen years old over barbed wire "in order to injure him" as prisoners arrive at the Dahariya prison, with no reaction by the officer observing, after vicious beatings of prisoners en route with clubs, plastic pipes, and handcuffs while their commanding officer looked on ("Israeli buses have become torture chambers," Knesset member Dedi Zucker reports, citing these and other atrocities). To rampage freely through

Jericho, breaking into houses, brutally beating and humiliating residents. To "run amok" through the Amari refugee camp, "knocking down doors, breaking into houses, smashing furniture, and beating residents, including children," then beating an ambulance driver who arrived on the scene after dragging him by his hair—an elite paratroop unit in this case, marauding with no provocation according to witnesses. To jail a prisoner "in perfect health," leaving him "paralysed and dumb," "apparently the result of severe beatings and torture ... he suffered while in detention" at the Jenin interrogation center. To acquit a young Arab imprisoned for setting fire to the car of a suspected police informant when it is discovered that someone else was responsible and that his confession was extracted by torture, but without any reference by the district attorney or the court to the false "confession extracted through severe beating," or what that implies. And on, and on.[26]

There are other variants. The commander of an elite unit, Willy Shlap, described his first week in the El Burj refugee camp near Jabaliya. An eleven-year-old boy was found throwing a stone and taken to his house, where his father was ordered to beat him. The father slapped him but the officer screamed "Is this a beating? Beat him! Beat him!" The tension mounted and the father "became hysterical," starting to beat the child brutally, knocking him on the floor and kicking him in the ribs as hard as he could. The soldiers were apparently satisfied. When atrocities became even more severe in the summer of 1988, as Wiesel published his reflections, the *Jerusalem Post* reported that, according to UNRWA relief workers and doctors at clinics, the victims of the sharp increase in brutal beatings were mostly "men [sic] aged 15 to 30," but the clinics had "also treated 24 boys and five girls aged five and younger" in the past weeks, as well as many older children, such as a seven-year-old boy brought to a clinic "with a bleeding kidney, and bearing club marks." Soldiers routinely beat, kick, and club children, according to doctors and relief officials.[27]

In a case that actually went to trial, and therefore received considerable attention (in Israel, that is), four soldiers of an elite unit of the Givati Brigade were arrested and charged with beating an inhabitant of the Jabaliya camp to death on August 22. The case was first reported in *Ha'aretz* a month later. After children had thrown stones, twenty soldiers broke into a home and began to beat the father of one of the suspected stonethrowers, Hani al-Shami. He was kicked and beaten with clubs and weapons. Soldiers jumped on him from the bed while he was lying on the floor, his head bleeding from blows with clubs. His wife was also beaten up by soldiers. An officer arrived, found the severely wounded man bleeding heavily, and ordered him taken to the Military Administration offices, not to a hospital; that is routine procedure. Later, the family was informed that al-Shami was dead. Two soldiers from the same unit said "it is true that we beat them up and very strongly too, but it is better to break bones than to shoot people," echoing the Minister of Defense. "We have lost our human image," they said.[28]

After the arrests were announced, other atrocities of the Brigade became public: for example, the story of a journalist from the El Bureij refugee camp, hospitalized after soldiers broke into his home, forced him to kneel on hands and knees and bray like a donkey while they beat him on the testicles, stomach, and back with clubs and electric wires for half an hour and smashed his glasses, shouting "now you will be a blind donkey." Soldiers described Givati as "a brigade without law," blaming the commander and the "right-wing orientation," with many units from the Hesder Yeshivot, military-religious training schools known for their ultra-right fanaticism.[29]

The courts released the four soldiers charged with the murder while the trial proceeded, as briefly noted without comment in the *Jerusalem Post*. The Hebrew press told the story that had been omitted from the version offered to the foreign reading public. A soldier testified at the trial that "the humiliation and the beatings were because of the need to pass the time." Another added that al-Shami's protruding belly particularly amused the soldiers and was "a target for the beatings." An officer testified that he had threatened to kill al-Shami because "his groans disturbed me"; "I shouted at him that he should shut up, or I will kill him." He testified further that in the military compound to which al-Shami had been brought after the beatings, he had asked a doctor to treat al-Shami, but the doctor had refused, only giving an order to wipe the blood from his face. On that day, the witness continued, many Arabs arrived at the command post with their hands tied and eyes covered, and were brutally beaten by officers and soldiers. Asked why he had not cared for al-Shami, the witness replied that "the wounded Arab did not interest me, because they are Arabs and want to kill us." Soldiers testified that "the moment you catch a rioter you beat him … even if he doesn't resist. It is to deter him." Troops are ordered "to break their legs so they won't be able to walk and break their hands so they won't throw stones." A company commander reported "unequivocal orders to beat any suspect" so as "to put him out of action for a month or two"; it is "necessary," he testified, because jailing suspects is "like taking them to a PLO training seminar." Beatings inside houses are "a daily matter" in Gaza.

The military court accepted the defense plea, ruling that "there is a basis to the claim that the deceased was beaten up in the military stronghold by soldiers whom to our sorrow the investigation did not succeed in identifying." Furthermore, the fact that the soldiers were detained for eighty-three days brings "a correct balance between the needs of the army and the nature of their innocence and the nature of justice." We are dealing with soldiers who "did their military duty and not with criminals," the court ruled. "Nobody had denied that they had brutally beaten an unarmed Arab inside his own home, that they had broken a club or two over his head in front of his children or jumped on him in their boots," Ziva Yariv commented; but there is no legal liability because these beatings might not have been the actual cause of death, "as if there were no law banning the brutal beating of civilians, or the breaking of a club over the body of an innocent man, as if there were no law against vicious attacks or grievous bodily harm."[30]

The military correspondent of Ha'aretz observed that there had been a decline in the number of "exceptions" brought to trial, the reason being that "exceptions have become the norm." The Givati soldiers, like the members of an elite paratrooper unit tried for rampaging in the Kalandia refugee camp, "did not understand what the fuss is about." They had behaved no differently from soldiers in other units and had been following orders, doing exactly what is expected of them. Brutal beating of prisoners or Arab civilians in their homes or on the streets is simply part of daily life, so they were unjustly tried. Evidently, the Court agreed. The Hebrew word "harig," literally "exception," by now seems to be used to mean little other than "atrocity."[31]

Atrocities are regarded as quite routine by the authorities. Dr. Marcus Levin, who was called for military service in the reserves at the Ansar 2 detention camp Medical Center, reports that he was assigned to check the prisoners "before and after interrogation." Asking why they had to be checked "after interrogation," Levin was informed by the doctors in charge that "It is nothing special, sometimes there are some broken limbs. For example, yesterday they brought in a twelve-year-old boy with two broken legs"—after interrogation. Levin, a sixteen-year army veteran, then went to the commander to tell him that "my name is Marcus Levin and not Joseph Mengele and for reasons of conscience I refuse to serve in a place that reminds me of South American dictatorships." Most, however, find their conscience untroubled, or look the other way. One doctor informed him that "in the beginning you feel like Mengele, but a few days later you become accustomed."[32]

The Israeli writer Dan Almagor recalled a TV film he had seen in England on the thirtieth anniversary of the outbreak of the second World War, in which several German officers who had been released from prison after serving their sentences as war criminals were asked why they had taken such care in filming the atrocities in which they participated. "We didn't film many of them for history," one officer said, but "so that there would be something to play for the children when we went home on weekends. It was very amusing for the children," who were deprived of Mickey Mouse films because of the war. Almagor was reminded of this film when he read the testimony of the Givati soldiers who described the amusement they felt over the "attractive" protruding stomach of Hani al-Shami, which provided such a fine "target for beatings." Almagor went on to describe a visit to the West Bank with a brigade educational officer, a Major, who described with pride how he beats people with a club and joined a group of other officers and enlisted men and women who were convulsed with laughter over stories told by one man from the religious ultra-right with a knitted skull cap about how he had bulldozed homes designated by the secret police, including one that was not marked but was between two that were, and had destroyed a store that was in his way when he wanted to turn the bulldozer. Almagor's bitter words brought back memories to me too, among them, an unforgettable incident forty years ago, when a horrifying Japanese documentary of the Hiroshima bombing was being shown, to much amusement, in the "combat zone" in downtown Boston, as a pornographic film. And a story in the *New York Times* in March 1968, right after the Tet offensive, describing with some annoyance how demonstrators had disrupted an exhibit at the Chicago Museum of Science where children could "enter a helicopter for simulated firing of a machine gun at targets in a diorama of the Vietnam Central Highlands," including a peasant hut, which particularly disturbed the obnoxious peaceniks.[33]

"It is already impossible, it seems, to relate these stories, to ask for an explanation, to seek those responsible. Every other day there is a new story." These are the despairing words of Zvi Gilat, who has been recording the atrocities in the territories with care and dedication as the armed forces resort to ever more savage measures to suppress the Palestinian uprising. He is describing the village of Beita, which gained its notoriety because a Jewish girl was killed there in early April 1988. She was killed by a crazed Israeli guard accompanying hikers, after he had killed two villagers. The sister of one of the murdered men, three-months pregnant, was jailed for throwing a rock at the killer of her brother and kept in prison until days before her child was due to be born; the Israeli guard who had killed three people was not charged because, army spokesman Col. Raanan Gissen said, "I believe the tragic incident and its result are already a penalty." Other Beita residents have remained in prison for eight months, with no sentence, and only one family member permitted to attend the sessions of the military court. The sentencing of four villagers to three years imprisonment for allegedly throwing stones before the Jewish girl was killed by her guard merited a few words in paragraph eleven of an AP report in the *Times;* ten days earlier, the *Times* reported the sentencing of a Jewish settler to 2½ years, the minimum sentence under law, for killing an Arab shepherd he found grazing sheep on land near his settlement. Beita residents were expelled from the country, houses were demolished including many not specifically marked for destruction, property was destroyed, the village was not permitted to export olive oil, its main source of income, to Europe; Israel refuses to purchase it. Two weeks before Gilat visited the village once again, a 12-year-old boy was shot in the back of his head at close range by Israeli soldiers, killed while fleeing from soldiers whom he saw when leaving his house, left to bleed on the ground for at least five hours according to witnesses. But though he has "no more strength, no more will," Gilat goes on with more and more tales of horror, cruelty, and humiliation, while senses become dulled even among those who read them, including very few of those who pay the bills.[34]

I cite only a tiny sample of the "regrettable exceptions" that are "no doubt" attributable to "inexperience" and "frustration," atrocities that mounted through mid-1988 as the U.S. media reduced their coverage under a barrage of criticism for their unfair treatment of defenseless Israel, if not their latent anti-Semitism. Meanwhile there were interspersed with quiet laments over Israel's tribulations, and occasional excesses, by some of those who helped create the basis for what they now fear. The atrocities go on, while the press looks the other way and those who might help mitigate them observe their vow of silence, assure us that nothing serious is happening, or warn of the problems Israel will face unless it takes some steps to recognize the human rights of Palestinians, not heretofore a matter of concern. The horror stories in the Israeli (mainly Hebrew) press barely skim the surface. An official of the Israeli Ministry of Foreign Affairs, returning from reserve service, reported that "the overwhelming majority of the severe and violent events in the territories do not reach the public at all." He estimated that about one in ten events reached the public during the escalation of violence that was becoming "a real war"—one largely kept from the eyes of the American taxpayer who funds it, a further contribution to state terror.[35]

Also largely kept from those who pay the bill are the current proposals that the solution may after all lie in simply "transferring" the recalcitrant population of the occupied territories, a venerable idea now again entering center stage, with opponents often objecting, in mainstream commentary and debate, on grounds that it is unfeasible. By mid-1988, some 40 percent of Israeli Jews favored expulsion of the Arab population, while 45 percent regarded Israel as too democratic and 55 percent opposed granting equal rights to Israeli Arab citizens (contrary to much propaganda, deprivation of equal rights, such as access to most of the country's land, has always been severe). Much Zionist literature has long regarded the Palestinians as temporary visitors in the Land of Israel, perhaps recent immigrants drawn by Jewish rebuilding efforts; this has been a popular tale among American intellectuals as well. The rising ultra-orthodox religious groups, with a strong base in the United States, are hardly likely to object to the removal of people who are inferior to Jews in their essential nature; thus, in the words of the revered Rav Kook, Chief Ashkenazic Rabbi from 1921 to 1935, "the difference between the Israelite soul ... and the soul of all non-Jews, at any level, is greater and deeper than the difference between the soul of a human and the soul of an animal, for between the latter [two categories] there is only a quantitative difference but between the former two there is a qualitative one."[36]

Those who believe that even the transfer solution would not find acceptance in some North American quarters are seriously in error. Respected figures of the social democratic left in the U.S. have long ago explained that the indigenous inhabitants of the former Palestine are "marginal to the nation" so that their problems might be "smoothed" by "helping people to leave who have to leave." Not a whisper was heard, Alexander Cockburn noted, when the Republican Party platform of 1988 "went so far as demurely to encourage the notion of transfer" with the words: "More jobs and more opportunities in adjoining countries might draw the energies of more young people into building a world for themselves rather than destroying someone else's"[37]—by struggling for their rights against a harsh military regime endorsed and funded by the United States.

3. The Summits[38]

In preparation for the Reagan-Gorbachev meetings at the Washington summit of December 1987, the news was carefully shaped to ensure that only proper thoughts would reach the public. Excluded were the overwhelming votes at the United Nations opposing the escalated arms race advocated by the United States in virtual isolation, definitely not a useful message at the moment when all attention was to be focused on Reagan's achievements in bringing about world peace. It was not only world opinion that had to be scrupulously censored from the independent media. The domestic peace movement is no less unworthy. In a summary of media coverage, the monitoring organization FAIR observed that "only rightwing critics of the INF Treaty were considered newsworthy." A sharp critique of the Reagan administration for reckless nuclear deployment by Republican Senator Mark Hatfield was "blacked out of the national media," as was SANE/Freeze, America's largest peace group. Its press conference on the peace movement's role in laying the basis for the INF agreement was ignored, but another the same day called by the Anti-Appeasement Alliance, where Reagan was denounced as a "Kremlin idiot," "became a big news story." Secretary of State George Shultz's denunciation of the peace movement and his call for them "to admit that they were wrong" was reported, but, SANE/Freeze peace secretary Brigid Shea comments, "We aren't even given one inch to tell our side of the story." Soviet charges about U.S. attempts to undermine the ABM treaty in its pursuit of Star Wars were dismissed as "doctrinaire" and "hostile" in TV news reports, which offered a "summit wrap-up" featuring Richard Perle, criticizing the INF Treaty from the hard right, and the hawkish Democrat Sam Nunn playing dove (Tom Brokaw, NBC). As usual, there is a debate, but within proper limits.[39]

The official agenda for the summit included Reagan's role as a peacemaker and his passion for human rights. The task for the media, then, was to emphasize these two notable features of the president's achievements. Proper filtering enabled the first requirement to be satisfied. The second was met with no less aplomb. As Gorbachev stepped onto American soil at the Washington airport before the TV cameras, CBS anchorman Dan Rather commented that Gorbachev will focus on arms reduction, but "Reagan will press the Soviet Union on broader issues such as human rights, Afghanistan, and Nicaragua."[40] Few were so gauche as to raise questions about Reagan's stellar human rights record (in Central America, for example), though not everyone went as far as Dan Rather, often denounced for his "ultraliberalism," in interpreting what has happened to Nicaragua as a Soviet transgression.[41]

In a front-page news story in the *New York Times*, Philip Taubman observed from Moscow that despite his promise, Gorbachev still has a good deal to learn. He continues to "articulate the orthodox Soviet view of life in the United States: A ruling class, dominated by a military-industrial complex, controls the Government and exploits the vast majority of Americans, creating a society of economic inequity and injustice." This "ideologically slanted" view is inconsistent with the "more sophisticated outlook of Soviet analysts and senior colleagues who are familiar with the United States," and therefore understand how remote this conception is from reality. The same issue of the *Times* includes an article by Adam Walinsky entitled "What It's Like to Be in Hell," describing the reality of life in the Chicago slums in this society free from economic inequity, injustice, and exploitation.[42]

The Moscow summit in June 1988 received similar treatment. With rare exceptions, commentary ranged from admiration of Reagan's courageous defense of human rights (in the Soviet Union) to criticism of his weakness for caving in to the Russians and his curious conversion to Leninism. Reagan's meeting with Soviet dissidents was featured; he is a man who "believes very firmly in a few simple principles, and his missionary work for human rights and the American way taps into his most basic values," the *New York Times* reported. In his "finest oratorical hour," the editors added, his speech to Moscow students "extended the President's persistent, laudable expressions of concern for human rights," a concern revealed, perhaps, by his fervent admiration for the genocidal killers in the Guatemalan military command and his organization of state terror in El Salvador, not to speak of his gentle treatment of the poor at home.[43]

A press conference at the Church Center near the United Nations called by a Human Rights Coalition fared differently. The national media ignored the plea for attention to human rights violations in the United States and countries dependent on U.S. aid, presented by the legal director of the ACLU, representatives of the Center for Constitutional Rights, the American Indian Movement, prison rights groups, and others.[44]

Some elements of the foreign press were more reluctant to adopt Washington's agenda. The Toronto *Globe and Mail* editors observed that just as Reagan "felt it necessary to lecture the Soviet Union on human rights" at the summit, the *New York Times* published some of the "shocking revelations" on the torturers whom the U.S. arms and advises in Honduras and the CIA's preference for inhuman methods that leave no visible trace, though the *Times* story refrained from citing the BBC report six months earlier that U.S. personnel were present at the meeting where the U.S.-trained death squad Battalion 316 ordered that an American priest, Father James Carney, be killed by throwing him from a helicopter.[45] The U.S. role in Honduras and its "quiet go-ahead" for the "dirty war" in Argentina are "not a proud record of respect for human dignity and freedom," the *Globe and Mail* editors observed, selecting some of the lesser examples that illustrate the point.

Note that the *New York Times* was quite capable of publishing this account while—unlike its Canadian counterpart—it perceived no conflict here with Reagan's "laudable expressions of concern for human rights," in the Soviet bloc.

The *New Statesman* in London added that "any claim which the American President makes to moral superiority must be accounted the most macabre of hypocrisies," noting the support of this "tribune of human rights" for state terrorists in El Salvador and Guatemala and for the "bloody terrorist campaign" against defenseless civilians in Nicaragua. The editors also commented on the "obvious irony" of Reagan's presentation to Gorbachev of a video-cassette of the film *Friendly Persuasion*, the only film in Hollywood history to be released with no screenplay credit because the scriptwriter was blacklisted in the days when Reagan was president of the Screen Actors Guild-Allied Artists, kicking "subversives" out of the union during the McCarthy witchhunt and later assuring us that "there was no such thing as a Hollywood blacklist." "The western media played Reagan's themes [in Moscow] for all they were worth," the editors observe; "the western media know their place." They are right with regard to the United States, where one would have to search far to find a similar discordant note.[46]

4. The Media and International Opinion[47]

The U.N. votes at the time of the December 1987 Washington summit, and the treatment of them noted in the text, illustrate a more general pattern. In recent years, the United States has been far in the lead in vetoing Security Council resolutions. From 1967 through 1981, the United States vetoed seven resolutions condemning Israeli practices in southern Lebanon, affirming Palestinian rights, and deploring Israel's changing of the status of Jerusalem and its establishment of settlements in the occupied territories. Each time, the United States was alone in opposition. There were thirteen additional vetoes by the Reagan administration on similar issues, the U.S. standing alone.[48] The United States has also been alone or in a small minority in opposing or vetoing U.N. resolutions on South Africa, arms issues, and other matters.

These votes are often not reported or only marginally noted. The occasional reports are commonly of the kind one might find in a state-controlled press, as examples already cited illustrate. To mention another, in November 1988 the General Assembly voted 130 to 2 (the United States and Israel) for a resolution that "condemns" Israel for "killing and wounding defenseless Palestinians" in the suppression of the Palestinian uprising and "strongly deplores" its disregard for earlier Security Council resolutions condemning its actions in the occupied territories. This was reported in the *New York Times*. The first three paragraphs stated the basic facts. The rest of the article (ten paragraphs) was devoted to the U.S. and Israeli positions, to the abstainers, and to the "relatively poor showing" of the Arab states on earlier resolutions. From supporters of the resolution, all we hear is reservations of those who found it "unbalanced."[49]

The isolation of the United States has aroused some concern. In 1984, the *New York Times Magazine* devoted a major story to the topic by its U.N. correspondent Richard Bernstein.[50] He observes that "there are many voices" asking "in tones of skepticism and anguish" whether there is any value to the United Nations at all. "There is a growing sense," he continues, "that the United Nations has become repetitive, rhetorical, extremist and antidemocratic, a place where the United States is attacked with apparent impunity even by countries with which it maintains cordial bilateral relations." "There can be little doubt that, over the years, the United Nations has come to be dominated by what might be called a third-world ideology"—that is, by the views of the majority of its members—and that its attacks on the United States are "excessive and one-sided."

This judgment holds despite the annual U.N. condemnations of the Soviet Union in Afghanistan and the regular U.N. reports on its human rights violations there, and the Security Council vote condemning the Soviet downing of KAL 007 over Soviet territory. The downing by the U.S. Navy of an Iranian civilian plane over Iranian territorial waters with 290 lives lost elicited no such reaction, and the U.S. attack against South Vietnam, later all of Indochina, was neither condemned nor subjected to inquiry; in fact, Shirley Hazzard observes, "throughout these years, the war in Vietnam was never discussed in the United Nations."[51]

Continuing his review of the decline of the United Nations, Bernstein observes that both the Security Council and the General Assembly condemned the U.S. invasion of Grenada, including most NATO countries and other U.S. allies. Even the efforts of U.N. Ambassador Jeane Kirkpatrick, "perhaps the most dazzling intellect at the world body" (a comment that must have elicited a few chuckles there), have been unavailing in stemming the tide of "prefabricated jargon about racism, colonialism and fascism" and "ritualistic" attacks on the United States in place of the "reasoned debate" in the good old days when there was "an automatic majority" to support the U.S. positions. "The question," Bernstein concludes,

> is not why American policy has diverged from that of other member states, but why the world's most powerful democracy has failed to win support for its views among the participants in United Nations debates. The answer seems to lie in two underlying factors. The first and dominant one is the very structure and political culture that have evolved at the world body, tending in the process to isolate the United States and to portray it as a kind of ideological villain. The other factor is American failure to play the game of multilateral diplomacy with sufficient skill.

The question, in short, is why the world is out of step, and the answer plainly does not lie in the policies of the United States, which are praiseworthy as a matter of definition, so that argument to establish the point would be superfluous.

A different view was expressed by Senator William Fulbright in 1972, when he had become quite disaffected with U.S. policies: "Having controlled the United Nations for many years as tightly and as easily as a big-city boss controls his party machine," Fulbright remarked, "we had got used to the idea that the United Nations was a place where we could work our will." In his *History of the United Nations*, Evan Luard observes that:

> No doubt, if they had been in a majority, the communist states would have behaved in much the same way. The conduct of the West ... was none the less an abuse of power. And it was an abuse that those same [Western] members were to regret more than most when the balance of power changed again and a different majority assumed control of the organization,

leading to "rage, but not, as yet, regret," as Shirley Hazzard comments, reviewing Luard's study.[52]

Hazzard goes on to describe how, with the complicity of Secretary General Trygvie Lie, the United States undermined the creation of an "independent international civil service" at the U.N. that "would impartially provide exposure and propose correctives to maintain the precepts to which governments nominally subscribed at San Francisco" when the U.N. was founded. She is referring to the U.S. insistence that the FBI be permitted to conduct a "witchhunt" to control selection of staff, opening "the floodgates ... to political appointments" and hopelessly compromising the organization.

In her own study of "the Self-Destruction of the United Nations," Hazzard describes the witchhunt in detail, revealing how "the *majority* of the 'international' United Nations Secretariat work force" was made subject to FBI screening and approval in a secret agreement with the State Department for which the only apparent partial precedent was an edict of Mussolini's concerning the League of Nations Secretariat. This secret agreement was "a landmark in United Nations affairs and the ascertainable point at which the international Secretariat delivered itself conclusively, in its earliest years, into the hands of national interest ... in direct violation of the United Nations Charter." She observes that had a similar compact been discovered with the Soviet Union, "the international outcry would have been such as, in all probability, to bring down the United Nations itself"; in this case, exposure passed in silence, in accordance with the usual conventions. The U.N. submitted in fear of losing U.S. appropriations. "The United States concept of the 'international'," Hazzard concludes, "was—as it continues to be—at best a sort of benign unilateralism through which American policies would work uncontested for everybody's benefit."[53]

This judgment explains the attitude of articulate U.S. opinion and the media towards the U.N. over the years. When the U.N. was a docile instrument of the United States, there was much indignation over Soviet negativism while distinguished social scientists reflected upon its sources in Russian culture and child-rearing practices. As the organization fell under "the tyranny of the majority"—otherwise called "democracy"—attitudes shifted to the current "skepticism and anguish," with equally profound musings on the cultural failings of the benighted majority.

The same attitudes are expressed towards other international organizations. When Latin American delegates, at a meeting of the Organization of American States, refused to bend to the U.S. will over the ham-handed efforts of the Reaganites to unseat General Noriega in Panama after he had outlived his usefulness, *Times* correspondent Elaine Sciolino observed sadly that "over the years, the O.A.S. has lost much of its authority as the conscience of Latin America" (Feb. 29, 1988)—in translation, it no longer follows U.S. orders.

Throughout, it is presupposed, beyond question, that what the United States does and stands for is right and good; if others fail to recognize this moral rectitude, plainly they are at fault. The naiveté is not without a certain childlike appeal—which quickly fades, however, when we recognize how it is converted into an instrument for inflicting suffering and pain.

As the world's richest and most powerful state, the United States continues to wield the lash. The *Times* reports that the O.A.S. "is likely to suspend its aid program for the rest of the year because of the worst financial crisis in its history." Half of the $20 million shortfall for 1988 results from a cut in the U.S. contribution; two-thirds of the $46 million in outstanding dues is owed by the United States, as of November 1988. "It's so serious that the essence of the organization is in danger," the Secretary General stated. O.A.S. officials warn that the fiscal crisis will cause curtailment of all development programs, adding that "the dispute grows out of sharply conflicting visions of the organization's role in the hemisphere," with the United States opposed to development programs that are favored by their beneficiaries. The drug program too "will be inoperative by the end of the year," the head of the Inter-American Drug Abuse Control Commission of the O.A.S. reported, while the Reagan administration lambasted the Latin American countries for their failure to control the flow of drugs to the United States. The U.S. cuts came against the background of criticism of the O.A.S. by administration officials and some members of Congress "for declining to take a more aggressive role against Nicaragua" and General Noriega.[54] A congressman explains that "we were not satisfied that we were getting a dollar's worth of performance for the American taxpayer." Reagan administration bully-boy tactics actually succeeded in creating hemisphere-wide support for the much-despised Noriega, in annoyance over blatant U.S. interventionism after the sudden turn against him.

The United Nations is facing the same problems now that it no longer has the wit to function as an organ of U.S. power. The United States is by far the largest debtor, owing $412 million as of September 1987; the next largest debtor was Brazil, owing $16 million. The Soviet Union had by then announced that it would pay all of its outstanding debts. In earlier years, when the U.S.S.R. was the culprit, the United States had backed a request to the World Court for a ruling on debt payment and had endorsed the Court ruling that all members must pay their debts. But now the grounds have shifted, and debt payment is no longer a solemn obligation. Unreported is the fact that according to the U.S. mission at the United Nations, the U.N. operation "funnels $400 million to $700 million per year into the U.S. and New York economies."[55]

The institutions of world order do not fare well in the media in other cases as well, when they serve unwanted ends. Efforts to resolve border tensions provide one striking illustration. These are rarely reported when the agent is an enemy state, particularly a victim of U.S. attack. Nicaraguan proposals for border monitoring are a case in point. To cite one additional example, in March 1988, during the Nicaraguan strike against the contras that apparently spilled a few kilometers into contra-held areas of Honduras, there was much indignant commentary about Sandinista aggression and their threat to peaceful Honduras. Nicaragua requested that a U.N. observer force monitor the Nicaragua-Honduras border—which would have put to rest these fears, had they been serious in the first place. Honduras rejected Nicaragua's call for U.N. observers, the U.N. spokesman told reporters. Nicaragua also asked the International Court of Justice to inquire into alleged Honduran armed incursions. There appears to have been no mention of these facts in the *New York Times*, which preferred to report that three months earlier Honduran Foreign Minister Carlos López Contreras had proposed monitoring of the border.[56]

5. Demolishing the Accords[57]

Given the policies it advocates in the Third World, the United States often finds itself politically weak though militarily strong, as commonly conceded on all sides in internal documents. The result is regular opposition to diplomacy and political settlement. Since the facts do not conform to the required image, considerable talent in historical engineering is required.[58] The problem has been a persistent one during the Central American conflicts of recent years.

The United States systematically blocked all efforts to use peaceful means to resolve what *Times* correspondent Shirley Christian calls "*our* Nicaraguan agony," describing our suffering in the course of our "basically idealistic efforts to deal with the situation," in which, "on balance, we may have had the best intentions of all the players."[59] The United States succeeded in blocking the Contadora initiatives, eliminating any recourse to the World Court and United Nations as required by international law and the supreme law of the land, and evading repeated Nicaraguan efforts to satisfy legitimate interests of the Central American countries—even the alleged U.S. security concerns, ludicrous as they are. The U.S. attempted to block the Arias proposals in 1987, succeeding through July with the cooperation of Salvadoran president Duarte. (See chapter 5.)

The Reagan-Wright proposals of August 5 were a final effort to sabotage any meaningful agreement that might result from the planned meeting of Central American presidents the next day. But this proved "an incredible tactical error," a Guatemalan diplomat observed, arousing "the nationalistic instincts of the Costa Rican and Guatemalan delegations," which felt "insulted" by these strong-arm methods.[60] On August 7, to the dismay of the U.S. administration, the Central American presidents agreed on the Esquipulas II Accord, "inspired by the visionary and permanent desire of the Contadora and the [Latin American] Support Groups."[61]

The unexpected August 7 agreement compelled the media to backtrack quickly from their advocacy of the Reagan-Wright plan as a forthcoming gesture for peace. On August 6, James LeMoyne had reported falsely that apart from Nicaragua, which risked isolation for its intransigence, the Central American presidents "were gratified" by the Reagan-Wright proposal—which Guatemala and Costa Rica dismissed with considerable irritation as an "insult." A day later, Washington now being isolated by the peace agreement of the Central American presidents, LeMoyne presented their accord as sharing "the central intent of Mr. Reagan's plan, which is to demand internal political changes in Nicaragua"; the Esquipulas Accord made no mention of Nicaragua, but was rather designed to apply simultaneously and comparably to all the Central American countries. The media proceeded to construct an interpretation which gave the United States the credit for having driven Nicaragua to negotiations by the use of force and the Reagan-Wright initiative. The purpose, apart from serving to conceal the consistent U.S. opposition to a peaceful settlement, was to legitimate state violence and thus prepare the ground for its renewal when needed, here or elsewhere.[62]

Some were unable to conceal their dismay with the developments. Former *New York Times* executive editor A.M. Rosenthal, whose regular columns since his retirement provide much insight into the thinking that animated the *Times* during his tenure, denounced "the pro-Sandinistas in press and politics"—a group that one might detect with a sufficiently powerful microscope—for their failure to stand by the Reagan-Wright plan after the Esquipulas Accord was signed. He assured the reader that the Central American presidents were "astonished" by this failure to pursue the proposal, which in Rosenthal's world they welcomed, while in the real world they had rejected it with contempt. Opponents of the Reagan-Wright plan, he wrote, are helping to kill "the peace proposals for Nicaragua"—that is, the Reagan-Wright plan, which, unlike the Esquipulas Accord, applied only to Nicaragua and therefore alone qualifies as a peace proposal for an American jingoist. Extolling the reliance on violence, Rosenthal wrote that "Secretary Shultz and Howard Baker, believing that the Sandinistas had been hurt severely enough to make negotiations feasible, got the President to agree." But now "the pro-Sandinistas in this country" are undercutting the Shultz-Baker achievements by advocacy of the Esquipulas Accord, and even "acted as if it were a damnable sin to suggest that the United States should not immediately destroy the contras, whose existence brought about the opportunity for negotiations."[63]

Most, however, preferred less crude means to convert the peace agreement to the basic structure of the Reagan-Wright plan. The Esquipulas Accord set in motion a U.S. government campaign to dismantle it and maintain the option of further attacks against Nicaragua accompanied with such state terror as might be required to keep the "fledgling democracies" in line. The enthusiastic cooperation of the media ensured the success of this endeavor. The desired result was achieved by January 1988, in a brilliantly executed government-media operation.

As discussed in chapter 4, the first task was to eliminate the provisions applying to the United States, namely, the one "indispensable element" for peace: the termination of any form of aid for indigenous guerrillas or the contras. U.S. aid for the contras attacking Nicaragua from Honduras and Costa Rica was already criminal, even in the technical legal sense, but the Esquipulas Accord raised a new barrier. By August 1987, supply flights to the contras had reached a level of one a day, in addition to the constant surveillance required to assure that barely defended targets can be safely attacked. The U.S. responded to the call for termination of such aid by escalating it. Supply flights doubled in September and virtually tripled in the following months. In late August, the CIA attempted to bribe Miskito leaders to reject Nicaraguan attempts at peaceful reconciliation and continue the war.[64]

These flagrant violations of the "indispensable element" for peace undermined the basis for the Esquipulas Accord. To assess the role of the media, we therefore ask how they dealt with these crucial facts. I will continue to keep largely to the *New York Times*, the most important newspaper and the one that provides the quasi-official record for history; the pattern elsewhere is generally similar.[65]

I was unable to find a single phrase in the *Times* referring to the bribes, the rapid U.S. escalation of supply and surveillance flights, or their success in escalating terrorist attacks against civilians.

The Esquipulas Accord designated the three-month period from August 7 to early November for initial steps to realize its terms, and the period from August 7 to mid-January as the first phase, after which the International Verification and Monitoring Commission (CIVS) was to present its report on what had been achieved. During the first three-month period, *Times* Nicaragua correspondent Stephen Kinzer had forty-one articles dealing with Nicaragua. The crucial events just described were omitted entirely. In fact, there were only two references even to the existence of supply and surveillance flights.[66] On September 23, Kinzer mentioned that "Thousands of contras inside Nicaragua now receive their supplies principally from clandestine airdrops run by the Central Intelligence Agency." On October 15, he wrote that "Planes that fly into Nicaragua at night to drop supplies to contras take off from Honduras." In later months, there are a few scattered references to these flights.[67]

In short, we find total suppression of the most critical facts concerning the fate of the accords, not to speak of the flagrant violation of international law and the dramatic proof of the artificial character of the implanted proxy army—a conclusion never drawn, as far as I can determine. The record provides impressive evidence of the dedication of the media to state propaganda and violence.

The *Times* was not content with evasion of the supply and surveillance operations and total suppression of the escalation of U.S. aid to its forces in an effort to undermine the Esquipulas Accord. It also resorted to outright falsification. In mid-November, President Ortega attended an OAS meeting in Washington, to which the U.S. brought its CIA-funded contra civilian directorate, much to the annoyance of the Latin American delegates. Ortega denounced the sharp increase in supply flights after they had been banned by the Accord, reporting 140 supply flights from August. Contra leader Adolfo Calero dismissed this estimate as far too low, stating that "his radar is not working very well." The *New York Times* reported the statements by Ortega and Calero, but with an editorial adjustment. Where they spoke of supply flights, the *Times* news report downgraded the reference to "surveillance flights," still a violation of international law and the Accord, but a less serious one, thus apparently less unacceptable.[68]

A few days later, Nicaragua's U.N. Ambassador Nora Astorga reported 275 supply and surveillance flights detected from August 7 to November 3. I found no notice in the press of this not entirely trivial allegation.[69]

By such means, the media succeeded in serving Washington's goal of eliminating two central provisions of the Accord: "Aid halt to irregular forces or insurrectionist movements," and "Non-use of territory to attack other states." With this implicit revision of the Accord, the United States was now free to act as it wished, with the endorsement of President Arias, according to the *Times* version, at least.[70]

The Esquipulas Accord called for "an authentic pluralistic and participatory democratic process to promote social justice, respect for human rights, sovereignty, the territorial integrity of states and the right of each nation to determine, freely and without any kind of external interference, its own economic, political and social model," as well as steps to ensure "justice, freedom and democracy," freedom of expression and political action, and opening of the communication media "for all ideological groups." They also called for "dialogue with all unarmed political opposition groups within the country" and other steps to achieve national reconciliation. Furthermore, "amnesty decrees will be issued setting out the steps to guarantee the inviolability of all forms of life and liberty, material goods and the safety of the people to benefit from said decrees."

El Salvador violated the amnesty condition at once by decreeing an amnesty that freed the state security services and their associates from the unlikely prospect of prosecution for their crimes. Human rights monitors denounced the step, predicting—accurately, as it turned out—that it would lead to an increase in state terror. The *Times,* however, lauded the amnesty. With regard to Nicaragua, the Washington-media interpretation was that the amnesty must apply far more broadly than the Accord specifies. We return to these matters.

The required steps towards democracy, social justice, safeguarding of human rights, and so on, plainly could not be enacted in Washington's terror states.[71] Therefore, the provisions had to be eliminated from the operative version of the Accord. The method pursued was, again, to suppress the facts and praise the terror states for their adherence to the accords that they were increasingly violating.

In September, the Inter-American Commission on Human Rights of the O.A.S. issued a report noting a "perceptible decline in the observance of human rights" in Guatemala, expressing concern over "the resumption of methods and systems for eliminating persons in mass and the reappearance of the dreadful death squads." The Costa Rican-based Commission for the Defense of Human Rights in Central America reported to the U.N. in November on the continuing terror by the Guatemalan security services and death squads, documenting some 175 cases of abductions, disappearances, and assassinations from August 8 to November 17, 1987, in addition to grenade attacks, a bomb thrown into a church, etc. The Guatemalan Human Rights Commission had recorded 334 extrajudicial executions and 73 disappearances in the first nine months of 1987. One of its directors reported in Washington that "the accords are being used as a smoke screen and the human rights situation is becoming much graver … [The accords have served] to allow violations with much more impunity." He added that the documented cases represent only a fraction of the abuses because most take place outside of the capital, citing also other government atrocities. The military also launched a new offensive in the mountains to try to drive the survivors of the near-genocidal campaigns of the early 1980s into "Development Pole villages" where they can be controlled by force.[72]

American readers were spared such facts. "During the first six months after the signing of the accords," Latin Americanist Susanne Jonas observes, "not one article on Guatemalan compliance appeared in the New York Times, and virtually none were printed in other major U.S. media." In a review of the *Times, Christian Science Monitor, Miami Herald,* and *Wall Street Journal* from October 1987 to March 1988, Alexander Cockburn found little comment on Guatemala at all, and no mention at all of the rising tide of political violence through November. As atrocities mounted further in December and January, there were two stories on Guatemala in the journals reviewed, both in the *Monitor,* both discussing rights abuses. The totals for October through January are over 500 dead and 160 disappeared, and two news stories. Combining the record of all papers reviewed over the entire period, Cockburn observes, "there is one critical story every 154 days on Guatemala in the US's most influential newspapers."[73]

In El Salvador, Tutela Legal, the human rights monitoring office of the Archdiocese of San Salvador, reported that recorded death squad killings doubled to about ten a month immediately after the accords, continuing through January; for the year, Tutela Legal's figures were 88 disappeared and 96 killed by death squads, the armed forces and civil defense, in addition to 280 killed, most presumed to be civilians, during army military operations.[74] Amadeo Ramos, one of the founders of the Indian Association ANIS, reported that an Indian settlement was bombed by the army and "the bodies of several Indians were found in a remote area thrown in a ditch" in mid-November; not being Miskitos in Nicaragua, their fate was of no interest. There were many other dramatic cases, ignored or barely mentioned. The Council on Hemispheric Affairs estimated eighty-seven civilians killed or "disappeared" by death squads during the August-January phase of the accords. Chris Norton, one of the few U.S. journalists based in El Salvador, reported abroad that the real numbers are unknown because, as in Guatemala, most death squad killings "have taken place in rural areas and few of them have been reported."[75]

Protection of the client regime of El Salvador is a particular imperative, reaching impressive levels. The fate of the Human Rights Commission CDHES is illustrative. The murder of its president, Herbert Anaya, was reported by James LeMoyne, with due respect for the official government story that the guerrillas were responsible. Omitted from his account was testimony to the contrary by his widow Mirna Anaya and others. Mirna Anaya, a Salvadoran judge until 1987, fled the country after her husband's assassination. Her statement that the security forces were responsible and that witnesses will so testify if granted protection was available to a Canadian audience, but *New York Times* readers were again spared such unpleasant facts, or her speech before the Human Rights Assembly of the United Nations identifying a death squad of "members of the hacienda police and National Police" as the assassins.[76]

It is of little moment that a former CDHES president, Marianela Garcia Villas, had been killed by security forces on the pretext that she was a guerrilla, while other members had been murdered or "disappeared" by the security forces. Herbert Anaya had been arrested and tortured by the Treasury police in May 1986, along with other Commission members. While in prison, they continued their work, compiling sworn testimony of torture by prisoners. They succeeded in smuggling out of the prison a document with detailed evidence on the torture of 430 prisoners along with a videotape of testimony. But this was evidence about torture by U.S. agents and clients (and a U.S. military officer in uniform, in one case), not about Cuban or Russian prisons. Hence these revelations aroused no interest, and nothing appeared in the national media (see appendix I, section 1). After Anaya was released in a prisoner exchange, he was denounced by the government and informed that he headed a list of Commission workers to be killed. Lacking the protection that might have been afforded by some media visibility, he was assassinated, probably by the security forces or their affiliates, as indicated by Archbishop Rivera y Damas in a homily at the Metropolitan Cathedral, unreported in the *Times,* in which he cited information that "a death squad was responsible."[77]

Systematically avoiding the undesirable facts about El Salvador, James LeMoyne assured his readers at the end of November that President Duarte "has gone considerably further [than the Sandinistas] in carrying out the letter of the treaty" though perhaps he too is not "particularly committed to its spirit of reconciliation," since he "is trying to split the leftist rebel alliance"—nothing more. LeMoyne also praised Duarte for having given the rebels "free access to the press"; the Council on Hemispheric Affairs, in contrast, reports that "journalists practice self-censorship to such an extent that papers will not print statements by opposition groups critical of the government."[78]

LeMoyne was also impressed with Duarte's having "permitted rebel civilian leaders to come home and actively pursue their political vision," asking whether "like the rebels in El Salvador, the contras may eventually ... take the risk of sending some representatives back to Nicaragua to test the Sandinistas' promise to offer genuine political freedom after eight years of single-party rule"—though there is reason to "doubt their sincerity" and willingness to "tolerate some political opposition."[79] LeMoyne is well aware that respected church leaders and intellectuals who have no connection with guerrilla movements have been forced to flee El Salvador and are unable to return for fear of assassination, while in Nicaragua the opposition have never faced anything remotely comparable to the terror of Duarte's security forces and their associates, and quite openly support the U.S. forces attacking the country, regularly identifying with them in public statements in *La Prensa*, publicly denouncing the government, and implicitly calling for further military aid to the contras when visiting Washington.[80]

As LeMoyne also knows full well, not only the pro-contra internal opposition, but even contra military leaders who decide to return to Nicaragua live and work there without concern for their lives. To cite only one of several cases, contra leader Fernando Chamorro returned to Nicaragua from Costa Rica and was named regional president of the Conservative Party, which openly supports the contras.[81] Consider in contrast Col. Adolfo Majano, not a guerrilla leader but the army officer who led the reformist military coup in October 1979 and was described by the U.S. press as "the symbol of American policy in this country" because of his efforts to move towards democracy and reform.[82] Majano was marginalized as the traditional repressive forces took over with U.S. government backing, and was removed from the junta in December 1980, when Duarte became president to preside over the slaughter then intensifying. He was forced to flee the mounting terror, returning after seven years in exile to test the "new democracy." Upon returning, he survived at least two assassination attempts by suspected death squads. A third occurred on August 25, 1988, when his car came under fire from two gunmen in a San Salvador shopping center and two bodyguards were killed. "This criminal attempt was aimed at myself and there is no doubt that it was carried out by the death squads," Majano said. The Archbishop agreed, stating in the Sunday mass three days later that the killings had been carried out by "the sinister death squads."[83] The assassination attempt took place immediately after a series of murders by security forces and presumed death squads. One suspects that similar events in Managua might have made the *New York Times*. Instead, we find philosophical reflections on the freedom and openness of El Salvador as compared with the brutal repression under the Sandinistas.

LeMoyne's zeal in applauding the encouraging developments in El Salvador as contrasted with repressive Nicaragua was sometimes excessive even by *Times* standards. Thus he reported the plans of the "rebel civilian officials" Rubén Zamora and Guillermo Ungo to return to El Salvador, where they hoped to survive by wearing bullet-proof vests, constantly changing residence, and carefully restricting their movements. "The two men's planned return," LeMoyne stated, "is in sharp contrast to the situation in neighboring Nicaragua, where the ruling Sandinistas have said they will jail any rebel leader who tries to return to carry out political activities." Five days earlier, Stephen Kinzer had reported President Ortega's statement that "any contras who stop fighting," including contra leader Adolfo Calero and military commander Enrique Bermúdez, "would be allowed to participate fully in Nicaraguan political life." He quoted Ortega as saying:

> A cease-fire is the immediate objective, but if the contras accept it, they can join political dialogue with other parties in Nicaragua. If Calero and Bermúdez accept this, they will be free to walk the streets of Managua, hold demonstrations and join the conservative party or whichever party they choose. No one will have to sign anything. By disarming, they will automatically receive amnesty.[84]

Unreported are the facts about Fernando Chamorro, Adolfo Majano, Horacio Arce, and others, or the Salvadoran government reaction when guerrilla commander Mario Aguiñada Carranza announced his intention to return to the country to take part in its political life. The government announced that it would bar his entry, and the army added that he would be captured and tried in the courts for his crimes.[85] The situation in the two countries is precisely the opposite of what LeMoyne conveys, as he can hardly fail to know.

Comparison of Zamora and Ungo with Bermúdez and Calero is a bit odd to begin with. Both Zamora (a left Christian Democrat[86]) and Ungo (a social democrat who shared the 1972 ticket with Duarte) fled from El Salvador in fear for their lives as their associates and relatives were assassinated. Among the victims was Rubén Zamora's brother, the Christian Democrat Attorney-General Mario Zamora. Two weeks after his associate was assassinated by a death squad, Duarte joined the junta, where he proceeded to legitimize the slaughter. Zamora and Ungo have maintained a political association with the Salvadoran guerrillas, most of whom were also driven to the hills by state terror. In contrast, Bermúdez is the contra military commander, formerly an officer of Somoza's National Guard; and Calero, at the right wing of the CIA-run "civilian directorate," is an avowed advocate of terror who had been excluded from visiting Costa Rica on these grounds. Furthermore, there is no comparison between the indigenous guerrillas in El Salvador and the U.S. proxy forces attacking Nicaragua. A closer comparison to Zamora and Ungo would be the internal opposition in Nicaragua, who have always been free to take part in political life if they choose, and face harassment but not state terror of the Washington-Duarte style. No hint of these truisms will be found in the *Times,* or, to my knowledge, elsewhere in the mainstream, with the rarest of exceptions.

The official story throughout has been that Duarte represents the "moderate center," unable to control the "violence by both ultra-rightists and by the Marxist guerrillas" (James LeMoyne); an accompanying photo shows New York Mayor Edward Koch being greeted by Duarte's Defense Minister, General Vides Casanova, who presided over much of the slaughter. A *Times* editorial noted the Anaya assassination—as a proof of Duarte's "courage" in "defying" the death squads. Buried in a news story, the same day, is the fact that the killers were using sophisticated weapons available only to the "right-wing death squads"—that is, the assassination squads of Duarte's security forces.[87]

Honduras made virtually no pretense of observing the Esquipulas Accord. The human rights violations that had become a serious problem as the United States converted it into a military base in the 1980s increased further after the Accord was signed. Ramón Custodio, president of the Commission for Defense of Human Rights in Central America and the Honduran Human Rights Commission (CODEH), reported in late October 1987 that killings by the security forces are becoming "more blatant," citing examples. As the first three-month period of the Accord passed, he stated at an international news conference that the worsening human rights situation deteriorated further in Honduras after the Accord was signed, and in El Salvador and Guatemala as well. These and other reports on growing human rights violations after the signing of the Accord were published in Canada and Mexico, but omitted from the *Times* through the August-January period.[88]

CODEH reported 263 judicial executions in Honduras in 1987, 144 more than in 1986, attributing 107 to the security forces, along with an increase in torture and illegal arrests. Honduran journalist Manuel Torres Calderón reported that economic decline in this U.S. dependency had "forced the state to intervene in the economy even more heavily than its much maligned neighbor, Nicaragua." Capital flight had reached such a level that "money leaves the country as fast as it comes in," a Honduran banker observed. Half the population has no access to health services and more than a million Hondurans live in overcrowded shantytowns, despite extensive U.S. aid and no guerrilla threat or foreign attack. Neither the increasing human rights violations nor the impact of U.S.-influenced economic management were on the media agenda.[89]

Also largely off the agenda is the hostility towards the contras in Honduras, not only among the thousands of peasants expelled from their homes in "contraland" in the south. Wire services reported that the conservative newspaper *La Prensa*, "which publishes several contra-inspired pages of information on Nicaragua, said an opinion poll carried out before the latest [March 1988] crisis erupted showed that 88.5 percent of Hondurans wanted the contras expelled." Such facts received little notice. Similarly, the media have been unable to discover the protest of the National Union of Campesinos in Honduras over contra recruitment among impoverished Honduran peasants with bribes of $500, an enormous sum by their standards, published in the major Honduran daily *El Tiempo*. Such facts, though plainly important and newsworthy, must be suppressed, because they are not conducive to the portrayal of the sturdy peasants of Nicaragua organizing to resist Sandinista depredations.[90]

Growing Honduran concerns over loss of national independence and integrity under U.S. influence have also not been a popular topic. As discussed earlier, the March 1988 Nicaraguan operations against the contras elicited irate denunciations of Sandinista aggressiveness and threat to Honduras in the U.S. media and Congress; also a bipartisan proposal for $48 million in aid, including arms, to the beleaguered freedom fighters so unfairly attacked. When the United States sent an airlift to "defend Honduras" against Sandinista aggression, there was much jingoist fanfare at home, and a reaction in Honduras that received somewhat less attention. Honduran journalists condemned the U.S. "invasion." *El Tiempo* denounced the government call for—or acquiescence in—the dispatch of U.S. troops as "not only illegal but shameful. It is telling the world that the state of Honduras does not exist." The journal described the U.S. troops as an "occupation force," while the Christian Democratic Party "said that the U.S. soldiers should fly home immediately" and its leader Rubén Palma "told reporters that Honduran President José Azcona had acted illegally in calling in foreign troops without parliament's authorization."[91]

One could learn little about such matters from the *New York Times*,[92] and not much elsewhere. Media reporting that departed from the U.S. government agenda would have allayed the widespread shock when Hondurans attacked the U.S. Embassy a few weeks later while police stood by, in an explosion of anti-U.S. sentiment.

Apart from the barriers to U.S. terror, overcome with media complicity as discussed earlier, two central features of the Esquipulas Accord were intolerable to Washington: the role given to international monitors, the CIVS, and the "symmetry" condition on which the agreements were based, requiring steps in parallel by all Central American countries. The former condition was unacceptable because it interferes with the U.S. ability to violate the Accord as it wishes; the latter, for the same reason, and because Washington's terror states cannot possibly live up to the provisions on democratization and human rights. The task of the media, then, was to eliminate these two unwanted principles. The agreement as revised by Washington must be focused solely on Nicaragua, with the international monitors dismissed. By these means, the unwanted Esquipulas Accord could be brought into line with the Reagan-Wright plan rejected by the Central American presidents in August.

The problem of international monitoring became serious in January 1988, when the CIVS was to present its findings to the Central American presidents after studying the five countries. Plainly, this was the central diplomatic event of the month; equally plainly, it was unacceptable, particularly when the Commission presented its conclusions. The CIVS singled out the United States for condemnation because of its continued assistance "to the irregular forces operating against the government of Nicaragua," thus violating "an indispensable requirement for the success of the peace efforts and of this Procedure as a whole." A CIVS official informed the press that Latin American representatives were "shocked by the attitudes of patent fear" expressed by trade unionists and opposition figures in El Salvador and Guatemala. He added that the CIVS could not provide details about compliance because of objections from Honduras, El Salvador and Guatemala—a clear indication of what the report would have said, had it not been blocked by the United States and its clients. The report praised Nicaragua's "concrete steps" towards democratization despite the difficulties it faced.

The facts were reported by several journals, but eliminated from the *New York Times*, where James LeMoyne, in a dispatch focusing on denunciations of Nicaragua, dismissed the CIVS report in one sentence, stating only that its meeting ended "with little agreement" (the report was adopted unanimously). The condemnation of the United States was briefly noted in an article on another topic nine days later by Stephen Kinzer, who added that "the commission fell out of favor in some circles when it reported that Nicaragua had taken 'concrete steps toward the beginning of a democratic process' "; like the O.A.S., the CIVS had thus "lost much of its authority as the conscience of Latin America."[93]

The Commission was disbanded under U.S. pressure, enabling the United States to pursue its terrorist exercises unhampered and permitting Duarte to continue to serve as a front man for repression and murder.

The "symmetry" problem was overcome by focusing virtually all coverage on Nicaragua, along with the constant pretense that whatever may appear in the text of the Esquipulas Accord, "there is no doubt that [the treaty's] main provisions are principally directed at Nicaragua and will affect Nicaragua more than any of the other nations that signed the accord" (James LeMoyne). That is quite true under the conditions dictated by Washington and observed by the press, though the conclusion has no basis in the text. As LeMoyne explained further, the Sandinistas are "in a somewhat exposed position" because they, and they alone, "are under close scrutiny for their efforts to carry out the Central American peace treaty."[94] Again true, on the tacit assumption that the Free Press must follow the marching orders that issue from Washington. His colleague Stephen Kinzer offered the same analysis, as did the media fairly generally.

The Media Alliance in San Francisco studied press samples during two periods of peak coverage of the peace plan (August 5 through September 15, 1987; January 5 through February 7, 1988). The *New York Times* devoted ten times as many stories to Nicaragua as to all the other countries combined in the first period, and eleven times as many in the second. Other media sampled had similar proportions.[95] Efforts to gain mainstream coverage for these reports failed.

The quality of coverage also differed radically. Thus a rock-throwing incident in Nicaragua on January 23 received front-page coverage in the *Washington Post* and prominent attention elsewhere, with the *Times* warning that the incident would "strengthen the argument" of the Reagan administration that Nicaragua is not complying with the peace plan. Similarly, extensive coverage was given to the January 16 detention of four members of the Nicaraguan opposition who had met with contras and the January 19 arrest of five opposition members, all released unharmed after several hours of questioning (in the *Times*, nineteen paragraphs and a headline across the page in the first case, and a front-page above-the-fold story in the second); months later, Roy Gutman, referring to this incident, observed in the *Washington Post* that "No government ordinarily allows a legal political party to negotiate a joint program with armed forces seeking the overthrow of that government." In contrast, the murder in Honduras of a human rights leader and a Christian Democratic Party leader on January 15 received 160 words in an un-headlined story, and no conclusions were drawn about compliance with the Accord. The disruption of a "Mothers of Political Prisoners" gathering by civilian Sandinista supporters warranted a major *Times* story and photo on January 23; the disruption of a "Mothers of Political Prisoners and the Disappeared" march by the Salvadoran riot police on December 21 was ignored.[96] The examples are typical, and again readily explained in terms of a propaganda model.

The readers of the Toronto *Globe and Mail* and the wire services could learn that in a one-week period in January, while compliance with the Accord was front-page news, ten people were found murdered in El Salvador in death squad style with signs of torture, including two women who had been hanged from a tree by their hair with their breasts cut off and their faces painted red. Later in the month, there were more killings, with the tortured bodies found in a traditional death squad dump. Foreign diplomats and Church leaders blamed the Salvadoran armed forces. Auxiliary Archbishop Rosa Chávez stated in his February 7 homily that "According to information compiled by our office [Tutela Legal], the captors [of two tortured and murdered laborers] were men in plain clothes and uniformed soldiers of the 1st Artillery Brigade's counter-insurgency section" (an elite U.S.-trained unit).[97] The readers of the *New York Times* were spared these facts, just as the *Times* had no interest in a televised mass on January 3 in which Archbishop Rivera y Damas once again denounced "the practice of torture used against many

Salvadorans by the death squads," stating that bishops in several provinces reported increased death squad murders and calling for an end to assassinations and torture.[98]

A few weeks later, as Duarte's security services and their associates extended their grim work while the *Times* obligingly looked the other way, the House of Representatives passed a resolution commending El Salvador's progress towards democracy. The proposed resolution stated that El Salvador has achieved a system "which respects human liberties," but liberal representative Ted Weiss of New York succeeded in having it changed to say only that the country has "sought to" establish such a system. "Give them a little credit for trying, Ted," said House Foreign Affairs Committee Chairman Dante Fascell. In December, as the terror was mounting after the signing of the Esquipulas Accord, the House of Representatives had overwhelmingly passed an amendment specifying a long list of "Actions Which Should Be Undertaken" to satisfy the high ideals of Congress—in Nicaragua. Representative Weiss sought to introduce a few changes, applying the conditions to "all countries in Central America" instead of only Nicaragua. This proposal was rejected by a large majority. Congress and the media share the same agenda.[99]

In subsequent months, state terror in El Salvador escalated, rarely reported. James LeMoyne was much exercised over *guerrilla* terror, devoting stories to the topic with such headlines as "Salvador Rebels Kill 12 in Raid on Town," "Guerrillas in Salvador Step Up Pre-election Terrorism," and "Salvador Rebels Target Civilians, Killing 3," repeatedly referring to the same alleged atrocities.[100] Terror by U.S. clients does not pass entirely unnoticed. Thus, he concludes one story with the words: "Such rebel violence has been reflected in a rise in political killings," its source unnamed. In a "review of the week" column, he describes a guerrilla shift to "terrorist tactics," then adds that "increasingly, the guerrillas and their sympathizers are also the targets of violence." Another report focuses on guerrilla terror, noting also that "the army appears to be returning to killing suspected leftists as an answer to sharply stepped-up guerrilla assassinations, bombings and other attacks."[101] The message is that the U.S.-installed government may not be perfect, but its deficiencies are a response to guerrilla atrocities. Readers familiar with such journalistic practice can try to read between the lines, and may surmise that the government is perhaps not judiciously observing its commitment to human rights under the accords. But they will learn little about the matter from this source. They may to turn to the foreign press to read, in the mainstream, that Europeans "want to see progress towards civilised politics not just in Nicaragua and Costa Rica, but also in Guatemala, Honduras and El Salvador, which lamentably continue to be by-words for barbarity."[102]

We should again observe that these devices to conceal atrocities provide a shield behind which the state terrorists can continue their work. The contribution of disciplined journalists to murder, torture, and general misery is not small.

The media campaign, only barely sampled here,[103] succeeded in demolishing what remained of the Esquipulas Accord by January. With the CIVS abolished under U.S. pressure, Ortega agreed to go far beyond the terms of the forgotten accords, abandoning the simulta-neity condition entirely. The "genius of the Arias plan," the *Times* editors explained, "is that it provides a means for Nicaragua to accommodate to neighbors without appearing to truckle to Washing-ton," not the simultaneity requirement that was recognized to be the "genius" of the plan when it was signed.[104] They may well be correct about what Arias had in mind, to judge by the references and quotes; but if so, that would simply show that he had no more interest in the implementation of the Esquipulas Accord than the *New York Times*.

Recognizing that the powerful make the rules, Ortega agreed that Nicaragua alone would enact the provisions of the accords, even calling for an international commission, including members of both U.S. political parties, to monitor Nicaragua's adherence alone.[105] The media reported that Ortega now promises to "comply with" the accords—that is, the version fashioned in Washington, which bears little resemblance to the text—while warning that his promises plainly cannot be trusted. No one else's promises were relevant, now that the accords had been consigned to oblivion. Citing unnamed "officials," LeMoyne portrayed Nicaragua as the villain of the piece, "the country most widely accused of bad faith," now "pressed to the wall by the other four Central American leaders" to implement the peace treaty. Readers could again turn to the foreign press to read that "Nicaragua has done more to comply with the terms of the Central American peace plan than any of the other five signatories, with the exception of Costa Rica," the judgment of the editors of the *Globe and Mail*, plainly accurate, but hidden by the U.S. media barrage with only an occasional glimpse of the unacceptable facts.[106]

Even critics were swept up in the propaganda campaign. Thus a *Nation* editorial (January 30) stated that Ortega "has made signifi-cant concessions to the Central American peace plan," namely, by agreeing to abandon it in conformity to U.S. demands. The terror states were now exempt, along with their sponsor.

Throughout this period, there was a simple algorithm to determine which features of the peace plan count. Violations by the United States and the "fledgling democracies" are off the agenda, as is any requirement to which Nicaragua conformed. For example, a central feature of the accords was establishment of a National Reconciliation Commission. Nicaragua alone complied in a meaningful way, selecting its severest critic, Cardinal Obando, to head the Commission. Duarte, in contrast, selected U.S. presidential candidate Alvaro Magaña as the head of the Commission, which did nothing. In the second U.S. dependency, Honduras, there was barely a show of forming a Commission, though it was not entirely inactive. We learn from the Honduran press that the National Reconciliation Commission was supervising the distribution of U.S. supplies to the contras and thus "helping to subvert" the March 1988 cease-fire.[107]

In accord with the algorithm just presented, the provisions of the Accord with regard to the National Reconciliation Commissions disappeared. Similarly, there is no utility to the unreported conclusion of the U.N. refugee commission (UNHCR) that repatriation of refugees has been more successful in Nicaragua than elsewhere because of the "excellent disposition of the Sandinista government."[108] Off the agenda, then, is the "sense of urgency" with which the Central American presidents committed themselves to the task of refugee repatriation in the Esquipulas Accord. The pattern is close to exceptionless.

Pursuing this procedure, the media, early on, reduced the Central American agreements to "two key points" (Stephen Kinzer): (1) Will Nicaragua offer an amnesty to what the U.S. government and the media call "political prisoners"?[109]; (2) Will Nicaragua agree to negotiate with the contra civilian directorate?

With regard to the first point, few readers would have been aware that in early November, 1987 the CIVS determined that amnesty provisions were to go into effect when the aggression against Nicaragua ceases, and even a real media addict would not have learned that a few weeks later in November, the Nicaraguan National Assembly decreed a complete amnesty and revoked the state of emergency, both laws to "go into effect on the date that the [CIVS certifies] compliance with" the commitments of the accords to terminate the attack against Nicaragua. These laws were formulated in terms of the simultaneity condition of the accords, which Nicaragua, in its naiveté, believed to be operative.[110] Thus, by November, Nicaragua had largely complied with the accords as they are actually written. It was alone in this regard apart from Costa Rica, as remained the case.

The U.S. government version of the accords was, however, quite different from that of the CIVS and the text. We can find it in State Department propaganda, or indirectly, in news reports in the *New York Times*, where Stephen Kinzer describes the contents of the accords as follows: "Under its provisions, no country in the region would be permitted to assist the contras once the Sandinistas establish full political freedom."[111] According to this useful version, as long as Nicaragua falls short of a Scandinavian democracy in peacetime, the United States is entitled to maintain its proxy army in the field attacking Nicaragua. Since the accords do not single out Nicaragua for special treatment, it also follows that on the *Times*-State Department version of the accords, they entitle the Soviet Union to send arms and supplies to the guerrillas in El Salvador with several flights a day from Cuba until a radical restructuring of Washington's terror state has been completed. This consequence, however, is unmentioned.

As noted earlier, El Salvador also declared an amnesty, though in a form that expressly violated the terms of the Esquipulas Accord. The *New York Times* lauded the decree as the Duarte government's "most concrete step toward complying with the regional peace accord," contrasting this forthcoming move with the refusal of the Sandinistas to comply apart from "tentative" and grudging steps[112]— steps that met the conditions of the Accord, as we have just seen, though the *Times* never reported the facts. The Toronto *Globe and Mail* chose different words, describing the Salvadoran edict as "an amnesty for the military and the death squads." This noble gesture was bitterly condemned by human rights groups, not only because it freed the assassins of tens of thousands of people from prosecution (hardly likely in any event, with the government under effective military control), but also, as María Julia Hernández of Tutela Legal observed after several more months of atrocities, because "it made the military feel secure that there would be no prosecutions for human rights" violations in the future. The amnesty "chiefly benefited the military-linked death squads," the *Globe and Mail* commented accurately.[113]

With regard to the second "key point," negotiations, the accords did not call for discussions with CIA-created front organizations of the classic Communist Party style. That the contra directorate is exactly that had long been known, and is documented in detail in an important (and unmentionable) monograph by Edgar Chamorro, who was selected by the CIA to serve as spokesman for the front created for the benefit of "enemy territory" at home.[114] In a memo released during the Iran-contra hearings, Robert Owen, Oliver North's liaison with the contras, described the civilian front as "a name only," "a creation of the United States government (USG) to garner support from Congress"; power lies in the hands of the Somozist-run FDN, headed by Adolfo Calero, who "is a creation of the USG and so he is the horse we chose to ride," though he is surrounded by people who are "liars and greed- and power-motivated" for whom the war is "a business" as they hope for the marines to restore them to the power they lost.[115]

Nevertheless, applying the algorithm for interpreting the accords, the media took their key feature to be negotiations between the Sandinistas and Washington's PR creation. The *New York Times* even went so far as to describe the Nicaraguan government and the contras as "the two factions" who must negotiate and reach a settlement, a difficult task because the government "faction" insists upon "an end to all outside support for the contras"—as the Esquipulas Accord stipulates, a fact unmentioned.[116] Another journalist, surveying the problems of the region, describes the contenders for power in Nicaragua as "the two hostile bands"; in El Salvador, in contrast, the civil war pits "the U.S.-supported government" against the "Marxist guerrillas."[117] Appropriate use of language has its role to play, alongside of careful selection, distortion, and outright falsehood.

The insistence on wide-ranging negotiations with the contra directorate was another part of the longstanding effort to establish the fiction that the proxy army is an indigenous force, comparable to the guerrillas in El Salvador who were largely mobilized by U.S.-backed state terror, have always fought within their country, receive little if any military aid from abroad, have nothing like the extraordinary intelligence and support system provided by the contras' superpower sponsor,[118] and face a military force that, on paper at least, is considerably more powerful than the army of Nicaragua. It is necessary to suppress the astonishing inability of the U.S. to construct a guerrilla army in Nicaragua despite support vastly exceeding anything available to authentic guerrillas, U.S. dominance of the media over much of the country through powerful radio stations, recruitment of mercenaries in Honduras and elsewhere, an economy that has collapsed as a result of U.S. economic warfare and terror, and denial, thanks to U.S. ideological warfare, of the right to employ the domestic measures regularly adopted by Western democracies under far less threatening circumstances. With a fraction of the outside support lavished on the U.S. proxy forces, the Salvadoran guerrillas would have quickly overthrown the U.S.-installed government, and one might suspect that a guerrilla movement could be successfully established in U.S. border regions with a comparable effort by some unimaginable superpower. This failure of the U.S. effort to organize a guerrilla force within Nicaragua or even one that could be sustained from abroad without unprecedented outside support and direction is most remarkable, and very informative, for anyone prepared to think about what it means. Therefore, the facts and their meaning must be scrupulously suppressed, as they are.

The U.S. foreign aid budget for fiscal 1989 contained $2 million to support opposition political groups and media in Nicaragua, the *Congressional Quarterly* (CQ) reported (June 25, 1988), some of which openly identify with the contra attack. None of these "democratic groups in Nicaragua," as CQ calls them, has the support of more than 3 percent of the population; combined, they have the support of 9 percent, less than one-third the support for the Sandinistas. These are among the results of polls taken under the auspices of the Centro Interamericano de Investigaciones in Mexico and the Jesuit University (UCA) in Managua. As for President Ortega himself, 42 percent ranked him "good/excellent" and 29 percent "fair." For comparison, in an UCA poll in El Salvador that received little notice, 6 percent of the respondents supported Duarte's Christian Democrats and 10 percent supported ARENA, while 75 percent stated that no party represented them.[119]

Other interesting results of the Salvadoran poll were that 95 percent preferred economic and humanitarian aid over any kind of military aid, 4 percent blamed "guerrilla or communist subversion" for the crisis, and only 13 percent rated Duarte as "good" or "excellent." Recall that only 10 percent of the population see any signs of a democratic process in El Salvador.[120] Another contrast between El Salvador and Nicaragua was that in the former, pollsters have found that

> certain political questions had to be carefully couched in non-incriminating language. A significant number of Salvadorans told us that they do not discuss politics—period—not even with their closest friends or relatives. By contrast, in our survey in Nicara-

gua in June, interviewers judged that 77 percent of some 1,129
respondents in Managua answered poll questions without apparent fear or distrust,

and the interviewers reported that "their biggest problem in the field
was the delay caused when respondents amplified their answers,"
giving explanations of their responses for or against the Sandinista
regime. In polls in Honduras in November 1987, 65 percent of respondents "said they believed Hondurans were afraid of expressing their
political opinions in public" and "interviewers judged that only 38
percent of their respondents answered questions without fear or
distrust."[121] The difference in climate between Nicaragua and El
Salvador has always been obvious, though the media have succeeded
in conveying the opposite impression.

Other unreported information on public opinion in El Salvador
provides a good deal of insight into U.S. policy and the real concerns
of the media. In 1988, the Archbishop of San Salvador organized a
national debate to consider the problems facing the country. Over
sixty organizations took part, "representing the private sector, professional associations, educational and cultural bodies, labor organizations, humanitarian groups, the displaced, religious institutions
and others."[122] There was near-unanimous (95-100 percent) agreement on "the failure of the Reagan Administration's project for El
Salvador"; support for negotiated settlement; increasing concern
over human rights violations and impoverishment of the majority
"while a few have become richer"; identification of the "root cause"
of the conflict not in "international communist aggression" but rather
"structural injustice, manifested in the unjust concentration of
wealth" in land, industry, and commerce and "exhaustion of the
capitalist, dependent agro-export model as part of an unjust structure
of international commerce."

The same proportions (95-100 percent) condemned:

1. The "subordination of political power to economic
   power"

2. The "direct, permanent interference by the military
   in the operation of the state and the society in support
   of the oligarchy and dominant sectors, and thus in
   support of North American interests" as the country
   is "subjugated to the interests of international capital"

3. "Mortgaging the national sovereignty and self-determination and the enormous interference of the U.S.
   in El Salvador's national affairs"

4. Foreign military aid

5. The "strong opposition by the United States" and its
   Salvadoran right wing and military allies to the Esquipulas Accord, to which El Salvador should be
   pressured to conform

6. The Amnesty Law which exculpated "those charged
   with war crimes and crimes against humanity."

Furthermore, 88 percent see "serious restrictions on the democratic process" and regard "Christian Democracy as a cover while
North American interference became more intensified"; attribute
principal responsibility for the armed conflict to "foreign intervention, especially that of the U.S."; and describe the armed struggle as
a response to "the impossibility of any genuine form of popular
participation." Most called for recognition of the FMLN guerrillas as
a "representative political force" that emerged in response to violence
and injustice (55-59 percent). The highly touted elections were described by 81 percent as "the fundamental instrument of the U.S.
counterinsurgency project, legitimizing the war and neutralizing the
popular movement."

The document has much to say about "the U.S. counterinsurgency project" and the likely prospects for this tortured country. It
was ignored in the United States, as were the polls.

The lack of attention to public opinion in El Salvador provides
interesting lessons about U.S. political culture and the societal function of the media. The United States has unleashed an enormous
military and repressive apparatus in El Salvador and has poured
huge sums of money into the country. If these efforts had even a
remote relation to the needs and concerns of Salvadorans, then, quite
obviously, their opinions would be front-page news in the U.S. media
and the subject of extensive commentary. What we discover, however, is that there is not the slightest interest in their opinions. It
would be misleading to say that the information is suppressed;
rather, the irrelevance of the people subject to our will is as elementary as the rules of arithmetic; to consider what they think would be
as absurd as to try to discover the attitudes of chickens or donkeys.

The conclusion is clear: U.S. planners, and the educated elites that comment and articulate positions on international affairs, care not a whit about the needs and concerns of the people of El Salvador. Their sole concern is the preservation of their own privilege and power. The rhetoric of "benevolence," "good intentions" that misfired, and so on, is mere deception, possibly comforting self-deception as well. The attitudes and opinions of Salvadorans are not only ignored, as of zero significance, but also happen to be diametrically opposed to those of their professed benefactors in Washington, New York, Cambridge, and elsewhere. This is a matter of no concern, not even a level of concern that would lead to attention to the facts. The disdain for subject peoples is merely a background fact, like the air we breathe.

New York Times correspondents regularly allege that polls are illegal in Nicaragua, citing no evidence and not reporting the statement of the respected Jesuit priest who is rector of UCA (which would normally be responsible for polling) that polls are permitted but that facilities are lacking; plausible, given the circumstances. The *Interamerican* report (see note 119) assumes that polls have been permitted since 1984, that the August 1987 accords further legitimize polls, and that "the present poll put that general understanding to the test." The poll was not reported in the *Times*. I noted little mention elsewhere, and that unreliable (see chapter 3, note 47).

Let us return to the fate of the Central American peace negotiations after the effective demolition of the Esquipulas Accord in January 1988. In subsequent discussion, the terms of the Accord are consistently understood in the Washington version, accepted under duress by Nicaragua: the expansive interpretation devised by Washington applies to Nicaragua alone. Thus, it is possible for news columns to assert that "other countries have done somewhat better" than Nicaragua in adhering to the accords with their requirement of "freedom for the press and opposition parties, an end to support for other countries' guerrillas and negotiations with Nicaragua's rebels," as the *Boston Globe* reported in August 1988; indeed, other countries *cannot* violate the accords, whatever the facts, under the conventions of government-media Newspeak.[123]

Putting aside the usual disregard for state terror in the "fledgling democracies" and Honduran support for the contras, the reference here to negotiations appears rather audacious; it was hardly a secret that Nicaragua alone had negotiated a cease-fire agreement. But one must understand the algorithm already described. When

Nicaragua entered into cease-fire negotiations and reached an agreement with the contras, this "key issue" was dropped from the agenda
as no longer serviceable.

It was also necessary to eliminate the inconvenient fact that El
Salvador and Guatemala, in opposition to the near-unanimous will
of the public,[124] were refusing to negotiate with the indigenous guerrillas. The *Times* did not interrupt its daily lambasting of the
Sandinistas in January 1988, the crucial month for dismantling the
accords, to report that "According to [FDR leader Guillermo] Ungo,
talks have not resumed, despite FMLN requests, because of pressure
exerted on Duarte by the Reagan administration as well as from the
country's security forces."[125] A February 8 appeal for dialogue by
Ungo was rejected by the government on grounds that it will "only
dialogue with legally registered political parties"; this was reported
prominently in the Mexican press, but not in the *Times*.[126] The
FMLN/FDR stated that this was Duarte's third rejection of renewed
talks since November. Neither this nor Archbishop Rivera y Damas's
homily hoping for a Duarte response appears to have been reported.
Rather, the *Washington Post* editors, in a fanciful construction, condemned the guerrillas for having "rejected [Duarte's] overtures,"
which "went substantially beyond the obligations placed on him by
the Central American peace plan." There was scant notice of subsequent rebel offers to negotiate, rejected by the government. Jeane
Kirkpatrick went so far as to denounce the guerrillas for rejecting all
of Duarte's "generous offers" for negotiations.[127] Again, the facts turn
into their opposite as they pass through the distorting prism of the
media.

In Guatemala, the Bishops' conference called for renewed negotiations on January 29; the guerrillas accepted, the army refused,
backed by President Cerezo. In late February, the rebels requested
talks again, to be mediated by the Archbishop; the government
refused. A rebel offer of negotiations in April, supported by President
Arias, who offered his country as a site, was rejected by Cerezo, and
a cease-fire proposal in June was dismissed by his government.[128] All
of this was unworthy of attention, on the principles already discussed.

The logic was explained further by George Shultz, in a letter
objecting to a congressional proposal that the president be required
to submit a report on Salvadoran government efforts to achieve a
cease-fire before all aid can be released. Its sponsors argued that
Congress would thereby be "making clear its support for a negotiated

end" to the civil war in El Salvador. Shultz replied that "it is wholly inappropriate to try to pressure the elected government to negotiate or to make concessions to the guerrillas, which would not be acceptable to any democratic government." Since Nicaragua, unlike El Salvador, has not achieved democracy and lacks an elected government, it is quite proper to subject it to terror and economic warfare to pressure it to negotiate with U.S. proxies.[129]

A cease-fire was reached in Nicaragua on March 23, 1988; again, Nicaragua was alone in implementing an element of the accords.[130] The agreement was at once undermined by congressional legislation, and the administration went still further, violating the legislation as well as the cease-fire agreement. The media went along, as discussed in the text. Further negotiations broke down in June as the contras, increasingly under hard-line leadership, followed the U.S. strategy to undermine them by constant demand escalation when agreement seemed near.

The Council on Hemispheric Affairs reported that

> the breakdown of the Nicaraguan talks also implemented the game plan urged several weeks ago by Assistant Secretary of State Elliott Abrams: that the administration was urging the contras not to sign a peace agreement with the Sandinistas, but go along with a prolongation of a de facto truce, hoping that some adventitious Sandinista military action, like shooting down a contra supply plane or opening fire on a contra unit, would enable the White House to seek a resumption of lethal military aid from Congress. According to Abrams this was the very least that he was hoping for. When asked what was the most that the United States would do if given such a pretext, he responded, "We'll flatten Managua."

Further elements of the "game plan" were for U.S. intelligence agencies to step up their activities within Nicaragua, "hoping to use internal opposition forces to discredit the Sandinistas and sow discontent," and to lay the basis for further military action; what is commonly and accurately referred to, outside the media, as "the Chilean method," referring to the means employed to replace Chilean democracy by a military dictatorship. As one example, COHA cited the arrest and brief detention of fifteen opposition leaders for demonstrating outside the National Assembly building after they had rejected a request that they obtain a permit. "It is widely believed in Washington," COHA continues, "that the opposition was acting at the behest of their CIA liaison to stage the unauthorized demonstration" and court arrest as proof of Sandinista bad faith.[131]

Reviewing the situation a few weeks later, Stephen Kinzer reported that "Administration officials attributed the collapse of the talks to Sandinista intransigence," mentioning no other possible explanation. The *Times* editors added that "without the war, and the damage to Nicaragua's economy, it's arguable that Managua wouldn't have signed the regional peace plan" of August 1987. They urged the administration "to work with Central Americans" to pressure the Sandinistas to accept "specific targets and timetables," against the threat of further sanctions; no suggestions are offered for other participants in the Central American drama. A few weeks earlier, James LeMoyne had observed that "there is little doubt that the pressure of the guerrillas [in El Salvador] has been the chief stimulus for positive political change here."[132] By the logic of the editors, then, we should support the indigenous guerrillas in El Salvador. Somehow, the logical consequence is not drawn.

As the first anniversary of the Esquipulas Accord approached, violations continued in the states now exempt from their terms. In El Salvador, the Church Human Rights Office documented "a startling increase" in political killings of civilians in 1988. The Archbishop, in a Sunday homily, condemned the "return to the law of the jungle" with increasing death squad violence; and Auxiliary Bishop Rosa Chávez, denouncing on national TV the killing of peasants associated with the labor union UNTS, declared that "All evidence points in only one direction—to the Salvadoran security forces." Peasants and members of the National Association of Indigenous Salvadorans were reported murdered after torture by soldiers, including a ninety-nine-year old man and his daughter in a recently resettled village. On July 28, Rigoberto Orellana, leader of the newly founded "Movement for Bread, Land, Work and Liberty," was killed, by security forces according to spokespersons of the organization. As the anniversary of the Accord passed, killing continued. On August 21, a Swiss physician, Jurg Weiss, was detained and then killed by the National Police, shot in the face in an apparent effort to conceal his identity. He was on his way to investigate reports of the bombing of a village. The army claimed he was killed in combat, but his colleagues allege that because of his humanitarian activity, he was targeted by security forces in their campaign of repression against humanitarian and religious volunteers. The murder was condemned in a resolution of the European Parliament on "growing escalation of state terrorism" in El Salvador. On the same day two young men were found shot to death in San Salvador, bringing the number to five for the week; all five victims showed signs of torture, according to the spokesman of the Human Rights Commission CDHES, who described the killings as intended to foster "psychological terror among the population." The attempt to assassinate Col. Majano took place four days later.[133]

There were lesser abuses as well. The army barred the Church from providing supplies to resettled refugee villages. In rural areas, police regularly broke up political meetings (Rubén Zamora). A July 21 demonstration calling for release of an abducted trade unionist was attacked by police, who fired with automatic weapons and tear gas, leaving many wounded. On July 12, troops using tear gas, rifle butts, and clubs had attacked a march of farmers and cooperativists attempting to deliver provisions to striking electrical workers; demonstrators were detained by the police (reports ranged from 1 to 100 detained). Earlier, in efforts to disrupt a May Day rally, the army bombed the UNTS office, and Treasury Police abducted and severely beat the man who operated the sound system after the regular UNTS soundman had kept away under death threat. Many organizers and demonstrators were detained in prison, and a leader of the striking metalworkers' union who had directed chants at the rally "disappeared." In Honduras the army prevented workers from attending May Day demonstrations in Danlí, organized by the major labor union of eastern Honduras; in mid-April, police in Tegucigalpa had shot in the air and used tear gas to prevent a protest march to the U.S. Embassy, and, according to human rights workers, "disappeared" a student, Roger González, arrested as other students were jailed in connection with the April 7 attack on the U.S. consulate while police stood by. In Costa Rica protesting farmers and cooperativists were harassed and detained by the Rural Guard, in one case, tear gas and physical force were used to prevent them from presenting a petition at the city hall.[134]

Neither the continuing atrocities nor the lesser abuses received coverage, apart from an occasional perfunctory notice. But denunciation of Sandinista iniquity continued at a fever pitch, particularly when Nicaragua briefly approached some of the regular lesser abuses of the U.S. client states in mid-July, eliciting a new round of indignant condemnations across the political spectrum and renewed support of congressional liberals for contra aid.

In her review of the first year of the Accord in August, Julia Preston observed that little was achieved apart from Nicaragua. In

Honduras, Azcona remains "another caretaker president for the powerful military"; the same is true, though unstated, in El Salvador and Guatemala. She cites an August 4 Americas Watch review of human rights, which reports that "Political murders by military and paramilitary forces continue on a wide scale in Guatemala and El Salvador and on a smaller scale in Honduras," along with several "reported in Nicaragua," Preston adds, "where they had not been common." "Nicaragua initially did far more than any other Central American country to comply" with the Accord until mid-July, ten months after it was signed; a long "initial" period, which terminated after the breakdown of the cease-fire negotiations, when Nicaragua "violently broke up a July 10 opposition rally [at Nandaime] and kept six leaders in jail during long trials, closed the Catholic radio [station] indefinitely, expelled U.S. ambassador Melton and expropriated the largest private sugar plantation in Nicaragua." The last two actions hardly qualify as violations of the Accord. Radio Católica reopened on August 18, leaving only the pro-Sandinista *La Semana Cómica* under government sanction, for publishing material degrading women.[135]

The events of mid-July—in Nicaragua, that is—aroused great horror. "Sandinistas will be Sandinistas," a radio commentator observed knowingly in one of the milder reactions when the police broke up the Nandaime rally, using tear gas for the first time—after having been "pelted ... with sticks and rocks," we learn in paragraph thirteen of Stephen Kinzer's report, a fact that disappeared from most later commentary.[136] There were front-page stories and regular reports and editorials on the Sandinista barbarity in breaking up the rally in the standard Salvadoran style, expelling the U.S. Ambassador with charges that he had been involved in organizing the pro-contra opposition, and nationalizing a private sugar plantation alleged to be nonproductive, a front-page story in the *Times*; references to the use of tear gas to break up the rally and to police violence continued to appear in the press, with appropriate horror, for months. Congress was so enraged that amidst renewed calls for arms for the contras, both Houses passed impassioned condemnations of Managua's "brutal suppression of human rights" by overwhelming margins (91 to 4 in the Senate, 358 to 18 in the House), the press reported approvingly.[137]

Recall that the "brutal repression of human rights" by the Sandinistas only began to approach, for a brief moment, some of the *lesser* abuses that are normal practice among the U.S. favorites in the region, and does not even come close to the regular exercise of their "pedagogy of terror." Recall also that as Duarte's security services and their death squads escalated their terror after the Accord was signed, there was no condemnation in Congress, but rather praise for their progress towards a system "which respects human liberties."

Congressional debate over how best to punish the Sandinistas for their July transgressions was no less interesting, even apart from the stirring rhetoric about our exalted libertarian standards and the pain inflicted upon our sensitive souls by any departure from them—in Nicaragua. The Senate passed the Byrd Amendment setting the conditions for renewed military aid to the contras.[138] Speaking for his colleagues, including some of the most prominent Senate liberals, majority leader Byrd warned the Sandinistas that they "can either fully comply with the requirements for democratization that they agreed to in the Arias peace plan and move into the mainstream of harmonious democratic relations with their neighbors," or they can continue "to blatantly violate the provisions of the peace accords," repress "the legitimate democratic aspirations of the Nicaraguan people"—and face the consequences: a "return to military pressure," that is, U.S.-sponsored international terrorism. Byrd was also concerned over the failure of the Reaganites "to press the Soviet leadership to cease and desist from its military aid program for the Government of Nicaragua," so that the only country in the region subject to foreign attack will also be the only country completely disarmed. Senator Dodd, perhaps the leading Senatorial dove with regard to Central America, was deeply impressed with these remarks and proposals and asked to "add my voice in praise of our leader," Senator Byrd. He was no less effusive in praising "the courageous leadership of President Arias, of Costa Rica; President Cerezo, of Guatemala; President Azcona, of Honduras; and President Duarte, of El Salvador, a great friend of this Congress"—if not of the people of El Salvador, who regard him with fear and contempt and see no signs of a democratic process in the country, as shown by polls that are suppressed as useless. Senator Dodd and other sponsors of the Byrd Amendment are well aware of the achievements of the military regimes of the U.S. terror states, and of the escalation, in response to the Esquipulas Accord, of the terror for which the official "moderates" provide a democratic cover for the benefit of Congress and the media. It simply doesn't matter.

It is "fine" for Congress "to take a good roundhouse swing at the Sandinistas for reverting to dictatorial form" and to "remind them that Americans are not divided over democratic rights and wrongs," the *New York Times* editors commented, admonishing the Democrats "to let the Sandinistas know publicly the dangers of their bad-faith actions." The editors are not "divided over democratic rights and wrongs" in El Salvador; they have utter contempt for democratic rights in El Salvador, as their silence indicates, not to speak of their constant praise for the progress of democracy in this terror state. Stephen Kinzer, who knows Guatemala well, went so far as to quote a senior Guatemalan official on the "palpable unhappiness" of his government over the despicable behavior of the Sandinistas. "There is a liberalizing trend in the whole world, and Nicaragua is practically the only nation that is resisting it," he says, speaking for a government that is indeed liberalizing in that its murders and disappearances are down to a rate of only a few a day according to human rights groups, definitely a marked improvement over earlier years.[139]

The editors of the *Washington Post* called upon the "Central American democracies" and "Democratic critics of contra aid" to join "wholeheartedly" in condemning the Sandinista violation of "their solemnly sworn democracy pledges" as they act "very much the Communist police state, busting heads, tossing people in jail, censoring the media"; imagine what terms would apply to El Salvador or Israel for their actions at the same time, by these standards. It was surely quite proper for the American Ambassador to offer "the extra help required by the opposition," the editors continue. As the Council on Hemispheric Affairs observed, few nations would tolerate such behavior; "Washington would view foreign governmental funding of U.S. dissident entities as an unfriendly if not outright illegal act" and would not be likely to "countenance the Soviet ambassador to Washington's participation in a local leftist group's rally which called for termination of the current government," let alone participation by the German or Japanese ambassador in 1942, to take a closer analogue. It is also less than likely that an Ambassador from a hostile power engaged in hostilities against the United States would have been admitted in the first place, particularly one who had duplicated Melton's performance as he was sworn in as Ambassador in Washington, announcing that "I want to make it crystal clear what America stands for and the values of democracy and how the Sandinistas don't meet even the minimal standards." There would be "no more compromising" with the Sandinistas, according to this protegé of Elliott Abrams, architect of the terrorist attack against Nicaragua.[140] But in the case of an official enemy, unique standards apply.

A few months earlier, Singapore had expelled a U.S. diplomat "on the grounds that he had improperly interfered in the domestic affairs of the country," Owen Harries writes in the right-wing journal he edits.[141] "Under the Vienna Convention governing diplomatic relations, such interference is impermissible," he continues, so "the United States had no option but to comply" when Singapore charged that the diplomat had "encouraged disgruntled Singaporeans in anti-government activities." Harries is writing in defense of Singapore against charges of improper behavior and police-state repression. Singapore is a semi-fascist country that offers a favorable investment climate, so the Vienna Convention applies. Not so, however, in the case of Nicaragua, designated by the authorities as an enemy.

Commenting further, the Council on Hemispheric Affairs observes that although Melton and members of his staff were expelled "for blatant interference in Nicaraguan internal affairs, the use of the U.S. embassy to fund, direct and coordinate disruptive activities by the civil opposition in Nicaragua in harmony with the actions of the contras ... continues," including almost $700,000 of U.S. government funds earmarked for opposition elements. The U.S. government "is making a clear effort to create a parallel government in Nicaragua" that might assume power under escalated attack or social collapse.[142]

In October 1988, Amnesty International (AI) released a document entitled *El Salvador: 'Death Squads'—A Government Strategy*, reporting that right-wing death squads had abducted, tortured, and killed hundreds of Salvadorans in the preceding eighteen months, often beheading the victims to spread fear.[143] The so-called "death squads" are an agency of the security forces of the U.S.-installed government, serving its strategy of intimidating any potential opposition. "Victims are customarily found mutilated, decapitated, dismembered, strangled or showing marks of torture ... or rape," AI reported. "The death squad style is to operate in secret but to leave mutilated bodies of victims as a means of terrifying the population." The victims include trade unionists, human rights workers, judges and jurors working on human rights abuse cases, refugees, church members, teachers, and students. "There can be no recourse to the police or military when they themselves carry out death-squad killings." The killings are carried out by plainclothes gunmen and by uniformed police and military units with the apparent acquiescence of the state: "the Salvadoran death squads are simply used to shield the government from accountability for the torture, disappearances and extrajudicial executions committed in their name." Members of the death squads, some living in hiding in the United States, told AI that the squads were drawn from specially trained police units, the Treasury Police and the National Guard. Church and human rights groups estimate that about a dozen bodies bearing the marks of death squad torture and execution were turning up every month on roadsides and in body dumps in 1987, the toll quadrupling in early 1988. AI reported that the resurgence of the death squads could be traced partly to the government amnesty of a year earlier, as had been widely predicted at the time while the *Times* hailed El Salvador's forthcoming steps towards compliance with the peace accord.

The AI report received no notice in the *New York Times*. The Senate passed a resolution, 54 to 12, warning *Nicaragua* "that continued Sandinista violation of regional peace accords would 'very likely' cause Congress to approve new military aid next year."[144] We see again the familiar pattern: U.S.-backed atrocities in its client states coupled with stern warnings to Nicaragua to improve its behavior on pain of intensified U.S. terror.

Also in October 1988, the Guatemala City journal *Central America Report* took as its lead story the just released Amnesty International annual review of human rights for 1987.[145] It reported that "some of the most serious violations of human rights are found in Central America," particularly Guatemala and El Salvador, where "kidnappings and assassinations serve as systematic mechanisms of the government against opposition from the left, the [AI] report notes"; recall that the situation deteriorated after the Esquipulas Accord, and became still more grim through 1988. The human rights situation is "less dramatic" in Nicaragua and Honduras, apart from "civilian deaths at the hands of U.S.-supported contra forces." While there have been "cases of kidnappings, tortures and extrajudicial killings in Honduras, Panama and Nicaragua, these actions have not been established as systematic government mechanisms."

A month later, the *New York Times* published a front-page story by Lindsey Gruson on atrocities in Guatemala.[146] In the past, Gruson observes, Guatemala City had been "a free-fire zone for political extremists" who carried out extensive terror; unmentioned is the fact that the "political extremists" responsible for the overwhelming majority of the atrocities were—and are—the agents of the U.S.-backed government. In fact, the U.S. role in Guatemala is unmentioned in this story. Gruson describes the increase in kidnappings, torture, and murder, the worsening situation in the cities, and the "de facto military dictatorship" in the countryside (quoting Americas Watch observer Anne Manuel). The main targets in the cities are "labor leaders, union organizers and leftists." A spokesman for an independent human rights organization says that "there's a democratic facade now, nothing more. The facade hides that all the power is held by the army and that the situation is getting worse." An Americas Watch report released two weeks later accused the government of prime responsibility for the serious increase in human rights abuses, now reaching a level of about two a day, presumably a considerable underestimate, Americas Watch concludes.[147]

As 1988 came to a close, government atrocities mounted in the client states. Several new death squads appeared. The dean of the Law School in Santa Ana, Imelda Medrano, was murdered on December 16 after returning from a university demonstration in San Salvador where she was a principal speaker; her house had been watched for two days by men in a jeep with darkened windows, a death squad trademark. Three powerful explosions destroyed the biology building of the National University on December 22. Attackers killed one watchman; a second described a heavily armed squad of about 50 men. The University Rector accused the military of planting the bombs: "This is the response of the Armed Forces to the stepped up war and their impotence in containing it," he said. The attack took place as soldiers were surrounding the campus and only the military would have been free to operate so openly, the Rector added. The director of Tutela Legal agreed that "These are actions of people with military training, heavily armed and moving with total liberty." Five days later, a bomb destroyed the offices of the Lutheran Church, which the army views with suspicion because of its work with refugees. Privately, church officials, who had received death threats, blamed the army. The West German Ambassador, who had condemned attacks against the Lutheran Church, received a death threat and left the country. A Western diplomat observed that "I see a military hand" behind the bombings. A source with close military contacts says the army feels it can counter the guerrillas only with "selective terror."[148] There was little news coverage, less concern, except for the possible threat to the Reagan project of bringing "democracy" to El Salvador.

The lesser abuses in the client states also continued. On September 13, soldiers and police attacked a student demonstration in San Salvador and broke up another in Santa Ana, while security forces surrounded the UNTS offices. Some 250 students and university workers were arrested; the rector of the university claimed that 600 students had been arrested and that the whereabouts of over 400 were unknown. "During the demonstration riot police fired volleys of shots and canisters of tear gas into the crowd of 3,000," wounding "scores of demonstrators" and apparently killing the operator of a police water cannon (*Central America Report*). Thirty local and foreign journalists "were ordered to the ground by security agents, who warned them not to move or take photographs" and at least ten foreign observers were detained. Sam Dillon reported in the *Miami Herald* that "angry riot police" had hurled tear-gas canisters at the students and workers, "firing their rifles skyward," "clubbing protestors and arresting 230." The director of Tutela Legal "said the police actions appeared designed to intimidate urban protesters at the beginning of a crucial election period." "The patience of the security corps has its limits, faced with street provocations," Defense Minister Vides Casanova told reporters: "We'll not tolerate any more violence." The day before, COHA reported, military forces had "attacked 500 demonstrators in Usulutan who were peacefully protesting the lack of government aid following heavy flooding," injuring fifteen and arresting eight.[149]

As before, these lesser abuses pale into significance before the government strategy of intimidation through sheer terror.

None of this elicited interest or concern, as distinct from the events at Nandaime that briefly approached some of the regular lesser abuses. These, as we have seen, aroused such horror that congressional doves were compelled to renew aid to their terrorist forces to punish the Sandinistas. Furthermore, the European allies of the United States refrained from more than token assistance after Hurricane Joan destroyed much of Nicaragua in October. The reason was their profound revulsion over the repression at Nandaime, which "many European governments view ... as open defiance by the Sandinistas of the regional peace process," Julia Preston reports, noting "the current displeasure in Europe with the Sandinistas"— though not with El Salvador and Guatemala, which continue to merit their support.[150] Again we see that hypocrisy has no limits, and also that Europe is far more colonized than it likes to believe.

As noted, the lesser abuses in the client states, generally ignored, were reported by Sam Dillon in the *Miami Herald*. In a later article, he reviews the increasing repression throughout the region, singling out Nicaragua as the worst offender, its most serious offense being "the gassing of a peaceful rally and jailing of top political leaders" at Nandaime. He goes on to describe how the Salvadoran military attacked "large but peaceful urban protests," which "angry riot police ... crushed ... with tear gas, clubbings and more than 250 arrests," along with arrests of many others "in night raids on the offices of two leftist unions and peasant groups." He briefly mentions the "dramatic" increase in "political killings by the army and death squads—as well as by guerrillas." He is plainly cognizant of the facts, but, as the facts pass through the ideological filter, large-scale slaughter, terror, and repression as a government strategy of intimidation in the U.S. client states become insignificant as compared with real but far lesser abuses in a country subjected to U.S. terror and economic warfare. Note that we are considering a reporter, and a journal, that are at least willing to report some of the facts.[151]

The client states continued to reject negotiations, while the U.S. government and the media railed at the Sandinistas for their failure to revitalize the negotiations stalled by the obstructionist tactics of the U.S. proxies. We learn from the Mexican press that President Cerezo "reiterated his rejection of a possible dialogue with the guerrilla army," adding that as long as the "subversives ... do not give up their belligerent position, we will not open direct talks with their leaders ... No dialogue can take place amidst weapons." In El Salvador, thousands of peasants, students and workers marched through the capital city to the hotel where an O.A.S. meeting was taking place to demand that the government negotiate with the guerrillas. The guerrillas had declared a unilateral truce for the duration of the meeting and "renewed a call for negotiations with the government," AP reported. President Duarte, in his address to the O.A.S. delegates, "said the guerillas' expressed desire to resume negotiations was merely 'tactical'. He accused the rebels of pursuing 'a strategic maneuver to destroy democracy through democracy's own liberties.'"[152]

The O.A.S. meetings were covered by Lindsey Gruson in the *New York Times*. Gruson referred bleakly to the "perversion" of the peace process in Central America. Predictably, only one example is cited: the Nandaime rally and the arrests of Nicaraguan peasants on suspicion of aiding the contras. These acts of repression have "undermined efforts to reinvigorate the negotiations," Gruson reports, citing U.S. diplomats. With regard to El Salvador, his only comment is that the October 1987 amnesty closed the books on earlier army assassinations; Guatemalan and Honduran abuses are unmentioned, and nothing is said about negotiations in El Salvador and Guatemala, or why they have not been "invigorated."[153] In short, a selective filter designed for the needs of government propaganda, and reflecting the insignificance of terror, torture, and repression when they do not serve these ends.

Gruson also notes that no agreement could be reached on a date for the planned Central American summit, for unknown reasons. The veil is lifted by the Mexican press, which reported that the Salvadoran government cancelled the Central American summit scheduled to take place in San Salvador, pleading "lack of economic capacity." The cancellation "came only a few hours after the visit to that country of the U.S. Special Ambassador to Central America, Morris Busby," and his meeting with President Duarte. Analysts are quoted as attributing the summit difficulties to "a boycott by the U.S., in which Morris Busby will not be exempt from 'chargeability' and which might have been devised as a reply to Cerezo's refusal to support belligerent action against Nicaragua." For President Cerezo, "it is vital that the presidential summit take place, observers indicate, because with this he is trying to distract attention from the violent problems of his country and to increase the international prestige that he has gained with his policies of active neutrality."[154]

The pattern is one that we have seen repeatedly: U.S. initiatives to obstruct a political settlement, Duarte's compliance, and the silence of the media.

The selection of issues and style of commentary illustrate the means employed to inculcate proper habits of thought. A particularly useful technique is uncritical citation of approved leadership elements. As the government and media sought to revitalize anti-Sandinista fervor in summer 1988, Stephen Kinzer reported a meeting of the United States and its four Central American allies. "All four countries disapprove of the Sandinistas and have urged them to liberalize their regime," he observed, "but they do not agree on how best to exercise such pressure." President Arias is quoted as saying that "Nicaragua has unfortunately failed us," expressing "my disappointment, my pain, my sadness," as he discussed abuses in Nicaragua with his colleagues from the terror states; about their practices he has expressed no disappointment, pain, or sadness, as least so far as the U.S. media report. President Cerezo added that he is "very distressed that the Sandinistas are not following the rules of democracy." George Shultz denounced the "Communist Government of Nicaragua—and the Communist guerrillas of El Salvador and Guatemala" as "a destructive and destabilizing force in the region," as "the Sandinista regime continues to rely on Soviet arms and to amass a military machine far in excess of its defense needs." "Mr. Shultz and the Foreign Ministers of Honduras, Guatemala, El Salvador and Costa Rica expressed 'their respect for the principles of peace, democracy, security, social justice and economic development'," Kinzer reports with no comment, and no detectable shudder.[155]

An accompanying article from Washington describes the consensus of Senators to approve further aid to the contras, and the concern of the Democrats that it would harm "their party's image" if the Sandinistas were to repress the internal opposition or "mount a military offensive against the contras"; "the party's image" is not damaged by its support for continuing atrocities in the terror states. A few days later, senatorial doves passed legislation permitting new military aid if the treacherous Sandinistas were to attack the contras within Nicaragua or receive more military aid than Congress considers appropriate.[156] AP quotes liberal Massachusetts Senator John Kerry, who supports "humanitarian aid to the rebels," with a vote on arms to follow in the event of "continued flow of Soviet weaponry into Nicaragua, violations of last year's regional peace accord by the Sandinistas and any attempt by the Nicaraguan government to militarily 'mop up' the rebel forces, Kerry said."[157]

All of this fits the standards for competent reporting. The quotes are presumably accurate, as are the descriptive statements. Lying behind the selection of facts and manner of presentation are certain unquestioned assumptions, including the following. Nicaragua alone is failing to "liberalize" and observe the Esquipulas Accord; the facts are different, but unwelcome, therefore scarcely reported. It is illegitimate for Nicaragua to defend itself from the terrorist attack of U.S. proxy forces based in Honduras by conducting military operations within its own territory, or by receiving arms from the only supplier that the United States will permit; but it is legitimate for the U.S. allies to refuse any dealings with the indigenous guerrillas (generally unreported) and to attempt to destroy them with U.S arms and advisers. The president of Costa Rica, whose business-run democracy survives on a U.S. dole, and who, if quoted accurately, cares little about continuing atrocities in the "fledgling democracies" or their gross violations of the minimal preconditions for democracy and of the peace treaty that bears his name in the media, is the arbiter of adherence to its provisions and of democratic practice. The president of the military-run state of Guatemala, which continues to terrorize and murder its citizens, though on a lesser scale than in earlier years, is in a position to condemn far less repressive and more open societies than his for failure to move towards "democracy." A U.S. official who bears major responsibility for the attack on Nicaragua, for traumatizing El Salvador, and for backing near-genocidal slaughter in Guatemala is, likewise, in a position to determine who is "destabilizing" Central America and what is an appropriate level of defense for the government subjected to U.S. armed attack. Aid to the U.S. proxy forces is "humanitarian," though international conventions, reiterated in the World Court ruling that the U.S. government rejects and the media ignore, are quite explicit in restricting the concept of "humanitarian aid" to aid to *civilians*, and civilians *on both sides*, without discrimination. It is only right and just for a "neutral agency" such as the State Department to administer such "humanitarian aid," and, if Nicaragua attempts measures of self-defense that would be normal and unquestioned in any Western democracy, it is proper for the CIA to supply its terrorist forces in the field within Nicaragua—unless they prove an "imperfect instrument" and thus contribute to "our Nicaraguan agony."

One can imagine a different style of reporting, not adopting these presuppositions of U.S. propaganda, citing other sources (the World Court, for example), and selecting relevant facts by different criteria (human rights and needs, democracy and freedom, the rule of law, and other values that are commonly professed). But such will rarely be found in the media. The constant barrage of properly selected material, with hardly a critical word or analytic passage, firmly instills the presuppositions that lie behind it, shaping the perceptions of the audience within the framework of acceptable doctrine more effectively than the productions of any Ministry of Truth. Meanwhile the media can plead that they are only doing their duty honestly—as they are, though not in exactly the sense they intend.

As throughout this horrifying decade, the worst human rights violators in Central America by a wide margin are the outright U.S. creations—the government of El Salvador and the contras—and the U.S.-supported regime of Guatemala. If the obvious significance of these facts has been discussed in the mainstream media and journals, I have not found it. The nature of these regimes is sometimes partially revealed; no conclusions are drawn concerning the U.S. role in Central America, U.S. political culture, and the moral standards of the privileged classes that construct and support these policies.

The conclusions that *are* drawn are quite different. *New York Times* diplomatic correspondent Robert Pear writes of the prospects for a "new policy of diplomacy in Central America" under the Bush administration. This hopeful new policy of President Bush and his pragmatic Secretary of State James Baker will emphasize working "more closely with Congress and with Latin American nations to put political pressure on the Sandinistas to allow elections [there having been none in Nicaragua by Washington edict], freedom of expression and other rights guaranteed under regional peace accords." To ensure that the reader understands the Party Line, Pear adds: "Nicaragua signed those accords in 1987 and 1988, but the United States and other nations say the Sandinistas have flouted many provisions." There is no hint that anything may be awry in the U.S. client states or that the actions of the United States itself might raise some questions.

The performance throughout would impress the rulers of a totalitarian state. The suffering that has resulted, and will yet ensue, is beyond measure.

Appendix V

1. The U.S. and Costa Rican Democracy[1]

As noted in chapter 5, the Costa Rican system established by the 1948 coup led by José (Don Pepe) Figueres satisfied the basic conditions required by U.S. global policy and ideology. Figueres aligned himself unequivocally with the United States. His government provided a favorable climate for foreign investment, guaranteed the domestic predominance of business interests, and laid a proper basis for repression of labor and political dissidence if required, even outlawing the Communist Party in its 1949 Constitution. Still, the United States remained dissatisfied.

Suspicions about Costa Rica were voiced early on, as the intelligence reports already cited indicate.[2] In 1952, the CIA warned that Guatemala "has recently stepped-up substantially its support of Communist and anti-American activities in other Central American countries," one prime example being the alleged gift of $300,000 to Figueres, then a candidate for election. The situation in Guatemala itself, of course, was regarded as "adverse to US interests" because of the "Communist influence ... based on militant advocacy of social reforms and nationalistic policies identified with the Guatemalan Revolution of 1944," which initiated the ten-year democratic interlude terminated by the CIA coup. Worse yet, the "radical and nationalist policies" of the democratic capitalist government, including the "persecution of foreign economic interests, especially the United Fruit Company," had gained "the support or acquiescence of almost all Guatemalans." The government was proceeding to create "mass support for the present regime" by labor organization and agrarian reform and "to mobilize the hitherto politically inert peasantry" while undermining the power of large landholders. Furthermore, "Guatemalan official propaganda, with its emphasis on conflict between democracy and dictatorship and between national independence and 'economic imperialism,' is a disturbing factor in the Caribbean area"; the background for the judgment is Washington's support for dictatorships and its natural fear of independent democratic tendencies. Also disturbing was Guatemalan support for "the 'democratic' elements of other Caribbean countries in their struggles against 'dictatorship'." The 1944 revolution had aroused "a strong national movement to free Guatemala from the military dictatorship, social backwardness, and 'economic colonialism' which had been the pattern of the past," and "inspired the loyalty and conformed to the self-interest of most politically conscious Guatemalans." Hence "Neither the landholders nor the [United] Fruit Company can expect any sympathy in Guatemalan public opinion." A "Commie display of strength" at a "gigantic May Day celebration" was particularly distressing, given what intelligence perceived to be their leading role in these ominous developments.[3] It was feared that Figueres might lend himself to similar Commie schemes.

American Ambassador Robert Woodward reported to Washington in 1955 that the Figueres government is "controversial" and not entirely reliable. True, Figueres had just "expressed appreciation for the activities of the United Fruit Company" and had "dislodged the commies from their powerful position" in the pre-coup government. But he "made himself suspect when he continued to support the Arbenz regime in Guatemala long after it was dominated by communists"; that is, long after this capitalist democracy was targeted for elimination by the CIA.

As yet, "the commies have presented no grave problem" in Costa Rica, Ambassador Woodward continued, noting that "the Constitution outlaws the Communist Party." But the commies represent "a potential danger" because they have not been rooted out of "the laboring class," and the suspect government "has made no move to stamp out the movement completely," as a solid commitment to democracy would require. With the "communists" not eliminated entirely, there might be problems in controlling banana workers and other dangerous elements. Who can tell when these subversives might try to organize to struggle for their rights? Thirty years later, the Twentieth Century Fund warns of the problems "brought on by the radicalization of the banana unions under Communist leadership," including "a lengthy strike in 1984 which resulted in violence—and several deaths." These and other problems had led the United Fruit Company "to turn some of its acreage over to palm oil—a less labor-intensive crop," so that such difficulties would not arise.[4]

Furthermore, Ambassador Woodward continued, the security forces "are handicapped in arresting communists because of the protection afforded the individual in the Costa Rican Constitution." But despite these unfortunate deviations from democracy, "it should not be too difficult to suppress communist publications," even though this risks "the hue and cry of the comrades against suppression of freedom of expression"; and "the application of limited force" should also be possible if we can provide the government with adequate intelligence and help them convince the public that "communism constituted a present menace." This public relations effort requires that the public be "conditioned" to "the use of force by the authorities," by means of "a strong propaganda campaign." Again, we see the importance of necessary illusions to lay the groundwork for the effective use of violence.

The policy recommendations, then, are that "the government should be urged to maintain closer surveillance over communists and prosecute them more vigorously" (by means that remain censored), and "the government should be influenced to amend the Constitution to limit the travel of communists, increase penalties for subversive activities and enact proposed legislation eliminating communists from union leadership," while the U.S. Information Agency programs "to condition the public to the communist menace" should be maintained. The United Fruit Company, which dominated much of the economy, should proceed to bring Figueres "to the point where he will become a Hemisphere-wide public relations agent for the Company." That should not be difficult, because he is already becoming "the best advertising agency that the United Fruit Company could find in Latin America."

To carry these efforts further, the Ambassador recommended that the United Fruit Company be induced to introduce "a few relatively simple and superficial human-interest frills for the workers that may have a large psychological effect." These recommendations should put to rest the calumny that the United States government lacks concern for the working class and the poor.

Ambassador Woodward's advice to United Fruit recalls a private communication of Secretary of State John Foster Dulles to President Eisenhower on how to bring Latin Americans into line with U.S. plans for their future as providers of raw materials and profits for U.S. corporations: "you have to pat them a little bit and make them think that you are fond of them."[5]

The State Department perceived "weaknesses" in Costa Rica "in the detection and investigation of communist activity" and "the absence of legal authority to move against communists." Another problem was the inadequate resources of the security services, who "can, therefore, contribute little to the surveillance and control of the international communist movement." While the media "make extensive use of news and special articles" from the U.S. propaganda services, more can be done in this regard to "encourage confidence in democracy and free enterprise"—the two being operationally equivalent—and to overcome the current "lackadaisical ... attitude of the government toward [the] suppression" of communists. The State Department recommended convincing the government to take measures to "Limit the international movement of communists, Increase penalties for communist activities, Eliminate communists from union leadership, Restrict communist propaganda," while continuing U.S. propaganda programs "to increase public support for anti-communist measures."

In short, the United States should foster democracy.

It should not be assumed that these are only the thoughts of the Republican Eisenhower administration. If anything, the Kennedy liberals were even more concerned to ensure that democratic forms remain within appropriate bounds.[6]

In later years, Don Pepe continued to serve the cause of the United States, as standard bearer of the Free World, while advocating probity in government, class collaboration, and economic development sensitive to the needs of business and foreign investors. In the Kennedy period he enlisted secret funding from the CIA for projects of the "Democratic Left," and dismissed later revelations of CIA funding as "silly and adolescent" while praising the CIA for the "delicate political and cultural tasks" it was performing "thanks to the devotion of the liberals in the organization." He particularly valued the contributions of Jay Lovestone and other U.S. labor bureaucrats, who had compiled an impressive record of undermining the labor movement in Latin America and elsewhere with CIA assistance.[7] He supported the Bay of Pigs invasion, anticipating "a quick victory by the democratic forces which have gone into Cuba," and later expressed his regrets for their "lamentable" defeat. He was concerned only that that his enemy Trujillo be deposed first, after which the Dominican Republic could be used as a base against Castro. When the Johnson administration invaded the Dominican Republic to prevent the re-establishment of the constitutional government under the democratic capitalist reformer Juan Bosch, under a series of fabricated pretexts including the usual rhetoric about takeover by Communists, Don Pepe reacted with ambivalence, pleading for understanding of Johnson's actions which, he held, were necessary, to avoid his impeachment.[8]

As the United States geared up for its attack on popular organizations and social reform in Central America in the 1980s, Costa Rica continued to cooperate, but with insufficient enthusiasm from the Reaganite perspective, particularly under the Arias government. Arias accepted the basic norms, lauding Washington's terror states as "democracies," condemning the Sandinistas for failing to observe the regional standards to which the U.S. clients conform, and assuring the press that "I told Mr. Shultz that the Sandinistas today are bad guys, and you are good guys, that they have unmasked themselves" by the repression at Nandaime.[9] But this level of support for U.S.-backed terror did not suffice for the jingoist right, offended by the fact that Arias joined general Latin American opinion in opposing overt U.S. violence in the region. In September 1987, according to the Council on Hemispheric Affairs (COHA), he was summoned to the White House to receive a "stern lecture" from Reagan, prepared by Elliott Abrams, warning him not to appeal directly to Congress to terminate contra aid. In previous months, delay of aid to Costa Rica and other pressures had served as a warning of what might be in store. When Arias responded with critical remarks about U.S. policy, COHA reports, "the outraged Reagan was heard to exclaim as Arias took his leave, "Who is that dwarf?" Since then, Arias has "not had the nerve to step over that limit established for him by Washington," risking the loss of the U.S. economic aid that maintains "the illusion of prosperity" that "is critical to preservation of the country's increasingly fragile democracy."[10]

Meanwhile, José Figueres became a nonperson—apart from ritual invocation of his name in the course of media denunciations of Nicaragua—because of his completely unacceptable reactions to the Sandinista revolution and the U.S. terrorist attack against Nicaragua, as discussed earlier. It is recognized that he "is still probably the most popular and powerful individual in the country," but he is "an erratic thinker and personality"—as shown now by his defense of the Sandinistas and "vociferous" opposition to "U.S. intervention against the Marxist Managua regime."[11] It is only reasonable, then, that the American public should be protected from the confusion that might be sown by exposure to the thoughts of the leading figure of capitalist democracy in Central America.

Costa Rica's external debt tripled from 1977 to 1981, and has since almost doubled to over $4 billion, with new loans of $500 million in 1988 and a trade deficit of $200 million a year. Current debt to private banks amounts to $200 million in interest alone, but though payment is largely suspended, the international lending institutions keep the funds flowing. "Costa Rica has lost the ability to determine its own economic future," the San José journal *Mesoamerica* concluded in mid-1988, reporting that real wages had fallen 42 percent in the preceding five years, as prices increased while subsidies for food and medicine were reduced or eliminated. The infant mortality rate had risen sharply in certain areas, primarily because of the economic crisis and increasing hunger, according to the University of Costa Rica's Institute for Health Research. The International Monetary Fund (IMF) demanded further cuts in social spending, lowering of the minimum wage, and cutting of government employees, "thus jeopardizing what had been one of the most enlightened social service programs in Latin America," *Mesoamerica* reports. Once self-sufficient in agriculture, Costa Rica is now importing staples as it shifts to largely foreign-controlled exports, including export crops, in line with traditional IMF-World Bank-USAID directives, a familiar recipe for disaster in Third World countries. "Arias's pro-big business economic strategy," COHA observes, may turn large numbers of once self-sufficient farmers to wage laborers on agribusiness plantations while profits are largely expatriated, "a major change of philosophy in a country that has had a strong state-directed welfare orientation."[12]

There is also growing civil unrest. Landless campesinos led by priests have occupied abandoned land, leading to arrests and forced expulsion. A report of the Human Rights Commission of Costa Rica documents dozens of complaints of illegal expulsion and abuse of authority during the past two years, including several assassinations, implicating the security forces, especially the Rural Guard, in violence against campesinos. Father Elías Arias, a priest imprisoned with 100 squatters, stated that "Costa Rica urgently needs land reform, but the legislators are reluctant to carry out this type of reform which is against their own self-interest. Instead of helping the campesinos, they have been protecting the property of John Hull," the wealthy U.S. landowner and CIA asset who was actively involved in the attack against Nicaragua from Costa Rican bases.[13]

Through the 1980s, Costa Rica was able to defer these problems thanks to rising U.S. aid, understood to be conditional on its general support for U.S. objectives in the region. It is only the enormous aid flow that has kept "Costa Rica's standard of living from plummeting even more disastrously and its society from collapse," Sanders observes, noting that it is possibly second only to Israel, a unique case in terms of foreign sustenance, in per capita foreign indebtedness. "Only the massive flow of American aid ... staves off catastrophe." The economic problems have been enhanced by massive capital flight and self-enrichment by the private sector. There are, he warns, severe dangers of a "nationalistic backlash that can be exploited by trouble-makers, particularly by the far left," encouraged by the evil Sandinistas leering across the border. This threat is less ominous than before; the crippling of the Nicaraguan economy and the "political oppression of the Sandinista regime" may have "inoculated the Costa Ricans for the time being against a shift to the left"—at least, those Costa Ricans who can see what Big Brother has in store for them.[14]

Leaving nothing to chance, the United States has been support-ing "parallel structures in Costa Rica, especially within the security services," COHA alleges, citing U.S.-backed military and paramilit-ary training programs and frequent reports, one verified personally by a COHA staff member in January 1988, of "U.S.-sponsored clan-destine arms deliveries to ... private paramilitary groups" associated with right-wing organizations and the Civil Guard, with Washington connections in the background.[15]

José Figueres observed that "the persecution of the Sandinistas is just one element of this trend" under the Reaganites that he deplored. "Another is the effort to undo Costa Rica's social institu-tions, to turn our whole economy over to the businesspeople, and to do away with our social insurance, our nationalized bank, our na-tionalized electric utility—the few companies we have that are too large to be in private hands. The United States is trying to force us to sell them to so-called private enterprise, which means turning them over to the local oligarchy or to U.S. or European companies. We're fighting back as best we can," with uncertain prospects.[16]

2. "The Evil Scourge of Terrorism"[17]

There is a standard device to whip the domestic population of any country into line in support of policies that they oppose: induce fear of some terrifying enemy, poised to destroy them. As discussed in chapter 5, "the evil scourge of terrorism" was a natural choice for this role in the early 1980s, as the United States sought to concoct an enemy weak enough to be attacked with impunity but sufficiently threatening to mobilize the general population in support of the Reaganite expansion of state power at home and violence abroad. The threat waned when it became necessary to face the costs of these policies a few years later. The media rallied enthusiastically to the enterprise.[18]

The meaning of the term "terrorism" is not seriously in dispute. It is defined with sufficient clarity in the official U.S. Code and numerous government publications. A U.S. Army manual on countering the plague defines terrorism as "the calculated use of violence or threat of violence to attain goals that are political, religious, or ideological in nature. This is done through intimidation, coercion, or instilling fear." Still more succinct is the characterization in a Pentagon-commissioned study by noted terrorologist Robert Kupperman, which speaks of the threat or use of force "to achieve political objectives without the full-scale commitment of resources."[19]

Kupperman, however, is not defining "terrorism"; rather, "low intensity confict" (LIC), a form of international terrorism, as the definition indicates and actual practice confirms. LIC is the doctrine to which the United States is officially committed and which has proven its worth in preventing successful independent development in Nicaragua, though it faltered in El Salvador despite its awesome toll. It must be emphasized that LIC—much like its predecessor, "counterinsurgency"—is hardly more than a euphemism for international terrorism, that is, reliance on force that does not reach the level of the war crime of aggression, which falls under the judgment of Nuremberg.

There are many terrorist states in the world, but the United States is unusual in that it is *officially* committed to international terrorism, and on a scale that puts its rivals to shame. Take Iran, surely a terrorist state, as government and media rightly proclaim. Its major known contribution to international terrorism was revealed during the Iran-contra scandal: namely, Iran's perhaps inadvertent involvement in the U.S. proxy war against Nicaragua, a topic of much attention by the media, which succeeded in not noticing this uncomfortable though perfectly evident fact. The U.S. commitment to international terrorism reaches to fine detail. Thus the proxy force attacking Nicaragua is directed to attack agricultural cooperatives— exactly what we denounce with horror on the part of Abu Nidal. In this case, the directives have explicit State Department authorization and the approval of media doves. The U.S.-organized security forces in El Salvador follow the same policy.[20]

"Terrorism is a war against ordinary citizens"; "the terrorists— and the other states that aid and abet them—serve as grim reminders that democracy is fragile and needs to be guarded with vigilance."

So George Shultz thundered at the very moment of the U.S. terrorist attack against Libya. "Negotiations are a euphemism for capitulation if the shadow of power is not cast across the bargaining table," he added, also condemning those who advocate "utopian, legalistic means like outside mediation, the United Nations, and the World Court, while ignoring the power element of the equation." The sentiments are not without precedent in modern history.[21]

It has required considerable discipline on the part of the "specialized class" to maintain its own studied ignorance while denouncing the terrorism of others on command and cue.

We learn just how impressive this achievement has been when we turn to the major examples of the plague. To avoid making the task of exposure too easy, let us put aside the extraordinary outburst of terror throughout Central America in the 1980s—overwhelmingly state-directed international terrorism, given the crucial U.S. role, hence an instance of the major crime of the period, according to the rhetoric of the 1980s, in fact by far the most extreme example.

Consider the year 1985, when media concern over terrorism peaked. The major single terrorist act of 1985 was the blowing up of an Air India flight, killing 329 people. The terrorists had been instructed in their craft in a paramilitary camp in Alabama run by Frank Camper, where mercenaries were trained for terrorist acts in Central America and elsewhere. According to ex-mercenaries, Camper had close ties to U.S. intelligence and was personally involved in the Air India bombing, allegedly a "sting" operation that got out of control. On a visit to India, Attorney-General Edwin Meese conceded in a backhanded way that the terrorist operations originated in a U.S. terrorist training camp, in statements that were barely reported in the press.[22] Any connection of a terrorist to Libya, however frail, suffices to demonstrate that Qaddafi is a "mad dog" who must be eliminated.

Turning to the Middle East, the primary locus of international terrorism according to state doctrine and the media, the major single terrorist act of 1985 was a car-bombing in Beirut in March that killed 80 people and wounded 200. The target was the Shi'ite leader Sheikh Fadlallah, accused of complicity in terrorism, but he escaped. The attack was arranged by the CIA and its Saudi clients with the assistance of Lebanese intelligence and a British specialist, and specifically authorized by CIA director William Casey, according to Bob Woodward's account in his book on Casey and the CIA.[23]

It follows that the United States easily wins the prize for single acts of international terrorism in the peak year of the official plague.

The U.S. client state of Israel follows closely behind. Its Iron Fist operations in Lebanon were without parallel for the year as sustained acts of international terrorism, and the bombing of Tunis (with tacit U.S. support) wins second prize for single terrorist acts, unless we take this to be a case of actual aggression, as was determined by a U.N. Security Council resolution, with the U.S. abstaining.[24]

In 1986, the major single terrorist act was the U.S. bombing of Libya—assuming, again, that we do not assign this attack to the category of aggression. This was a brilliantly staged media event, the first bombing in history scheduled for prime-time TV, for the precise moment when the networks open their national news programs. This convenient arrangement, which the media pretended not to comprehend, allowed anchor men to switch at once to Tripoli so that their viewers could watch the exciting events live. The next act of the superbly crafted TV drama was a series of news conferences and White House statements explaining that this was "self-defense against future attack" and a measured reaction to a disco bombing in West Berlin ten days earlier for which Libya was to blame. The media were well aware that the evidence for this charge was slight, but the facts were suppressed in the general adulation for Reagan's decisive stand against terrorism, echoed across the political spectrum.

Media suppression began from the first moment, when the journalists at the televised press conference loyally averted their eyes from evidence readily at hand that raised very serious doubts about the claims they were hearing, such as the report from Berlin, half an hour before the U.S. attack on Libyan cities, that U.S. and West German officials had no evidence of Libyan involvement in the disco bombing in Berlin, only "suspicions," contrary to administration claims of certain knowledge ten days earlier; at the TV press conference, none of the intrepid members of the White House press corps asked how it could be that Washington had certain knowledge ten days earlier of what remained unknown to U.S. and West German intelligence. Within weeks, it was published prominently in Germany—and in obscure publications here—that the West German police intelligence team investigating the bombing had no knowledge, and had never had any knowledge, of any "Libyan connection." Again, the facts were suppressed, even by journalists interviewing the high German officials who were providing the information to anyone who wanted to hear. Further evidence about U.S. government lies was published abroad but silenced here apart from marginal publications. Thus, the dramatic stories of high administration officials about the alert called in West Berlin after the alleged Libyan "intercepts," which failed by only fifteen minutes to save the victims at the bombed disco, were revealed to have been complete fabrication; no alert had been called, West Berlin police informed the BBC. It was finally conceded quietly that the charges of Libyan involvement had little if any substance, though they continue to be presented as fact; thus, the *Business Week* Pentagon correspondent writes that "by ordering the 1986 bombing of a West Berlin disco in which two American servicemen were killed, Qadaffi provoked a violent response—a massive air raid"; the practice is quite common. But despite the occasional concession in the small print that there is no basis for the tales that are still widely relayed, no conclusions were drawn about the U.S. bombing itself, hitting civilian targets, with about 100 reported killed in "retaliation" for a bombing in which two people had been killed, one an American serviceman. Nor were conclusions drawn about the conscious media collusion in this act of large-scale terrorism, which goes well beyond what is sampled here.[25]

In this case too, the discipline of the specialized class has been impressive throughout, particularly when we bear in mind that the media had been subjecting themselves to disinformation campaigns concerning Libya from the first months of the Reagan administration,[26] recognizing each time that they had been "fooled," but eagerly returning to savor the experience on the next round.

For 1986 too the United States appears to win the prize for international terrorism, even apart from the wholesale terrorism it sponsors in Central America, including what former CIA director Stansfield Turner describes as our "state-supported terrorism" in Nicaragua.[27]

The full range of terrorist actions by the United States and its clients in the 1980s is remarkable. In Central America alone, tens of thousands of murdered, tortured, and mutilated victims can be charged directly to the account of the Reaganites and their accomplices. It is therefore only to be expected that Reagan should be lauded for his contribution to the cause of human rights, one of his major "triumphs," we read in the *New Republic*—without great surprise, considering the meaning of the phrase "human rights" in a journal that urged Reagan to support state terror in El Salvador "regardless of how many are murdered, lest the Marxist-Leninist guerrillas win." At the liberal extreme, editor Hendrik Hertzberg lists the "things about the Reagan era that haven't been so attractive, like sleaze, homelessness, Lebanon [meaning, presumably, dead Marines, not dead Lebanese and Palestinians], yuppie scum," and other forms of ugliness and lack of taste. Tens of thousands of tortured and mutilated bodies in Central America do not qualify as "not so attractive."[28]

International terrorism is, of course, not an invention of the 1980s. In the previous two decades, its major victims were Cuba and Lebanon.

Anti-Cuban terrorism was directed by a secret Special Group established in November 1961 to conduct covert operations against Cuba under the code name "Mongoose," involving 400 Americans, 2,000 Cubans, a private navy of fast boats, and a $50 million annual budget, run in part by a Miami CIA station functioning in violation of the Neutrality Act and, presumably, the law banning CIA operations in the United States.[29] These operations included bombing of hotels and industrial installations, sinking of fishing boats, poisoning of crops and livestock, contamination of sugar exports, blowing up of civilian aircraft, etc. Not all of these actions were directly authorized by the CIA, but we let no such niceties disturb us when condemning officially designated terrorist states.

Several of these terrorist operations took place at the time of the Cuban missile crisis of October-November 1962. In the weeks before, Raymond Garthoff reports, a Cuban terrorist group operating from Florida with U.S. government authorization carried out "a daring speedboat strafing attack on a Cuban seaside hotel near Havana where Soviet military technicians were known to congregate, killing a score of Russians and Cubans"; and shortly after, attacked British and Cuban cargo ships and again raided Cuba among other actions that were stepped up in early October while Congress passed a resolution "sanctioning the use of force, if necessary, to restrain Cuban aggression and subversion in the Western Hemisphere" and voted to withhold aid from any country trading with Cuba. At one of the tensest moments of the missile crisis, on November 8, a terrorist team dispatched from the United States blew up a Cuban industrial facility after the Mongoose operations had been officially suspended. In a letter to the U.N. Secretary General, Fidel Castro alleged that 400 workers had been killed in this operation, guided by "photographs taken by spying planes" (referring to testimony by the captured "leader of a group of spies trained by the CIA and directed by it"). This terrorist act, which might have set off a global nuclear war, was considered important enough to merit passing reference in a footnote in an article on the missile crisis in the journal *International Security*, but no media attention, to my knowledge. Attempts to assassinate Castro and other terror continued immediately after the crisis terminated, and were escalated by Nixon in 1969.[30] There is no known example of a campaign qualifying so uncontroversially as terror that approaches this one in scale and violence.

Turning to the second major example of the pre-Reagan period, in southern Lebanon from the early 1970s the population was held hostage with the "rational prospect, ultimately fulfilled, that affected populations would exert pressure for the cessation of hostilities" and acceptance of Israeli arrangements for the region (Abba Eban, commenting on Prime Minister Menachem Begin's account of atrocities in Lebanon committed under the Labor government in the style "of regimes which neither Mr. Begin nor I would dare to mention by name," Eban observed, recognizing the accuracy of the account).[31] Notice that this justification, offered by a respected Labor Party dove, places these actions squarely under the rubric of international terrorism by any reasonable definition, unless, again, we consider them to fall under the more serious crime of aggression—as of course we would if an enemy state were the agent of the crimes.

Thousands were killed and hundreds of thousands driven from their homes in these terror attacks. Little is known about them because it was a matter of indifference that Arabs were being murdered and their villages destroyed by a Western state armed and supported by the United States. ABC correspondent Charles Glass, then a journalist in Lebanon, found "little American editorial interest in the conditions of the south Lebanese. The Israeli raids and shelling of their villages, their gradual exodus from south Lebanon to the growing slums on the outskirts of Beirut were nothing compared to the lurid tales of the 'terrorists' who threatened Israel, hijacked aeroplanes and seized embassies." The reaction was much the same, he continues, when Israeli death squads were operating in southern Lebanon after the 1982 Israeli invasion. One could read about them in the *London Times,* but U.S. editors were not interested. Had the media reported the operations of "these death squads of plainclothes Shin Beth [secret police] men who assassinated suspects in the villages and camps of south Lebanon," "stirring up the Shiite Muslim population and helping to make the Marine presence untenable," there might have been some appreciation of the plight of the U.S. Marines deployed in Lebanon. They seemed to have no idea why they were there apart from "the black enlisted men: almost all of them said, though sadly never on camera, that they had been sent to protect the rich against the poor." "The only people in Lebanon they identified with were the poor Shiite refugees who lived all around their base at the Beirut airport; it is sad that it was probably one of these poor Shiites ... who killed 241 of them on 23 October 1983." If any of these matters had been reported, it might have been possible to avert, or at the very least to comprehend, the bombing in which the Marines were killed, victims of a policy that "the press could not explain to the public and their information officers could not explain to the Marines themselves"—and which is now denounced as unprovoked Arab terrorism by George Shultz and the commentators who admire his "visceral contempt for terrorism."[32]

The effect of removing Egypt from the conflict at Camp David was that "Israel would be free to sustain military operations against the PLO in Lebanon as well as settlement activity on the West Bank," Israeli strategic analyst Avner Yaniv observes ten years later; the point was obvious at the time, but remains an unacceptable insight in the euphoria about American "peace-making."[33] Predictably, then, Israeli terror in Lebanon continued after the Camp David agreements, probably escalating, though reporting was so scanty that one cannot be sure. There was enough to know that Palestinians and Lebanese suffered many casualties. Sometimes the Israeli operations were in retaliation or alleged retaliation; often there was no pretext. From early 1981, Israel launched unprovoked attacks which finally elicited a response in July, leading to an exchange in which six Israelis and several hundred Palestinians and Lebanese were killed in Israeli bombing of densely populated civilian targets. Of these incidents, all that remains in the collective memory of the media is the tragic fate of the inhabitants of the northern Galilee, driven from their homes by katyusha rockets.[34]

After a cease-fire was arranged under U.S. auspices, Israel continued its attacks. The Israeli concern, according to Yaniv, was that the PLO would observe the cease-fire agreement and continue its efforts to achieve a diplomatic two-state settlement, to which Israel and the United States were strongly opposed. In the following year, Israel attempted with increasing desperation to evoke some PLO response that could be used as a pretext for the planned invasion of Lebanon, designed to destroy the PLO as a political force, establish Israeli control over the occupied territories, and—in its broadest vision—to establish Ariel Sharon's "New Order" in Lebanon and perhaps beyond. These efforts failed to elicit a PLO response. The media reacted by urging "respect for Israel's anguish" rather than "sermons to Israel" as Israel bombed targets in Lebanon with many civilian casualties.[35] Israel finally used the pretext of the attempted assassination of Ambassador Argov by Abu Nidal—who had been at war with the PLO for years and did not so much as have an office in Lebanon—to launch Operation Peace for Galilee, while the *New York Times* applauded the "liberation of Lebanon," carefully avoiding Lebanese opinion. "Calling the Lebanon War 'The War for the Peace of Galilee' is more than a misnomer," Yehoshafat Harkabi writes. "It would have been more honest to call it 'The War to Safeguard the Occupation of the West Bank'." "Begin's principal motive in launching the war was his fear of the momentum of the peace process."[36]

It was clear enough at the time that the perceived threat of the PLO was its commitment to a political settlement and renunciation of terror. PLO terror, in contrast, was no problem, in fact was desirable as a means for evading political settlement.

The United States backed these policies; accordingly, the actual reasons and background for them are completely foreign to the media, which assure us that the U.S.-Israeli search for peace has been thwarted by PLO terror. After the Israeli invasion, with perhaps 20,000 or more civilian casualties, Israeli terrorist actions in Lebanon continued, as they do today, though these are no part of "the evil scourge of terrorism." We may occasionally read that Lebanese farmers "working in fields near Ain Khilwe were killed when the Israeli planes dropped incendiary bombs," but nothing is suggested by this casual observation in the final sentence of a brief article on the shelling of the refugee camp at Rashidiye by Israeli gunboats, the day after forty-one people were killed and seventy wounded in the bombing of the refugee camp at Ain Khilwe.[37] Other terrorist attacks against Arabs, even against U.S. installations in Arab countries and a U.S. vessel in international waters with many casualties (the *U.S.S. Liberty*), are also readily absorbed when the agent is a client state.

In the light of such facts as these, how is it possible for scholars and the media to maintain the required thesis that the plague of the modern age is conducted by the Soviet-based "worldwide terror network aimed at the destabilization of Western democratic society," as proclaimed by Claire Sterling, who, Walter Laqueur assures us, has provided "ample evidence" that terrorism occurs "almost exclusively in democratic or relatively democratic countries"? How is it possible for the media to continue to identify Iran, Libya, the PLO, Cuba, and other official enemies as the leading practitioners of international terrorism? The answer is simplicity itself. It is only necessary, once again, to recall "the utility of interpretations." Terrorism is terrorism only when conducted by official enemies; when the United States and its clients are the agents, it is defense of democracy and human rights.

The media are not called upon to defend the doctrine, only to adhere to it. The scholarly literature has a more demanding task. As an example, consider the contributions of the highly regarded ter-rorologist Walter Laqueur[38]—a respected scholar whose insight into international affairs is illustrated by his declaration elsewhere that "unlike the Soviet Union, the U.S. does not want to convert anyone to a specific political, social, or economic system."[39]

A primary concern of Laqueur's scholarly study of terrorism is "international state-sponsored terrorism." His study contains many innuendos and charges about Cuban sponsorship of terrorism, with little pretense of evidence. But there is not one word on the U.S. terrorist operations against Cuba. He writes that in "recent decades ... the more oppressive regimes are not only free from terror, they have helped to launch it against more permissive societies." His intent, of course, is to imply that the United States, a "permissive society," is one of the victims of the plague of international state-sponsored terrorism, while Cuba, an "oppressive regime," is one of the agents. What in fact follows from his statement is that the United States is a "more oppressive regime" and Cuba a "more permissive society," given that the United States has undeniably launched major terrorist attacks against Cuba and is relatively free from terror itself. The careful selection of evidence and allegations is designed to prevent understanding of these simple facts.

Employing the same doctrinal filters, Laqueur states that the 1982 Israeli invasion of Lebanon was a response to PLO "attacks against Israel"; the actual facts of the matter, as we have seen, are radically different. In earlier years, he asserts, the PLO "stormed Damour," killing "some 600 civilians," after they had decided, for no suggested reason, to support the Lebanese National Movement against the Maronites. The terrorist attacks of the Israeli-backed Maronites that drew the PLO into the civil war and led to the retaliatory terror at Damour pass without mention; rather, Laqueur writes that "even if [the PLO] had kept scrupulously neutral, which they certainly did not, their mere physical presence would have ... acted as a provocation." He does not elaborate on how they might have kept "scrupulously neutral" after murderous attacks on Pales-tinians and Lebanese allied with them.[40] But just as a propaganda agent for the United States will see no U.S. terror against Cuba, only Cuban support for terror, so an Israeli propagandist understands that the task is to demonize the PLO and thus to provide implicit justification for continued Israeli control over the occupied territories—what Laqueur calls "the Left Bank."

Laqueur observes that terrorism "has been a factor of some importance in El Salvador and Guatemala," referring not to the awesome display of state terrorism orchestrated and backed by the United States but to guerrilla terror—real, but not remotely comparable to the "international state-sponsored terrorism" that he evades when the agents are the wrong ones for his purposes. Laqueur mentions that six Americans "perished in the civil war in El Salvador." They are not further identified, but he presumably has in mind the four American churchwomen raped and murdered by the Salvadoran National Guard supported by the U.S. and directed by General Vides Casanova, who was promoted to Defense Minister under the Duarte government in the "fledgling democracy"; and two Americans working on land reform, assassinated in a restaurant by soldiers under orders from officers of the National Guard and the chief of staff, who were never charged. None of these facts are mentioned, and they occasion no thoughts on the source of terrorism in that traumatized country. One might also ask whether the phrase "perished in the civil war" does justice to the element of "international state-sponsored terrorism" in these atrocities. But if the task is to provide a cover for U.S.-backed atrocities so that they can proceed with impunity while demonizing enemies of the state, facts can be dismissed as a mere annoyance.

Laqueur refers to Sheikh Fadlallah, though not to the CIA-initiated car-bombing in March 1985 that killed eighty civilians in a failed effort to assassinate him. Car-bombs in Lebanon and elsewhere are within the scope of his concept of terrorism. Thus "the car-bomb attacks against US marines in the Lebanon" fall within the canon of terrorism, but the car-bomb attack initiated by the CIA that was the major single act of international terrorism in the Middle East in the peak year of the plague does not. Similarly, the use of letter-bombs and "a primitive book-bomb" is discussed, but there is no mention of the sophisticated book-bomb used by Israeli intelligence to kill Egyptian General Mustapha Hafez in Gaza in 1956, at a time when he was responsible for preventing Palestinian Fedayeen from infiltrating to attack Israeli targets.[41] Laqueur's review of the use of letter-bombs also does not include the testimony of Ya'akov Eliav, a commander of the terrorist group headed by the current Prime Minister of Israel, Yitzhak Shamir (*Lehi*, the "Stern gang"). In a 1983 book, Eliav claims to have been the first to use letter-bombs. Working from Paris in 1946, he arranged to have seventy such bombs sent in official British government envelopes to all members of the British cabinet, the heads of the Tory opposition, and several military commanders, marked "personal and secret" so that the intended victim would open them himself. In June 1947, he and an accomplice were caught by Belgian police while attempting to send these letter-bombs, and all were intercepted.[42]

Laqueur refers to North Vietnamese-guided terrorism in South Vietnam in the late 1950s and early 1960s, avoiding the basic facts of the matter, available in any reputable scholarly study: that Hanoi authorized violence only after several years of pleas by southerners who were being wiped out by the U.S.-Diem terrorist assault that had decimated the anti-French resistance, that "the government terrorized far more than did the revolutionary movement" and well before violence was authorized in response to U.S.-sponsored terror, and that this authorization of force came long after the United States and its client had undermined the Geneva Accords that established a temporary demarcation line between North and South Vietnam.[43]

Laqueur also discusses narco-terrorism on the part of Soviet-bloc countries, notably Laos, which even grows opium, an extreme proof of Soviet iniquity, the reader is to understand. He concedes that "there were some rumours—and perhaps more than rumours—about links between the production of drugs in the 'golden triangle' in South-east Asia and various local warlords and insurgencies." But his discussion of narco-terrorism carefully skirts the leading role of the CIA in the drug trade, particularly in Laos and the golden triangle. The facts would be useless for the intended goals, so they are again consigned to the memory hole and Laos becomes an example of *Soviet*-backed narco-terrorism. One must at least admire the audacity. Laqueur is not the only scholar to voice concern over a possible Soviet role in the drug trade. To mention another, Oxford history professor Norman Stone, warning that the West should not be carried away by Gorbachev's trickery, refers ominously to "the alleged Soviet involvement in the drugs trade, to demoralise the West," but not to the well-established U.S. government involvement in the drug trade since shortly after World War II.[44]

Terrorism in the Western democracies became a problem in the 1960s, Laqueur continues, when "political violence became intellectually respectable ... in some circles," and the terrorist groups, mostly left-wing, launched a "terrorist wave" with foreign support. He does concede that right-wing terrorism existed, even noting that "the terroristic outrages which involved most victims in Europe," one in Munich and two in Italy, "were not carried out by left-wing groups"—his way of saying that this was right-wing terror. He adds that "the Munich bomb had almost certainly exploded inadvertently," so presumably the right is at least partially exculpated; left-wing bombs always aim directly at civilians. Despite the fact that the worst terror in Europe was attributable to the right wing, "it could still be argued," he goes on, that right-wing terror "was far less frequent and systematic." This serviceable argument is facilitated by entirely ignoring the exploits of right-wing extremists, for example in Italy, where fascist elements integrated with the military and the secret services may have almost come within reach of taking over the state during a period of "terrorist outrages" for which the right was largely responsible.[45]

Left-wing terror in the United States, apart from Blacks, was apolitical, Laqueur explains. It grew from "the crisis of identity, suburban boredom, the desire for excitement and action, a certain romantic streak—in short terrorism as a cure for personality problems." So Laqueur has determined, doubtless on the basis of profound psychological study of the participants. In particular, this was true of the Weathermen. Surely they were merely suffering from "personal hangups" enhanced by "immense intellectual confusion" and "an absence of values," not reacting to such trivialities as the treatment of Blacks, the U.S. wars in Indochina, or the kinds of values exhibited by the Laqueurs who supported aggression and massive atrocities until they became too costly to the perpetrator, or simply kept their silence.[46]

A problem in dealing with terrorism is that the media provide such a favorable image to the terrorists, whom they so admire. Thus, "the attitude of television to terrorism has spanned the whole gamut from exaggerated respect to sycophancy," apparently not including a critical word. As throughout, evidence is eschewed in favor of *obiter dicta* that are useful for ideological warfare.

There "has been no Western equivalent of terrorism of the kind practised by the various Abu Nidals and Carlos" and other official terrorists; surely nothing like the car bombing in Beirut in March 1985, the attacks on agricultural cooperatives in Nicaragua, or the achievements of Operation Mongoose in Cuba, for example. Rather, "state-sponsored terrorism" is directed against democratic societies. The reasons for the abstention from terrorism on the part of the United States and its allies is that "the Western countries are *status-quo* orientated" and "want to prevent insurgencies and other forms of destabilization." This explains why the United States has been so scrupulous in preserving the status quo in Cuba, Chile under Allende, and Nicaragua, among many other cases, and has refrained from intervention and other forms of destabilization throughout its history. Furthermore, the Soviet Union can make use of proxies "such as Cuba or Bulgaria," but America "has no such substitutes," and is therefore reduced to rank "amateur[ism]" in comparison with the "professionals" of the Soviet bloc. The United States cannot turn to the neo-Nazi generals of Argentina, or to Taiwan, Israel, and other client states to aid the contras (perhaps that was the lesson of the Iran/contra hearings) or to support state terrorism in Guatemala, and is thus unable to compete with its Soviet opponent.

If international terrorism increases, this highly regarded expert advises, "the obvious way to retaliate is, of course, to pay the sponsors back in their own coin," difficult as such legitimate response may be in the Western societies that find it so hard to comprehend that others do not share their "standards of democracy, freedom and humanism." Legitimate response does not, however, include the bombing of Washington and Tel Aviv, thanks to the familiar utility of interpretations.

It is necessary to recall that all of this is taken quite seriously in the media and general intellectual culture. In reality, Laqueur's scholarship, not untypical of the genre, is an ideological construction, only occasionally tainted by the world of fact. Not surprisingly, it is highly welcomed for its contribution to establishing the images required for state propaganda. The media can then refer to the scholarly literature and call upon the practitioners of the art for solemn commentary and advice, as they serve their own function.

3. Heroes and Devils[47]

As the authors of children's tales understand, life is simple when there are heroes to admire and love, and devils to fear and despise. One goal of a well-crafted propaganda system is to dull the mental faculties, reducing its targets to a level at which they will respond with appropriate enthusiasm to slogans carrying a patriotic message. Accordingly, the cast of characters in international affairs includes heroes, who stand for freedom, democracy, reform, and all good things, and devils, who are violent, totalitarian, and generally repellent. Most of the players are irrelevant, part of the background scenery. Entry into the two significant categories is determined by contribution to elite interests, or harm caused them.

Iran provides an interesting example.[48] Nationalist currents developed during and after World War II as Britain and the Soviet Union jockeyed for influence, and the United States extended its presence as part of its growing role in the region, control over oil being a major factor. U.S. pressures were instrumental in expelling the Soviet Union from northern Iran at the Soviet border in 1946. The oil resources of the country remained a British monopoly, though the British were wary of U.S. intentions. The nationalist movement crystallized around Muhammad Mossadeq, whom James Bill describes as "an old-fashioned liberal," "a beloved figure of enormous charisma to Iranians of all social classes."[49] Mossadeq became Prime Minister in 1951, heading the nationalist bloc, committed to the nationalization of Iranian oil. By 1953, the United States agreed with Britain that he had to go. A CIA coup overthrew the parliamentary regime, restoring the Shah. One consequence of the coup was that U.S. oil companies took 40 percent of the Iranian concession, part of the general takeover of the world's major energy reserves by the United States.[50] The Shah remained in power, with constant U.S. support that reached an extraordinary level in the Nixon-Kissinger years, through 1978, when he was overthrown by a popular mass movement.

Our assumptions would lead us to predict that Mossadeq would pass from insignificance to the devil category as the United States determined to overthrow him, while the Shah, generally supportive of U.S. goals, would be a hero until the Peacock Throne began to totter, at which point other devils would arise. In brief, that is the story told by William Dorman and Mansour Farhang in their review of press coverage of Iran over this period.[51]

When Mossadeq became Prime Minister in 1951, the United States was "generally supportive of Iranian demands" concerning oil policy, Dorman and Farhang observe, perhaps because "U.S. officials saw an opportunity to gain a foothold for American companies at the expense of British interests." Correspondingly, the press "portrayed Iran's position in relatively evenhanded terms." But after nationalization, the U.S. government reversed its stand, and "a new frame began to take shape in the press." "Over about a two-year period, then, Mossadeq's portrait would change from that of a quaint nationalist to that of near lunatic to one, finally, of Communist dupe." In fact, he remained an anti-imperialist nationalist seeking to maintain Iran's independence. It was U.S. plans, not Mossadeq, that had changed; the media shifted course, hardly a step behind state policy.

The *New York Times* observed that there are lessons to be learned from the restoration of the Shah in 1953 and the establishment of the U.S. concession. Crucially, "Underdeveloped countries with rich resources now have an object lesson in the heavy cost that must be paid by one of their number which goes berserk with fanatical nationalism," attempting to control its own resources. "It is perhaps too much to hope that Iran's experience will prevent the rise of Mossadeghs in other countries, but that experience may at least strengthen the hands of more reasonable and far-seeing leaders."[52] A sage warning from the independent media.

As the United States geared up to overthrow the Mossadeq government, his media image deteriorated and he was routinely condemned as a dictator. The Shah, however, was virtually never described in such terms as long as his power held. From his restoration by the CIA coup in August 1953 until the revolution of 1978, the *New York Times* used the phrase once, referring to the Shah as a "benevolent dictator" in 1967, and "did not publish a major story on human rights violations in Iran" during the period when the Shah was identified by Amnesty International and others as one of the worst human rights violators in the world. During the year of revolution in 1978, Dorman and Farhang found *one* reference to the Shah as a dictator, and that in a positive context, when a *Washington Post* editorial wondered why he did not use the power available to him as "a dictator" to suppress the population even more violently.

Though Mossadeq's "style of rule was far more democratic than anything Iran had known," Dorman and Farhang observe, and surely more so than that of the Shah, it was Mossadeq who was called an "absolute dictator" while the Shah was a benevolent progressive reformer who "demonstrated his concern for the masses" (*New York Times*). "It is no exaggeration," they continue, "to say that the *Times* demonstrated more concern for Iran's constitutional system during the single month of August 1953 [when the U.S. was moving to "save" it by a military coup] than it would during the following quarter of a century." A familiar tale.

A plebiscite called by Mossadeq was denounced by the *New York Times* as "more fantastic and farcical than any ever held under

Hitler or Stalin." A plebiscite conducted by the Shah ten years later "under far more questionable circumstances," with a 99 percent vote in favor of the Shah, was lauded by the *Times* as "emphatic evidence" that "the Iranian people are doubtless behind the Shah in his bold new reform efforts." The Shah's fraudulent elections were lauded with equal enthusiasm.

While the *Times* was fully aware of the CIA role in the 1953 coup within a year, Dorman and Farhang conclude, seventeen years went by before the fact received passing mention. "Clearly Mossadeq was the single most popular leader until the rise of Khomaini," they observe, but for the U.S. press, it was clear that "the great majority of Iranians all but worship" the Shah (*Washington Post*). While strikes in Poland received enthusiastic applause, Dorman and Farhang could find not "a single editorial or column" that "commented favorably on the strikes" in Iran at the same time in the course of the popular uprising against the Shah.[53]

The fall of the Shah elicited the first serious concern in twenty-five years for civil and human rights in Iran, with impassioned congressional and media commentary and the first Senate resolution condemning repression; "longtime apologists for the shah and his government" such as Senators Jacob Javits and Henry Jackson were particularly outspoken in condemnation of human rights violations—after the brutal tyrant was deposed.[54] The media reaction was the same.

In these respects, the pattern is virtually identical to Nicaragua. From 1960 through 1977, the *New York Times* had three editorials on Nicaragua (1963, 1967), and even the final paroxysm of terror in 1978-79 received little comment. Other media coverage was similar, as we have seen. Through the 1980s, the pattern changed dramatically as "for the first time" Nicaragua came to have "a government that cares for its people," in the words of the unreportable José Figueres in 1986. In accordance with the dictates of the State Department Office of Latin American Public Diplomacy, the Sandinistas are totalitarian monsters who must be removed or at least "contained," as we "restore democracy" and defend human rights in fulfillment of our mission—miraculously activated on July 19, 1979.

The pattern is characteristic. These quick transitions and their obvious cause scarcely arouse a second thought, another illustration of the effectiveness of indoctrination among the educated classes.

The sudden discovery of human rights problems in Iran in 1979, as the U.S. client was displaced, had other consequences. Reviewing media coverage of the Kurds, Vera Beaudin Saeedpour observes that "beginning in 1979, the Kurds of Iran captured the attention of the *Times*" as they took up arms against the Khomeini regime.[55] Subsequent press coverage treated the Kurdish problem as "a variable in the power struggle." The basic question was whether whether U.S. interests would benefit or suffer if Iran were to be dismembered; coverage of the rights and travail of the Kurdish people rose or fell according to this criterion.

There is, however, another condition under which repression of the Kurds becomes a legitimate issue of concern: if it can be exploited to support Israeli power. Thus, *Times* columnist William Safire has written favorably of Kurdish aspirations for autonomy and respect for their culture, then coming to the point: "PLO leader, Yasir Arafat, who wants not only sovereignty in the West Bank but claims all of Israel, has embraced the Ayatollah in Iran" and does not defend the Kurds; and the "Soviet-backed" Iraqis are equally hypocritical, attacking the "non-Arab Kurds" but calling for independence for Palestinian Arabs. "Kurdish rights are ignored wherever PLO supporters are lionized," Safire concludes, also a common theme in the *New Republic* and other publications of the Israeli lobby.

Safire "championed the Kurds of Iraq" from 1976, Saeedpour observes, writing of the betrayal of the "non-Arab Kurds" and the hypocrisy of Arabs who "talk of 'legitimate rights' of Palestinians" but "fall silent at the mention of the Kurds." In 1980, he advocated arming the Kurds against the regime in Iran. Even Israel has done nothing for the suffering Kurds in Iran and Iraq, he protests. "Yet to this day," Saeedpour continues, "Mr. Safire has produced not a single essay on the Kurds in Turkey," where they have been subject to extreme repression under the U.S.-backed regime (and Israeli ally). Only their fate in enemy Iran and Arab Iraq evokes indignation and humanitarian concern.

Coverage of the Kurds in Iraq received brief notice in 1975 when the cynical manipulation of their struggle by Nixon and Kissinger, and their abandonment to Iraqi terror when they were no longer needed, was revealed in the leaked secret report of the House Pike Committee. Since then, Iraqi terror against the Kurds has been an intermittent theme, largely insofar as their plight can be exploited as an anti-Arab weapon. And the repression of Kurds in Iran occasionally arises as an issue in the context of U.S. strategic interests.

Harsh treatment of the Kurds in Turkey, a U.S. ally, has no such value or utility. Coverage is therefore markedly different, as Saeedpour shows. In Turkey, Kurdish separatism is not to be advocated; indeed there are no Kurds, our Turkish ally alleges, and even use of the language is criminal. The media adhere closely to the Turkish government perspective. Though there was some limited notice of anti-Kurdish repression after the U.S.-backed military coup of 1980, subsequently the Kurds were denounced as "Marxist and terrorist" while the brutal Turkish state was presented as a "secular democracy" beleaguered by terrorism. The tales spun about the KGB-Bulgarian plot to kill the Pope, using a Turkish fascist transmuted by the propaganda system into a Communist agent, helped establish this image. The "acquiescence of the American press in the Turkish interpretations of events," Saeedpour writes, is shown in the reports on Turkish attacks against Kurds in Iraq in cross-border raids, allegedly in retaliation against "unidentified aggressors." Similar reports on violence in Kurdish areas of Turkey, based on Turkish news agencies, imply that Kurds are killing Turks. The press, echoed by some scholars, alleges that the Kurds in Turkey do not support the "militants," a claim that "borders on the absurd," Saeedpour comments, since for a Turkish Kurd to avow such support would be "tantamount to committing suicide." Kurdish opinion cannot even be sampled in a country where their ethnic identity is illegal.

In short, atrocities against the Kurds, and their search for self-determination, are proper themes—but only when they are useful for other ends.

4. The "Peace Process" in the Middle East[56]

The task of "historical engineering" has been accomplished with singular efficiency in the case of the Arab-Israeli conflict, arguably the most hazardous issue in world affairs, with a constant threat of devastating regional war and superpower conflict. The task has been to present the United States and Israel as "yearning for peace" and pursuing a "peace process," while in reality they have led the rejectionist camp and have been blocking peace initiatives that have broad international and regional support. This remained the case as 1988 came to an end with the diplomatic flurry discussed in chapter 4, to which we return.

From the late 1960s there has been a substantial consensus in favor of a political settlement on the internationally recognized (pre-June 1967) borders, with perhaps minor modifications. In the early stages, the terms of this broad consensus were restricted to the rights of existing states, and were, in fact, very much along the general lines of official U.S. policy as expressed in the Rogers plan of December 1969. By the mid-1970s the terms of the consensus shifted to include the concept of a Palestinian state in the West Bank and Gaza Strip, with recognized borders, security guarantees, and other arrangements to safeguard the rights of all states in the region. At this point, the PLO and most Arab states approached or joined the international consensus. Prior to this, the consensus was strictly rejectionist, denying the right of self-determination to one of the two contending parties, the indigenous population of the former Palestine.

To avoid misunderstanding, I should stress that I am departing from standard convention and am using the term "rejectionist" with its actual meaning, referring to the position that rejects the right of self-determination of one of the contending parties. Thus, I am not adopting the conventional usage, which applies the term "rejectionist" only to those who deny the right of self-determination to Jews. The strictly racist conventional usage is designed to fortify, by tacit assumption, the doctrinal requirement that Palestinians lack such rights. Note also that evaluation of the status of such rights, in one or the other case, is a separate matter, which I do not address here.

The United States has been opposed to all of the arrangements of the international consensus, both the earlier plan that conformed to official U.S. policy and offered nothing to the Palestinians, and the later nonrejectionist alternative that recognized the parallel rights of both Israeli Jews and Palestinian Arabs. The United States preferred to block a political settlement that might have been feasible, and (rhetoric aside) to fund and support Israeli expansion into the territories. Both major political groupings in Israel have always adamantly opposed any political settlement that does not grant Israel effective control over the resources and much of the land in the occupied territories; they differ only in the modalities of this rejectionist stance, which denies the right of self-determination to the indigenous population.[57] The U.S. administrations have generally supported the position of the Israeli Labor Alignment, which calls for a form of "territorial compromise" that would satisfy these basic demands. U.S.-Israeli rejectionism has been so extreme that Palestinians have even been denied the right to select their own representatives for eventual negotiations. Thus, the United States and Israel have adopted a position comparable to the refusal in 1947 to allow Jews to be represented by the Zionist organizations in the negotiations of that time, a position that would have been regarded as a reversion to Nazism had it been put forth.[58] One would be hard put to find any questioning in the media of the U.S.-Israeli position in this regard, a fact of no small interest for those intrigued by the primitive nature of contemporary Western culture.

The media have had the task of presenting extreme rejectionism as accommodation and the soul of moderation, and suppressing the efforts of the Arab states and the PLO to advance a nonrejectionist settlement, depicting the PLO in particular as violent extremists. These responsibilities have been fulfilled with dedication, skill, and great success.[59]

U.S. efforts to derail a political settlement can be traced to 1971, when the administration opted for Kissinger's policy of "stalemate" and backed Israel's rejection of a full-scale peace proposal by President Sadat of Egypt that was framed in terms of the international consensus and official U.S. policy. These events therefore had to be excised from history. Consequently, standard doctrine holds that that it was only six years later, in 1977, that "Egyptian President Anwar Sadat broke through the wall of Arab rejectionism to fly to Jerusalem and offer peace to Israel in the Israeli Knesset"[60]—on terms less acceptable to Israel than those of his rejected proposal six years earlier, which offered nothing to the Palestinians. It would be difficult to discover anyone who is willing to break ranks on this crucial doctrine of the propaganda system.

In the years between, the October 1973 war had taught Kissinger and the Israeli leadership that Egypt could not simply be dismissed with contempt, as had been assumed in the mood of post-1967 triumphalism. They therefore moved to the next best policy of excluding the major Arab deterrent from the conflict so that Israel would be free, with U.S. support reaching phenomenal levels, to integrate the bulk of the occupied territories and attack its northern neighbor while serving the United States as a "strategic asset." This policy was consummated—whatever the intentions of the participants might have been—at Camp David in 1978-79. In this context, Sadat's 1977 peace initiative was admissible.

An associated doctrine is that Sadat's "break with Arab rejectionism" in 1977 remains unique. It is therefore necessary to expunge from the record such events as the session of the U.N. Security Council in January 1976, when the United States vetoed a resolution advanced by Jordan, Syria, and Egypt, supported by the PLO and even "prepared" by it according to Israel, which called for a two-state diplomatic settlement in the terms of the international consensus, with territorial and security guarantees. On the rights of Israel, the proposal of the Arab "confrontation states" and the PLO reiterated the wording of U.N. Resolution 242, calling for "appropriate arrangements ... to guarantee ... the sovereignty, territorial integrity and political independence of all states in the area and their right to live in peace within secure and recognized boundaries." This is the first of many endorsements of U.N. 242 by the PLO, with the backing of the major Arab states.

These facts are unacceptable. Accordingly, they quickly disappeared from official history and have remained unmentionable. The same is true of the unanimous endorsement by the Palestine National Council (PNC) in April 1981 of a Soviet peace proposal with two "basic principles": (1) the right of the Palestinians to achieve self-determination in an independent state; (2) "It is essential to ensure the security and sovereignty of all states of the region including those of Israel." It has also been necessary to suppress a series of initiatives over the years by the PLO and others to break the diplomatic logjam and move towards a two-state peaceful settlement that would recognize the right of national self-determination of Israeli Jews and Palestinian Arabs, regularly blocked by U.S.-Israeli rejectionism.

The general Washington-media position has been that Palestinians must be satisfied with Labor Party rejectionism, which grants Israel control over the occupied territories and their resources, while excluding areas of dense Arab settlement so that Israel will not have to face the "demographic problem," a term devised to disguise the obviously racist presuppositions. In these areas, the population will remain stateless or be administered by Jordan. These options are overwhelmingly rejected by the people of the territories, but that fact is deemed irrelevant on the traditional principle that people who are in our way are less than human and do not have rights.

During these years, the rejectionist stand of the United States has been taken as a historical given in the media and the intellectual community generally, hence not subject to discussion. Thus, *Times* correspondent Thomas Friedman writes that Arafat "has to face the choice of either going down in history as the Palestinian leader who recognized Israel in return for only, at best, a majority of the West Bank or shouldering full responsibility for the Palestinians' continuing to get nothing at all."[61] These are the only choices, for the simple and sufficient reason that only these options are permitted by the United States. In a *Times Magazine* article of October 1984 deploring the growing strength of "extremists, and all those in the Middle East who reject compromise solutions," Friedman places primary blame on the Arabs, particularly Yasser Arafat: "By refusing to recognize Israel and negotiate with it directly, the Arabs have only strengthened Israeli fanatics like Rabbi Kahane, enabling them to play on the legitimate fears and security concerns of the Israeli public," which still has "a majority for compromise." This was a few months after Arafat had quite explicitly called for negotiations with Israel leading to mutual recognition, a call officially rejected by Israel, dismissed without comment by the United States, and unreported in the *New York Times*, which even refused to publish letters referring to it.[62] But no matter: Arafat's call for negotiations and mutual recognition is an "extremist" refusal "to recognize Israel and negotiate with it directly," and the refusal of the Israeli Labor Party to consider this possibility is moderation and search for compromise. Pursuing the familiar conventions, Friedman writes that "it took Anwar Sadat to bring out the moderate in Moshe Dayan and Menachem Begin," referring not to his rejected peace offer of 1971, which is ideologically unacceptable and therefore does not exist, but to the less forthcoming proposals of 1977, admissible to the historical record because they were issued after the United States and Israel had recognized that their larger goals were unattainable.[63]

For the *Times* editors, the willingness to accord both contestants equal rights is defined as "rejectionism"; that is, nonrejectionism is rejectionism, another example of the utility of interpretations. It is fair, they say, to criticize "Israel's hard-fisted repression," but it is necessary "to complete the record" and recall the background reasons, specifically, the "sterile rejectionism" of the Palestinians, and the Arabs generally, which leaves Israel little choice. Deploring the "intransigence" of "the Arab heads of state" in June 1988, the editors write that "while they didn't reject the Shultz peace plan outright or insist on Palestinian statehood, they hardened their stance on the need for Israeli withdrawal from all occupied territories." This is unfortunate: "Rejectionism is a formula for endless paralysis." "Rejectionism" here means not rejection of the right of one or the other of the contending national groups to self-determination, but rather rejection of the Shultz peace plan, which denies this right to the Palestinians but is moderate and forthcoming by definition, because it is advanced by the United States. The editors call upon "the West Bankers," who "have been ill-used by PLO exiles and their let's-pretend declarations" calling for Palestinian self-determination, to go beyond "defying occupying soldiers" and "to take the harder step," that is, to accept the U.S.-Israel conception of peace *without* Palestinian self-determination. The editors even state that "Israel can't be blamed because Palestinians spurned Security Council peace plans"; for example, the two-state Security Council resolution supported (or "prepared") by the PLO in January 1976, and vetoed by the United States—but nonexistent, because inconsistent with ideological requirements.[64]

The attitude is reminiscent of a stubborn three-year-old: I don't like it, so it isn't there. The difference is that in this case, the three-year-old happens to be the information services of the reigning superpower.

The option of a nonrejectionist settlement that accords Palestinians the same human rights as Jews does not exist, because the United States and Israel oppose it; that is a simple, unchallengeable fact, the basis for further discussion. Similarly, it has been taken for granted that the Palestinians, unlike the Jews, do not have the right to select their own representatives, a particularly extreme form of rejectionism. The "peace process" must be crafted so as to protect these principles from scrutiny and awareness. Success has been brilliant, as I have documented at length elsewhere.[65]

As the quasi-official Newspaper of Record, the *New York Times* must be more careful than most to safeguard the preferred version of history. As already noted, when Yasser Arafat issued a call for negotiations leading to mutual recognition in April-May 1984, the *Times* refused to print the facts or even letters referring to them. When its Jerusalem correspondent Thomas Friedman reviewed "Two Decades of Seeking Peace in the Middle East" a few months later, the major Arab (including PLO) initiatives of these two decades were excluded, and attention was focused on the various rejectionist U.S. proposals: the official "peace process." Four days later, the *Times* editors explained that "the most important reality is that the Arabs will finally have to negotiate with Israel," but Yasser Arafat stands in the way "and still talks of an unattainable independent state" instead of adopting a "genuine approach to Israel" to "reinforce the healthy pragmatism of Israel's Prime Minister Peres" by agreeing to accept King Hussein as the spokesman "for West Bank Palestinians"—regardless of their overwhelming opposition to this choice, irrelevant in the case of people who have no human rights because they stand in the way of U.S. designs. That Peres's "healthy pragmatism" grants Israel control over much of the territories and their resources is also unmentioned. Shortly after, in yet another review of the "peace process" under the heading "Are the Palestinians Ready to Seek Peace?," diplomatic correspondent Bernard Gwertzman asserted—again falsely—that the PLO has always rejected "any talk of negotiated peace with Israel."[66]

Note that Gwertzman need not ask whether Israel or the United States is "ready for peace." For the United States, this is true by definition, since "peace" is defined as whatever Washington is prepared to accept. And since the Israeli Labor Party, with its "healthy pragmatism," is basically in accord with U.S. rejectionism, it too is automatically "ready for peace."

The commitment to falsifying the record on this crucial matter reaches impressive levels. On December 10, 1986, Friedman wrote that the Israeli group Peace Now has "never been more distressed" because of "the absence of any Arab negotiating partner."[67] A few months later, he quoted Shimon Peres as deploring the lack of a "peace movement among the Arab people" such as "we have among the Jewish people," and saying that there can be no PLO participation in negotiations "as long as it is remaining a shooting organization and refuses to negotiate."[68] Recall that this is almost three years after the Israeli government's rejection of Arafat's offer for negotiations leading to mutual recognition.

Six days before Friedman's article on "the absence of any Arab negotiating partner," a headline in the mass-circulation Israeli journal *Ma'ariv* read: "Arafat indicates to Israel that he is ready to enter into direct negotiations." The offer was made during the tenure of the "healthy pragmatist" Shimon Peres as Prime Minister. Peres's press advisor confirmed the report, commenting that "there is a principled objection to any contact with the PLO, which flows from the doctrine that the PLO cannot be a partner to negotiations." Labor party functionary Yossi Beilin observed that "the proposal ... was dismissed because it appeared to be a tricky attempt to establish direct contacts when we are not prepared for any negotiations with any PLO factor." Yossi Ben-Aharon, head of the Prime Minister's office and Yitzhak Shamir's political adviser, explained that

> There is no place for any division in the Israeli camp between Likud and the Labor Alignment. There is in fact cooperation and general understanding, certainly with regard to the fact that the PLO cannot be a participant in discussions or in anything ... No one associated with the PLO can represent the issue of the Palestinians. If there is any hope for arrangements that will solve this problem, then the prior condition must be to destroy the PLO

> from its roots in this region. Politically, psychologically, socially,
> economically, ideologically. It must not retain a shred of influ-
> ence ... The Israeli opposition to any dealings with the PLO will
> lead to the consequence that it will weaken and ultimately
> disappear ... This depends to a considerable extent upon us. For
> example, no journalist may ask questions about the PLO or its
> influence. The idea that the PLO is a topic for discussion in the
> Israeli press—that is already improper. There must be a consen-
> sus here, and no debate, that the PLO may not be a factor with
> which Israel can develop any contact.[69]

None of this was reported in the mainstream U.S. media, though
Friedman was alone in using the occasion to issue one of his periodic
laments over the bitter fate of the only peace forces in the Middle East,
which lack any Arab negotiating partner.

Friedman's services are much appreciated. The *Times* promoted
him to chief diplomatic correspondent, and in April 1988, he received
the Pulitzer Prize for "balanced and informed coverage" of the Middle East, of which these are a few samples. This is his second such
award. He received the first for his work in Lebanon, but he observed
that at that time the pleasure was marred because the award came
just after the bombing of the American Embassy in Lebanon, at "a
moment very much bittersweet." This time, however, the award was
"unalloyed, untinged by any tragedy," an interesting reaction on the
part of a journalist covering Jerusalem and the occupied territories,
where apparently everything had been just fine in the preceding
months of violent repression of the Palestinian uprising.[70]

On the occasion of his receipt of the Pulitzer Prize, Friedman
had several long interviews in the Israeli press,[71] in which he repeated
some of the fabrications he has helped establish, for example, that the
Palestinians "refuse to come to terms with the existence of Israel, and
prefer to offer themselves as sacrifices." The tone of racist contempt
is no less noteworthy than the falsehood. He went on to laud his
brilliance for having "foreseen completely the uprising in the territories"—which will come as something of a surprise to his regular
readers—while writing "stories that no one else had ever sent" with
unique care and perception; prior to his insights, he explained, Israel
was "the most fully reported country in the world, but the least
understood in the media." Friedman also offered his solution to the
problem of the territories. The model should be south Lebanon,
controlled by a terrorist mercenary army backed by Israeli might. The
basic principle must be "security, not peace." Nevertheless, the Palestinians should not be denied everything: "Only if you give the

Palestinians something to lose is there a hope that they will agree to moderate their demands"—that is, beyond the "demand" for mutual recognition in a two-state settlement, the longstanding position that Friedman refuses to report and consistently denies. He continues: "I believe that as soon as Ahmed has a seat in the bus, he will limit his demands."

The latter phrase is interesting. One can imagine a similar comment by a southern sheriff in Mississippi thirty years ago ("give Sambo a seat in the bus, and he may quiet down"), though it is hard to believe that a U.S. reporter could make such a statement today about any group other than Arabs. In fact, anti-Arab racism is prevalent in respectable circles in the United States, a matter to which we return.

After being promoted to chief diplomatic correspondent of the *Times* in recognition of his achievements in having provided "balanced and informed coverage" of the Middle East, Friedman turned to the broader responsibilities of this new position, informing the reader, for example, that in Central America, "after eight years of a failed Reagan Administration approach, Washington has one realistic option—to seek change through the diplomatic initiative opened by the leaders of Costa Rica, Guatemala, El Salvador and Honduras"—and opposed throughout, we are of course to understand, only by the totalitarian Sandinistas.[72] It is impressive to see how little effort it takes for the well-trained intellectual to learn the lines. Another Pulitzer Prize doubtless awaits.

A year after Shimon Peres's rejection of "direct negotiations," the Hebrew press in Israel headlined Arafat's statement that "I am ready for direct negotiations with Israel, but only as an equal among equals," and Shimon Peres's report that "the PLO is ready for direct negotiations with Israel without an international conference."[73] Israel again rejected the offer. A few days later, Arafat reiterated the PLO call for "an independent Palestinian state in any part of the territory of Palestine evacuated by the Israelis or liberated by us," adding that this state should then form "a confederation with the Jordanians, the Egyptians, the Syrians, and why not, the Israelis."[74] Again, the North American reader was spared knowledge of these facts.

On January 14, 1988, Arafat stated that the PLO would "recognize Israel's right to exist if it and the United States accept PLO participation in an international Middle East Peace conference" based on all U.N. resolutions, including U.N. 242.[75] Once again the *New York Times* refused to publish Arafat's statement, or even to permit letters referring to it—though the facts were buried in an article on another topic nine days later. Arafat had expressed a similar positions many times, for example, a few months earlier in an interview in the *New York Review of Books*, and in a September speech at a U.N. Nongovernmental Organization (N.G.O.) meeting, also unreported in the Newspaper of Record, in which he called for an "International Conference under the auspices of the United Nations and on the basis of international legality as well as of the international resolutions approved by the United Nations relevant to the Palestinian cause and the Middle East Crisis, and the resolutions of the Security Council, including resolutions 242 and 338."[76]

In March 1988 the *New York Times* at last permitted readers a glimpse of the facts,[77] but in an interesting manner. A front-page headline read: "Shamir and Arafat Both Scornful of U.S. Moves for Mideast Peace." Two stories follow on the villains who scorn the peace process. One deals with Yitzhak Shamir, who says that "The only word in the Shultz plan I accept is his signature"; the other, with Yasser Arafat, who repeats his endorsement of all U.N. resolutions including 242 and 338, once again accepting Israel's existence in return for withdrawal from the occupied territories and calling for Palestinians to be represented in negotiations through their chosen representatives.[78] George Shultz soberly and honorably pursues the peace process; the extremists on both sides scorn his efforts.

In a similar vein, the press reported in 1984 that the Israeli Supreme Court would permit "two extremist political parties" to run in the elections, one of them Rabbi Kahane's Kach party, which "advocates the eventual expulsion of all Arab residents of Israel and the West Bank of the Jordan River," and the other, the Progressive List, which "wants Israel to recognize the Palestine Liberation Organization and form a Palestinian state on the West Bank"—the two forms of extremism.[79]

In April 1988, Arafat again endorsed partition, referring explicitly to the *principle* of a two-state political settlement, not the borders of the original U.N. Resolution of 1947. The next day, Defense Minister Rabin (Labor) announced that Palestinians must be excluded from any political settlement, and that diplomacy can proceed only "on a state-to-state level." A few days earlier, Prime Minister Yitzhak Shamir (Likud) had informed George Shultz that "U.N. Resolution 242 does not contain territorial provisions with regard to Jordan," meaning that it excludes the West Bank; the government of Israel is thus on record with a flat rejection of U.N. 242, as understood anywhere else in the world. In February, the Platform Committee of Herut, the core of the governing Likud coalition, had reiterated its longstanding position that the right of the Jewish people to the Land of Israel, including all of Jordan, is "permanent" and "not subject to any higher authority," though they do not "propose to go to war on Amman," at least now. Deputy Prime Minister Roni Milo (Likud) had announced earlier that "we have never said that we renounce our right to [Jordan], though in the context of negotiations with Jordan we might agree to certain concessions in Eastern Transjordan," granting Jordan some of its current territory (the reference is presumably to the largely uninhabited desert areas). Later in April 1988, the Labor Party once again adopted a campaign platform rejecting Israeli withdrawal from the occupied territories, and Rabin clarified that the plan was to allow 60 percent of the West Bank and Gaza Strip to be part of a Jordanian-Palestinian state, with its capital in Amman. Both major Israeli political groupings thus confirmed their extreme rejectionism, though in their characteristically different guises. The respected Israeli diplomat Abba Eban, an advocate of the Labor Party variety of rejectionism, comments on "the awkward fact that the Israeli government does not support [U.N. 242] at all"; specifically, "there is no trace of [resolutions 242 and 338] whatever in the Israeli coalition agreement because the Likud negotiators in 1984 resisted the Labour proposal to include 242 as one of the sources of Israeli governmental policy."[80]

All of this passed without notice in the mainstream press.[81] The press did, however, report that George Shultz, pursuing his "peace mission" in Jordan, announced that the PLO or others "who have committed acts of terrorism" must be excluded from peace talks, which would leave the bargaining table quite empty and surely would exclude the speaker. He also "explained his understanding of the aspirations of Palestinians," *Times* reporter Elaine Sciolino wrote, by citing the example of the United States, where he, Shultz, is a Californian, and George Bush is a Texan, but they have no problem living in harmony. The Palestinian aspirations into which he shows such profound insight can be handled the same way.[82]

At the Algiers meeting of the Arab League in June 1988, the PLO circulated a document written by Arafat's personal spokesman Bassim Abu Sharif, submitted to the major U.S. media and reported in a cable to the State Department on June 8. The document once again explicitly accepted U.N. resolutions 242 and 338, explaining why the PLO will not accept them in isolation. The reason, long understood, is that "neither resolution says anything about the national rights of the Palestinian people, including their democratic right to self-expression and their national right to self-determination." "For that reason and that reason alone," Abu Sharif continued, "we have repeatedly said that we accept Resolutions 242 and 338 in the context of the U.N. Resolutions which do recognize the national rights of the Palestinian people." The same considerations are what underlie the insistence of the United States and Israel that the PLO accept U.N. 242 and 338 in isolation, thus implicitly abandoning their right to self-determination. The Abu Sharif statement was published in the small democratic socialist weekly *In These Times*. The *Washington Post* refused publication. The *New York Times* published excerpts as an opinion column, accompanied by a front-page news story headlined "An Aide to Arafat Comes Under Fire: Hard-Line Palestinian Groups Criticize the Adviser's Call for Talks With Israelis." The article focuses on the condemnation of Abu Sharif by George Habbash's Popular Front for the Liberation of Palestine and groups that oppose the PLO, barely mentioning the contents of the proposal. It is possible that the *Times* withheld publication until they could frame the story in this manner.[83]

Recall that it was *after* all of this that the *Times* editors condemned the "sterile rejectionism" and "intransigence" of the Palestinians and the Arabs generally, in their June 13 editorial cited above. A few weeks later, Faisal Husseini, a leading West Bank moderate, was again placed under administrative detention, this time for publicly advocating the Abu Sharif proposal at a Peace Now meeting, a fact too insignificant to merit a story in the *Times* (see below). Peace Now's association with Husseini in mid-1988 could be interpreted as indicating oblique support for the nonrejectionist two-state proposal that Husseini advocated, though subsequent Peace Now statements make this interpretation doubtful.[84] Husseini had emphasized—accurately—that he was taking a position long advanced by the PLO. If Peace Now did intend to signal in an ambiguous way its support for something like Husseini's position, then we could conclude that for the first time, Israel has a nonrejectionist peace movement comparable to the PLO, apart from the margins of the political system. These words, though accurate, would be virtually incomprehensible in respectable political discourse in the United States.[85]

The events of late 1988 again revealed the utility of this extensive government-media campaign to eliminate Arab and PLO initiatives from the historical record while depicting U.S.-Israeli efforts to derail a political settlement as "the peace process" and their rejection-ism as moderation. As noted in the text, the Palestine National Council, meeting in Algiers, called for an international conference based on U.N. Resolutions 242 and 338 (which recognize Israeli rights but say nothing about the Palestinians) along with the Palestinian right of self-determination. One might have imagined that this very clear reaffirmation of the rights of both Israelis and Palestinians would have raised some problems for U.S.-Israeli rejectionism. The expected PNC announcement did, in fact, arouse such fears. They were expressed, for example, in a headline in the more dovish seg-ment of the American Jewish press reading "Israel girding itself for Arab peace offer," all pretense that Palestinian moves towards peace would be welcome having been abandoned as the dread moment approached.[86]

But the fears of peace were quickly put to rest as the PNC peace proposal passed through the media filter. For the editors of the *New York Times*, it was simply "the same old fudge that Yasir Arafat has offered up for years," a "wasted opportunity," another refusal to abandon "the rejectionist formulas." Once again, a clear nonrejection-ist stance is "rejectionism" because it does not accord with the U.S.-Israeli position rejecting Palestinian national rights. With regard to the PLO's reiteration of the position on terrorism endorsed by the entire world apart from the United States, Israel, and South Africa this is just "the old Arafat hedge," the editors scornfully observed.[87]

A few weeks later, the ever-annoying Arafat stated explicitly in Stockholm that the PNC declaration had "accepted the existence of Israel as a state in the region," reiterating in a joint declaration with American Jews that the PLO affirms "the principle incorporated in those United Nations resolutions that call for a two-state solution of Israel and Palestine" and calls for an international conference "to be held on the basis of U.N. Resolutions 242 and 338 and the right of the Palestinian people of self-determination without external interfer-ence." The *Times* again reacted with contempt, as did both major Israeli political groupings and the U.S. government. The editors explained that once again, "the endorsement of Resolutions 242 and 338 also contains vague allusions to other U.N. declarations, not excluding those that impugn Israel's legitimacy." That statement is flatly false: the only U.N. resolutions to which Arafat made reference are 242, 338, and those that recognize the right of the Palestinians to self-determination. The editors also reiterated the official position that Arafat did not go far enough in "rejecting terrorism," meaning that he did not join the U.S. government and the *Times* in their splendid isolation off the spectrum of world opinion, a simple matter of fact that the Newspaper of Record has refused to publish.[88]

The *Times* editors went on to say that the PLO "seems to have crept closer to accepting Israel's right to exist" though "how far the P.L.O. has moved is hard to tell." The U.S. must therefore stand fast, and "keep the pressure" on Arafat "for more clarity." Their meaning is transparent. Only when the Palestinians explicitly and without equivocation abandon their claim to human and national rights, in accord with State Department-*Times* directives, will their position be sufficiently clear to merit consideration.

The *Los Angeles Times* described the Algiers declaration as "the first official hint of a PLO interest" in abandoning their claim for "sovereignty over the whole of Palestine," though "it would be stretching things to use any word stronger than 'hint' to describe what came out of the PLO meeting in Algiers." The PLO proposals for a two-state settlement incorporating the right of all states to live in peace within secure and recognized boundaries, negotiations leading to mutual recognition, etc., for well over a decade, do not qualify as "hints" because they have been excised from the historical record. Particularly troublesome, the editors continue, was that "the PLO's proclamation doesn't define the boundaries of a Palestinian state"; Israel's refusal to do the same from its founding has never been troublesome. The *Washington Post,* anticipating the PNC statement, was hopeful, because "for the first time reasonable people can ask if Palestinians are at least moving toward peace"; fair enough, on the assumption that historical facts do not exist if they would compel us to acknowledge unpleasant truths about ourselves.[89]

Among columnists, the spectrum extended from doves who described the Algiers declaration as "a clumsy but potentially significant move" (Judith Kipper of the Brookings Institution), to George Will, who explained that the German word for "two-state settlement" is "Endloesung, meaning 'final solution'." At the dovish extreme, Anthony Lewis applauded this move "in a constructive direction" even though the resolution "was not as clear as we would like," and the PLO must still be excluded from negotiations because of its failure to "unambiguously renounce all terrorism"—that is, to join the United States and Israel (and, of course, South Africa) in defiance of the world. Boston University history professor Allen Weinstein, president of the Center for Democracy, questioned whether we can trust Arafat's alleged "moderation." We can test it, he suggested, by calling upon him to order a unilateral pause in the Palestinian uprising (Intifada) "as a valuable good faith gesture in shaping future US response to the legitimate demands of the Palestinian people"; Weinstein does not indicate what the United States and Israel would then do to meet these "legitimate demands," or why they did not respond to them prior to the Intifada.[90]

One of the most intriguing reactions was in the *Christian Science Monitor*, which has been unusual in its occasional willingness to recognize that Palestinians too might have human rights, including the right to national self-determination that is accorded to Israeli Jews. The *Monitor* presented two columns: the president of the American Jewish Committee presented the case for denying a visa to Arafat and thus sending a message to the PLO that "it must stop trying to destroy Israel," while *Monitor* correspondent Scott Pendelton, representing the opposite pole of expressible opinion, urged Shultz to reconsider the decision to bar Arafat from speaking at the United Nations. After all, Pendelton argued, "with the United States' encouragement, PLO moderation had been learning to crawl. Our ultimate aim, supposedly, was to help it to walk." Facts aside, the racist arrogance of the formulation is worthy of note. Pendelton goes on to sketch the outlines of a fair settlement. Since "our primary concern is Israel's security," the only question is: "How far can we go toward addressing Palestinians' grievances?" The basic principle, then, is that the indigenous population simply does not have the human rights of Jews. "Giving Palestinians something to lose would guarantee their good behavior," Pendelton urges, adopting the Thomas Friedman stance. So they ought to be granted some kind of "state," but "Israel should expect to retain military bases in the West Bank and Gaza, overflight rights, and lots more stuff"; this "stuff" remains unspecified, except that it will allow Israel to "walk away with everything it needs" in addition to peace. As for the Palestinians, they should understand that if they "so much as look funny at Israel, we'll step back and let Israel annex your new state and drive all you people into the sea." "If Arafat agrees to such a brutally blunt condition," then he will have made a statement of "honest intentions" that is clear enough for us, the advocate of the doves concludes.[91]

In short, sheer unalloyed rejectionism throughout, laced with racist contempt for the lesser breeds. The entire spectrum is a counterpart to extremist elements among the Arabs.

Much attention is given throughout to the reaction of American Jewish leaders and organizations. The doves among them described

Arafat's explicit acceptance of Israel in a two-state settlement as "a further small step on the road, though there were reasons to fear that the expressed attitudes would not survive a political settlement" (Arthur Hertzberg). The director of the Anti-Defamation League criticized Arafat's statement as "encumbered" and "conditional," when what is needed is "utter clarity" (Abraham Foxman). The chairman of the Conference of Presidents of Major American Jewish Organizations" described Arafat's declarations as "a thinly disguised version of the same old propaganda line" and dismissed his acceptance of Israel as a "meaningless" recognition of existing reality; his desire to destroy Israel is "unmitigated," and that is all that counts (Morris Abram).[92] In short, the only satisfactory step for the Palestinians is national suicide, with "utter clarity." The meaning of these positions is not discussed.

In Israel, Peace Now reacted to these developments by taking a "new position" that "has surprised many," the Israeli press commented: namely, Peace Now published an advertisement calling for negotiations with the PLO, thus abandoning the extreme form of rejectionism that denies the Palestinians even the right to select their own representatives for negotiations. Peace Now did not, however, move towards a political position of the sort that the PLO had advanced in January 1976 and repeatedly since, calling for a peaceful two-state political settlement. The Peace Now ad asserted falsely that "in Algiers the PLO abandoned the path of rejection ... and adopted the path of political compromise"; that step had been taken thirteen years earlier when the PLO backed (or, if the president of Israel can be believed, "prepared") the proposals rejected by Israel and the United States, and that step had yet to be taken by Peace Now. The ad urged that Israel "speak with the PLO" to determine "if the PLO has really adopted the path of peace as declared in Algiers." The advice is sound, except that it omits the major question: has Israel, or Peace Now, finally adopted the path of peace? Peace Now spokesman Tsali Reshef stated that "It isn't we who have undergone a transformation so much as the PLO," with its "revolutionary change" in Algiers, recognizing U.N. 242 and a two-state settlement. The change in Algiers was anything but revolutionary, as the record clearly indicates. What had changed was that Peace Now had now separated itself slightly from Labor Party rejectionism, moving along with mainstream opinion—which, a few months later and after no further change of any significance in the PLO position as we will see, registered support for negotiations with the PLO by a margin of 54 percent to 44 percent.[93]

While one can, quite properly, point to ambiguities in PLO formulations, to their corruption, deceit, foolishness, and terror, that shameful record is praiseworthy in comparison with that of the Israeli Labor Party and Peace Now, which still had not reached the level of commitment to a peaceful settlement articulated by the PLO and the "confrontation states" well over a decade earlier.

Notably missing from the discussion in the U.S. media was any suggestion that the United States or Israel should depart from their clear and unambiguous rejection of Palestinian rights, or should renounce terrorism.[94] There is no thought that denial of Palestinian self-determination is a form of "Endloesung." The only question that may be considered is whether the Palestinians have moved far enough towards our position, which is by definition the right one, therefore unquestioned. The doves say that the Palestinians are learning, and we should reward them for their painfully slow progress; the hawks warn that it is all fraud and delusion. The more forthcoming argue that for the first time the Palestinians have made sounds that reasonable people might listen to, departing from the "old Arafat fudge": namely, endorsement of a two-state settlement based on the right of self-determination of both peoples, the call for negotiations and mutual recognition, and the other proposals that do not even qualify as "hints." The tough-minded refuse to concede even that. A well-crafted history is a powerful instrument.

December 1988 brought a series of events that provide yet another dramatic indication of the ability of the media to adapt instantaneously to the needs of state propaganda. The media consensus, as expressed by the editors of the *New York Times*, is that in mid-December the PLO underwent a "seismic shift of attitude," for the first time "advanc[ing] towards a serious negotiating position." Recognizing that the PLO had now met all U.S. demands, Washington made the "momentous decision" to talk with them. It is now "reality time" in the Middle East, Thomas Friedman added; whether there will be any progress depends "in large part on how the P.L.O. leadership responds to the dose of reality they are expected to get in their talks with United States diplomats."[95]

Let us now turn to what actually occurred.

We must, first of all, not overlook the broader context. The Palestinian uprising from December 1987 undermined the assumption that the Palestinians could simply be disregarded. Their resis-

tance was becoming costly to Israel on many levels, a threat to its
services to the United States and perhaps even to its social and
economic integrity. Israeli rejectionists of both Labor and Likud
began to recognize that the Palestinians could not be as easily suppressed as they had supposed, joining a few others who had already
come to this conclusion. U.S. analysts were drawing the same conclusions. The rejectionism of the U.S. intellectual community, overwhelmingly dominant, also was beginning to erode, accelerating as
the costs of the Intifada to Israel became clear. Even some of the
leading hatchet men, who for years had been denouncing advocates
of a political settlement as left fascists, self-hating Jews, and the like
while producing a steady stream of apologetics for Israeli repression
and atrocities, began to fashion for themselves a role as long-term
advocates of a political settlement and critics of Israel's lack of compassion (typically blaming the Likud government and exculpating
Labor, which has a comparable record, worse in some respects).[96]
Israel's costly failures in Lebanon from 1982 had led to a similar
reassessment, as had Arab military successes in the October 1973 war,
which made it clear that the Arab states could not simply be ignored
and that it would be best for Israel and the United States to arrange
a Sinai settlement. Some change in policy towards the Palestinians,
at least at a symbolic level, was therefore likely, on the basis of a
reassessment of costs. Against this background, it was becoming
increasingly difficult to maintain the illusions that had served for so
long. Correspondingly, from early 1988 Arab peace initiatives began
to be reported, however deceptively, and to elicit some kind of
limited reaction.

Turning to the events of December 1988, after the November
Algiers declaration the United States refused to permit Arafat to
address the U.N. General Assembly in New York, in clear violation
of law. The Assembly session was moved to Geneva, where Arafat
essentially repeated the positions already articulated. Washington's
response was that Arafat had not met its conditions, which were, once
again, clearly stated:

1. "Acceptance of Resolutions 242 and 338"

2. "Recognition of Israel's right to exist"

3. "Rejection of terrorism in all its forms"

These U.S. positions must be adopted by the PLO "clearly,
squarely, without ambiguity," the State Department continued. The

media endorsed this stand. The *New York Times Magazine* ran a cover story entitled "The Ambiguous Yasir Arafat," and others deplored his evasiveness as well. The concept of "ambiguity" was explained by John Chancellor of NBC: "The trouble with Yasser Arafat is that his native language seems to be ambiguity. He never quite says what you want him to say."[97] How unreasonable.

Recall what is at stake in the three conditions. Resolutions 242 and 338 call for the right of all *states* in the region to "live in peace within secure and recognized boundaries." This condition had been endorsed by the PLO in January 1976 in those very words, and repeatedly since. But the PLO had always added a "qualification." It also insisted upon those U.N. resolutions that recognize the right of the Palestinians to national self-determination in a state alongside of Israel. The first of the State Department requirements is that the PLO abandon this "qualification," thus abandoning the right to self-determination.

The second point is a bit different. No state in the international system is accorded an abstract "right to exist," though states are accorded the right to exist in peace and security. The difference is fundamental. Thus, the United States explicitly denies the "right to exist" of the Soviet Union in its present form (as demonstrated, for example, in Captive Nations Week, or in high-level planning documents such as NSC 68). But it agrees that the U.S.S.R. has the right to be free from foreign attack or terror, that is, to live in peace and security. For the Palestinians to agree to Israel's abstract "right to exist" would be for them to accept not only the *fact* but the *legitimacy* of their dispossession from their land and homes. That is why Israel and the United States insist on this precise wording. "It is essential that these words be spoken," a State Department Middle East expert asserts. It is not the "existence" of Israel but the "right" of existence that is at issue, National Security Adviser Colin Powell insists: "It's the right of Israel to exist that is the essential acknowledgement that we need."[98] Israel naturally agrees. The U.S. media and intellectual community do so as well, for only such total humiliation and renunciation of even abstract rights on the part of the Palestinians will justify the attitudes that intellectual circles had displayed towards them for many decades.

The third point we have already discussed. It is not sufficient for the PLO to take the position on terrorism held by virtually the entire world; it must join the United States, Israel, and South Africa off the spectrum of world opinion, clearly and unambiguously renouncing the right of people to struggle for self-determination against racist and colonialist regimes or foreign occupation. Again, the media agree with near unanimity, while continuing to suppress the fact that this is precisely what is at issue.

The alleged reasons for the U.S.-Israeli stand are "security"; only if Arafat says the magic words will Israel be secure, according to government-media doctrine. The absurdity is transparent. Suppose that Arafat were to waltz into the Knesset wearing a yarmulke and singing *Hatikva*, proceeding to pledge undying loyalty to the State of Israel while condemning Palestinians as undeserving sinners, temporary visitors in the Land of Israel who will be eternally grateful if the rightful owners of the entire land grant them the gift of a mini-state in the West Bank and Gaza. Israel's security would not be enhanced one iota. Security is based on facts, not words. In fact, the idea that the Palestinians threaten Israel's security can hardly be taken seriously; if the longstanding PLO proposals for a two-state diplomatic settlement were accepted, it would be the Palestinian state that would face security problems, contained within the traditional tacit alliance between Jordan and Israel, the regional superpower. Israel doubtless faces severe security problems, in part of its own making because of its rejection of the possibilities for diplomatic settlement since 1971. But the Palestinians pose a security threat only in that Israel's capacity to defend itself against really dangerous enemies will doubtless erode as its military forces are trained not to fight wars but to break the bones of children. The threat is understood by Israeli military specialists, and is one reason why the Intifada is leading them to reconsider the wisdom of holding the territories. One well-known military historian, Martin van Creveld, observes that "What used to be one of the world's finest fighting forces is rapidly degenerating into a fourth-class police organization. To realize the way such a force will fight when confronted by a real army, one need look no further than the Argentinians in the Falkland Islands."[99]

The issue of Arafat's refusal to pronounce the words written for him by the State Department—what the media term his "ambiguity"—is not at all "frivolous," as the editors of the *Washington Post* rightly assert while misstating the reasons.[100] If the PLO were to accept the State Department position clearly and unambiguously, it would fall into a diplomatic trap. It would then have renounced its right to national self-determination (the "qualification" to 242), accepted the legitimacy of everything that had happened to the Palestinians in the past, and renounced any right to struggle for self-determination—for example, the right to endorse popular committees in a "liberated village," or the right to approve if the inhabitants of the village throw stones at army units invading to prevent such attempts at self-government and to arrest, torture, beat, or kill the perpetrators of such crimes. PLO agreement to these terms would be a substantive achievement for U.S.-Israeli rejectionism. It would mean that if the Palestinians made any move towards self-determination, or even spoke words to that effect, they could be accused of reneging on their solemn commitments, proving that they are mere barbarians as the United States and Israel had always known, and abandoning any rights whatsoever. They could then be "driven into the sea" or the desert, in accordance with the prescriptions of the doves, as we have seen. Whatever Israel and the United States now choose to do to them would be legitimate, after this demonstration of their worthlessness. The weapon would always be available, held in reserve, if the PLO were to accept the demands of the U.S. government and the media.

By mid-December 1988, the U.S. government was becoming an object of ridicule outside of the United States for its insistence that Arafat not only accept the positions long regarded as reasonable in the international community, but pronounce the exact words written for him by the State Department. Boxed into an untenable position, Washington turned to the usual technique of the powerful: the "Trollope ploy" (see chapter 4, note 40): When the adversary refuses to accept your position, pretend that he has done so, trusting the media to fall into step. In the world of necessary illusions, then, the adversary will indeed have accepted your position, and you may proceed as if that had happened, punishing him as required for any departure from the solemn commitments that you have invented for him. An added benefit is the psychological satisfaction derived from the claim that Third World nuisances have been humiliated, while in return we now grant them the great gift of admission to the master's chambers for some meaningless conversation. Furthermore, these pretenses have the practical advantage of reinforcing the doctrine that a stern and uncompromising stance is the only way to deal with the lesser breeds. Recall the reinterpretation of the diplomatic defeat of the United States in August 1987 as a proof that our resort to violence finally compelled the reluctant Sandinistas to accept U.S. terms. The actual facts are quite irrelevant if the information system can be trusted to obey and if its power to mold opinion is sufficient in the countries that matter (the Western allies). This is the device that Nixon and Kissinger used to destroy the Paris peace agreements in

1973, and that the Reagan administration adopted to undermine the Esquipulas Accord. In fact, it is virtually a reflex, and it typically works like a charm.

Adopting this procedure, the State Department announced that in a news conference in which he said nothing new of any moment, Arafat had finally accepted the U.S. position on all three issues, so that now, in our magnanimity, we would agree to talk to the PLO (and to inform them, politely, that Palestinians have no rights or claims). As more perceptive analysts recognized, this "sudden and dramatic reversal of US policy ... got the Reagan administration out of a corner into which it had been painting itself" as the administration "snatched the slender straw of Arafat's press conference in Geneva as an elegant way out of an increasingly untenable position."[101] The standard media interpretation was, however, quite different: the U.S. had not changed its position at all; rather, firmness had paid off and forced the ambiguous Mr. Arafat to accede to Washington's just demands, proving that the U.S. should continue to "hang tough," as the *Washington Post* editors put it.

The news columns of the *New York Times* reported that "State Department officials declined to speculate about what may have convinced Mr. Arafat to embrace the American formula after so many years of refusing to do so." Over and over, they reiterated that the PLO had met the U.S. terms "by renouncing terrorism, recognizing Israel's right to exist and accepting important United Nations resolutions on the Mideast." The *Washington Post* praised the Reagan administration for having "scored an unexpected diplomatic coup by drawing the Palestine Liberation Organization into formal acceptance of the state of Israel." There was much derision of "Palestinian semantics." The story was that Arafat had tried to evade the stern U.S. requirements, but finally succumbed, there being no further escape. Thus, after much squirming, Arafat had finally spoken the words that gave the PLO the privilege of an invitation to lunch with U.S. officials. This "stunning breakthrough" is a triumph of U.S. diplomacy, the *Times* editors announced, admonishing Secretary Shultz to "hold Arafat responsible" for any "violence within Israel and the occupied territories." The *Boston Globe* editors asserted that "Yasser Arafat has spoken the words he had to say in order to meet American conditions for open contacts with the PLO," including "his belated declaration of Israel's right to exist in peace and security." "Henceforth," the editors warned, "the PLO can be held to the pledges he made." Columnists added that the United States should persist in the "tough approach" that had "got Mr. Arafat this far along by repeating the same three conditions year in, year out"; this steadfastness should force Mr. Arafat the rest of the way, to accommodating the "legitimate interests" of Israel and Jordan by abandoning even marginal claims for self-determination (Daniel Pipes). Thomas Friedman spelled out "reality": Arafat had finally recognized "Israel's right to exist," and must now talk to the Israelis just as Sadat, "during his first negotiations with Israel after the 1973 war," finally understood that Egypt "would have to talk to Israel directly and in language that Israelis would find sincere" (recall that Egypt had offered a full peace treaty in 1971, recognized as such officially by Israel, but rejected because the Labor government felt that they could gain territorial concessions by holding out, as they frankly explained). As the U.S. proceeds to administer a "dose of reality" to the PLO, Friedman continued, it should advise the Palestinians to "agree to a two-month cease-fire in the uprising, in exchange for Israeli agreement to allow them to hold municipal elections." Note that it is the *Palestinians* who must "agree to a cease-fire" in the occupied territories, from which the reader is to understand that it is the Palestinians who have been "firing" on the Israeli army.[102]

Subsequent commentary proceeded along the same lines, virtually (or perhaps even completely) with no exception. President Bush, in his first news conference, explained that we agreed to "communicate" with the PLO (but not "deal with" them, as he hastened to emphasize, correcting a slip of the tongue), because of "their acceptance of three principles," those we had formulated for them; "As long as they stay hooked and stay committed to those three principles, we will have quite appropriate meetings with the P.L.O." What has changed is that the PLO has "dramatically I'd say—agreed to the—to the principles that are part of our policy," saying the magic words. *Times* correspondent Joel Brinkley, along with many others, went further, adding that "Yasir Arafat, the P.L.O. leader, is saying openly for the first time that he wants to solve the Palestinian problem through negotiation," a real breakthrough, an offer that the U.S. and the world have "tentatively accepted." Recall that Brinkley's comment is quite accurate in the world of necessary illusion that the *Times* has so carefully crafted over many years; Arafat's repeated proposals to solve the Arab-Israeli conflict through negotiation exist only in the irrelevant world of reality, from which readers of the *Times* have been scrupulously protected.[103]

Turning to the facts, which quickly disappeared from the scene as anticipated, in his magic words Arafat recognized "the right of all parties concerned in the Middle East conflict to exist in peace and security, and, as I have mentioned, including the state of Palestine, Israel and other neighbors, according to the Resolution 242 and 338"; thus he "accepted the state of Israel" in the terms he had offered thirteen years earlier, and repeatedly since, with the same "qualifications" as always and with no endorsement of Israel's abstract "right to exist." He "renounced" terrorism in all its forms (the State Department had insisted only on "rejection"), while he and other officials made it clear in accompanying statements that the PLO "would not abandon either attacks on military targets in Israel or the year-old uprising in the Israeli-occupied West Bank and Gaza Strip."[104]

In short, Arafat repeated the former PLO positions. The only changes were that whereas in January 1976 (and often since) the PLO adopted the wording of U.N. 242, endorsing the right of all parties "to live in peace within secure and recognized boundaries," Arafat now spoke of their right "to exist in peace and security"; the change is zero. As before, he insisted on the "qualification" that the Palestinians have the right of self-determination, clearly referring to "the State of Palestine" alongside of Israel. He refused to accept Israel's abstract "right to exist," on which the U.S. had insisted as the crucial point. Instead of "condemning" and "rejecting" terrorism as before (see chapter 4), he "renounced" terrorism, while retaining the internationally recognized right of struggle for self-determination against racist and colonialist regimes and foreign occupation.

The version presented by the State Department and the media is false in virtually every particular. That fact, however, makes not the slightest difference. The necessary illusions have been established. Accordingly, Arafat can be held to the "pledges" that he has not made, and the Palestinians can be punished if they fail to live up to these solemn commitments. Note again the close similarity to the techniques adopted to undermine the Esquipulas Accord, among other familiar cases.

Seeking to extract what advantages one might from these developments, William Safire expatiated on the crucial difference between the words "condemn" and "renounce." True, he conceded, Arafat had previously "condemned" terrorism (as well as "rejecting" terrorism, he fails to add), but now he had followed our orders and "renounced" it, tacitly conceding that he had previously endorsed it. From the point of view of the security of Israel—Safire's alleged concern—or any other issue of possible human significance, the difference is so small as to be near invisible. What impresses Safire, however, is that the United States has imposed a satisfying form of humiliation on the victims of U.S.-Israeli repression and rejectionism, righteously forcing them to concede that they, and they alone, have sinned.[105] At the other extreme of the acceptable political spectrum, Paul Berman urges Israel to "take your enemy's watery words and dig a moat for them, and ... try to seal your enemy behind a channel of his own promises. By making him repeat his words endlessly, and linking big words to tiny measurable commitments, and the tiny to the large." There has been progress, "if only that Arafat's lies flow today in a better direction than when he was dazzling his own people with news of the secular democratic state to come," Berman continues, while extolling Abba Eban (the "grand veteran of Israeli Labor," and long-time advocate of its rejectionism) and Irving Howe ("easy and weighty, socialism's truest voice," long known for silence over Israeli atrocities or denial of them, and venomous denunciation of Daniel Berrigan, the New Left from Palo Alto to Scarsdale, and an array of other villains whose crime was to tell truths that he preferred not be heard). Neither Safire nor Berman, nor the spectrum between, call upon Israel and the United States to "renounce" their terrorism and their rejection of any political settlement; there are no injunctions that these regimes must be sealed behind a channel of their own promises, compelled to repeat their words of contrition and renunciation endlessly, and to direct their lies along a better course. And the necessary illusions about the diplomatic history remain firmly in place. The imperial arrogance and racist contempt for those in our way are as striking as the easy dismissal of unacceptable fact.[106]

While all eyes were focussed on Palestinian ambiguity, the press reported that "soldiers raiding the West Bank village of Deir al-Ghusun" shot and killed an Arab, among the many who were killed and wounded in a new outburst of Israeli violence with daily killings. To further underscore the U.S.-Israeli attitude towards terrorism, the U.S. vetoed a Security Council resolution deploring a large-scale Israeli armed attack near Beirut. Shimon Peres, praised in the media as Israel's leading dove, explained that there is no Palestinian partner for negotiations and that Palestinians have no right of national self-determination because Israel determines that their cultural relations with Jordan bar any "notion of artificially dividing the Palestinian people"—though Israel will allow the people of the West Bank and Gaza "free and secret elections" without Israeli interference, once they abandon in advance the one principle that they would uphold, with near unanimity, in free elections. Israel formed a coalition government based on the familiar demands of both major political groupings: "No talks with the P.L.O. for sure, no Palestinian state between Jordan and the Mediterranean, and no retreat to the 1967 borders." The coalition agreement also called for up to eight new settlements a year in the occupied territories, with U.S. funds.[107]

There are no ambiguities here. Similarly, the media remain unwavering in their services to derailing any possible peace process as long as Washington persists in its own unambiguous rejectionism.

One aspect of this service is suppression of the position of the United States after the spectacular achievement of U.S. diplomacy. According to the Israeli press, Washington advised Israel to stop requesting that the United States terminate its dialogue with the PLO because these requests "only add significance to the dialogue." Defense Minister Rabin expressed his great satisfaction with the dialogue in late February because it was a delaying action, intended to grant Israel at least a year to suppress the Intifada by "harsh military and economic pressure." This interpretation is reinforced by the protocols of the first meeting between the United States and the PLO in Tunis. These were leaked to the Egyptian journal *Al-Mussawar*, which is close to President Mubarak, and published in translation by the *Jerusalem Post*, which could hardly contain its pleasure over the fact that "the American representative adopted the Israeli positions." U.S. Ambassador to Tunisia Robert Pelletreau stated two crucial conditions: the PLO must call off the Intifada, and must abandon the idea of an international conference, accepting the U.S. demand for direct negotiations between the PLO and Israel (which Israel, incidentally, refuses). With regard to the Intifada, the U.S. position is that

> Undoubtedly the internal struggles that we are witnessing in the occupied territories aim to undermine the security and stability of the State of Israel, and we therefore demand cessation of those riots, *which we view as terrorist acts against Israel*. This is especially true as we know you are directing, from outside the territories, those riots which are sometimes very violent.[108]

The U.S. position, then, is that the Palestinian uprising is terrorism aimed at destruction of Israel, and the PLO must order it to cease. Once the Intifada is brought to a halt, matters will revert to the situation that prevailed before, when the U.S. government cheerfully supported and lavishly funded Israel's brutal repression of the population and its steps towards integration of the territories within Israel, while the media systematically avoided the ongoing atrocities, praised the "benign" occupation, and hailed the occupiers as "a society in which moral sensitivity is a principle of political life" (*New York Times*, right after the Sabra-Shatila massacres); and the left-liberal intelligentsia praised this "ebullient democracy" striding towards democratic socialism (Irving Howe) while slandering those who called for a political settlement and had the impudence and temerity to observe, quite inadequately, that all was not quite as delightful as was being depicted.[109]

With regard to direct negotiations, the matter is hardly more subtle. The international community supports a political settlement; the United States does not. Therefore, the international community must be excluded from any role, because it would be an irritant, pressing for the kind of political settlement that the U.S. has rejected for many years. More generally, as we have seen in other contexts too, the international community must be excluded as much as possible from interfering on U.S. turf—much of the world, including the Middle East—though the U.S. is willing to turn to it when preferred methods of exercising control have failed. In "direct negotiations," without the interference of those who might press for peace, Israel can continue (with U.S. support) to reject any proposal for meaningful negotiations or political settlement, even if Israel can be brought to take part in the charade.

The "dose of reality" administered to the PLO is, therefore, very much along the lines of what the *Times* chief diplomatic correspondent thought necessary, and conforms exactly to the demands of Israeli rejectionism, as the *Jerusalem Post* editors exulted. The United States has succeeded, once again, in throwing a wrench in the "peace process" and blocking the prospects that appeared to be developing, much to the consternation of Washington and Tel Aviv.

All such matters must be excluded from discussion in the media, and are, even in the glare of publicity over the remarkable and spectacular U.S. diplomatic achievements of December 1988.

While the United States won a major diplomatic and propaganda victory, forces may be set in motion that Washington cannot control, exactly as in the other cases we have discussed. The world is not as easily managed as the media. That, however, is another topic.

This is only a brief sample of a very large record. One has come to expect such services on the part of the *New York Times*, which, *Boston Globe* Middle East correspondent Curtis Wilkie observes, "has historically been Israel's chief conduit for news for American consumption."[110] But the pattern is far more pervasive, virtually exceptionless.

I mentioned earlier that one should not dismiss the undercurrent of racism that runs through the discussion of the Israel-Arab conflict. That is the meaning of the tacit assumption that the indigenous population does not have the human and national rights that we naturally accord to the Jewish immigrants who largely displaced them. The assumption is rarely challenged, or apparently even perceived. That is true when the denial of Arab rights is merely presupposed, and remains so even when the expression of racist attitudes is crude and explicit. A number of examples have been mentioned. It would be an error to think of them as merely scattered cases.

Consider, for example, a *New York Times Magazine* article by Thomas Friedman entitled "Proposals for Peace," outlining his ideas about a peaceful resolution of the Arab-Israel conflict. He begins by introducing "an elderly curmudgeon named Sasson," a representative of "the Israeli silent majority." The article asks what will convince this silent but reasonable ordinary man—whose alleged views turn out to be remarkably like Friedman's—to agree to a political settlement. "Sasson is the key to a Palestinian-Israeli peace settlement," Friedman holds. Two proposals are offered that might satisfy Sasson; these are presented as speeches by some Israeli political figure who would be farsighted enough to listen to Friedman's advice. One is Friedman's south Lebanon proposal, already discussed: place the territories under the control of a mercenary force backed by Israeli might, and warn the Palestinians that if "they put one of ours in the hospital, we'll put 200 of theirs in the morgue," and Israel will "obliterate" whatever the Palestinians construct if they threaten Israel "in any way." The second is a "diplomatic solution" along the lines of Labor Party rejectionism, with enough power deployed to convince Israelis "to ignore Palestinian poetry" that they do not like.[111] Again, the familiar racist arrogance.

Notably missing is any Palestinian Sasson, or indeed any recognition that it might matter what Palestinians think or want. The discussion of proposals for peace is based on the assumption that all that matters is what is good for the Jews. Friedman takes great pains to explain to American readers Jewish attitudes into which he feels he has much insight: the attitudes of Sasson, or Ze'ev Chafets, the American-born former director of the Israeli Government Press Office, sympathetically portrayed as he calmly explains that his son would drop a nuclear bomb on the Rashdiye refugee camp "without a second thought" if he felt that Israel's security were threatened. There is no indication that Friedman understands anything about the Palestinians, or cares to. They are a nuisance that Israel cannot get rid of, and for its own good, Israel should give Ahmed a seat on the bus to shut him up. That ends the discussion.

The racism is often not subtle at all. We read that *Times* correspondent Stephen Kinzer is offended by the willingness of the Sandinistas "to express solidarity with Palestinians, M-19s, and other Third World detritus" (Joe Klein); replace "Palestinians" with "Jews" and no one will fail to recognize the echoes of *Der Stuermer*. The same reaction would be elicited by a complaint that New York is "underpopulated," meaning that it has too many Blacks, Hispanics, and Jews and too few WASPs; but there is no reaction to a reference to the "underpopulated Galilee," meaning that it has too many Arabs and too few Jews (*Dissent* editor Irving Howe in the *New York Times*). Liberal intellectuals express no qualms about a journal whose editor reflects on "Arab culture" in which "no onus falls on lying," on a "crazed Arab," but "crazed in the distinctive ways of his culture. He is intoxicated by language, cannot discern between fantasy and reality, abhors compromise, always blames others for his predicament, and in the end lances the painful boil of his frustrations in a pointless, though momentarily gratifying, act of bloodlust" (*New Republic* editor Martin Peretz). Comparable statements about "Jewish culture" would be recognized as a reversion to Nazism. Gary Hart was forced to terminate his presidential candidacy because of alleged indiscretions, which did not include his withdrawal of money from a bank when he learned it had Arab investors: "'We didn't know it was an Arab bank,' said Kenneth Guido, special counsel to the Hart campaign. 'We got him (Hart) out of it as soon as we knew'." Nor was Walter Mondale accused of racism when he returned campaign contributions he had received from Arab-Americans or, in one case, a woman with an Arab-American surname, "for fear of offending American Jews," the *Wall Street Journal* reported; or when he accepted the endorsement of the *The New Republic*. Change a few names, and the meaning of these facts is evident enough. In the *New York Times*, William Safire condemns "the world's film crews" for their coverage of "a made-for-TV uprising of a new 'people' … in Israel's West Bank"; such derision of Jewish resistance to comparable abuses would be unthinkable, apart from neo-Nazi publications, but this passes without notice. It is pointless to discuss the journal of the American Jewish Committee, considered one of the most respectable voices of conservative opinion, where a lead article seethes with bitter scorn about "the Palestinian Arabs, people who breed and bleed and advertise their misery"; this is "the obvious key to the success of the Arab strategy" of driving the Jews into the sea in a revival of the Nazi *Lebensraum* concept, the author of these shocking words continues. We may, again, imagine the reaction if a respected professor at a major university were to produce the same words, referring to Jews.[112]

There is no space to comment here on the vicious racist depiction of Arabs in novels, television, cartoons and cinema, or the crucial support in the American Jewish community for Rabbi Kahane, who is commonly denounced as a Nazi in Israeli commentary, and for other groups within Israel that are only marginally less extreme in their intentions with regard to the Arab population and attitudes towards them.

Those who express their fear and concern over manifestations of anti-Semitism among Blacks and others might be taken seriously if they were to pay even the slightest attention to what is said by their friends and associates. They do not.

The matter of racism and the Arab-Jewish conflict is more complex. The anti-Arab racism that has become so familiar as to be unnoticed has been accompanied by apparent concern over anti-Semitism; that the qualification is accurate is evident from a closer look at the revision that the concept of anti-Semitism has undergone in the process. There have long been efforts to identify anti-Semitism and anti-Zionism in an effort to exploit anti-racist sentiment for political ends; "one of the chief tasks of any dialogue with the Gentile world is to prove that the distinction between anti-Semitism and anti-Zionism is not a distinction at all," Israeli diplomat Abba Eban argued, in a typical expression of this intellectually and morally disreputable position.[113] But that no longer suffices. It is now necessary to identify criticism of Israeli policies as anti-Semitism—or in the case of Jews, as "self-hatred," so that all possible cases are covered.

The leading official monitor of anti-Semitism, the Anti-Defamation League of B'nai Brith, interprets anti-Semitism as unwillingness to conform to its requirements with regard to support for Israeli authorities. These conceptions were clearly expounded by ADL National Director Nathan Perlmutter, who wrote that while old-fashioned anti-Semitism has declined, there is a new and more dangerous variety on the part of "peacemakers of Vietnam vintage, transmuters of swords into plowshares, championing the terrorist P.L.O.," and those who condemn U.S. policies in Vietnam and Central America while "sniping at American defense budgets." He fears that "nowadays war is getting a bad name and peace too favorable a press" with the rise of this "real anti-Semitism." The logic is straightforward: Anti-Semitism is opposition to the interests of Israel (as the ADL sees them); and these interests are threatened by "the liberals," the churches, and others who do not adhere to the ADL political line.[114]

The ADL has virtually abandoned its earlier role as a civil rights organization, becoming "one of the main pillars" of Israeli propaganda in the U.S., as the Israeli press casually describes it, engaged in surveillance, blacklisting, compilation of FBI-style files circulated to adherents for the purpose of defamation, angry public responses to criticism of Israeli actions, and so on. These efforts, buttressed by insinuations of anti-Semitism or direct accusations, are intended to deflect or undermine opposition to Israeli policies, including Israel's refusal, with U.S. support, to move towards a general political settlement. The ADL was condemned by the Middle East Studies Association after circulation of an ADL blacklist to campus Jewish leaders, stamped "confidential." Practices of this nature have been bitterly condemned by Israeli doves—in part because they fear the consequences of this hysterical chauvinism for Israel, in part because they have been subjected to the standard procedures themselves, in part simply in natural revulsion.[115]

Anti-Semitism, in short, is not merely conflated with anti-Zionism, but even extended to Zionists who are critical of Israeli practices. Correspondingly, authentic anti-Semitism on the part of those whose services to Israeli power are deemed appropriate is of no account.

These two aspects of "the real anti-Semitism," ADL-style, were illustrated during the 1988 U.S. presidential campaign. The Democratic Party was denounced for anti-Semitism on the grounds that its convention dared to debate a resolution calling for a two-state political settlement of the Israeli-Palestinian conflict. In contrast, when an array of Nazi sympathizers and anti-Semites were exposed in August 1988 in the Bush presidential campaign, the major Jewish organizations and leaders were, for the most part, "curiously blasé about both the revelations and Bush's response to them," largely ignoring the matter, John Judis comments.[116] The *New Republic* dismissed as a minor matter the "antique and anemic forms of anti-Semitism" of virulent anti-Semites and Nazi and fascist sympathizers at a high level of the Republican campaign organization. The editors stressed, rather, the "comfortable haven for Jew-hatred on the left, including the left wing of the Democratic Party," parts of the Jackson campaign, and "the ranks of increasingly well-organized Arab activists," all of whom supported the two-state resolution at the Party convention and thus qualify as "Jew-haters."[117]

The point is that the ultra-right Republicans are regarded as properly supportive of Israel by hard-line standards, while the Democratic Party reveals its "Jew-hatred" by tolerating elements that believe that Palestinians are human beings with the same rights as Jews, including the right of national self-determination alongside of Israel. Following the lead of the major Jewish organizations, the Democrats carefully avoided the discovery of anti-Semites and Nazis in the Republican campaign headquarters and the continuing close links after exposure.

The same point was illustrated by the revelation, at the same time, that the Reagan Department of Education had once again refused federal funds for a highly praised school history program on the Holocaust. It was first rejected in 1986 "after a review panel member complained that the views of the Nazi Party and the Ku Klux Klan were not represented." Republican faithfuls charged the program with "psychological manipulation, induced behavioral change and privacy-invading treatment" (Phyllis Schlafly); citing "leftist authorities" such as *New York Times* columnist Flora Lewis, British historian A.J.P. Taylor, and Kurt Vonnegut; being "profoundly offensive to fundamentalists and evangelicals"; and even being "anti-war, anti-hunting" and likely to "induce a guilt trip." A senior Education Department official attributed the rejections to "those on the extreme right wing of the Republican Party." In 1986 and 1987, this particular program had been "singled out for a refusal." In 1988, when the program "was the top-rated project in the category [of history, geography, and civics], created by then-Education Secretary William J. Bennett," the entire category was eliminated.[118]

But "the extreme right wing of the Republican Party," whatever its attitudes towards Nazis and the Holocaust, is adequately pro-Israel. There was no detectable protest, and the issue did not arise in the last stages of the election campaign.

The cheapening of the concept of anti-Semitism and the ready tolerance for anti-Arab racism go hand-in-hand, expressing the same political commitments. All of this, again, is merely "antique and anemic anti-Semitism."

Media services to Israel have gone well beyond praising the "benign" occupation while Palestinians were being subjected to torture, daily humiliation, and collective punishment; suppressing the record of Israeli terror in Lebanon and elsewhere and its conscious purpose of blocking steps towards political accommodation on the part of the PLO; hailing the "liberation of Lebanon" in 1982; and properly engineering the historical record on such matters as diplomacy and terror. The media have also been "surprisingly uncurious" on the Israeli nuclear threat, as observed by Leonard Spector, specialist of the Carnegie Endowment for International Peace on nuclear proliferation. They remained so even after ample evidence had appeared on Israel's nuclear forces and its testing of a nuclear-capable missile with range sufficient to "reach the Soviet Union." In 1984, Spector's Carnegie Foundation study of nuclear proliferation identified Israel as "by far the most advanced of eight 'emerging' nuclear powers, surpassing the nuclear capabilities of earlier contenders such as India and South Africa," the *Los Angeles Times* and *Boston Globe* reported.

The *Globe* headline read: "Israel may have 20 nuclear arms, report says." The *New York Times* report of Spector's study by Richard Halloran the same day is headlined "Nuclear Arms Races in Third World Feared." It mentions Israel once, namely, in having helped to *reduce* the danger of nuclear proliferation by bombing the Iraqi nuclear reactor in 1981. Spector's 1987 study on nuclear proliferation was reported in the *Boston Globe* on page 67, in the Amusements section, under the headline "Report says Israel could 'level' cities," quoting him as saying that Israel may have acquired enough nuclear weaponry "to level every urban center in the Middle East with a population of more than 100,000." The *New York Times* report by Michael Gordon the same day makes no mention of Israel. It opens by warning of Libyan efforts to acquire a nuclear capacity, then turns to suspicions about Pakistan, Iran, and India.[119]

The *London Sunday Times* revelation of Mordechai Vanunu's testimony on Israel's nuclear arsenal with an across-the-page front-page headline on October 5, 1986 was barely noted in the U.S. press. The *New York Times* eliminated a brief wire service report from its national edition, publishing a few words on Israel's denial of the charges the next day, and other major journals were hardly different. Reviewing media coverage, Nabeel Abraham found "no editorials or commentaries, pro or con, ... on Israel's new status as the world's sixth nuclear power" in the following six months, and only a few news references, mostly downplaying the story or fostering doubts about its authenticity (citing Thomas Friedman of the *New York Times*, November 9).[120]

Also unmentioned was an interesting observation by the scientific head of France's atomic energy establishment during the period when France helped Israel build its nuclear weapons plant in Dimona, reported in the *London Sunday Times* on October 12, 1986. He commented that

> We thought the Israeli bomb was aimed against the Americans, not to launch it against America but to say "if you don't want to help us in a critical situation we will require you to help us, otherwise we will use our nuclear bombs"

—a conception of some potential interest to the American public, one might think, particularly in the light of its earlier roots, going back many years.[121]

Vanunu's abduction by Israeli intelligence and his secret trial in Israel also received little notice. When his trial opened three weeks after the *London Sunday Times* had prominently reported the details of his abduction in Europe, the *New York Times* reported only that "it is still not entirely clear how Mr. Vanunu, who disappeared from London last September, was brought back to Israel to stand trial."[122]

There are many similar cases of protection of Israel in the media, some already discussed; to add another, consider the September 1987 statement by Foreign Ministry Director General Yossi Beilin (a Labor dove) that Israel's sanctions against South Africa are "symbolic, psychological," and will not hurt the $240 million yearly trade between the two countries, unreported in the *New York Times*.[123] South Africa too benefits from selective attention. Thus, when a South African naval force attacked three Russian ships in the Angolan harbor of Namibe in June 1986, sinking one, using Israeli-made Scorpion missiles, there was no mention in the *New York Times, Wall Street Journal, Christian Science Monitor*, the news weeklies, or other journals listed in the magazine index; the *Washington Post* published only a 120-word item from Moscow reporting Soviet condemnation of the attack, on page 17.[124] The reaction might have been different if a Libyan naval force had attacked U.S. commercial vessels in the port of Haifa, sinking one, using East German-made missiles.

5. The Best Defense[125]

Despite the extraordinary protection the media have afforded Israel since 1967, and the demonizing of its enemies, many are not satisfied and bitterly condemn the media for their unfair treatment of Israel and their tilt towards the PLO and the Arabs generally (see appendix I). These attacks then lead to thoughtful reflections on the "double standard" that Israel must suffer and the reasons for it. This is a virtual reflex when some Israeli atrocity, such as the war in Lebanon or the violent repression of the Palestinian uprising from December 1987, becomes impossible to overlook, so that the media present a glimpse of what they generally dismiss or deny while continuing to ignore (or sometimes falsify) the background and causes.

The arguments offered on the "double standard" are often startling. In the *Jerusalem Post,* Eliahu Tal ("perhaps Israel's leading mass communicator") describes the work he is completing in cooperation with the Anti-Defamation League that shows how Israel is losing the propaganda war because of the "anti-Israel bias and double standards" of the media and the "clever trick" devised by Arab propagandists: "deliberately using women and kids as targets for the camera"—a remark reminiscent of the insight in *Commentary* about "the Palestinian Arabs, people who breed and bleed and advertise their misery."[126] Another typical refrain is that those who do not live in Israel and suffer its problems at first hand are dishonest and unfair when they interfere with its affairs by criticizing its policies—though they are permitted to laud and admire Israel in public, and there are no similar strictures with regard to criticism of the PLO or the Soviet Union on the part of people who do not live in refugee camps or in Leningrad. Also exempt from the doctrine are the extreme pressures on Israel from the American Jewish community, even blocking formation of a functioning government for several weeks after the November 1988 Israeli elections and significantly influencing its character, when it seemed that the government might change the wording of its Law of Return in a manner unacceptable to diaspora Jewry.

The reaction to media coverage of Israel makes a certain kind of sense: attack is always the best defense, particularly when one can expect to control the terms of the discussion, and charges, however outlandish, will be granted a certain credence.

A number of examples have already been discussed. Another typical case is an ABC TV "news viewpoint," moderated by Peter Jennings.[127] In accordance with the regular pattern, two positions are represented: the media are attacked as too adversarial, unfair to Israel in this case; and they are defended as doing a creditable job under difficult circumstances. There is barely a nod given to the possibility that they might be guided by a different bias. In a question from the audience, media analyst Dennis Perrin asked ABC Israel Bureau Chief Bill Seamans why the media continue to claim that the PLO refused to recognize Israel's rights in the face of a series of statements by Arafat, which he cites, "calling for mutual security guarantees and mutual recognition." Seamans's response is that Arafat "has not made a clearcut, definitive statement recognizing Israel's right to exist," but has always added qualifications. Panelist Howard Squadron of the American Jewish Congress then dismisses Perrin's comments as "utter nonsense," and there the matter ends.

Seamans's comment is quite accurate: Arafat has added the qualification that Palestinians should have rights comparable to those accorded Israeli Jews. It is also true that U.S.-Israeli statements have no taint of ambiguity, being unfailingly rejectionist. That stand, by definition, conforms to the requirements of peace, moderation, and justice, so nothing need be said about it.

But no review of the actual facts can be expected to diminish the drumbeat of criticism of the "pro-PLO" media, which, in a major "scandal," have accorded the PLO "moral and political prestige" (Leon Wieseltier) and have provided the organization with "its stellar media presence" (Daniel Pipes). The adulation of the PLO and the unfair double standard imposed on defenseless Israel are to be explained, perhaps, on the basis of "the irrational attitude of the Western world toward Jews" that lies "deep in the psyche" of Christian civilization, so Israeli President Chaim Herzog ruminates.[128]

Such perceptions have a familiar ring. The regime of the Shah received overwhelmingly positive coverage, but that did not prevent him from charging the Western media with a "double standard for international morality: anything Marxist, no matter how bloody and base, is acceptable; the policies of a socialist, centrist, or right-wing government are not." Similarly, in internal government discussions on the eve of the overthrow of the government of Guatemala in 1954, Secretary of State John Foster Dulles "expressed very great concern about the Communist line being followed by Sydney Gruson in his dispatches to the *New York Times*," which President Eisenhower then described as "the most untrustworthy newspaper in the United States." CIA director Allen Dulles "pointed out some very disturbing features of Sidney Gruson's career to date" and the assembled dignitaries decided "to talk informally to the management of the *New York Times*"—successfully, it appears; Gruson was sent to Mexico after Allen Dulles communicated to the top *Times* management suspicions that Gruson and his wife, *Times* columnist Flora Lewis, were Communist agents or sympathizers, asking the *Times* to remove him from Central America during the coup. This was during a period when the *Times* and other media were being spoon-fed appropriate material by the public relations specialists of the United Fruit Company, though, as its PR director Thomas McCann later wrote: "It is difficult to make a convincing case for manipulation of the press when the victims proved so eager for the experience."[129]

One finds similar perceptions among respected political figures, scholars, and journalists. Zbigniew Brzezinski writes that "it is scandalous that so much of the conventionally liberal community, always so ready to embrace victims of American or Israeli or any other unfashionable 'imperialism,' is so reticent on the subject" of Afghanistan. Surely one might expect liberals in Congress or the press to desist from their ceaseless labors on behalf of the PLO and the guerrillas in El Salvador long enough to notice some Soviet crimes; perhaps they might even follow Brzezinski to the Khyber Pass to strike heroic poses there before a camera crew. Political scientist Robert Tucker writes that "numerous public figures in the West, even a number of Western governments [... have] encouraged the PLO in its maximalist course" of "winner-take-all," that is, destruction of Israel; he too fails to cite names and references, for unsurprising reasons. One of the most audacious examples was a media triumph by journalist William Shawcross, who succeeded—easily, given the serviceability of the thought—in establishing the doctrine that there was relative silence in the West during the Pol Pot atrocities, when there was in fact a vast chorus of indignation, and that this silence was attributable to the formidable left-wing influence over media and governments that is so striking a feature of Western society. My co-author Edward Herman and I were even granted magical powers in Shawcross's construction: he cited alleged comments of ours that went to press in February 1979 and appeared the following November as the source and agency of this influence from 1975 through December 1978.[130] None of this affected the respectful reception for these thoughtful insights in the slightest.

A variant is that the universities have been taken over by Marxists and (other) left-wing fascists. Commenting on the "new generation" in the field of Soviet studies, University of Massachusetts sociologist Paul Hollander, a fellow of the Harvard Russian Research Center, writes that "many academics of this generation believed that no social-political system could be worse than their own ... For them, it was easier to discern political pluralism in the U.S.S.R. than in the U.S." Historian John Diggins sees Marxism as having "come close to being the dominant ideology in the academic world." New York University historian Norman Cantor deplores the failure of the Reaganites to overcome the dominance of academic life by "the radical left," who "indoctrinate" the children of the middle class "in European socialist theory." This is a symptom of the deeper failure to develop "a comprehensive rightist doctrine," he explains. The "ingredients" for such a doctrine existed "in interwar European Fascism," but "recourse to this intellectual reservoir was never attempted" because of the "discrediting of intellectual Fascism by World War II, Vichy, Mussolini, Nazism and the Holocaust"—which, we are apparently to understand, had nothing to do with the heritage of intellectual Fascism. What a shame that the Reaganites missed the opportunity to revive these valuable ideas.[131]

There are many similar examples, specifics invariably omitted for understandable reasons. It is superfluous to comment on the relation to reality of such pronouncements about the left-wing take-over of the academic world (or perhaps the whole world). It may well be, however, that they are seriously intended; apparently they are respectfully received. The point is that to those who demand strict obedience to authority, even the slightest sign of independence of thought is enough to evoke the fear that all is lost.

6. *La Prensa* and its Colleagues[132]

Through the 1980s, Nicaragua has been quite unusual in the openness of its society in a time of crisis. Hostile journalists who are hardly more than agents of the great power attacking Nicaragua travel and report freely throughout the country.[133] Bitterly anti-Sandinista U.S. officials and other advocates of the U.S. terrorist attack are permitted to enter and deliver public speeches and news conferences, calling for the overthrow of the government, and to meet with the U.S.-funded political opposition, segments of which declare the same ends and barely conceal their support for the contras.

Domestic media that identify with the attack against Nicaragua and serve its purposes, and are funded by the foreign power attacking the country, have been subjected to harassment, censorship, and periodic suspension; but neither they, their editors and staff, nor opposition figures with the same commitments have faced anything remotely like the repression of media and dissidents in the U.S.-backed "fledgling democracies," and the record compares favorably with that of other U.S. allies or the United States itself, surprising as the conclusion may be to people who have not sought to determine the facts.

Furthermore, in a most remarkable display of arrogance and willful ignorance, none of this is so much as noticed in the United States. Similarly, it is considered obviously appropriate—and therefore requires no comment or even reporting in the national media—for the United States to impose barriers to freedom of travel unknown in a weak and tiny country under U.S. attack: to bar entry of tortured mothers from El Salvador who have been invited to speak in small towns, or opposition parliamentarians from Nicaragua who oppose contra aid, or critics of the Vietnam war, years after it terminated.

Since its reopening in October 1987 under the Esquipulas Accord, the opposition journal *La Prensa* has made little effort to disguise its role as an agency of U.S. propaganda, dedicated to overthrowing the government of Nicaragua by force. The journal publishes bizarre tales about Sandinista atrocities (comparing the Sandinistas to the Nazis), virtually calls for resistance to the draft, and is full of praise for the contras, who are portrayed as freedom fighters in the Reagan style.[134]

I reviewed *La Prensa* from its opening in October 1987 through December 23.[135] There is no pretense of meeting minimal journalistic standards. Rather, the journal follows the standard procedures of U.S. psychological warfare to a degree that is almost comical, presenting a general picture along the following lines.

The background theme throughout is that there is a close analogy between the current conflict and the struggle against Somoza. In the current conflict, the Sandinistas (FSLN) play the role of Somoza, but they are much worse, because at least he was a native Nicaraguan while the Sandinistas are agents of Soviet imperialism (the U.S. is a benevolent, if sometimes confused outsider). The contras are the guerrillas fighting Somoza, and the internal opposition is the opposition to Somoza, with *La Prensa* taking up the mantle of the journal with the same name of the Somoza years. For the most part the theme is insinuated; sometimes it is directly expressed, under such headlines as "Threats of FSLN Recall Somocism" (Dec. 15). The Sandinistas, the new Somoza clique, attack, torture, rob, and exploit the people, living a life of luxury while the people starve under their oppressive rule. The United States is almost entirely missing from the picture, though it does provide heroes: for example, avid contra enthusiast Jeane Kirkpatrick, who declares in the lead story of October 12 that "Nicaraguans are not alone," she is with them; and Elliott Abrams, who calls for "total democratization, or indefinite struggle" (Oct. 23, Nov. 11). Other heroes include the U.S. Senate, which provided $250 million for "democratic institutions" in Nicaragua, including *La Prensa* (Oct. 7); and parts of the U.S. press, for example, the editors of the *Baltimore Sun*, who call for contra aid as a "sensible and modest" means to maintain the "anti-Sandinista resistance" (Dec. 17). The visit of U.S. congressmen supporting the contras, with applause and ovations in public meetings, is hailed as a "historic moment" in the struggle for freedom (Dec. 16, 18).

The complementary aspect of this CIA construction is that the people "unanimously" oppose the Sandinistas, denouncing Ortega "unanimously" (all social classes, etc.) for failing to comply with the accords, all of this being reminiscent of the similar conditions under the Somoza dictatorship (Nov. 6). Ortega is also denounced for insulting Reagan (another hero) and American soldiers who died in foreign wars (including those who helped "liberate the USSR from Hitler," the editors add, in an interesting version of history). Through early December we read that peasants complain about Sandinista injustice, townspeople about the oppressive Sandinista officials, mothers about sons in prison and the army, prisoners about torture and terrible conditions, workers about suffering and oppression. There are fires, accidents, disasters, inflation, rampaging soldiers, protests against military service. Campesinos protest that government agencies are not selling them bread, there is hunger, they are too poor to buy on the black market. And so on, with no variation. In short, a picture of unmitigated oppression of the general population who unanimously oppose the foreign-imposed dictatorship, which tortures the suffering people for no reason apart from their own greed and service to their foreign master, while profiting from the drug racket (Nov. 24).

The line is precisely as laid down by the U.S. Embassy. Thus, compliance with the peace accords is defined strictly in the terms determined by the United States. The lead headline on October 30 reads "FSLN says no to peace," with an AFP story reporting that the

FSLN refuses to dialogue with the civilian leadership of the contras and will maintain the emergency until the aggression stops—both steps in conformity with the accords, as already discussed.[136] The United States has defined the matter differently, and for *La Prensa*, as for the U.S. media, that is where it ends.

A summary review of the peace accords (Dec. 4) is entirely negative, blaming everything on the Sandinistas. There is only one good feature of the developments since August: the cease-fire negotiations "have legitimized the Nicaraguan Resistance" (the contras) and thus permitted the internal opposition to enter into "open negotiations with the Nicaraguan Resistance without danger of delegitimizing themselves." The program of the contras "coincides fully with the position of the fourteen political organizations of the civilian opposition in the national dialogue."

Throughout, *La Prensa* identifies with the contras, often quite openly. In an interview with Pedro Joaquín Chamorro on "his experience as a member of the Nicaraguan Resistance" (Dec. 12), he is identified as "the co-director of La Prensa who has chosen to fight from outside the country against the Sandinista dictatorship"; he was at the time a member of the CIA-established "civilian directorate." The interview describes his struggles in support of democracy and his international awards for his valiant struggle against the Sandinista dictatorship. He took the decision "to conduct the civic conflict at a different level, in a different context." In short, there is no difference between *La Prensa* and the contras, apart from tactical decisions.

Similarly, a November 13 article states that the Sandinistas "have recognized the contras" by agreeing to cease-fire talks. Conservative Party leader Mario Rappacioli, the same day, states that the agreement to negotiate with the contras through Cardinal Obando amounts to "recognition of their legitimacy," and makes the contras a "legitimate part of the Nicaraguan community with all rights," a matter of "enormous significance." The contras now have the right to act politically within Nicaragua, and the opposition can openly identify with them without delegitimization. In short, the internal opposition has been pro-contra all along, but now can be so openly, because of this "recognition of the contras" by the Sandinistas.

On November 30, contra leader Adolfo Calero is asked to comment on these remarks of Rappacioli, in an interview. He strongly supports them, and suggests that "the principal political currents that exist in Nicaragua" (which he identifies as the opposition political parties, the Sandinistas not being a political element but rather a foreign-imposed dictatorship) should work together with the contras for democracy and free elections; this is quite in line with Pedro Joaquín Chamorro's expressed view that after the contra victory, the Sandinistas should have no "representation in the governing junta" in the "democracy" that will be established.[137] The contras and the internal opposition have the same objectives, Calero continues, and *La Prensa* obviously endorses this position, again identifying itself with the contras, in fact, their most extreme terrorist element. On December 3, the Secretary-General of the Social Christian Party makes the same point, emphasizing that the Resistance proposals correspond to those of the fourteen internal opposition groups.

It was hardly accurate for Stephen Kinzer to report subsequently that "For the moment, at least, it seems that virtually any criticism will be tolerated in Nicaragua as long as it does not endorse the one point of view that is still officially taboo: support for the contras."[138] Such support had been quite open in *La Prensa* and in statements of the political opposition. It is scarcely imaginable that any Western democracy would tolerate a newspaper, or an internal opposition, that openly identifies with the proxy army of a foreign power attacking the country from abroad, maintained in the field with constant supply flights violating the national territory.

The war is barely covered in *La Prensa*, though this was a period of heightened contra attacks against civilians as the U.S. desperately sought to undermine the Esquipulas Accord by escalating the war. Sometimes fighting is reported with a twist that implies that the area is under attack by the Sandinistas, terrifying the population (lead headlines, Nov. 18; "Bombing terrifies peasants," Dec. 19; etc.). There are also allegations of use of cluster and phosphorus bombs against contras in Honduras. I found no mention of the increase in CIA supply flights, except obliquely in the context of the report of Ortega's O.A.S. speech in November.

All of this is not dissimilar to reporting in the United States. In fact, at times *La Prensa* is more honest. Thus, as we have seen, the *New York Times* simply falsified Ortega's and Calero's reference to supply flights; *La Prensa* reported it accurately. On December 17, there is an editorial condemning the United States for sending advanced F-5 jet fighters to Honduras; this was not condemned, in fact not even reported, in the *New York Times*—right at the moment when they were denouncing the Sandinistas in article after article for allegedly requesting vintage 1950s jet interceptors to defend their territory from the illegal flights by the CIA and the U.S. military that provide arms and intelligence for contras attacking "soft targets."

La Prensa reported the facts more or less accurately when the Interior Ministry stated that "Radio Católica may broadcast news, but must apply for the legally required permission for the program and register the name of its director, the broadcast time and other information."[139] In contrast, Stephen Kinzer reported falsely that "a spokesman for the Interior Ministry had no comment," in an article headlined "Sandinistas Ban Station's Plan for Radio News" which opens by stating that "the Government today forbade Nicaragua's newly reopened Roman Catholic radio station to broadcast news." Two days later, Kinzer reported falsely that "the Government refused to allow the newly reopened Roman Catholic radio station to broadcast news. The Government has given no indication as to whether it intends to open up broadcasting to dissenting views, although this is required by the peace agreement." In a Sunday "week in review" column three days later, Kinzer asserted falsely that "the Interior Ministry forbade the church radio station to broadcast news," again refusing to report the Ministry statement. The false claim was also reiterated by his colleague James LeMoyne.[140]

Presumably, those who prepare the material for *La Prensa* understand that the journal must maintain some degree of credibility within Nicaragua if the project of disinformation and disruption is to succeed. Within the United States itself the contraints are much weaker.

While the tribulations of *La Prensa* receive extensive and anguished coverage in the United States and Europe, the media elsewhere in Central America merit little attention; being firmly under right-wing control through the workings of the market guided by state terror when needed, they raise few problems for dedicated defenders of freedom of the press.

Harper's editor Francisco Goldman published a review of the Central American press in August 1988.[141] As others have observed, he writes that in Guatemala and El Salvador, censorship is hardly necessary: "you have to be rich to own a newspaper, and on the right politically to survive the experience. Papers in El Salvador don't have to be censored: poverty and deadly fear do the job." Correspondingly, the security forces are immune from any criticism, though political figures who do not completely conform to the agenda of the right-wing business class and oligarchy are fair game, often with "hallucinatory disinformation" of the sort familiar as well in

Nicaragua's *La Prensa*. Journalistic standards are abysmal. The war and terror barely exist. Apart from "multi-page, technicolor sports supplements ..., these newspapers seem made up almost entirely of society pages: the whole country dresses well and spends all its time floating from one baby shower to another."

In Honduras too, "the army is above criticism or investigation." And in keeping with the status of Honduras as a client state under effective military rule, "Honduran reporters have long been banned from firsthand reporting in the southern chunk of their country occupied by the *contras*."

Elsewhere we learn that American reporters are allowed in, but choose not to report on the hundreds of thousands of people starving to death or the many driven from their homes, despite pleas from the Church and relief workers. Rather, they report on the state of the "democratic resistance," which has "staged a number of scenes for their benefit" and provides them with footage that provides "more exciting news segments" and that creates "a good impression of the *contras*," including faked battle scenes, supply drops, and mining (with actual mines later laid by the CIA). It was also "a common tactic of the FDN [contras] to take reporters on a tour through the country-side, telling them that they were travelling through Nicaragua, when often they were still in Honduras." Another device was "to draw parallels with the Salvadoran guerrilla opposition" so as "to confuse the public, and make FDN forces appear roughly equivalent to the Salvadoran guerrillas" while concealing the fact that they were a CIA "proxy army ... working for *American* goals." These and other mech- anisms of media manipulation are described by Edgar Chamorro, the CIA-selected press spokesman for the contras, in his unmentionable study of how the U.S. media were handled.[142]

"Nicaragua at this moment has the freest print media in Central America," Goldman continues; its media have been incomparably freer than those in El Salvador and Guatemala through the 1980s, if only because journalists do not have to fear the retribution of the security forces. The Sandinista journal *Barricada*'s "generally suffo- cating earnestness bears some relation to reality: there's often a real attempt to explain perhaps inexplicable Sandinista policies here (if no room to refute them) ... with the occasional light touch thrown in to remind readers that even party militants are irrepressibly Nicara- guan." Examples, in fact, are not uncommon in *Barricada*, though in three months of *La Prensa* I found no such departures from its mission. *La Prensa* is "relentlessly ideological, propagandistic, one-sided, sensationalistic, negative and even dishonest." It is also unique: *La Prensa*, "alone of all the Central American newspapers can print whatever it wants against its country's 'ruling power'," though it "seems no more enlightened, or enlightening, than Guatemala's *Prensa Libre* or any of El Salvador's politicking rags." Reviewing some fabrications about Sandinista atrocities, Goldman observes that no other newspaper in Central America could long survive after "leveling such accusations against its national army." One can hardly ignore the fact that "*La Prensa* has been cozy with our efforts (CIA, National Endowment for Democracy, Ollie North) to topple the Nicaraguan government." In reality, it is not only in Central America that such a newspaper would not long survive, under such conditions. An analogue in the history of the Western democracies is not easy to find; I know of none.

Accordingly, in the pages of the *Washington Post* and *New York Times*, *La Prensa* is a paragon of virtue, Nicaragua is a repressive dictatorship that bars freedom of expression, and the free press in democratic El Salvador represents all points of view.[143]

In Costa Rica, the government has a system of obligatory press licensing condemned by the Inter-American Human Rights Court in 1985. President Arias disagreed with the ruling that state licensing limits freedom of expression, and refused to comply with it. Though the media are free from censorship or state terror, "in practice, however, Costa Ricans often can obtain only one side of the story, since wealthy ultraconservatives control the major daily newspapers and broadcasting stations."[144] In particular, the major journal *La Nación* and others have been engaged in a feverish anti-Sandinista campaign of distortion and disinformation—with considerable effect, according to the unreportable José Figueres.[145]

La Prensa uses rather crude methods in portraying the government as the new Somoza regime opposed unanimously by the population that it robs and oppresses. In the United States, the project of "demonizing the Sandinistas" in accord with the directives of the Office of Latin American Public Diplomacy is conducted in a more subtle way. One device is careful selection of sources. A Stephen Kinzer article on the opening of *La Prensa* and the Catholic Radio station in October 1987 presents a sample of public opinion: the proprietress of a store "in a poor section of town" who says that "Truth is what I want, and La Prensa is the truth"; a banana vendor who predicts that the journal will soon be closed "and we'll be under twice as much pressure as before"; a laborer reading *La Prensa* aloud to friends who is saving it for his grandchildren; a truck driver who hasn't read a newspaper since *La Prensa* was suspended but doubts that this good fortune will last. In short, the People, United.

The device recalls standard Communist Party Agitprop. Given the poll results (which Kinzer did not report) indicating that support for all opposition parties combined amounts to nine percent, less than one-third that of the support for the Sandinistas (and much less than the personal approval for President Ortega), one might suppose that there would be some other reactions, but if so, they are unreported— just as no opinions were quoted when *La Epoca* opened in Guatemala or when it was destroyed by terror a few weeks later, or when the independent Salvadoran press was demolished by murder and violence, the agents being the security forces backed by the U.S. government, Congress, the media, and the intellectual community quite generally.[146] In some variants, the voices of "the people" are counterbalanced by quotation of some government official, again helping to establish the required image of the oppressive government versus the suffering population.

In fact, readers of the *Times* could plausibly conclude that support for the Sandinistas is virtually non-existent, outside of the government itself. In a sample of forty-nine Kinzer articles from the signing of the peace accords in August 1987 through mid-December, I found two references to the possible existence of such people. One is in paragraph eighteen of one of the many articles condemning the Sandinistas on the matter of amnesty, where a mother of a Sandinista soldier killed in action is quoted as opposing amnesty for "the people who killed our sons." A second is in an insert in a survey of the land crisis in Central America, quoting cooperative members who express appreciation for land reform measures.[147] The articles are largely devoted to diplomatic maneuverings and the tribulations of the internal opposition, who are presented as the true voice of Nicaragua. One learns next to nothing about the country, not an untypical feature of media coverage.

The procedure of highly selective sourcing is second nature even among journalists who take some pains to keep independent of government propaganda. Thus Roy Gutman of *Newsday*, in a book critical of Reagan administration policy in Nicaragua as flawed and incompetent, reconstructs the events of a highly controversial rally at Chinandega in 1984, when the CIA-subsidized candidate Arturo Cruz was allegedly harassed by Sandinista mobs. This was taken to be a critical event demonstrating Sandinista intransigence, if not totalitarian commitment, by Cruz adviser and contra lobbyist Robert Leiken, who was the *New York Review of Books* and *New Republic* commentator on Nicaragua, and by Reaganite propaganda generally. In a footnote, Gutman states that his account is based on interviews with Cruz and five other members of the U.S.-backed political opposition, the U.S. Ambassador and the National Security Adviser, and an unnamed senior U.S. official in Central America.[148] Not surprisingly, his account—stated as fact, with no qualifications—is very favorable to Cruz and critical of the Sandinistas. Such practice would arouse a storm of protest and derision if the choice of sources were reversed, in an account unfavorable to the U.S. and its clients. In this case, it passes completely without notice on the part of reviewers who praise Gutman's critical and independent stance—a judgment that is correct, relative to the permissible spectrum.

In yet another variant, a *Times* photograph of a November 7, 1987 rally in Managua on the completion of the first period of the accords carries the caption: "Nicaraguans cheering President Daniel Ortega Saavedra as he announced that his Sandinista Government would agree to indirect negotiations with the contras on a cease-fire." The reader is to understand, then, that the people of Nicaragua are overjoyed over what the accompanying story by James LeMoyne depicts as a major victory for the contras and the United States.[149] The people are indeed cheering, but, to judge by the signs and T-shirts, they are enthusiastic Sandinista supporters. Peter Ford, who covered the rally, reported that "the tens of thousands of Sandinista supporters in Revolution square offered no response when the President announced ... talks with the contra leadership," and other steps highly touted here were "met with a baffled silence," though his defiant challenge to "aggression against the Nicaraguan people" received "enthusiastic applause."[150] The Newspaper of Record chose to convey a different image.

Similarly, in a sarcastic report on how "in an effort to persuade Congress to defeat President Reagan's request for new aid to the contras, the Sandinista Government has mounted a campaign of good deeds," Kinzer writes that "the Government's campaign against contra aid is receiving strong support from *one quarter*—the estimated 2,000 Americans who live in Nicaragua" (my emphasis). He proceeds to quote a number of Americans working in Nicaragua, the insinuation being obvious, though Kinzer knows that opposition to contra aid is overwhelming; the polls that he did not report, after long claiming that polls are illegal, show 85 percent opposed to contra aid and 9 percent in favor—perhaps the same 9 percent that supported all opposition parties.[151]

In El Salvador, where the image to be conveyed is the opposite, the method of sampling is reversed. Thus, in discussing growing anxiety in El Salvador, James LeMoyne quotes government officials, an army officer, a young businessman, an unidentified visitor, the guests at "a dinner of upper-class businessmen and their wives," a painter "in his spacious studio," and an American official—but no one in the slums, refugee camps, or villages, who might have rather different concerns in the "fledgling democracy." Their actual concerns can be discovered outside the bounds of the Free Press, in public opinion surveys and responses to the Church-organized National Debate, unreported as we have seen.[152]

Rather similar conceptions of "the people" are often to be found in domestic reporting. Clyde Farnsworth reports from Washington on the U.S. embargo against Nicaragua, which "Appears of Little Effect," the headline assures us; in reality, it achieved its predicted effect of destroying private enterprise and reducing the economy to bare survival, but the Party Line requires that all problems be attributed to Sandinista incompetence and malevolence. "Those opposing the embargo," Farnsworth reports, say that it will not achieve U.S. goals. But all agree that the sanctions "will be in place a long time," because "by and large leading multinational companies have not been affected." "No important domestic [U.S.] constituency has been seriously hurt by the trade rupture, and therefore *no one* is arguing strenuously that it be mended" (my emphasis). Here the phrase "no one" is to be understood in the conventional sense of "no one who counts." A great many people were calling for ending of these—literally murderous—measures, not on grounds of harm to themselves, and doing so quite strenuously. They continued to do so after the embargo was declared unlawful by the World Court to no effect and with little notice. But they do not conform to the dictates of the powerful, so they fall under the category of nonpersons for the independent media.[153]

A related technique is selective quotation of such figures as Oscar Arias. He receives wide coverage when he denounces the Sandinistas. Sometimes, however, he joins José Figueres beyond the pale. During the government-media campaign to focus the peace accords on negotiations between what the *Times* calls the two Nicaraguan "factions," Stephen Kinzer reported that neither side shows a "willingness to compromise," noting Ortega's insistence that "the negotiations would cover only technical aspects of how the contras would lay down their weapons and receive supplies while they prepare to stop fighting"—exactly as required by the peace accords, he failed to add. He did not report Arias's view that "the agenda should be restricted to reaching a ceasefire. It will not be a political dialogue in which you can introduce any topic." Kinzer is, of course, aware that "the Central America peace accord signed in August does not require governments to negotiate political matters with armed groups," as he had observed a few weeks earlier, but these facts were quite regularly omitted in commentary on Sandinista "intransigence."[154]

The vast array of daily examples of the relatively subtle means employed to establish the required version of reality should not obscure the more direct contributions, as in the fabrications about Nicaraguan support for Colombian terrorists or the case of Radio Católica, and numerous others. To take merely one additional case, consider Kinzer's report on the attempted assassination of contra leader Edén Pastora at La Penca on May 30, 1984. In his June 1 report of the bombing, Kinzer quoted Pastora as blaming the Sandinistas. Pastora, however, says that he blamed the CIA: "I never said it was the government of Nicaragua. I would feel ashamed if I had said that."[155]

James LeMoyne's reporting in the *Times* provides many other examples, some already discussed.[156] Another is his report of the contra attacks on three mining towns in northeastern Nicaragua in late December 1987, close to the contra supply lines from Honduras. This account appeared while great efforts were being made to depict the contras as a serious military force with growing political appeal. LeMoyne was one of several journalists flown to the site. His version of the incident, which happened to accord with the requirements of State Department propaganda, was challenged in a story by journalist Mark Cook, who was in the same party. Cook's account found no media outlet, but parts appeared in a column by Alexander Cockburn. LeMoyne responded to the criticisms by "someone named Mark Cook" (whom he knows perfectly well) in a long letter, citing eyewitnesses who, he claimed, substantiated his account. These sources, however, explicitly *denied* LeMoyne's version of what had happened and what they had said.[157]

LeMoyne's reporting from El Salvador, where the priorities are reversed (we support the "democratic" government and oppose the terrorist guerrillas), is no less suspect. I have already mentioned a number of examples, including his loyalty to State Department propaganda on the "symmetry" between the contras and the FMLN in El Salvador, which he claims, could hardly survive without the constant flow of (undetectable) arms from Nicaragua; and his attempts to conceal and downplay state terror either by refusing to report it, or attributing it to right-wing extremists, or describing it as a response to the guerrilla terror on which he focuses attention. To demonstrate the political weakness of the Salvadoran guerrillas, LeMoyne reported that the 1988 May Day parade of the UNTS labor federation declined sharply from 40,000 in 1986 to "perhaps 3,000 supporters." He had given the figure of about 20,000 in attendance, not 40,000, in his report of the 1986 march, and journalists from AP, UPI, PBS *Frontline* (public TV), and the newspaper of the Jesuit University estimated the crowd at 20,000, not 3,000, in 1988, up from half that in 1987. LeMoyne's story also avoided the fact that the army blocked major roads to keep *campesinos* away and the violent government attacks on labor in preceding months, including bombing of the UNTS office two days before the march. An accurate headline would have read "Support for Rebel-Linked Union Doubles Despite Army Scare Tactics," Alexander Cockburn observes, reviewing these facts.[158]

The systematic evasion of government repression is the most striking feature of LeMoyne's reporting on El Salvador, but his accounts of guerrilla atrocities also merit some skepticism. Direct evidence is rarely offered, and attempts to check his stories raise questions, to say the least. In the course of its campaign to prove that the guerrillas were disrupting the 1988 elections in El Salvador, the State Department circulated a February 29 story by LeMoyne in which he reported that "villagers say guerrillas publicly executed two peasants ... because they had applied for and received new voter registration cards ... According to the villagers, the guerrillas placed the voting cards of Juan Martin Portillo and Ismael Portillo in their mouths after executing them as a warning to others not to take part in the elections."

In this case there was an independent investigation by journalist Chris Norton, who discovered that the incident never happened. It was "invented by a Salvadoran army propaganda specialist ... who placed it with one of his contacts in the local Salvadoran media," from which LeMoyne lifted the story without attribution. The State Department then included the *Times* story in a pre-election booklet to highlight the guerrilla "campaign of intimidation and terrorism." The booklet was mailed to Congress, newspaper editors, and other opinion makers. The Church human rights office had sent a team to investigate the story, reporting that only one of the two men pronounced dead actually exists while the other is alive and well, according to local sources. We thus have an army allegation, probably fabricated, converted into an authoritative account of guerrilla terrorism via the *New York Times*, then circulated as State Department propaganda.[159]

Yet another example appears in a letter to the *New York Times Magazine*, where Ines Murillo, a Honduran victim of torture, responds to LeMoyne's version of the interview with her that was the basis for an article of his on torture. She notes a series of distortions and falsehoods, which "have caused great damage to me and my family" and "could be used to justify the kidnapping, disappearance and assassination of hundreds of people" in Honduras, a rather serious matter. LeMoyne's response takes up none of her specific points.[160]

Such particular examples can be placed alongside of the systematic crusades, such as LeMoyne's contributions to undermining the Esquipulas accords and the history of the "ample evidence" for Sandinista arms to the Salvadoran guerrillas on which they relied for survival, already discussed.

What reaches the general public, and establishes the framework of interpretation and discussion, is the version of the facts presented by the Kinzers and the LeMoynes; the refutations and the crucial omissions can be discovered only by those who look beyond, no easy task.

The message is: *caveat emptor*, particularly when a journal is so fervently committed to some cause: in this case, the cause of "demonizing the Sandinistas" and protecting the U.S. terror state of El Salvador.

7. "The Courage to Preserve Civil Liberties"[161]

In discussing the chasm between the real and professed concerns for freedom of expression among political commentators in chapter 5, I compared the reaction to the legal structures and practices in the enemy state of Nicaragua and in the state that dwarfs all others in the scale of U.S. aid and support, "the symbol of human decency," as the *New York Times* editors described it while soldiers and settlers were conducting pogroms in villages and refugee camps under the official policy of "force, might, beatings." It is the State of Israel, Supreme Court Justice William Brennan observes, that "provides the best hope for building a jurisprudence that can protect civil liberties against the demands of national security" and may provide us with "the expertise to reject the security claims that Israel has exposed as baseless and the courage to preserve the civil liberties that Israel has preserved without detriment to its security."

Some examples of the Israeli record, and the U.S. reaction to it, have already been reviewed. A closer look provides further insight into the real attitudes towards freedom of expression among those most outspoken in condemning official enemies.

Israeli censorship is very broad. Wiretapping by the military and censorship of mail are routine and unconcealed. People report actual interruption of telephone calls by censors; one letter of mine reached the addressee with the word "nivdak" ("inspected") stamped on the envelope, with a date. Press censorship extends far beyond security matters, including coverage of what are termed "hostile organizations," water supplies, road conditions, loans to Israel, nuclear research, border settlements, and aerial photographs; it also covers previously published material.[162]

Censorship is particularly harsh in the occupied territories, where it reaches such extremes as banning notices and press releases of the respected human rights group Law in the Service of Man (Al-Haq) and articles describing its human rights work, on grounds that these are "likely to disturb the public peace"; arrest of union leaders for pamphlets educating Palestinians about their work rights, and closing of print shops on grounds of the need "to guarantee public safety" (General Amram Mitzna, July 28, 1987); detention of journalists without charge, or expulsion; the jailing of a Palestinian artist for having painted a picture that uses the colors of the Palestinian flag; and so on. Similar measures are applied in East Jerusalem, annexed by Israel and theoretically subject to Israeli laws. Telephone connections are often cut and distribution of journals banned as a means of collective punishment and control of information. When the Palestine National Council issued its independence declaration in Algiers in November 1988, the government cut telephone and power lines to the West Bank and Gaza to prevent access by radio or television and banned public celebrations, while the U.S. media scoffed that the declaration was aimed at the American public. On that occasion, the government also censored news broadcasts within Israel to protect the public from hearing the Algiers declaration and

Arafat's statements, at the request of Defense Minister Rabin, though Israeli Television did present Arabist Ehud Ya'ari to rebut the banned material.[163]

Arab journalists are routinely arrested and imprisoned for months without charge, sometimes in the grim prison camp Ketziot-Ansar 3 in the Negev. Often the arrests appear to be capricious. One among the many Arab journalists imprisoned was Nahida Nazzal, a resident of the village of Kalkilya (subject to regular terror and curfew). She was arrested in the Jerusalem office of *Al-Awdah*, where she wrote on society and family matters. She had dealt with no political topics and had never been involved in any political activities. After five months' imprisonment under terrible conditions, she still had no idea what the charges might be. There may well be none; the intent is probably general intimidation. A particular target is journalists, lawyers, and others who have been in contact with Israeli doves and who seek political settlement. On the other hand, fundamentalist religious leaders who circulate rabid anti-Semitic propaganda are left untouched, the residue of a policy of support for uncompromising religious fundamentalist elements in preference to secular nationalists who seek political settlement. In 1988 the Institute for Family Welfare in El-Bireh, which had operated for twenty years, was closed by the security forces, and its sixty-five-year-old chairperson, Samikha Khalil, was arrested and charged with "incitement against the state, an attempt to influence public opinion in a way which will cause harm to peace and public order, and possession and distribution of hostile material." The specific charges submitted to the military court of Ramallah were that in ceremonies within her institution she had made a "V" sign and that she had "made speeches in which she emphasized the connection between the Palestinian people and its land with the hope of the establishment of an independent Palestinian state." She was also accused of participating in the writing of a book entitled *Intifadah*, which was not published, and having in her possession a copy of a widely circulated Cyprus journal.[164]

The measures of coercion and control are applied without mercy, as in the case of Mahmoud al-Hatib, editor of the Jerusalem journal *Al-Shaab*, a "gifted journalist" expelled in 1974, Pinhas Inbari reports. His sons founded the Jerusalem journal *Al-Mithaq*, since closed by the state authorities, a journal that was critical of the policies of Israel, Jordan, and the PLO. Al-Hatib lived in Amman, where he had "refrained from any political activity in the hope that someone would have pity upon him" and permit him to see his family again.

In November 1987, he was allowed to return to his home in Jerusalem for a week when his wife died. He was then again expelled to Jordan, where "the old father lives isolated and alone, without a family," unable to visit his children in Jerusalem, who are also forbidden to visit him. All appeals were rejected.[165]

Within the pre-1967 borders, draconian laws also apply, usually against Arabs as in several cases already mentioned, and sometimes against Jews as well, including banning of theatrical productions in recent years. It has long been predicted that the repressive practices of the harsh military occupation would spill over to Israeli Jews as well, and as Palestinian resistance increased, the signs began to appear. In March 1987, the American-Israeli Civil Liberties Coalition addressed a letter to Prime Minister Yitzhak Shamir protesting "the closing of the Alternative Information Center [by police in West Jerusalem on February 16], the suspension of [its publication] *News from Within*, the arrest of its staff, and the extended incarceration of [editor] Michael Warshavsky," at first "in solitary confinement without reading or writing materials." The letter noted further that "it is probably not irrelevant that Michael Warshavsky is married to Lea Tsemel, one of the two women Jewish lawyers who regularly represent Palestinians, and that the Center disseminated otherwise unavailable information about government actions in the territories to the Israeli and foreign press." The Israeli Embassy in Washington responded to inquiries on the matter with letters claiming that the Center "cynically used the masquerade of 'journalism' solely to obfuscate its intelligence-gathering function on behalf of the notorious 'Popular Front for the Liberation of Palestine,' the PLO terrorist gang led by George Habash." The closure of a "terrorist front" and its director are "not an infringement of 'civil liberties.' No one has a civil liberty to assist in the violent destruction of the State of Israel." The actual charge was that Warshavsky arranged for the typesetting of a PFLP manuscript "advising members of the PFLP how to withstand detention and security service interrogations" (i.e., torture) and articles for "PFLP periodicals illegally distributed in the territories," and others unspecified; and that he had in his possession unspecified documents of the PFLP.[166] Prosecution is pending as I write. Closure of the offices merited brief notice in the *New York Times*.[167]

In 1988, the Hebrew journal *Derech Hanitzotz* was shut down and its editors arrested. Bail was denied on grounds that they had "crossed the borders of the national consensus" (Judge Barak), as distinct from the soldiers of the Givati Brigade who had beaten Hani al-Shami to death or near-death in his home but were released, not having crossed these borders. Its Arabic-language sister journal was also closed. Its editor, Ribhi al-Aruri, was adopted as an Amnesty International "prisoner of conscience" after he was given six months' detention without charge and interrogated with torture, he alleges; the detained Jewish editors also allege torture and inhuman treatment.[168]

One of the charges against the editors is "contact with a foreign agent," illegal under Israeli law. In June 1988, four Israeli Jews were convicted under this law, charged with having conducted a political discussion with Palestinians in Rumania. The court agreed that the meeting was solely "devoted to the subject of peace," but held that "a country in a state of emergency has [the] right" to curtail citizens' rights by barring political discussion on reaching peace with members of an organization designated as "terrorist."[169] Discussions of political settlement are, in fact, considered particularly threatening.

In accord with the same logic, Israel once again sentenced the Palestinian intellectual Faisal Husseini to six months in prison without trial in July 1988 immediately after he had appeared as the principal speaker at a meeting organized by Peace Now exploring the possibilities for a peaceful settlement of the Israel-Palestine conflict, and only hours before a scheduled meeting with Peace Now activists to implement the proposals discussed. The Israeli press observed that Husseini, the leading (unofficial) spokesman for the PLO in the occupied territories and one of the most respected Palestinian intellectuals, surely appeared with prior PLO authorization. At the Peace Now meeting, Husseini endorsed the two-state settlement proposal advanced by PLO spokesman Abu Sharif and called for "mutual recognition of the two sides," proposing that the Palestinians create a demilitarized state in the currently occupied territories. The *New York Times* did not consider these events significant enough for a news story, but they did run a picture with a caption reporting his arrest and the closing of the Arab Studies Center that he directed.[170]

This was Husseini's third administrative detention in two years. The first was a week after a meeting with Soviet dissident Natan Sharansky, whom Husseini had approached on a civil rights issue. The second was shortly after a meeting with Likud activist Moshe Amirav, with whom Husseini prepared a plan for a peaceful political settlement. Professor Yehoshua Porath, Israel's leading specialist on Palestinian nationalism, commented that Husseini and his Center were alone among Palestinian intellectuals and institutions in seeking contact with Israeli research institutions and scholars and calling for cooperation among Israelis and Palestinians. The government reaction is typical of the official response to the threat of moderation and political settlement.[171]

One will learn virtually nothing about these matters here, and they do not affect the doctrine that Israel and the United States can find no Palestinians who share their deep commitment to peace.

The Husseini-Sharansky interchange merits further attention. Husseini approached Sharansky to ask his assistance in the matter of Akram Haniye, editor of the Jerusalem journal *Al-Shaab*, who had been ordered expelled from the country by the military authorities. The expulsion was protested by the International Red Cross and the twelve countries of the European Community, which condemned Israel's actions as a breach of international law. Not Sharansky, however. After coming under attack by the Israeli right for meeting with Husseini on the Haniye matter, Sharansky published advertisements expressing his "full confidence" in the actions of the Israeli government and security forces, including the expulsion of the editor. He endorsed these actions as "in no way a violation of human rights" and as furthering "the highest goals of humanity in preserving the nation of Israel and in combating a pestilence that threatens all civilised people"; the wording is interesting, considering the memories it will evoke in the minds of every Jewish reader. A few weeks later he described Israel as "an absolutely free society." The same week, he received the "Jewish Settlement in the Gaza District Award" at Yeshivat Hesder Yamit, a right-wing military-religious school named after the town of Yamit, established by Israel in northeastern Sinai after thousands of Bedouins were expelled, their homes, schools, lands, cemeteries, and mosques destroyed; on the contribution of these institutions to military terror, see p. 210. At the ceremony, Sharansky called for "freedom to settle anywhere in Israel," meaning the occupied territories.

On arriving in Israel after nine years of courageous resistance in Soviet prisons, Sharansky had assured the press that "his broad concern for human rights remains undiminished" and "his sensitivity to human rights ... would inevitably lead him to study closely their observance here." With regard to the Arabs, he said that "whether we want them or not, there are many Arabs in Israel, and I think we must, from time to time, try to talk to them"—a good indication of what was to come. A reviewer in the *New York Times* praises his "high spirited and generous faith" and his "political engagement to include the cause of human rights everywhere," where "everywhere" presumably is intended to include the place where he lives. The proposal to appoint him as Israel's ambassador to the United Nations aroused much acclaim. He would be "an inspired choice," the editors of the *New Republic* felt: "He may be the single most morally alert public figure of our time, and he is keenly alert to the grievance of the Palestinians."[172]

Whatever one's judgment may be about Israeli law and regular practice, one thing is clear. If Nicaragua were to follow the legal principles and regular practice of the state of Israel under far less threatening circumstances, the internal political opposition would have been jailed or expelled long ago and all their publications closed. If four anti-contra Nicaraguan dissidents were convicted, sentenced, and fined "for violating a law that bars contacts with the contras" after a meeting abroad to discuss the possibilities of a peaceful political settlement, the *New York Times* might have thought that the matter deserved more than the buried hundred-word item devoted to exactly these events, with "Nicaragua" and "contras" replaced with "Israel" and "PLO"[173] Much the same is true of the other examples cited, and many more like them.

Similarly, if Nicaragua were to bomb a contra radio station in a refugee camp deep inside Honduras, "firing 30 missiles in 15 sorties over two hours," killing three people and bringing the death toll from such bombings to sixty for 1988 through mid-August, the *Times* might devote more than the 190 words it used to describe exactly these events, except that it was Israeli jets bombing "a site in Mieh Mieh [refugee camp in Lebanon] used as a transmitter by the Voice of Palestine, a P.L.O. radio station" that "broadcasts reports designed to incite what the Israeli [spokesman] called 'terrorist activity' in the West Bank and the Gaza Strip"[174]—that is, the Intifada, which has been remarkable for how little violence has been elicited by the extreme brutality of the occupying military forces, and which is, furthermore, an extraordinary expression of courage, integrity, and the will for freedom. The comparison is far from exact; the Voice of Palestine is not a Soviet-run station so powerful as to dominate the airwaves in the occupied territories and much of Israel, and the "terrorist activity" of the Intifada falls somewhat short of the behavior of those who proudly designate themselves "the sons of Reagan" when they swoop down upon civilian settlements to murder, pillage, torture, rape and kidnap. Nevertheless, in this case there was no notice or reaction.

It is, of course, unthinkable that Israel would permit free entry by journalists and political figures from the PLO and the Arab states, in sharp contrast to the practice of the "totalitarian Sandinistas." Nor has anything similar ever been tolerated by the United States, even under far lesser threat. The demands upon Nicaragua that are standard in U.S. commentary conform to libertarian standards that are appropriate, in my view, though held by virtually no one, surely not by those who indignantly invoke them in the media in the case of official enemies, as the simple test of sincerity discussed earlier conclusively demonstrates. The application of these standards to Nicaragua by Western elites has been a display of crude hypocrisy, yet another tribute to the effectiveness of thought control and the vulgarity of the intellectual culture.

Such considerations are off the agenda in U.S. commentary. Thus, in a departure from the Washington line, Stephen Kinzer observes that

> during the recent negotiations in Managua, contra leaders dominated the radio airwaves, appearing on morning and evening news programs and giving live statements as the talks proceeded. They were jubilantly received at La Prensa's offices. That would have been unthinkable until a few months ago, and would be unheard of in a truly Marxist regime.[175]

We are to assume, then, that it would be standard procedure in Western democracies under attack by the terrorist forces of a superpower, or even far lesser threat—an evident absurdity.

Quite generally, no notice is given and no concern aroused in the case of repression in the Western democracies of a sort that arouses much ire when conducted in Nicaragua, under threat of destruction. In 1988, when congressional liberals and media doves were berating the Sandinistas for harassment of the media and political opposition, and calling for escalation of the military attack if this display of communist totalitarianism does not cease forthwith, the government of France, under no threat, "prohibited the sale, circulation and distribution" of a Basque book on grounds that it "threatened public order," and banned publication of the journal *El-Badil Démocratique* that supports Algerian dissidents on grounds that "this publication might harm the diplomatic relations of France with Algeria." The director of the Basque journal *Abil* was sentenced to twenty months in prison by the French courts for having published an "apology for terrorism," while the Spanish courts fined a Basque radio station for having broadcast insults to the King on a call-in radio show and the government brought three activists of a political group to trial on charges of "publication, circulation and reproduction of false information that might disturb public order," among many other cases of punishment of public statements and cancellation of peaceful demonstrations.[176] Such events do not arouse the civil libertarian passions of Western elites, or call for harsh retribution by the guardians of democratic principles.

8. The Continuing Struggle[177]

As intimated by the remarks of Justice Brennan cited earlier, freedom of speech is by no means a deeply entrenched tradition even in the United States, which by comparative standards is quite advanced in this regard.[178] The same is true of other rights. Half a century ago, the anarchist writer Rudolf Rocker observed that

> Political rights do not originate in parliaments; they are rather forced upon them from without. And even their enactment into law has for a long time been no guarantee of their security. They do not exist because they have been legally set down on a piece of paper, but only when they have become the ingrown habit of a people, and when any attempt to impair them will meet with the violent resistance of the populace.[179]

History provides ample warrant for this conclusion.

As is well known, even the right to vote was achieved in the United States only through constant struggle. Women were disenfranchised for 130 years, and those whom the American Constitution designated as only three-fifths human were largely denied this right until the popular movements of the past generation changed the cultural and political climate. While the franchise has slowly been extended through popular struggle, voting continues to decline and to become a concomitant of privilege, largely as a reflection of the general depoliticization of the society and the disintegration of an independent culture challenging business dominance, along with popular groupings to sustain it. What formal participation remains is often hardly more than a gesture of ratification with only limited content, particularly at the higher levels of political power.

The same is true of freedom of speech. Though these rights appear to be granted in the First Amendment, as interpreted in practice the grant was limited. At its libertarian extreme, the legal doctrine remained that of Blackstone, reiterated in 1931 by Chief Justice Hughes in a decision regarded as a landmark victory for freedom of expression: "Every freeman has an undoubted right to lay what sentiments he pleases before the public; to forbid this, is to destroy the freedom of the press; but if he publishes what is improper, mischievous or illegal, he must take the consequence of his own temerity." Prior restraint is barred, but not punishment for unacceptable thoughts.[180]

In a review of "the history and reality of free speech in the United States," David Kairys points out that

> no right of free speech, either in law or practice, existed until a basic transformation of the law governing speech in the period from about 1919 to 1940. Before that time, one spoke publicly only at the discretion of local, and sometimes federal, authorities, who often prohibited what they, the local business establishment, or other powerful segments of the community did not want to hear.

He is referring not to the more subtle means of control that I have been discussing throughout, but to the legal right of freedom of speech, a fragile construct that has not withstood the test of even very limited threat falling far short of crisis.[181]

A measure of the weight of concern over freedom of speech is given by the fact that from 1959 to 1974 the Supreme Court dealt with more First Amendment cases than in its entire previous history, the process of establishing these rights in the law having begun seriously after World War I. The Sedition Act of 1798 was not tested in the Courts until 1964, when it was declared "inconsistent with the First Amendment." Justice Brennan's opinion in this case overturned a decision in which the *New York Times* was condemned for having published an advertisement sponsored by a civil rights group that allegedly defamed the police commissioner of Montgomery, Alabama. Thus in 1964, for the first time, the Supreme Court "made explicit the principle that seditious libel—criticism of government—cannot be made a crime in America and spoke in this connection of 'the central meaning of the First Amendment'."[182] Commenting on this decision, Harry Kalven observes that seditious libel is "the hallmark of closed societies throughout the world" and its status in law "defines the society"; if "criticism of government is viewed as defamation and punished as a crime," then "it is not a free society, no matter what its other characteristics."[183] By that reasonable measure, the United States passed one of the crucial tests of a "free society" as the bicentennial celebration of its Declaration of Independence approached.

The Espionage Act of 1917 made it a federal crime during times of war to "willfully make or convey false reports or false statements with intent to interfere with the operation or success of the military or naval forces of the United States or to promote the success of its enemies," to "willfully cause or attempt to cause insubordination, disloyalty, mutiny, or refusal of duty" in the armed forces or to "willfully obstruct the recruiting or enlistment service of the United States."[184] In 1918 more offenses were added, including "uttering, printing, writing, or publishing any disloyal, profane, scurrilous, or abusive language, or language intended to cause contempt, scorn, contumely or disrepute as regards the form of government of the U.S., the Constitution, the flag, the uniform of the Army or Navy, or any language intended to incite resistance to the U.S. or promote the cause of its enemies."[185]

Postmaster General Albert Burleson, charged with the responsibility of purifying the mails, announced that no one could write "that this government got in the war wrong, that it is in it for wrong purposes, or anything that will impugn the motives of the Government for going into the war. They can not say that this Government is the tool of Wall Street or the munitions-makers" or "campaign against conscription and the Draft Law." His decisions were consistently approved by the courts, which held that "We must in good faith and with courage accept the reasons which the authorities have deemed sufficient to justify war" (Judge Aldrich, District of New Hampshire). Burleson barred a pamphlet on the suffering under British Rule in India, and removed from a Catholic journal a statement by the Pope in which he said that "no man can be loyal to his country unless he first be loyal to his conscience and his God." Washington's Committee on Public Information, the government propaganda bureau, was permitted "to circulate the official portrait of Lenin," but the Rand School in New York was not allowed "to circulate Lenin himself," among many other cases.[186]

This state repression was accompanied by extensive mob violence on the part of a public inflamed by jingoist appeals and encouraged by state authorities.[187] The same period saw severe weakening of unions and political organizations, sentencing of presidential candidate Eugene Debs (in 1919) to ten years' imprisonment for a pacifist speech, internment of the conductor of the Boston Symphony Orchestra for declining to play the national anthem, barring of dozens of newspapers from the mails, and so on, all of this minor in comparison to Woodrow Wilson's "Red Scare."[188]

There were some 2,000 criminal prosecutions for unacceptable dissent. Reviewing these, Harvard Law School professor Zechariah Chafee observed that

> the courts treated opinions as statements of fact and then condemned them as false because they differed from the President's speech or the resolution of Congress declaring war ... [I]t became criminal to advocate heavier taxation instead of bond issues, to state that conscription was unconstitutional ..., to urge that a referendum should have preceded our declaration of war, to say that war was contrary to the teachings of Christianity. Men have been punished for criticizing the Red Cross and the Y.M.C.A.[189]

"None of the Espionage Act convictions was reversed by the Supreme Court on First Amendment grounds," Kairys observes.

This extraordinary assault on freedom of expression, it should be recalled, took place at a moment when the country had incomparable wealth and growing power, and faced no threat.

In a 1943 review, the ACLU praised the "state of civil liberty" during World War II in contrast to World War I, when governmental and other pressures "resulted in mob violence against dissenters, hundreds of prosecutions for utterances; in the creation of a universal volunteer vigilante system, officially recognized, to report dissent to the FBI; in hysterical hatred of everything German; in savage sentences for private expressions of criticism; and in suppression of public debate of the issues of the war and the peace."[190] But this positive evaluation of the state of civil liberty during World War II should be tempered in the light of the (Court-approved) dispatch of 110,000 Japanese-Americans to concentration camps; the 1940 Espionage Act and Smith Act,[191] initiation of repressive activities of the FBI that persisted at a high level for at least thirty years; government strike-breaking and destruction of the Socialist Workers Party; full-scale martial law in Hawaii barring trial by jury, *habeas corpus,* and other due process rights; jailing of dozens of people for such seditious acts as counselling draft opposition; barring of dissident press from the mails and seizure of newspapers and other publications; surveillance of all international message traffic under wartime censorship; brutal treatment of conscientious objectors, etc.[192] Meanwhile, left-liberal opinion called for restricting the Bill of Rights to "friends of democracy" and "exterminating" the "treason press," while Reinhold Niebuhr stressed the "greater measure of coercion" required during a national emergency and approved infringements on "the freedom of organizations to spread subversive propaganda" and community drives "to eliminate recalcitrant and even traitorous elements."[193]

All this was at a time when opposition to the war was minuscule, the United States was by far the richest and most powerful state in the world, and its national territory had not been threatened with attack since the War of 1812.

The opinions of Holmes and Brandeis after World War I constituted the first significant break in the pattern of state control of expression, but in a limited way. In 1919, Justice Holmes formulated the "clear and present danger" test, regarded as a significant victory for civil liberties. The doctrine is hardly a forthright defense of freedom of speech, particularly when the circumstances are considered. In this opinion, Holmes affirmed the conviction of a Socialist Party leader whose crime was to have distributed a leaflet to draftees criticizing World War I and urging them to challenge their conscription, which he alleged to be unconstitutional, on legal grounds and by legal means. It was not until 1969 that the Supreme Court held that the "clear and present danger" test was inadequate, adopting instead the criterion of direct incitement for the banning of speech by the state.[194]

Implicitly endorsing the perspective outlined by Rocker in the remarks quoted above, Kairys makes the important point that "the periods of stringent protection and enlargement of civil rights and civil liberties correspond to the periods in which mass movements posing a credible challenge to the existing order have demanded such rights," that is, have demanded the enforcement of the theoretical right to free expression: primarily the left, labor, and other popular movements, again in the 1960s.

To this analysis, one should add that dominant classes have their own reasons to oppose state power that might infringe on their rights, and will often protect the rights of which they are the primary beneficiaries. Others, particularly those who share privilege, will then benefit as well from these constraints on state power, including dissidents. In a well-functioning capitalist society, everything becomes a commodity, including freedom; one can have as much as one can buy, and those who can buy a lot have every reason to preserve an ample supply.

Throughout, I have been keeping largely to the liberal side of the spectrum, which tends to endorse at least the abstract right of freedom of expression, and to the more subtle—though very effective—measures of control of thought and expression that result from the normal workings of the sociopolitical system. But as American history to the present shows with great clarity, there is a persistent strain of opposition to the entire concept of freedom of speech and association. We see this clearly in the experience of the World Wars and the postwar repressions, the wave of political firings in the universities to try to hold back the challenge to elite authority that arose in the 1960s, the FBI COINTELPRO operations that peaked during the liberal administrations of the 1960s and the quite limited concern evoked when they were exposed during the furor over Watergate, and much else. We see it again in the vulgar jingoist rhetoric of the Bush presidential campaign of 1988 (the demand that the state should force children to pledge allegiance to the flag, for example, vigorously endorsed by many opponents of freedom in the mainstream), in the significant impact of religious fundamentalism, and other noteworthy phenomena.

There also continue to be those who are not satisfied with the kind of popular vigilantism sponsored by the government during World War I, and who want the state itself to register and identify those thoughts that it is impermissible to think. It is important to bear in mind that they are by no means regarded as quasi-fascist extremists. To illustrate, I will review only one interesting recent example.

Consider historian Guenter Lewy, whose concept of the writing of moral-historical tracts, highly praised as "sophisticated and profound," is misrepresentation of documents, uncritical regurgitation of government claims, and dismissal of annoying facts that contradict them, and whose concept of morality is such as to legitimate virtually any atrocity against civilians once the state has issued its commands.[195] Writing on the "basic ground rules" required for the marketplace of ideas to function properly, he assures the reader of his support for freedom of speech and free exchange of ideas, and then outlines just how these values are to be understood. His basic conception is that because of the threat of subversion, the inadequacy of private vigilantism, and the limits imposed upon the state authorities, the state must find novel means to protect the public from contamination by subversives and to "energize the democratic forces." Without the intrusion of the state to keep the marketplace fair and the contest equal, he holds, the "democratic forces" of the mainstream lack the means to "counteract falsehoods propagated by extremist groups" and their "deception."[196]

The problems that trouble Lewy arose as state and popular vigilantism declined by the late 1950s. The country "completely lost interest in the issue of communist subversion," Congress "called for abandoning the term 'subversion'," and "Attorney General Edward H. Levi confined the domestic intelligence function of the FBI to activities that involve a violation of federal law." It is doubtful, he warns, that the FBI "is keeping adequate track of [groups other than the Communist Party] that act directly or indirectly under the direction of Cuba, Nicaragua, Communist China, or other hostile states" (quoting "a well-informed student of the subject").

Since the 1960s, Lewy continues, "the United States has had to cope with the New Left," a broad category in his account, and apparently not part of the United States; "the United States" is implicitly identified with the state authorities who have to "cope with" improper thoughts and must have the means to do so.

Resolutely addressing the problems posed by the tolerance and naive liberalism of the post-McCarthy era, the state must take action against "the ever-changing scene of loosely organized groups" that constitute the New Left. These organizations, Lewy asserts, have a "hidden agenda" which "makes them subversive and therefore unacceptable." "Rather than acknowledge their espousal of Cuban-style Communism or their solidarity with Marxist-Leninists in Central America, New Left groups pretend to defend peace and justice and talk of a progressive social and economic order. Some speak of using a Marxist paradigm though in fact they are fully committed to Communism (or Marxism-Leninism, the currently fashionable term that appears to sound more benign)." Open espousal of Marxism-Leninism is "unacceptable" in a democratic society, even "subversive," and those who conceal this "hidden agenda" are even more dangerous. It may be, he concedes, that some New Leftists "act from a deep alienation more than from allegiance to communism, but this is irrelevant from the viewpoint of surveillance" by the state authorities. That these subversives might have some motives other than hidden allegiance to Communism or psychic disorders is plainly inconceivable. Presumably, then, New Leftists who condemn Marxist-Leninist theory and practice in a manner far more serious and searching than will be found in Lewy's pronouncements must be laboring to conceal their "hidden agenda."

Such techniques of Straussian interpretation, discerning hidden agendas whatever actual texts may say, is a most useful device for the guardians of authority and propriety. These methods provide an automatic "proof" for virtually any desired conclusion. If the conclusion is unsupported by any textual evidence, or even directly refuted by the texts, that merely shows that the authors are even worse criminals, not merely pursuing their evil ways but attempting to conceal them by pretense and cunning. We must not be misled by the trickery of these sly dogs, readily unravelled by the mind of the commissar. By Lewy's logic, it would be child's play to demonstrate that he and his publishers are agents of the Third Reich, working to reverse its unfortunate defeat.

Some of these subversives, Lewy continues, are virtual foreign agents. He quotes sociologist James Q. Wilson on the "maddeningly difficult" problem of determining which "dissident groups" fall into this category; when, for example, should it include someone "who travels to a foreign country to receive training, or who accepts foreign money to cover the expenses of his organization, or who secretly collaborates, without pay, with foreign powers in the pursuit of their policy objectives?" The tasks of the commissar are indeed daunting. One doubts, incidentally, that Lewy and Wilson have in mind the more obvious cases that fall within their paranoid constructions, American Zionists, for example.

Yet another problem, in Lewy's view, is that the FBI "now ignores the entire range of subversive activities that are neither illegal nor linked to a foreign power." The "United States" is thus deprived of means previously available to "cope with" enemies who are so deceitful as to operate within the law, and who are "politically dishonest by hiding one's true political aims or knowingly planting lies and disinformation." Prominent in this category are the church-based groups and others that opposed the Vietnam war and are carrying out similar "calculated political deception" with regard to our crusade for freedom in Central America. The "lies and disinformation" of these subversive elements in the service of their hidden agendas or foreign masters "may poison the marketplace of ideas and damage a democratic society more seriously than the overt advocacy of forceful overthrow." A serious problem indeed, for those committed to "democracy."

"Private initiatives" to control these subversives and foreign agents are inadequate to the awesome task, Lewy concludes. This is so despite the contributions by groups that "expose leftist-sponsored manipulation," including the John Birch Society, "the American Security Council, established in the mid-fifties to help corporations check the political background of potential employees" (evidently a worthy objective in a free society), and "Lyndon Larouche, founder of the U.S. Labor party."[197] It is therefore necessary for the state itself to assume the "valid undertaking" of "throwing light on subversive designs."

The state must become directly engaged in a form of "consumer protection" to ensure that the public will "know when an individual or organization is in effect an agent of a foreign state" and to protect the public "against deception in the marketplace of ideas." "Ideas should compete openly and honestly," but "with full information available about the motives of those who would sway the body politic," information that must be provided by the state authorities. The state, then, must register what is True and identify those who deny Official Truth as subversive if not foreign agents, exposing their hidden motives and deceitful practice, and letting the public "know when an individual or organization is in effect an agent of a foreign state." In this way, it can guard against "subversion of the democratic process."

Given that the state is all-knowing and wise, we need not be concerned that it will err in its formulation of Official Truth and exposure of "deception," "subversive designs," "disinformation" and other devices of those who pursue their malicious "hidden agendas" while publicly professing a concern for peace, justice, international law, human rights, and other values. And those who are devoted to (a certain conception of) democracy must therefore accord the state the right, even the duty, to conduct this enterprise.

But identification of hidden foreign agents and subversives who dare to question what the state determines to be True does not suffice. Lewy urges that the state also maintain surveillance and "gather information on *potentially subversive groups*," thus enabling it to "protect citizens from falsely labelled ideas as it does already protect them from falsely labelled commercial products" (to be sure, "without infringing on individual rights," in his conception of such rights, at least). He suggests the model of the West German Basic Law of 1949, which permits state authorities to "focus the glare of publicity on anti-democratic political forces—an innovative and successful feature of West Germany's 'militant democracy' that bears a closer look." While the FBI "probably" cannot use such techniques as robbery, break-in, and electronic surveillance freely, it can still find means "to publicize the activities of extremists" and thus "check the machinations of the enemies of the democratic system *before* they constitute a 'clear and present danger'."[198]

To guarantee the workings of the free market, there must be "accurate labels on the package" (quoting Morris Ernst), and it is the responsibility of the state to provide these labels for ideas. It is necessary to expose the hidden Communist agenda of such segments of "the radical left" as Clergy and Laity Concerned about Vietnam, which secretly sought "victory for North Vietnam" and "worked to create a political climate in which the United States was seen as the aggressor and perpetrator of evil in Vietnam," conclusions which must be labelled by the state authorities as False, because Lewy asserts them to be false. Departing from his general procedure, Lewy actually provides evidence for his charges about the hidden agenda of Clergy and Laity Concerned and the Washington-based Indochina Resource Center. The evidence is that "Fred Halstead, a member of the (Trotskyite) Socialist Workers Party and one of the movement's leading figures, revealed after it was all over that 'our central task ... was to put maximum pressure on the U.S. to get out of Vietnam'" and thus "help the Vietnamese revolution." Halstead and the SWP said exactly the same thing, quite openly, long before "it was all over," indeed always; and Clergy and Laity Concerned, the Indochina Resource Center, and other "New Left" criminals will be intrigued to learn that Halstead was one of their leaders—or will at least feign surprise, in pursuit of their hidden agenda.

Similarly, those who "allege that the Sandinistas are democratic socialists and dedicated to Christianity ... are not staking out another legitimate political position but are manipulating a falsehood," and such misdeeds must be exposed by the state authorities, to protect democracy and the free market of ideas; the state "consumer protection" agency must act, for example, when Conor Cruise O'Brien, in the *Atlantic Monthly*, deceitfully pretends to discern Christian elements in the Sandinista revolution. The same is true of those who "deny or minimize Soviet-bloc support for the Marxist-Leninist guerrillas of Central America" (joining ex-CIA analyst David MacMichael and the International Court of Justice, among other subversives) while "decrying U.S. aid for the democratic regimes" of Central America, just as their predecessors claimed "to seek peace while surreptiously working for a communist victory" in Vietnam (the entire New Left). Among those pursuing such subversive designs in secret are the liberal lobbying group Coalition for a New Foreign and

Military Policy, the research organization NACLA, Women's Strike for Peace, and others who try to conceal their "hidden agendas" with their "machinations." All such elements should be identified by the state authorities in "an American report on extremism and subversion irrespective of whether they have formal links with the Soviet Union or other communist regimes."

To a totalitarian, Lewy observes, "an opponent is by definition subversive" (quoting Jean François Revel). This point, at least, is accurate, as he demonstrates throughout, apparently unwittingly.

Such thoughts elicit neither contempt nor ridicule. Rather, they appear in the respected journal of the Foreign Policy Research Institute in Philadelphia edited by Daniel Pipes, with a distinguished board of editors.

I have mentioned only one case, admittedly extreme. But there are substantial currents that resonate to such sentiments, and other forms of attack on free expression are all too easily illustrated. The victories for freedom of speech that have been won are far from stable.

Still, there have been victories. In other domains as well, there is detectable progress in the guarantee of fundamental human rights, difficult as it may be to pronounce such words in the century that has given us Hitler and Stalin, agonizingly slow as the process may be. There remains a long path ahead, and without constant vigilance and popular determination, there is no "guarantee of security" for what has already been attained.

Notes

Chapter 1

1. José Pedro S. Martins, *Latinamerica Press* (Lima), March 17, 1988.

2. See Philip Lee, ed., *Communication for All* (Orbis, 1985); William Preston, Edward S. Herman, and Herbert Schiller, *Hope and Folly: the United States and UNESCO, 1945-1985* (U. of Minnesota, forthcoming).

3. "Freedom of the Press—Anthony Lewis distinguishes between Britain and America," *London Review of Books*, Nov. 26, 1987.

4. M. P. Crozier, S. J. Huntington, and J. Watanuki, *The Crisis of Democracy: Report on the Governability of Democracies to the Trilateral Commission* (New York University, 1975).

5. See my *Turning the Tide* (South End, 1985, chapter 5) and *On Power and Ideology* (South End, 1987, lecture 5). For detailed examination of these matters, see Thomas Ferguson and Joel Rogers, *Right Turn* (Hill & Wang, 1986). For a summary of the domestic consequences, see Emma Rothschild, "The Real Reagan Economy" and "The Reagan Economic Legacy," *New York Review of Books*, June 30, July 21, 1988.

6. FAIR, Press Release, July 19, 1988. Poll on Constitution, *Boston Globe Magazine*, Sept. 13, 1987, cited by Julius Lobel, in Julius Lobel, ed., *A Less than Perfect Union* (Monthly Review, 1988, 3).

7. *New York Times*-CBS poll; Adam Clymer, *NYT*, Nov. 19, 1985.

8. Kissinger and Vance, *Foreign Affairs*, Summer 1988. As one example, among twenty industrialized countries the U.S. ranks 20th in infant mortality rates, with rates higher than East Germany, Ireland, Spain, etc. *Wall Street Journal*, Oct. 19, 1988. For a survey of the deepening poverty, particularly under the Reagan administration, see Fred R. Harris and Roger Wilkins, eds., *Quiet Riots* (Pantheon, 1988).

9. *Globe and Mail*, March 28, 18, 5, 1986.

10. For a sample, see Mark Green and Gail MacColl, *Reagan's Reign of Error* (Pantheon, 1987).

11. John P. Roche, *Washington Star*, Oct. 26, 1977.

12. Peter Braestrup, *Big Story* (Westview, 1977).

13. Landrum Bolling, ed., *Reporters under Fire: U.S. Media Coverage of Conflicts in Lebanon and Central America* (Westview, 1985, 35, 2-3).

14. Justice Holmes, dissenting in *Abrams v. United States*, 1919.

15. Benjamin Ginsberg, *The Captive Public* (Basic Books, 1986, 86, 89). Ginsberg's study is short on evidence and the logic is often weak: for example, his belief that there is a contradiction in holding both that Star Wars "could not protect the United States from a nuclear attack" and that it might "increase the probability that such an attack would occur," part of his argument that the advocacy of their causes by "liberal political forces" is motivated by "political interest"; but there is plainly no contradiction, whatever the merits of his conclusion about liberal political forces. He also believes that "student demonstrators and the like ... have little difficulty securing favorable publicity for themselves and their causes," particularly anti-Vietnam war protestors, and accepts uncritically familiar claims about "the adversary posture adopted by the media during the sixties and seventies," among other untenable assumptions.

16. Putting the point slightly differently, V. O. Key observes that "newspaper publishers are essentially people who sell white space on newsprint to advertisers." Cited by Jerome A. Barron, "Access to the Press—a New First Amendment Right," *Harvard Law Review*, vol. 80, 1967; from Key, *Public Opinion and American Democracy*.

17. Sir George Lewis, cited in James Curran and Jean Seaton, *Power without Responsibility* (Methuen, 1985, 31); Paul Johnson, *Spectator*, Nov. 28, 1987.

18. A panel of media critics organized annually by Carl Jensen, who select the "ten most censored stories" of the year, gave the first prize for 1987 to a study of these issues by Ben Bagdikian, referring of course not to literal state censorship but to media evasion or distortion of critical issues.

19. *Economist*, Dec. 5, 1987.

20. For more extensive study of these matters, see Edward S. Herman and Noam Chomsky, *Manufacturing Consent: the Political Economy of the Mass Media* (Pantheon, 1988), chapter 1.

21. For some discussion, see appendix I, section 1.

22. Bolling, *op. cit.*, 8.

23. Herman and Chomsky, *Manufacturing Consent*; Chomsky, *The Culture of Terrorism* (South End, 1988). See also our two-volume *Political Economy of Human Rights* (South End, 1979), an extension of an earlier study that was suppressed by the conglomerate that owned the publisher; see the author's preface for details. See also Herman, *The Real Terror Network* (South End, 1982); my *Pirates and Emperors* (Claremont, 1986; Amana, 1988); and much other work over the past twenty years. Also James Aronson, *The Press and the Cold War* (Beacon, 1970); Michael Parenti, *Inventing Reality* (St. Martin's, 1986).

24. For some further comments on these topics, discussed more extensively in the references of the preceding footnote, see appendix I, section 1.

25. On the role of Freedom House as a virtual propaganda arm of the government and international right wing, see Edward S. Herman and Frank

Brodhead, *Demonstration Elections* (South End, 1984, appendix I), and *Manufacturing Consent*. According to a memo of NSC official Walter Raymond, Freedom House was one of the recipients of money raised by the Reagan administration propaganda apparatus (see note 45, below), a charge denied by Sussman, speaking for Freedom House. See Robert Parry and Peter Kornbluh, "Iran-Contra's Untold Story," *Foreign Policy*, Fall 1988; correspondence, Winter 1988-89. To demonstrate the impartiality and *bona fides* of Freedom House, Sussman states that "we cited the deplorable human rights record of the Sandinistas, as we publicize violators of human rights in many other countries, such as Chile and Paraguay." Nicaragua, Chile, and Paraguay are the three Latin American countries that the Reagan administration officially condemns for human rights violations, and, to the surprise of no one familiar with its record, Freedom House selects these three examples. Sussman does not, however, select El Salvador and Guatemala, where human rights violations are vastly beyond anything attributable to the Sandinistas, but are not deplored by the Reagan administration, which bears much of the responsibility for them. The fact that Freedom House is taken seriously, in the light of its record, is startling.

26. Martin Peretz, *New Republic*, Aug. 2, 1982. See my *Fateful Triangle* (South End, 1983), for more on this curious document and others like it; and appendix I, section 2.

27. See appendix I, section 1, for some comment.

28. Bolling, *op. cit.*. See appendix I, section 2, and *Manufacturing Consent* on the Vietnam war TV retrospective and others. On public attitudes towards the media as not critical enough of government and too readily influenced by power generally, see Mark Hertsgaard, *On Bended Knee* (Farrar Straus Giroux, 1988, 84-85).

29. Former *Time* senior editor Timothy Foote, who asserts that "any attentive reader" of that journal will know that its bias is sometimes "as obvious as the faces of Mount Rushmore" (Review of William Rusher, *The Coming Battle for the Media*, *WP Weekly*, June 27, 1988). Rusher condemns the "media elite" for distorting the news with their liberal bias. Press critic David Shaw of the *Los Angeles Times*, reviewing the same book in the *New York Times Book Review*, responds with the equally conventional view that "journalists love to challenge the status quo," and are "critics, nitpickers, malcontents" who "complain about everything."

30. For detailed analysis of media coverage of Cuba, see Tony Platt, ed., *Tropical Gulag* (Global Options, 1987). Wayne Smith, formerly head of the U.S. Interests Section in Havana and a leading Cuba specialist, describes the study as offering "devastating" confirmation of the "overwhelmingly negative" treatment of Cuba in the media, in conformity with "the Department of State's version," citing additional examples of "lack of balance" and refusal to cover significant evidence refuting Reaganite charges; *Social Justice*, Summer 1988. See also appendix I, section 1.

31. Cited by Ginsberg, *Captive Mind*, 34.

32. Distaste for democracy sometimes reaches such extremes that state control is taken to be the only imaginable alternative to domination by concentrated private wealth. It must be this tacit assumption that impels Nicholas Lemann (*New Republic*, Jan. 9, 1989) to assert that in our book *Manufacturing Consent*, Herman and I advocate "more state control" over the media, basing this claim on our statement that "In the long run, a democratic political order requires far wider control of and access to the media" on the part of the general public (p. 307). This quoted statement follows a review of some of the possible modalities, including the proliferation of public-access TV channels that "have weakened the power of the network oligopoly" and have "a potential for enhanced local-group access," "local nonprofit radio and television stations," ownership of radio stations by "community institutions" (a small cooperative in France is mentioned as an example), listener-supported radio in local communities, and so on. Such options indeed challenge corporate oligopoly and the rule of the wealthy generally. Therefore, they can only be interpreted as "state control" by someone who regards it as unthinkable that the general public might, or should, gain access to the media as a step towards shaping their own affairs.

33. Appleby, *Capitalism and a New Social Order* (NYU, 1984, 73). On the absurd George Washington cult contrived as part of the effort "to cultivate the ideological loyalties of the citizenry" and thus create a sense of "viable nationhood," see Lawrence J. Friedman, *Inventors of the Promised Land* (Knopf, 1975, chapter 2). Washington was a "perfect man" of "unparalleled perfection," who was raised "above the level of mankind," and so on. This Kim Il Sung-ism persists among the intellectuals, for example, in the reverence for FDR and his "grandeur," "majesty," etc., in the *New York Review of Books* (see *Fateful Triangle*, 175, for some scarcely believable quotes), and in the Camelot cult. Sometimes a foreign leader ascends to the same semi-divinity, and may be described as "a Promethean figure" with "colossal external strength" and "colossal powers," as in the more ludicrous moments of the Stalin era, or in the accolade to Israeli Prime Minister Golda Meir by Martin Peretz from which the quotes just given are taken (*New Republic*, Aug. 10, 1987).

34. Frank Monaghan, *John Jay* (Bobbs-Merrill, 1935); Richard B. Morris, *The Forging of the Union* (Harper & Row, 1987, 46-47, 173, 12f.). See *Political Economy of Human Rights*, II, 41ff. on the flight of refugees after the American revolution, including boat people fleeing in terror from perhaps the richest country in the world to suffer and die in Nova Scotia in mid-winter; relative to the population, the numbers compare to the refugee flight from ravaged Vietnam. For a recent estimate, including 80,000-100,000 Loyalists, see Morris, 13, 17.

35. *The American Revolution Reconsidered* (Harper & Row, 1967, 57-58).

36. See Joshua Cohen and Joel Rogers, *On Democracy* (Penguin, 1983), for a perceptive analysis, and next chapter for some further comments.

37. For some discussion and further references, see *Turning the Tide*, 232f.

38. Editorials, *El Tiempo*, May 5, 10; translated in *Hondupress* (Managua), May 18, 1988, a journal of Honduran exiles who fear to return to the "fledgling democracy" because of the threat of assassination and disappearance. For more on the Salvadoran polls, see *Culture of Terrorism*, 102, and appendix IV, section 5. I found no reference in the media, though there is a regular chorus of praise for the progress of this noble experiment in democracy under U.S. tutelage.

39. Alex Carey, "Reshaping the Truth," *Meanjin Quarterly* (Australia), 35.4, 1976; Gabriel Kolko, *Main Currents in American History* (Pantheon, 1984, 284). For extensive discussion, see Alex Carey, "Managing Public Opinion: The Corporate Offensive," ms., U. of New South Wales, 1986.

40. For references, see my *Towards a New Cold War* (Pantheon, 1982, chapter 1). Niebuhr, *Moral Man and Immoral Society* (Scribners, 1952, 221-23, 21; reprint of 1932 edition); also Richard Fox, *Reinhold Niebuhr* (Pantheon, 1985, 138-39). For more on his ideas, and their reception, see my review of several books by and on Niebuhr in *Grand Street*, Winter 1987.

41. Bailey, cited by Jesse Lemisch, *On Active Service in War and Peace: Politics and Ideology in the American Historical Profession* (New Hogtown Press, Toronto, 1975). Huntington, *International Security*, Summer 1981.

42. *England in the Age of the American Revolution* (Macmillan, 1961, 40); cited by Francis Jennings, *Empire of Fortune* (Norton, 1988, 471).

43. Defense Minister Frits Bolkestein, *NRC Handelsblad*, Oct. 11, 1988. He is commenting (indignantly) on material I presented on this topic as a Huizinga lecture in Leiden in 1977, reprinted in *Towards a New Cold War*, chapter 1.

44. Fyodor Dostoyevsky, *The Brothers Karamazov* (Random House, 1950).

45. Alfonso Chardy, *Miami Herald*, July 19, 1987. The State Department Office of Public Diplomacy operated under CIA-NSC direction to organize support for the contras and to intimidate and manipulate the media and Congress. On its activities, condemned as illegal in September 1987 by the Comptroller General of the GAO, see Staff Report, *State Department and Intelligence Community Involvement in Domestic Activities Related to the Iran/Contra Affair*, Committee on Foreign Affairs, U.S. House of Representatives, Sept. 7, 1988; Parry and Kornbluh, *op. cit.* Also *Culture of Terrorism*, chapter 10, referring to Chardy's earlier exposures in two outstanding though generally neglected articles in the *Miami Herald*.

Chapter 2

1. See chapter 1, note 32. There are various complexities and qualifications, of course, when we turn from very general features of the system to fine details and minor effects. It should be understood that these are features of the analysis of any complex system.

2. See their *On Democracy*, where more wide-ranging consequences are elaborated.

3. Christopher Hill, *The World Turned Upside Down* (Penguin, 1984, 60, 71), quoting contemporary authors.

4. Edward Countryman, *The American Revolution* (Hill and Wang, 1985, 200, 224ff.)

5. James Curran, "Advertising and the Press," in Curran, ed., *The British Press: A Manifesto* (London: MacMillan, 1978).

6. Lawrence Shoup and William Minter, *Imperial Brain Trust* (Monthly Review, 1977, 130), a study of the War and Peace Studies Project of the Council on Foreign Relations and the State Department from 1939 to 1945.

7. See appendix II, section 1, for further discussion.

8. Exceptions were tolerated in the early years because of the special need for recovery of the centers of industrial capitalism by exploiting their former colonies, but this was understood to be a temporary expedient. For details, see William S. Borden, *The Pacific Alliance: United States Foreign Economic Policy and Japanese Trade Recovery, 1947-1955* (Wisconsin, 1984); Andrew J. Rotter, *The Path to Vietnam: Origins of the American Commitment to Southeast Asia* (Cornell, 1987).

9. *WP Weekly*, Dec. 28, 1987.

10. Lippmann and Merz, "A Test of the News," Supplement, *New Republic*, Aug. 4, 1920. Quotes here from citations in Aronson, *The Press and the Cold War*, 25f.

11. See appendix II, section 1.

12. H. D. S. Greenway, *Boston Globe*, July 8, 1988. On the backgrounds, see *Turning the Tide*, 194f., and sources cited; Christopher Simpson, *Blowback* (Weidenfeld & Nicolson, 1988).

13. By the late 1960s, it was already clear that these were the basic factors behind the U.S. intervention in Southeast Asia, which, in U.S. global planning, was to be reconstituted as a "co-prosperity sphere" for Japan, within the U.S.-dominated Grand Area, while also serving as a market and source of raw materials and recycled dollars for the reconstruction of Western European capitalism. See my *At War with Asia* (Pantheon, 1970, introduction); *For Reasons of State* (Pantheon, 1973); Chomsky and Howard Zinn, eds., *Critical Essays*. vol. 5 of the *Pentagon Papers* (Beacon, 1972); and other work of the period. See also, among others, Borden, *Pacific Alliance*; Michael Schaller, *The American Occupation of Japan* (Oxford, 1985); Rotter, *Path to Vietnam*.

14. Acheson, *Present at the Creation* (Norton, 1969, 374, 489); Borden, *op. cit.*, 44, 144.

15. See appendix II, section 2.

16. Carey, "Managing Public Opinion."

17. *Ibid.*, citing Bell, "Industrial Conflict and Public Opinion," in A. R. Dubin and A. Ross, eds., *Industrial Conflict* (McGraw-Hill, 1954).

18. See appendix V, section 5.

19. Carey, "Managing Public Opinion." On the purge of the universities in the 1950s, see Ellen Schrecker, *No Ivory Tower* (Oxford, 1986). For a small sample of the later purge, see several essays in Philip J. Meranto, Oneida J. Meranto, and Matthew R. Lippman, *Guarding the Ivory Tower* (Lucha publications, Denver, 1985).

20. For some discussion, see my article "Democracy in the Industrial Societies" in *Z Magazine*, Jan. 1989.

21. The Food for Peace program (PL 480) is a notable example. Described by Ronald Reagan as "one of the greatest humanitarian acts ever performed by one nation for the needy of other nations," PL 480 has effectively served the purposes for which it was designed: subsidizing U.S. agribusiness; inducing people to "become dependent on us for food" (Senator Hubert Humphrey, one of its architects in the interest of his Minnesota farming constituency); contributing to counterinsurgency operations; and financing "the creation of a global military network to prop up Western and Third World capitalist governments" by requiring that local currency counterpart funds be used for rearmament (William Borden), thus also providing an indirect subsidy to U.S. military producers. The U.S. employs such "export subsidies (universally considered an 'unfair' trading practice) to preserve its huge Japanese market," among other cases (Borden). The effect on Third World agriculture and survival has often been devastating. See Tom Barry and Deb Preusch, *The Soft War* (Grove, 1988, 67f.); Borden, *Pacific Alliance*, 182f.; and other sources.

22. *NYT*, Oct. 30, 1985.

23. See *Political Economy of Human Rights* and *Manufacturing Consent*.

24. *NYT*, March 25, 1977; transcript of news conference.

25. *Los Angeles Times*, Oct. 25, 1988; Robert Reinhold, *NYT*, same day.

26. For comparative estimates at the time, see *Political Economy of Human Rights*, II, chapter 3.

27. *NYT*, March 3, 1985.

28. T. Hunter Wilson, *Indochina Newsletter* (Asia Resource Center), Nov.-Dec. 1987. Mary Williams Walsh, *Wall Street Journal*, Jan. 3; George Esper, AP, Jan. 18; *Boston Globe*, picture caption, Jan. 20, 1989.

29. Walsh, *Wall Street Journal*, Jan. 3, 1989. Robert Pear, *NYT*, Aug. 14; Elaine Sciolino, *NYT*, Aug. 17; Paul Lewis, *NYT*, Oct. 8; Mary Williams Walsh, *Wall Street Journal*, Sept. 1, 1988. In her Jan. 3, 1989 article, Walsh notes, a touch ruefully, that "the release of the Afghan maps could even count as a small propaganda victory for the Kabul regime, since its enemies in Washington" have yet to do as much fourteen years after their departure. The propaganda

victory will be extremely small, since there is no recognition that the U.S. has failed to provide this information, or has any responsibility to do so.

30. Barbara Crossette, *NYT*, Nov. 10, 1985.

31. Crossette, *NYT*, Feb. 28; E. W. Wayne, *Christian Science Monitor*, Aug. 24, 1988.

32. Anderson, "The Light at the End of the Tunnel," *Diplomatic History*, Fall 1988.

33. Lee H. Hamilton, "Time for a new American relationship with Vietnam," *Christian Science Monitor*, Dec. 12, 1988; Frederick Z. Brown, *Indochina Issues* 85, Nov. 1988; *Boston Globe*, July 8, 1988.

34. Jennings, *Empire of Fortune*, 215.

35. Kapeliouk, *Yediot Ahronot*, April 7, 1988; also April 1, 15.

36. Ziem, *Indochina Newsletter* (Asia Resource Center), July-August 1988; Susan Chira, *NYT*, Oct. 5, 1988; *Wall Street Journal*, April 4, 1985. See *Manufacturing Consent* on how the tenth anniversary retrospectives (1985) evaded the effects of the war on the South Vietnamese, the main victims of the U.S. attack.

37. NSC 144/1, 1953; NSC 5432, 1954; and many others. For more detailed discussion, see *On Power and Ideology*. The basic principles are reiterated constantly, often in the same words.

38. On this propaganda device, aimed at the home front, see Herman and Brodhead, *Demonstration Elections*.

39. Jorge Pinto, *NYT* Op-Ed, May 6, 1981; Ricardo Castañeda, Senior Partner of a Salvadoran law firm, Edward Mason Fellow, Kennedy School, Harvard University, p.c.; "Salvador Groups Attack Paper and U.S. Plant," World News Briefs, *NYT*, April 19, 1980. The information on *Times* coverage is based on a search of the *Times* index by Chris Burke of FAIR.

40. "Sad Tales of La Libertad de Prensa," *Harper's Magazine*, Aug. 1988. See appendix IV, section 6, for further discussion.

41. Deirdre Carmody, *NYT*, Feb. 14, 1980. Perhaps we might regard the brief notice of April 19, cited above, as a response to his plea.

42. *NYT*, Editorial, March 25, 1988.

Chapter 3

1. *New Republic*, April 7, 1917.

2. For quotes, references, and background, see my *Towards a New Cold War*, chapter 1, and sources cited.

3. For some examples, see *Manufacturing Consent*, 343n.

4. *American Foreign Policy* (Norton, 1969).

5. Thomas Paterson, *Meeting the Communist Threat* (Oxford, 1988, 82-83), quoting a Truman official and political scientist Gabriel Almond.

6. Melvyn Leffler, "Adherence to Agreements: Yalta and the Experiences of the Early Cold War," *International Security,* Summer 1986.

7. Robert W. Tucker, "Reagan's Foreign Policy," *Foreign Affairs,* "America and the World 1988/89," Winter 1989, featured lead article. John Lewis Gaddis, *The Long Peace* (Oxford, 1987, 129). The effort to liberate Indochina from the U.S.-backed French forces was in part a civil war, as is generally true of struggles against foreign occupation and colonial rule—the American revolution, for example. It should be clear that this fact adds no credibility to the bizarre notion that the U.S. was "deterring aggression" by aiding the French effort to reconquer Indochina, even contemplating the use of nuclear weapons for this purpose.

8. See appendix V, section 8, for an example, though one beyond the norm.

9. Neil Lewis, *NYT,* Dec. 6, 1987.

10. *Daily Telegraph* (London), Jan. 28, 1988.

11. *NYT,* June 2, 1956. The charge was made by Assistant Secretary of State Walter Robertson. We can still read of "the south's memory of democracy" (Clayton Jones, *Christian Science Monitor,* Jan. 19, 1989)—under the military dictatorships imposed by U.S. violence.

12. Sidney Hook, "Lord Russell and the War Crimes 'Trial'," *New Leader,* Oct. 24, 1966; "Politics Tests Philosophy's Meaning," Review of Alan Ryan, *Bertrand Russell: A Political Life, Insight* (published by the *Washington Times*), Oct. 3, 1988. Hook's commentary on Russell will be familiar to anyone acquainted with attacks on dissidents in the Communist Party press in the Stalinist years.

13. *Boston Globe,* Jan. 15, 1988.

14. *NYT,* Aug. 6, 1987.

15. For one forthright exception, see "Talk of the Town," *New Yorker,* Feb. 1, 1988.

16. Editorial, *WP Weekly,* April 4, 1988.

17. Bruce Cameron and Penn Kemble, "From a Proxy Force to a National Liberation Movement," ms., Feb. 1986, outlining how the U.S. should act to effect this transition. Edgar Chamorro, *Packaging the Contras: A Case of CIA Disinformation,* Institute for Media Analysis Monograph Series, No. 2 (New York, 1987, 49); Chamorro was the CIA-selected spokesman for the contra directorate from December 1982 until he quit the organization in December 1984.

18. *Davar,* July 8, 1988. For a detailed record of the reporting of these operations, see appendix III.

19. *Manchester Guardian Weekly* (London), Dec. 18, 1988. Julie Flint reports from Lebanon in the same issue that this "bizarre and probably bungled operation" left no visible effects except for the remnants of human bodies and "two dead mastiffs strapped with explosives." An Israeli officer was killed, elite commandoes had to be rescued clinging to helicopter skids after they abandoned their equipment and arms (which were proudly exhibited in Lebanon), and there is "no evidence that the Israelis destroyed a single ammunition dump—and these hills are littered with them—or inflicted casualties that would justify the size of the attack force." The failure of the raid may reflect the decline in combat effectiveness of the Israeli forces that has been a source of much concern in military circles for some years, and that has probably accelerated as the military forces have been assigned the mission of terrorizing defenseless civilians in the territories.

20. AP, Dec. 14; *NYT*, Dec. 15, 1988. The brief *Times* report quotes the Lebanese ambassador as saying that Israel "attaches no concern or importance to non-Israeli peoples." What he actually said is that Israel could hardly be expected to "show any mercy to animals" given that it attaches no importance to non-Israeli people. He had repeated the charge that Israeli forces used dogs strapped with explosives and tear gas canisters to attack people hidden in underground tunnels, then adding the comment of which a few words reached print. Dead Dobermans with explosives strapped to their body had been displayed by guerrillas (William Tuohy, *Los Angeles Times*, Dec. 10, 1988; see preceding note).

21. *NYT*, Feb. 19, 1988; *WP*, June 30, 1985. On the attack on the school in Damour, see Liston Pope, *City Sun*, June 1-7, 1988; Pope, who was teaching English at the school, writes that the attack, one of many, received 20 words in the *New York Times*. See my *Pirates and Emperors*, chapter 2, on the Iron Fist operations and the Bekaa valley bombings.

22. See chapter 5, below, and *Pirates and Emperors*, chapter 2, for many details.

23. *Ibid.*, chapters 1, 2, and *Fateful Triangle*, on media protection of Israel. For updates, see my articles in *Z Magazine*, May, June 1988, and "The U.S. and the Middle East," talk given at Tel Aviv university in April 1988, to appear in Zachary Lockman and Joel Beinin, eds., *Intifada: the Palestinian Uprising against Israeli Occupation* (South End, 1989).

24. *Boston Globe*, Nov. 9, 1984.

25. For details, see my article in *Z Magazine*, March 1988.

26. *Ibid.*, for details, including subsequent reference in quotes from Ortega and Arias buried in articles on other matters.

27. Editorial, *El Tiempo*, May 5, 1988; reprinted in *Hondupress*, May 18, 1988.

28. They know, of course, as an occasional throw-away line indicates.

29. *Towards a New Cold War*, 51.

30. *Congressional Record,* Senate, Aug. 5, 1988, S 11002; Susan Rasky, *NYT,* Aug. 11, 1988.

31. Robert Pear, *NYT,* May 25, 1988.

32. See appendix IV, section 4; and section 5, on public support for the political opposition. On opposition backing for the contras, see appendix V, section 6.

33. *Congressional Record,* Aug. 5, 1988, S 10969f.; AP, *NYT,* Aug. 4; Bryna Brennan, AP, *WP,* Aug. 4, a much fuller account; *Barricada* (Managua), Aug. 3; Julie Light, *Guardian* (New York), Aug. 17, 1988. The *Boston Globe* ran a tiny item featuring a contra denial, Aug. 4.

34. Vaky, *Foreign Policy,* Fall 1987. On support for the political opposition within Nicaragua, see appendix IV, section 5.

35. Pastor, *Condemned to Repetition* (Princeton, 1987, 32), his emphasis.

36. See *Culture of Terrorism* for references on Barnes and many similar examples. Barnes was regarded as "the ring leader" of the congressional opposition to the illegal Reagan administration programs of domestic propaganda and contra terror. He had to be "destroyed" politically as an "object lesson to others," according to memos of one of the "private" affiliates of these operations (run by Carl Channell, who pleaded guilty for serving as a conduit for tax-exempt money for contra weapons). Barnes was defeated after an ad campaign run by Channell depicting him as a Sandinista sympathizer, a message not lost on Congress. See Parry and Kornbluh, *op. cit.*

37. U.S. Senate, Committee on Foreign Relations, Feb. 27, 1986.

38. *NYT,* March 14, 1986.

39. Editorial, *WP Weekly,* March 1, 1986.

40. *New York Times Book Review,* April 12, 1987. See letters, *Z Magazine,* January 1989, for Morley's interpretation of the quoted phrase.

41. *Wall Street Journal,* March 26, 1987.

42. John E. Rielly, ed., *American Public Opinion and U.S. Foreign Policy 1987,* Chicago Council on Foreign Relations, March 1987. "Leaders" are defined as "prominent individuals in the United States from government, business, labor, academia, the mass media, religious institutions, private foreign policy organizations and special interest groups."

43. For a sample, see *Culture of Terrorism,* chapter 11.

44. Andrew Reding, interview with Figueres, *World Policy Review,* Spring 1986; *Culture of Terrorism,* 206-7, for longer excerpts from an interview published by COHA, *Washington Report on the Hemisphere,* Oct. 1, 1986.

45. *NYT Magazine,* Jan. 10, 1988.

46. James LeMoyne, "Bitterness and Apathy in Nicaragua," *NYT,* Dec. 29, 1987. Chamorro, *Update,* Central American Historical Institute, Georgetown University, Nov. 13, 1987; *Extra!* (FAIR), Oct./Nov. 1987. Having been in

Managua at just the time that LeMoyne stopped by briefly, I am personally aware of how distorted his rendition was. Others with personal experience will draw their own conclusions. The point, however, is that it is LeMoyne's version, not other reactions, that can reach the general public. Only certain kinds of responses—in fact, those that conform to the conditions of the propaganda model—pass through the media filter, with only occasional exceptions.

47. Mary Speck, "Nicaragua's Economic Decline Takes Toll on Health," *Miami Herald*, Sept. 15, 1988; William Branigin, "Let Them Eat Fruit Rinds," *Washington Post Weekly*, Oct. 10-16, 1988. Consistent with the media policy of downplaying the U.S. role in Nicaragua's distress, Branigin alleges that a June 1988 poll shows that only 19 percent of Managua residents regard "U.S. aggression in any of its forms" as "the main cause" of the economic problems. But, relying on a secondary source, he misread the poll results (see appendix IV, section 5). The question asked was to identify "the country's main economic problems." Two-thirds of respondents selected inflation, shortage of goods, low wages, deficient production, and "other"; 8 percent selected "bad government"; and Branigin's 19 percent chose "war," "economic blockade," or "aggression." Plainly, the responses were heterogeneous. Doubtless many of the 67 percent who identified specific economic problems would have agreed that they were attributable to U.S. intervention and economic warfare; even right-wing pro-Somoza businessmen are clear about this matter.

48. Thomas W. Walker, *Nicaragua* (Westview, 1986, 67).

49. See my introduction to Morris Morley and James Petras, *The Reagan Administration and Nicaragua*, Institute of Media Analysis, Monograph Series No. 1 (New York, 1987), for a detailed survey, noting some marginal exceptions and nuances and also discussing one of the more outlandish contributions, that of Ronald Radosh, now in his "God that failed" phase and therefore with ready access to the media, previously denied. Also my chapter "U.S. Polity and Society: the Lessons of Nicaragua" in Thomas Walker, ed., *Reagan versus the Sandinistas* (Westview, 1987).

50. *NYT*, Dec. 31, 1987.

51. See Appendix I for discussion of these predictions.

52. *NYT*, Feb. 10.

53. *NYT*, Feb. 14.

54. Editorials, *WP*, Jan. 9, March 11; Buckley, *WP*, May 21, 1987.

55. Rosenthal, *NYT*, March 8; Rosenfeld, *WP*, April 24, 1987.

56. Stephen Vaughn, *Holding Fast the Inner Lines* (U. of North Carolina, 1980, 194).

57. Kenneth Roth, letter, *NYT*, Aug. 17, 1988; *BG*, Dec. 26, 1988. Advocates of U.S. violence condemn Americas Watch because its careful and judicious

reporting does not satisfy their standards of loyalty to state doctrine. Thus *New Republic* editor Morton Kondracke charges that Americas Watch and State Department propagandists "deserve each other," each exaggerating and distorting in their partisan endeavors, protecting Nicaragua and the U.S. clients, respectively ("Broken Watch", *The New Republic*, Aug. 22, 1988; for some examples of Kondracke's appreciation for successful violence, and other views, see *Culture of Terrorism*; also appendix I, section 2). In fact, Americas Watch has bent over backwards to detect and denounce Nicaraguan abuses, devoting far more attention to them than the comparative facts would warrant. It has gone so far as to say that it would oppose support for Nicaragua if that were at issue, because of its abuses, though it has not proposed that the U.S. terminate aid to El Salvador, where the abuses are vastly worse; nor have the Watch groups called for termination of aid to Israel and other major violators of human rights (see Americas Watch, *Human Rights in Nicaragua*, March 1986). But Americas Watch has kept to the determinable facts, scandalizing assorted commissars.

58. Bernard Diederich, *Somoza* (E.P. Dutton, 1981, 74). *Memorandum* from Secretary of Defense Robert McNamara to McGeorge Bundy, June 11, 1965; for further details, see *On Power and Ideology*, 22f. and bibliography.

59. Schoultz, *Human Rights and United States Policy toward Latin America* (Princeton, 1981, 7).

60. Cited by F. Parkinson, *Latin America, The Cold War, and The World Powers* (London, 1974), 40.

61. See my article "Democracy in the Industrial Societies" in *Z Magazine*, Jan. 1989, for discussion and references.

62. *Torture in Latin America*, LADOC (Latin American Documentation), Lima, 1987.

63. Secretary Shultz, "Moral Principles and Strategic Interests: The Worldwide Movement Toward Democracy," State Dept. Bureau of Public Affairs, *Current Policy* no. 820, address at Kansas State University, April 14, 1986; LeMoyne, *NYT*, Feb. 7, 1988.

64. See *The Political Economy of Human Rights*, vol. I; Lars Schoultz, *Comparative Politics*, Jan. 1981. See also his *Human Rights and United States Policy toward Latin America*.

65. *NYT*, March 15, 1987.

66. AP, Feb. 1, 1988.

67. Editorial, *WP Weekly*, March 31, 1986; Pamela Constable, *BG*, March 15, 1987.

68. For a detailed analysis, see Morley and Petras, *op. cit.*

69. See my article in Walker, *Reagan vs. the Sandinistas*; *Culture of Terrorism*, 219f.; *WP*, Oct. 15, 1985; Peter Kornbluh, *Nicaragua* (Institute for Policy Studies, Washington, 1987).

70. *Ibid.*

Chapter 4

1. Hearings of the Senate Committee on Foreign Relations, August 31, 1966; cited by Aronson, *The Press and the Cold War,* 226.

2. There are exceptions when interfering factors distort the operation of the system. Even powerful segments of the corporate world may be barred from ready access to the public forum; for one case, see the next chapter.

3. *Turning the Tide,* 72f., and my article in Walker, *Reagan versus the Sandinistas.* See also Michael Parenti, "Afterword," in Morley and Petras, *The Reagan Administration in Nicaragua,* and Michael Linfield, *Human Rights in Times of War,* ms., 1988.

4. Spence, "The U.S. Media: Covering (Over) Nicaragua," in Walker, *Reagan vs. the Sandinistas.* On the election coverage, see appendix I, section 1, and sources cited.

5. Council on Hemispheric Affairs (COHA), "News and Analysis," Feb. 29, 1988.

6. More generally, it would be very difficult to find in the media any discussion of the impact of the Alliance for Progress in intensifying the crisis, with its emphasis on development programs that increased both GNP and human suffering (for example, by shifting production from subsistence crops to beef for export), led to serious ecological damage, and in general were a human catastrophe even where they were a statistical success.

7. For example, Katsuichi Honda published in the Japanese press extensive studies of life in villages controlled by South Vietnamese resistance forces and under U.S. attack, but the English translation found no takers. Cambodia specialist Serge Thion reported his visit to Cambodian guerrillas in 1972 in *Le Monde,* but the *Washington Post* turned it down. *Le Monde* southeast Asia specialist Jacques Decornoy published first-hand reports of the devastating U.S. bombing of Laos in 1968, but despite repeated efforts, no U.S. journal was willing to reprint his articles or even to mention the facts. Reports on the atrocities of U.S.-backed Salvadoran forces by foreign journalists and even direct testimony by House members were ignored. See *For Reasons of State, Towards a New Cold War, Manufacturing Consent,* on these and other examples.

8. Cambodian refugees on the Thai border in the late 1970s were not more accessible than Cambodia refugees in Phnom Penh a few years earlier, but the former had a useful tale to tell and the latter did not, and were therefore ignored. The Thai border camps were also not more accessible than Lisbon or Australia despite some remarkable claims by journalists who surely know better, but what the Timorese refugees had to say conflicted with the requirements of U.S. power, as distinct from those who fled Pol Pot atrocities. See

Political Economy of Human Rights and *Manufacturing Consent* for discussion and details, in these and other cases.

9. Seattle Central America Media Project, *Out of Balance*, n.d. See also appendix V, section 6, on *Times* choice of sources within Nicaragua.

10. Donald Fox and Michael J. Glennon, "Report to the International Human Rights Law Group and the Washington Office on Latin America," Washington D.C., April 1985, 21, referring to the State Department reaction to their revelation of contra atrocities. Most studies were, like this one, ignored or dismissed.

11. For a review of *New York Times* editorials on El Salvador and Nicaragua from 1980 through mid-1986, see my article in Walker, *Reagan vs. the Sandinistas*. For comparison of the image of Duarte here and in Latin America, including El Salvador, see *Culture of Terrorism*, 101f. On Duarte's record and media appreciation for it, see *Turning the Tide*, chapter 3, sec. 5.2; Cooper, "Whitewashing Duarte," U.S. Reporting on El Salvador, *NACLA Report on the Americas*, Jan./March 1986.

12. See sources cited above for explicit references and further detail, here and below; appendix V, section 6, on the Central American media.

13. Lydia Chavez, *NYT*, April 24, 1983. Defense Minister Gen. Vides Casanova cited by Ray Bonner, *Weakness and Deceit* (Times Books, 1984, 106).

14. See appendix IV, section 1, for a few of the many examples. For many other cases, see *Political Economy of Human Rights* and other sources cited earlier.

15. For a review of media performance in El Salvador as the terror mounted in 1980 and early 1981, see *Towards a New Cold War*, introduction; reprinted in part in *The Chomsky Reader*. For more on the refusal of the media to report government atrocities, see Ed Harriman, *Hack: Home Truths about Foreign News* (Zed, 1987); Harriman covered El Salvador for British media. There followed a brief period of serious reporting as atrocities reached extreme levels, but when it seemed that U.S.-organized terror might well succeed and demonstration elections were held, the pattern returned to the earlier norm of apologetics and neglect, with sporadic exceptions. The withdrawal of Ray Bonner by the *Times* was also important. "U.S. embassy officials boasted in 1982 that they had forced [Bonner] out of the country because of his unfavorable [and accurate] reporting on the Salvadoran government," Parry and Kornbluh report (*op. cit.*).

16. See appendix IV, section 2.

17. *NYT Magazine*, April 6, 1986.

18. *NYT Magazine*, May 25, 1980. Oduber, in Kenneth M. Coleman and George C. Herring, eds., *The Central American Crisis* (Scholarly Resources Inc., 1985, 196).

19. There were exceptions, but the media reaction was generally similar, sometimes reaching surprising extremes. Thus the *Washington Post* turned for comment to contra lobbyist Robert Leiken, who "blamed the court, which he said suffers from the 'increasing perception' of having close ties to the Soviet Union"; the Soviet judge had withdrawn from the case, but evidently his subjects performed their assigned tasks (Jonathan Karp, *WP*, June 28, 1986). For more on the appeal of Leiken's Maoist line and his interesting media role as the Latin American specialists largely refused to join the cause, see *Culture of Terrorism*, 205f.

20. *NYT*, May 12, 1986.

21. *NYT*, June 29, 1986.

22. *Extra!*, journal of the press monitoring organization FAIR, Dec. 1987. World Court announcement, AP, *WP*, Aug. 4, 1988, a brief item; *Boston Globe*, 29 words.

23. U.N. Press Release GA/7572, Nov. 12; AP, Nov. 12; Paul Lewis, *NYT*, Nov. 11, 13, Dec. 26, 1987.

24. On coverage of the December 1987 and June 1988 summit meetings, see appendix IV, section 3.

25. U.N. Press Release GA/7591, 30 November; AP, Nov. 30; William Broad, "Star Wars is Coming, but Where is it Going?," *NYT Magazine*, Dec. 6, 1987.

26. Paul Lewis, *NYT*, Dec. 2, 1987.

27. U.N. Press release GA/7603, Dec. 7, 1987.

28. Excerpts from the U.S. Government translation appear in the *New York Times*, Nov. 17, 1988.

29. Yehoshafat Harkabi, *Israel's Fateful Hour* (Harper and Row, 1988, 31).

30. See appendix V, section 4.

31. Editorial, *NYT*, Nov. 16; Lewis, *NYT*, Dec. 1, 1988. In the liberal *Boston Globe*, for example, when the U.S. government agreed to talk to the PLO on the pretense that they had accepted U.S. demands, two columns appeared to reveal the diversity of opinion on the topic, under the heading "Taking Arafat's 'yes' for an answer" (*BG*, Dec. 24, 1988). The hawks were represented by a leader of the Boston Jewish community, Philip Perlmutter, warning of Arafat's deception and duplicity; the doves, by former Israeli ambassador Benno Weiser Varon, who declared "I am no peacenik, and disliked viscerally 'Breira,' 'The New Agenda' and 'Peace Now'"—but Israel's interests require recognition of reality (Breira and the New Jewish Agenda are dovish Zionist groups, the former driven out of existence by effective defamation; Peace Now has ambiguous credentials as an Israeli peace group). See next chapter and appendix V, section 4, for further detail.

32. See appendix V, section 4, for further comment.

33. Paul Lewis, *NYT*, March 11; Joseph Treaster, *NYT*, May 31, 1988. See Karen Wald, *Z Magazine*, July-August 1988, for a different view on the U.N. Cuba debate.

34. AP, March 11, 1988.

35. For further comment, see appendix IV, section 4.

36. See *Culture of Terrorism*, chapter 7, for a longer excerpt, and further details on the diplomatic maneuverings and the peace plan, through October 1987. See my articles in *Z Magazine*, January and March 1988, for discussion of the events and the services of the media through February 1988. See these sources for references, where not cited below.

37. Dennis Volman, *Christian Science Monitor*, June 26, 1987.

38. *El Tiempo*, July 3, 1987, citing the journal of the Guatemalan Latinamerican Agency of Special Information Services (ALASEI).

39. Cf. appendix IV, section 5, for further documentation and references. For reasons of space, I will largely keep to the Newspaper of Record. For further details, see the references of note 36, including some exceptions to the general pattern, primarily in the *Christian Science Monitor* and *Los Angeles Times*, and editorials in the *Boston Globe*.

40. See *Manufacturing Consent*, chapter 5, and sources cited. A variant of this diplomatic strategy was called "the Trollope ploy" by the Kennedy intellectuals during the Cuban missile crisis, when they sought to evade a proposal by Khrushchev that they recognized would be regarded generally as a reasonable way to terminate the crisis; the "ploy" was to attribute to Khrushchev a different and more acceptable stand, just as the heroine of a Trollope novel interprets a meaningless gesture as an offer of marriage. The December 1988 reversal on speaking to the PLO is another example; see appendix V, section 4.

41. A classified background paper for the National Security Council after the U.S. had scuttled the 1984 opportunities exulted that "we have trumped the latest Nicaraguan/Mexican effort to rush signature of an unsatisfactory Contadora agreement," namely the one that the U.S. had been vigorously advocating until Nicaragua announced its support for it. See Kornbluh, *Nicaragua*, 181f.

42. A further Dukakis flaw is that he "would now deny the Nicaraguan rebels even economic aid" (as required by the 1987 peace accords, the editors neglect to add; these accords they constantly applaud—when they can be employed as an anti-Sandinista weapon). Editorial, *NYT*, Aug. 28, 1988.

43. AP, Jan. 29, 1988, reporting a Witness for Peace study. There is a mention by Julia Preston, *WP*, Feb. 4.

44. Ortega, *Barricada Internacional*, Dec. 22, 1988, Review of 1988 (POB 410150, San Francisco CA 94103); also AP, Dec. 15, 1988 (since the information was on the wires, it was readily available to every segment of the mass media).

On one contra attack in November, see Ellen V.P. Wells, letter, *NYT*, Dec. 31, 1988. Commenting on a *Times* report that the contras had passed into history, Wells reports her experience as a Witness for Peace observer living with farmers in Jinotega province. On November 18, contras raided their cooperative, killing two, destroying houses, supplies, harvested coffee, and a health clinic (a prime target for many years). In an August 17 raid, four children had been killed.

45. See appendix IV, section 5, for further details on these matters.

46. Kirkpatrick, *WP*, June 6, 1988. See appendix IV, section 5, for details.

47. LeMoyne, *NYT*, March 26; Susan Rasky, *NYT*, March 29, 30, 1988.

48. Letter of the Secretary General of the OAS to George Shultz, April 25, 1988.

49. *NYT*, April 1. Susan Rasky reported that Adams also "said that even humanitarian aid for the rebels amounted to support of a fighting force," perhaps an oblique reference to the World Court decision.

50. Robert Pear, *NYT*, April 6; COHA *Washington Report on the Hemisphere*, May 11; AP, May 12, 11; Reuters, *BG*, May 13, 1988.

51. "Special Report," DSG, May 16, 1988.

52. LeMoyne, *NYT*, May 12; Pear, *NYT*, May 10, 1988.

53. John Goshko, *WP*, May 14; John McCaslin, *WT*, June 14, 1988; COHA press release, May 12, 1988; Don Podesta, *WP*, Sept. 21, 1988.

54. *NYT*, Peter Kilborn, April 5; editorial, *BG*, April 17, 1988.

55. Center for International Policy, "The Nicaraguan Cease-Fire Talks: a Documentary Survey," June 13, 1988; see also *Cease-Fire Primer, International Policy Report*, CIP; Julia Preston, *WP*, June 10, 1988.

56. COHA, "A Critique of the Dole Amendment," Aug. 1, 1988, referring to the events of July; see appendix IV, section 5, also chapter 3.

57. Cited by Michael Conroy, in Thomas Walker, ed., *Nicaragua: The First Years* (Praeger, 1985, 232f).

58. Julia Preston, *WP Weekly*, Jan. 2-8, 1989; the latter comment referring to Jalapa in the far north. On the curious amalgam of Maoism and right-wing jingoism that was concocted in the early 1980s when authentic Latin America specialists refused to perform the services expected of them by government and media, see *Culture of Terrorism*, 205f. On Kirkpatrick's psychiatric insights into Sandinista paranoia as she spun a web of lies about U.S. policies, see Holly Sklar, *Washington's War on Nicaragua* (South End, 1988, 114f.).

59. *BG*, Dec. 25, 1988.

60. See chapter 3, note 47.

61. *BG*, Oct. 30, 31, Nov. 1, 1988. The series also contains many distortions and outright lies, for example, the claim that in December 1987 Defense Minister Ortega "announced his objective of military forces of 600,000 men

by 1995," which will add to those "legions of troops [that] produce nothing." As Sheehan and the editors know full well, Ortega announced a planned *reduction* of the military forces, with light arms to be distributed to the general working population. Useful propaganda fabrications are not readily abandoned.

62. See appendix V, section 3, for reference and background.

63. Preston, *WP Weekly*, Jan. 2-8, 1989. On U.S. dominance of the information system in large areas of Nicaragua, see Howard Frederick, "Electronic Penetration," in Walker, *Reagan vs. the Sandinistas*.

64. Thomas Walker, in Coleman and Herring, *The Central American Crisis*; Carlin, *Independent* (London), Feb. 1, 1988.

Chapter 5

1. Milton, *Paradise Lost*, Bk. III, 682-84; Pascal, *Provincial Letters*, Letter VI. For a perceptive account of how the wealthy and the business community transmute tax reform to serve their interests, using the device of "confusion of the public" to make this happen "while appearing not to happen," see Linda McQuaig, *Behind Closed Doors: How the Rich Won Control of Canada's Tax System* (Penguin, 1987). Her study deals specifically with Canada, but the conclusions are more general.

2. Churchill, *The Second World War*, vol. 5 (Houghton Mifflin, 1951, 382).

3. See p. 49.

4. U.S. government scholar Douglas Pike, *Viet Cong* (MIT, 1966).

5. Editorial, *NYT*, Dec. 22, 1965. Washington took credit for helping to prepare the ground for the military coup, and a more direct U.S. role in the coup and its aftermath is hardly unlikely; see *Culture of Terrorism*, 181, and an important study by Peter Dale Scott, "The United States and the Overthrow of Sukarno, 1965-1967," *Pacific Affairs*, Summer 1985. Lyndon Johnson's National Security Adviser McGeorge Bundy commented in retrospect that "our effort" in Vietnam was "excessive" after these events in Indonesia, which helped inoculate the region against Vietnamese-inspired nationalism, a perceptive insight into the backgrounds for the Vietnam war, amply supported by other evidence; *Manufacturing Consent*, 174.

6. Sam Pope Brewer, "Iran is Reported Subversion Free," *NYT*, Dec. 2, 1956; *NYT*, Aug. 30, 1960. Cited by William A. Dorman and Mansour Farhang, *The U.S. Press and Iran* (California, 1987, 77, 72).

7. UPI, *BG*, July 27, 1987.

8. See *Turning the Tide*, 161.

9. *NYT*, Sept. 25, 1988. Apart from the efficacy of quasi-fascist measures, the economic successes reflect the crucial priming effect of America's Asian wars and the lingering impact of Japanese colonialism, which exploited its colonies

in a different manner from the West, "bringing industry to the labor and raw materials rather than vice versa," Bruce Cumings observes, commenting on the renewal of the industrial development that had been initiated under Japanese imperialism with state-corporate guidance ("The origins and development of the Northeast Asian political economy," *International Organization* 38.1, Winter 1984).

10. *FRUS*, 1955-57, Vol. VII, 88f., NIE 82-85. For more on this enlightening document, reflecting intelligence analysis at the highest level, see my "Agenda of the Doves," Z *Magazine*, September 1988.

11. John Murray Brown, *CSM*, Feb. 6, 1987; *Economist*, Aug. 15, 1987. On media coverage of East Timor, see *Political Economy of Human Rights, Towards a New Cold War*, and *The Chomsky Reader*, the latter including some discussion of the remarkable subsequent apologetics by Western journalists. There is a great deal to add about later efforts to cover up this dismal record, but I will not pursue it here. Though at a lesser scale, the terror and repression continue, with little notice.

12. For a record, see *Manufacturing Consent*, chapter 6. The U.S. bombings of rural Laos shortly before were also suppressed during the worst period; *ibid.*, and sources cited.

13. *Ibid.*, and sources cited; Ben Kiernan, "The American Bombardment of Kampuchea," *Vietnam Generation* 1.1, Winter 1989.

14. Editorial, *NYT*, July 16, 1988. On the U.S. role during the period of "indifference," see *Manufacturing Consent*, chapter 6.

15. Elaine Sciolino, *NYT*, Oct. 16; Clayton Jones, *CSM*, Aug. 24, 1988. On what he properly calls the "hypocrisy" of the West on this issue, see Peter Carey, *Far Eastern Economic Review*, Dec. 22, 1988. He points out that thanks to "generous supplies of Chinese arms and money" and "Western food aid" sent via the U.N., "the Khmer Rouge has become a formidable fighting force," well established in parts of Cambodia. Thai military authorities play a crucial role in allowing Khmer Rouge bases and "terror enclaves" to operate within Thailand. Much of the fighting has been between the Khmer Rouge and its non-Communist coalition partners that the U.S. claims to support, one of which (Son Sann's KPNLF) has been "almost eliminated" and the other (Sihanouk's army) "badly mauled." With the aid of the Thai and Chinese allies of the United States, the Khmer Rouge may be able to take over after the Vietnamese withdrawal that is the alleged goal of U.S. policy. These developments have been clear enough for several years. See *Manufacturing Consent* for earlier references.

16. For references, see *Turning the Tide*, chapter 3, section 5.2.

17. See my article "Democracy in the Industrial Societies," Z *Magazine*, January 1989.

18. See Victor Bulmer-Thomas, review of *On Power and Ideology, Third World Quarterly*, January 1988.

19. Connell-Smith, *The Inter-American System* (Oxford, 1966).

20. Charles Ameringer, *Don Pepe* (U. of New Mexico, 1978, 114).

21. LaFeber, *Inevitable Revolutions* (Norton 1983, 187, 105); Charles F. Denton and Preston Lee Lawrence, *Latin American Politics: a Functional Approach* (San Francisco, 1972), quoted by LaFeber; Ameringer, *op. cit.*, 105.

22. *FRUS*, 1952-54, vol. IV, 1170, notes of meeting of Guatemala group, at State Dept., June 16, 1954; See pp. 1157f. for the text of the resolution. Guatemala would, it was hoped, be compelled to turn to the Soviet bloc for arms, other sources having been barred by the United States. As explained by Guatemala City embassy officer John Hill, stopping ships in international waters might "disrupt Guatemala's economy." This would in turn "encourage the Army or some other non-Communist elements to seize power," or else "the Communists will exploit the situation to extend their control," which would "justify the American community, or if they won't go along, the U.S. to take strong measures" (Bryce Wood, *The Dismantling of the Good Neighbor Policy* (Texas, 1985, 177).) We thus compel Guatemala to defend itself from our threatened attack, thereby creating a threat to our security which we exploit by destroying the Guatemalan economy so as to provoke a military coup or an actual Communist takeover which will justify our violent response, in self-defense. Here we see the real meaning of the phrase "security threat," spelled out with much insight.

23. LaFeber, *op. cit.*, 105-6.

24. Cf. p. 63. For further details, see appendix V, section 1.

25. For an account of the origins and progress of this propaganda campaign, see, among others, Herman, *The Real Terror Network*, and my *Towards a New Cold War* (introduction), *Fateful Triangle*, and *Pirates and Emperors*; see these for references, where not cited below.

26. See appendix V, section 2.

27. Martha Crenshaw, ed., introduction, *Terrorism, Legitimacy and Power: The Consequences of Political Violence* (Wesleyan, 1983).

28. Dodd, AP, Nov. 25; Shultz, Robert Pear, *NYT*, Nov. 28, 1988. An accompanying article by Alan Cowell refers to the "protestations of outrage" on the part of the Arab nations after Arafat was excluded. Shultz feels genuine "visceral outrage"; Arabs produce "protestations," perhaps merely for show. Apple, Dec. 15, 1988.

29. Editorial, *WP Weekly*, Dec. 5-11, 1988.

30. Szep, *BG*, Dec. 4, 1988. In print, allusions to the same matters in a column by *Globe* editor Randolph Ryan, Dec. 2, are the only questioning note I detected, though the point is so transparent that there must have been some others among the flood of obedient reports and commentary.

31. For some comparative assessments, see the sources cited earlier in note 25.

32. See *Pirates & Emperors*, chapter 2.

33. *Ibid.*, 87f.; *Al-Fajr*, Aug. 2, 1987; Danny Rubinstein, *Ha'aretz*, Aug. 29, 1987; Committee against State Terrorism at Sea, *State Terrorism at Sea* (Jerusalem, n.d.); Joseph Schechla, "Israel's Piracy on the High Seas," *The Return* (September 1988); Joost Hiltermann, *Middle East International*, Oct. 10, 1987.

34. Wire services, *BG*, Oct. 5, 4; Joel Greenberg, *Jerusalem Post*, Sept. 28; Mary Curtius, *BG*, Sept. 28, 1988.

35. *BG*, Oct. 10, 1988.

36. For one informative case, see appendix V, section 3.

37. Michael Wines and James Gerstenzang, *LAT*, Jan. 26, 1988.

38. Robert Pear, *NYT*, July 3, 1988; *LAT*, July 17, 1988.

39. See appendix V, section 4, for further comment.

40. Montague Kern, *Television and Middle East Diplomacy: President Carter's Fall 1977 Peace Initiative* (Center for Contemporary Arab Studies, Georgetown, Occasional Papers Series, 1983).

41. See appendix V, section 5.

42. Niebuhr, *Moral Man and Immoral Society*, 95.

43. Kempton, *NYRB*, Nov. 26, 1986; Bob Woodward, *Veil* (Simon & Schuster, 1987, 113); editorial, *WP*, March 29, 1987. See John Spicer Nichols, *Columbia Journalism Review*, July/August 1988, on the funding for *La Prensa* by the U.S. government, the North network, and other sources linked to the U.S. government and the contras; also letters, *CJR*, Sept./Oct. According to sources reported by the Council on Hemispheric Affairs, Violeta Chamorro was paid a CIA stipend and the journal received at least $500,000 from the CIA and other U.S. sources; *Washington Report on the Hemisphere*, March 16, 1988.

44. *South*, Oct. 1988.

45. Editorial, *WP*, April 25, 1988. See chapter 4 and appendix IV, section 5.

46. *Central America Report* (Guatemala City), June 10, 17, 1988; Jean-Marie Simon, ed., *Guatemala News in Brief*, no. 23, May 11-July 1988, Americas Watch; Human Rights Watch, *The Persecution of Human Rights Monitors*, Dec. 1988.

47. A month later, the seventeenth paragraph of a story on Guatemala by Stephen Kinzer mentions the bombing of *La Epoca*, which "some diplomats attributed to the security forces," and it was mentioned again in August in the *Times* book review in a report on a conference of Central American writers. Kinzer, *NYT*, July 6, 1988; David Unger, *NYT Weekly Book Review*, Aug. 7, 1988. The home of the TASS correspondent had been firebombed shortly before the destruction of *La Epoca*, and the correspondents for TASS and the Cuban *Prensa Latina* had been forced to leave the country after death threats; two traditional death squads, linked to the security forces, took credit.

48. "Freedom of the Press," NACLA *Report on the Americas*, May/June 1988.

49. Wire services, *Boston Globe*, Sept. 5, 1988.

50. See appendix V, section 6.

51. Kinzer, *NYT*, April 20, 1987. Elsewhere, Kinzer writes that "In 1980, La Prensa was shaken by internal conflict when a group of employees objected to its increasingly anti-Sandinista line. The dissident employees, led by Xavier Chamorro Cardenal, a brother of the late publisher, quit and founded their own paper, Nuevo Diario" (*NYT*, Oct. 2, 1987). Omitted is the fact that Xavier Chamorro was the editor and that the "dissident employees" constituted 80 percent of the staff.

52. Chamorro, *WP*, April 3, 1986; Nichols, *op. cit.*; see appendix V, section 6.

53. For comparison of Nicaraguan practices with those of the U.S. and Israel, see references of chapter 4, note 3.

54. AP, Dec. 22, 1987; Cal Thomas, *BG*, Jan. 3, 1988.

55. *Al-Hamishmar*, July 25, Aug. 13; *Jerusalem Post*, Aug. 12, 24; *Al-Hamishmar*, July 25, Aug. 13, 1986.

56. *Yediot Ahronot*, Aug. 16, 1987, translated in *The Other Israel* (Israeli Council for Israeli-Palestinian Peace), Sept. 1987; *Ha'aretz*, Jan 1, 1988; AP, Oct. 25, 26. On the state of emergency, see Avigdor Feldman, B. Michael, *Hadashot*, Aug. 14, 1987.

57. *NYT*, Oct. 26, 1987.

58. Simon Edge, *Middle East International*, Jan. 20, 1989.

59. The plea that we did not know is valid for passive consumers who believe that the media present the world as it actually is. It is not valid for those who have any familiarity with the ideological institutions or participate in them, and who therefore must surely be aware that it takes effort and enterprise to find important and unwelcome facts.

60. Leah Enbal, *Koteret Rashit*, June 8, 1988, also citing a series of recent cases of state repression of Israeli Jews. Moshe Negbi, *Politika*, Sept. 1986; "Press in Chains," *Shomer Hanitzotz*, May 1988 (published in protest over the suppression of the Hebrew newspaper *Derech Hanitzotz* and the arrest of its editors); "Paper Tiger: The Struggle for Press Freedom in Israel," *Jerusalem Quarterly*, #39, 1986. *Ha'aretz*, September 29, 1986.

61. *Fateful Triangle*, 139.

62. Avigdor Feldman, *Hadashot*, Nov. 18, 1988. See appendix V, section 7, for further comments.

63. Rosenthal, *NYT*, May 27, 1988.

64. For example, Dan Fisher, *Los Angeles Times*, Oct. 5, 1985.

65. Jo Ann Boydston, ed., *John Dewey: The Later Works*, vol. II, from *Common Sense*, Nov. 1935.

66. See appendix V, section 8.

67. Quoted by Hill, *The World Turned Upside Down*, 72.

68. *Ibid.*, 385, 353.

69. See Mark Hollingsworth, *The Press and Political Dissent* (Pluto, London, 1986), for which Mill's statement serves as epigraph.

70. Barron, "Access to the Press," 1656.

71. *St. Louis Post-Dispatch*, Aug. 24, 1967, cited by Jerome A. Barron, "An Emerging First Amendment Right of Access to the Media?," *George Washington Law Review* (March 1969), 498. See Aronson, *The Press and the Cold War*, 273-74, for discussion.

72. See *Towards a New Cold War*, 36-37, 228, for further detail and some very marginal exceptions.

73. Dianna Melrose, *Nicaragua: The Threat of a Good Example?* (Oxfam, London, 1985).

74. *NYT*, Dec. 29, 1987.

75. Thomas Friedman, *NYT*, Oct. 16; photo, p. 1. AP, Oct. 15, 1986.

Appendix I

1. Addendum to p. 9.

2. See the references of chapter 1, note 23, for extensive discussion of cases cited here without specific reference.

3. See the review of media coverage of Cuba in 1986 in Platt, *Tropical Gulag* (chapter 1, note 30, above). Quotes are from *WP*, Stephen Rosenfeld (July 18), Stephen Cohen (July 26), Charles Krauthammer (Dec. 14); *NYT*, Ronald Radosh, June 8; *Time*, June 30; *Miami Herald*, "President hails Valladares, raps Cuba on prisons," Dec. 11, 1986. The study reports that the national press accepted Valladares's charges without qualification or attempt at verification and ignored entirely the Cuban government version of the story and the documentation offered to support it, with one exception (Tad Szulc, *WP*, Aug. 4, 1986, who briefly notes that the book had "inaccuracies" and that "Cuban officials portray [Valladares] as unreliable and unsavory"). They found "professional coverage of the issue" with "lengthy columns pro [R. Emmett Tyrell] and con [Warren Hinckle] Valladares" only in the *San Francisco Examiner* (July 29, 1986).

4. See pp. 228f. The sole exception to suppression of the CDHES study, apart from Alexander Cockburn in the *Nation*, was, again, the *San Francisco Examiner*. See CDHES, "Torture in El Salvador," Sept. 24, 1986; and for further details, *Culture of Terrorism*, 227f.

5. See p. 12-13; Mona Charen, "A double standard on human rights," *Boston Globe*, Jan. 2, 1989.

6. For detailed examination by the former method, see *Manufacturing Consent*, chapter 3; also Spence, *op. cit.*. On the second method, see the references of notes 7, 8, below.

7. On popular support for the opposition parties even after years of war and suffering, see appendix IV, section 5.

8. Alfonso Chardy, *Miami Herald*, July 19, 1987, citing "an intelligence source familiar with North's relationship with" the Office of Latin American Public Diplomacy, the main propaganda agency of the Reagan administration, later more fully exposed. For further comment, see *Manufacturing Consent*, 137f. See also Walter LaFeber's review of the book, *NYT Weekly Book Review*, Nov. 6, 1988, and an exchange of letters with Edward Herman, Dec. 11. LaFeber describes the later phase of the disinformation effort as a "key exception" to the propaganda model; as just discussed, it fits the model closely. He notes that a later *Newsweek* article (Nov. 26) "did question the MIG mirage"—well after it was agreed, from top government on down, that there were no MiGs. That the media questioned what was openly conceded by the government to be false is not a very persuasive demonstration of their independence from power.

9. *NYT*, Dec. 27, 1985.

10. See a forthcoming study by Dennis Driscoll, Faculty of Law, University College, Galway, Ireland, for comparative analysis of the U.S. and foreign media in this and other critical cases.

11. Jennifer G. Schirmer, "What You See Is What You Get: Comparing Realities of the U.S. and European Press Coverage of the 1982 and 1984 Elections in El Salvador," forthcoming in *Creating Reality: Media Coverage of International Affairs*, based on Summer Seminar presentations at Center for International Affairs, Harvard (CFIA Publishers, Cambridge Mass., 1989), directed by Dennis Driscoll.

12. See *For Reasons of State*, 232-23; *Manufacturing Consent*, 181.

13. *Ibid.*, 177, 191.

14. Bill Keller, *NYT*, Jan. 21, 1988; Paul Quinn-Judge, *Christian Science Monitor*, July 21, 1987; *Extra!*, monthly of FAIR, December 1987, for Sakharov letter. Danchev, see the excerpts from "Manufacture of Consent" in Peck, *Chomsky Reader*, 223f.

15. See *Manufacturing Consent*, chapters 5 and 6 and appendix III.

16. *NYT*, April 30, 1987.

17. Lemann, *New Republic*, Jan. 9, 1989; see chapter 1, note 32. Michael Pollan, *NYT Book Review*, April 6, 1986, reviewing Parenti, *Inventing Reality*.

18. I mention merely one, because Lemann gives it as the clinching evidence of our lack of "commitment to truth": "Herman and Chomsky say that 'principled and courageous resistance' was a more common response of draft-age Americans to Vietnam than the seeking of deferments." The quoted

phrase can be found on page 252, in the course of our discussion of how the PBS series on the Vietnam war gave "short shrift" to the peace movement. As one example, we noted that the search for deferments "hardly defined 'the spirit of the times'" as the series claimed (interviewing Lemann's colleague James Fallows), "although it is a facet of this 'spirit' that is far more acceptable to mainstream opinion than the principled and courageous resistance of many thousands of young people." Lemann's falsification of this accurate statement merely shows that he falls within the mainstream, as there described, putting aside the matter of "commitment to truth."

19. Letters, *The New Republic*, March 6, 1989. Romero was murdered on March 24, 1980; Popieluszko was abducted on October 20, 1984, then murdered. One natural comparison, then, is the columns of the *New York Times* index for El Salvador in 1980 and for Poland from August 1984 through July 1985 (the comparable period), obviously excluding the coverage of these incidents themselves. Coverage of El Salvador is slightly higher by this measure.

20. The few studies that do exist confirm the conclusion. See *Manufacturing Consent* on studies of the impact of the media, primarily television, in mobilizing support for the Vietnam war, including the self-refuting study published by Freedom House on coverage of the Tet offensive.

21. Cases offered are often quite absurd (see the next section for some examples), but real ones can be found. See my *Fateful Triangle*, 371, on major slaughters that were suppressed while the media briefly focused attention on the Sabra-Shatila massacres, before adopting the conclusions of the Israeli government's Kahan investigating commission. This selective focus does merit the charge of hypocrisy leveled by the Israeli government and its apologists, as discussed in *Fateful Triangle*. The Kahan Commission report was a shameful whitewash; see *Fateful Triangle*, chapter 6, and Shimon Lehrer, *Ha'ikar Hehaser* ("The Missing Crucial-Point"; Amit, Jerusalem, 1983). In a close critical analysis of the events and the Kahan Commission report, Lehrer shows that its conclusions were untenable and argues that the Defense Minister and Chief of Staff should have faced 20-year jail sentences for premeditated murder under Israeli law. While sharply criticized in Israel, in the U.S. the Kahan Commission report was depicted, without analysis, as most impressive or even approaching the sublime.

22. It would be interesting, for example, to compare the coverage of the Israeli elections with that of the Canadian elections at the same time, a neighboring country voting on an issue quite significant for U.S. business interests, the "free trade" agreements.

23. See *Manufacturing Consent*, chapter 1, for discussion of some others.

24. In fact, an early 1974 version of this study was suppressed by the conglomerate that owned the publisher, which even went to the extent of putting the publisher out of business to prevent distribution; see the prefatory note to the 1979 published version of *Political Economy of Human Rights* for details. The matter was brought to the attention of some noted civil libertar-

ians, but they found it of no interest, presumably, because no state censorship was involved, only corporate censorship that is considered legitimate on the assumption that the distribution of power in the civil society is legitimate.

25. Recall that the book went to press immediately after the Vietnamese invasion that overthrew Pol Pot, just before a flood of refugee testimony became available. At the time we wrote, virtually all evidence had to do with the years 1975-77, and almost nothing was known about the 1978 massacres in the Eastern Zone, by far the most extensive of the Pol Pot period, according to the current scholarly literature. See Michael Vickery, *Cambodia* (South End, 1983), the most detailed scholarly source, widely and favorably reviewed in England by Indochina scholars and journalists, virtually ignored in the United States. On other studies, see my review in *Inside Asia*, reprinted in *The Chomsky Reader*, 289f. As Vickery observes, the great mass of evidence that subsequently appeared, while enriching understanding of the period, suggests no significant revision of what we published in 1979. Although the parallels between Timor and Cambodia, and the assessments by relief officials, other observers, and area specialists, were widely recognized by the early 1980s, it is unlikely that these facts will be permitted to survive the historical engineering of the future.

26. In fact, this was only one false claim. Lacouture's article was presented as a review of François Ponchaud's *Cambodge année zéro*, but there was barely a reference to the book that was near accurate. In a sequel that far transcends the predictions of a propaganda model, Lacouture's false claims were widely quoted as established truth long after his retraction appeared. See *Political Economy of Human Rights* for details on these revealing facts.

27. I stress: *under the Khmer Rouge*. Atrocities in the first half of the decade for which the U.S. bore primary responsibility were very much downplayed, and still are. See *Manufacturing Consent*, chapter 6, for details.

28. *Ibid.*, for discussion.

29. There are actually two such discussions, a lengthy one in *Political Economy of Human Rights*, volume II, and a a 1977 review-article in the *Nation* that briefly raised similar points.

30. See Vickery, *op. cit.*, 308, 310.

31. For examples of both absurdity and lies, see the *Political Economy of Human Rights*, vol II, chapter six, and *Manufacturing Consent*, chapter six, section 6.2.8; also appendix V, section 5, below. For an example of a weird array of inventions and falsehoods in what some regard as "scholarship," see Leo Labedz, "Chomsky Revisited," *Encounter*, July 1980; the article is also notable for its apologetics for the Western-backed atrocities in Timor. That the lies were conscious in this case is indicated by the fact that the journal refused to permit a response that exposed the falsifications point by point, so that the article can therefore be quoted, reprinted with acclaim, etc. It is standard for dissidents to be denied the right of response to personal attacks, and it is

reasonable to suppose that in such cases the journal recognizes the need for protection of fabrications that would be all too readily exposed if response were not barred.

32. *NYT Book Review,* Dec. 27, 1970.

33. For some examples, see Russell, *War Crimes in Vietnam* (Monthly Review, 1967); Barry Feinberg & Ronald Kasrils, *Bertrand Russell's America: 1945-1970* (South End, 1983). The books also contain material on the hysterical abuse elicited by his exposure of unwelcome truths, for which he was never forgiven by the commissars.

34. Addendum to p. 12.

35. For completeness, we may also find those who explain why the media err in their defiance of authority, thus reinforcing the required premise by tacit assumption.

36. Landrum R. Bolling, ed., *Reporters Under Fire: U.S. Media Coverage of Conflicts in Lebanon and Central America* (Westview, 1985).

37. These are mostly excerpts, though a few are given in full.

38. One might, for example, test Bolling's judgments in the Third World countries that regard Cuba as "an international superpower" because of the teachers, construction workers, physicians, and others involved in "international service" (Michael Stuehrenberg, *Die Zeit* (West Germany), *World Press Review,* Dec. 1988.) In 1985, he reports, 16,000 Cubans worked in Third World countries, more than twice the total of Peace Corps and AID specialists from the United States; "Today, Cuba has more physicians working abroad than any industrialized nation, and more than the UN's World Health Organization." Most of this aid is uncompensated, and Cuba's "international emissaries" are "men and women who live under conditions that most development aid workers would not accept," which is "the basis for their success." For Cubans, he continues, "international service" is regarded as "a sign of political maturity" and taught in the schools as "the highest virtue."

39. On these matters, see *Manufacturing Consent,* chapters 5, 6.

40. Some have been misled by the fact that one journal, the *New York Review of Books,* was open to dissident opinion during the peak years of popular protest. Those doors closed in the early 1970s, however, and there were few other examples.

41. For an account of some of its exploits, see Robert I. Friedman, "Selling Israel to America: the Hasbara Project Targets the U.S. Media," *Mother Jones,* Feb./March 1987.

42. See Edward S. Herman and Frank Brodhead, *The Rise and Fall of the Bulgarian Connection* (Sheridan Square Publications, 1986); *Manufacturing Consent,* chapter 4.

43. See, *inter alia,* my *Fateful Triangle* and the references of chapter 3, note 23.

44. In my *Pirates & Emperors*, chapter 2, note 26, I stated erroneously that the ADC document was not included. Much of the same material appears, with the same error, in my chapter in Edward Said and Christopher Hitchens, eds., *Blaming the Victims* (Verso, 1988).

45. This citation is excluded from the excerpt that appears in *Reporters under Fire*. For a detailed analysis of the ADL report, see *Fateful Triangle*, 284f.

46. Reuven Padhatzur, *Ha'aretz*, Nov. 14, 1983; Ya'acov Friedler, *Jerusalem Post*, Feb. 24, 1984; Drew Middleton, *NYT*, Feb. 26, 1984.

47. See appendix V, section 4, for some further comment.

48. See *Fateful Triangle*, 221f.

49. *Ibid.*, 184f., and sources cited.

50. Naomi Joy Weinberger, *Syrian Intervention in Lebanon* (Oxford, 1986, 179); Dov Yermiya, *My War Diary* (South End, 1983, 62) (translated from the Hebrew original); Laqueur, *The Age of Terrorism* (Little, Brown and Co., 1987, 218); Silver, *Manchester Guardian Weekly*, Oct. 3, 1982; Schiff and Ya'ari, *Israel's Lebanon War* (Simon and Schuster, 1984, 87). On Laqueur's treatise, see appendix V, section 3.

51. Rabinovich, *The War in Lebanon* (Cornell, 1984, 57). He is referring to the 1975-76 period, when the overwhelming majority of casualties occurred.

52. *Fateful Triangle*, 188f.

53. *Ibid.*, 243f., for a sample, partly from the Lebanese press. I know of no other.

54. For reference to a few examples from the *Los Angeles Times*, *Christian Science Monitor*, and *Washington Post*, see the reprinted comments by *Post* Ombudsman Robert McCloskey, who, however, feels that the *Post* report was belated. Also David Shipler, *NYT*, July 25, 1982.

55. Mansour, *Ha'aretz*, July 27, 1982. See also Benny Morris and David Bernstein, *Jerusalem Post*, July 23, 1982. Both reviewed in *Fateful Triangle*, 186f., among other sources. See Shipler, *op. cit.*, during the same days, for a report of a very different kind in the U.S. press, focusing on PLO repression.

56. Porath, *Ha'aretz*, June 25, 1982; Yaniv, *Dilemmas of Security* (Oxford, 1987, 52-3, 67ff., 100-101). Harkabi, *Israel's Fateful Hour*, 100-1. Eitan, quoted by Rafi Ga'on, *Ha'aretz*, Dec. 27, 1983. Eitan also dismisses the protests by Yesh Gvul and others, asking where they were when Israel spent 6 years at the Suez canal, where "we destroyed three of their cities (Suez, Ismailia, Port Said), carried out deep-penetration bombing, killed civilians, and even shot down a civilian Libyan plane that wandered off course and all its passengers were killed." On the background of Israeli provocations leading to the 1982 invasion of Lebanon, see *Fateful Triangle* and Schiff and Ya'ari, *Israel's Lebanon War*.

57. See *Fateful Triangle* for some discussion of the former.

58. Information here is from the *Times* Database.

59. *NYT*, March 29, 1983.

60. Council on Hemispheric Affairs, *Washington Report on the Hemisphere*, Nov. 23, 1988; the context is Washington's refusal to provide assistance to Nicaragua after the devastating hurricane of October 1988.

61. Center for Cuban Studies, New York, Oct. 28, 1983.

62. Knight-Ridder Service, *BG*, Oct. 27; *WP*, Oct. 27; *NYT*, *BG*, Nov. 20. Also *Latin America Regional Reports Caribbean*, Nov. 4, 1983; Michael Massing, *Atlantic Monthly*, Feb. 1884, two sentences on an inside page.

63. Thomas, *NYT*, Nov. 1; editorial, *NYT*, Nov. 10, 1983.

Appendix II

1. Addendum to p. 25.

2. John Lewis Gaddis, *Strategies of Containment* (New York, 1982, viiin), his emphasis; *The Long Peace*, 43.

3. Wm. Roger Lewis, *Imperialism at Bay: the United States and the Decolonization of the British Empire, 1941-1945* (Oxford, 1978, 481). On Grand Area planning, see Shoup and Minter, *Imperial Brain Trust*. For remarks on this and competing models, and applications in the Far East, see Bruce Cumings, introduction, in Cumings, ed., *Child of Conflict* (Washington, 1983).

4. Lewis, *op. cit.*, 550; Christopher Thorne, *The Issue of War* (Oxford, 1985, 225, 211).

5. Gaddis, *The Long Peace*, 10-11, 21; Andy Thomas, *Effects of Chemical Warfare* (SIPRI, Taylor & Francis, 1985, 33f.), reviewing newly released British state archives.

6. Gaddis, *The Long Peace*, 37, 11.

7. In earlier years, military spending was selected as the major device to overcome the "dollar gap" of the U.S. allies and to ensure that they would remain securely within the U.S.-dominated world system, after the failure of aid programs to achieve their ends. See Borden, *Pacific Alliance*, for extensive discussion of these themes, which were given their first comprehensive analysis by Joyce and Gabriel Kolko, *The Limits of Power* (Harper & Row, 1972).

8. A closer examination shows that the figures were misrepresented to exaggerate the impression of Soviet military expenditures and Western weakness, also a familiar pattern over the years.

9. Kennedy, "Tremors that should be felt in Washington," *Christian Science Monitor*, Dec. 28, 1988.

10. *Strategies of Containment*, 356-57, his emphasis.

11. Addendum to p. 29.

12. See Murray B. Levin, *Political Hysteria in America* (Basic Books, 1972); Richard G. Powers, *Secrecy and Power* (Free Press, 1987); Aronson, *The Press and the Cold War*.

13. David Brion Davis, ed., *The Fear of Conspiracy* (Cornell University Press, 1971). A fifth anarchist committed suicide before the sentence of death could be executed. Three others were sentenced to hanging as well, but were not executed. No proof was offered that any of the eight had been involved in the bomb-throwing. On "moral responsibility," see the excerpt from Michael J. Schaack, *Anarchy and Anarchists* (Chicago, 1889), in Davis's collection. A Chicago police captain, Schaack "was widely credited with having uncovered the anarchist conspiracy" (Davis).

14. See excerpts from Palmer in Davis, *op. cit.* On the role of the press, see Levin, *op. cit.*

15. Powers, Aronson, *op. cit.*

16. Davis, Powers, *op. cit.*

17. Robert J. Goldstein, *Political Repression in Modern America* (Schenkman, 1978).

18. Levin, *op. cit.*

19. Dulles, *The Road to Teheran* (Princeton, 1945), cited by Levin, *op. cit*; Gaddis, *The Long Peace*, 37.

20. On the continuing FBI policies of subversion and repression, often they were allegedly terminated, see Ward Churchill and James Vander Wall *Agents of Repression* (South End, 1988) and *Cointelpro Papers* (South End, 1989).

21. The bombing of Cambodia did enter the proceedings, though not the final indictment, but in a specific form: not the murder of tens of thousands of people and the destruction of rural Cambodia, but the failure to notify Congress properly. Again, the prerogatives of the powerful are the criterion.

Appendix III

1. Addendum to p. 52.

2. Editorial, *Globe and Mail*, March 18, 1988.

3. AP, March 17; Alan Cowell, Jerusalem, *NYT*, March 18; UPI, *Boston Globe*, March 20; *NYT*, March 24; *NYT*, March 25; AP, March 24; *NYT*, March 31, 1988.

4. UPI, *BG*, March 24; AP, March 24; UPI, *BG*, March 31, 1988.

5. AP, *BG*, Oct. 22, 1988 (my emphasis); *NYT*, same day.

6. AP, *BG*, Oct. 27; *NYT*, Oct. 27, Nov. 2, Nov. 7; AP, Nov. 22, 25, 1988.

7. AP, *NYT*, Jan. 12, 1989, a brief note reporting new raids "aimed at pre-empting attacks on Israel," the army said.

8. AP, Feb. 1, 5; Julie Flint, *Guardian* (London), Jan. 26, Feb. 9; Jim Muir, *Christian Science Monitor*, Feb. 9, 1989.

Appendix IV

1. Addendum to p. 80.

2. AP, *NYT*, Jan. 5; Stephen Kinzer, *NYT*, Jan. 6; AP, *BG*, Jan. 8; editorial, *NYT*, Jan. 8; Bernard Weinraub, *NYT*, Jan. 15; Abrams, Op-Ed, *NYT*, Jan. 15; David Shipler, *NYT*, Feb. 26, 1986.

3. Beecher, "Pressuring Nicaragua," Jan. 17, 1986.

4. Hamilton, ms., 1987.

5. For extensive documentation on how charges known to be false are maintained for propaganda purposes, and the interesting reaction to the exposure of these facts, see references cited in appendix I, section 1.

6. *NYT*, Aug. 13, 1987.

7. For a detailed review of the major State Department allegations, see Morley and Petras, *The Reagan Administration and Nicaragua*.

8. *Extra!*, Oct.-Nov. 1987. In a letter of March 11, 1988, Lelyveld informed FAIR that he had instructed LeMoyne "to devote an entire article to what the current evidence shows on this point" (*Extra!*, Sept./Oct. 1988, pointing out that "six months later, no such article has appeared"). See below.

9. Humberto Ortega, FBIS-LAT-87-239, Dec. 14, 1987; LeMoyne, Dec. 20, 1987.

10. *NYT*, Dec. 18, 1987.

11. *NYT*, Jan. 18, 1988.

12. J. D. Gannon, *Christian Science Monitor*, Aug. 26, 1988.

13. *NYT*, Feb. 7, July 4, 1988; my emphasis.

14. Trainor, *NYT*, April 3, 1988; Rivera y Damas, Oct. 26, 1980, cited by Bonner, *Weakness and Deceit*, 207.

15. "Salvador Rebels: Where Do They Get the Arms?", *NYT*, Nov. 24, 1988. Whether by accident or not, this article appeared a month after FAIR had made public the failure of the *Times* to deal with the issue despite the promise of the foreign editor; see note 8.

16. See my introduction to Morley and Petras, *Reagan Administration and Nicaragua*.

17. Others too have put the doctrine aside. *Newsweek* Central America correspondent Charles Lane writes in the *Wall Street Journal* (always irate about Sandinista attempts to overthrow the government of El Salvador and others) that the Salvadoran guerrillas "capture or make most of their own weapons." Still, history has passed them by, he writes, in part because of the "disillusioning Sandinista experiment," a "once-promising revolution" (we now

read) that "turned into an embarrassing Cuban-style economic basket case [for unstated reasons] and a U.S.-Soviet battleground" (*WSJ*, Dec. 23, 1988).

18. On the Miranda testimony and the media-State Department version of it, see my article in *Z Magazine*, March 1988; Sklar, *Washington's War on Nicaragua*, 383f.

19. Marcio Vargas, Mexico City, interview with Arce, *Central America Information Bulletin*, Dec. 21, 1988; Rubén Montedonico, *El Día* (Mexico City), Nov. 6, 7, 1988, reprinted in translation in *Honduras Update*, Nov./Dec., 1988. On Lau, see *Turning the Tide*, 104.

20. Addendum to p. 81.

21. For discussion of one example, see my review of Saul Bellow's *To Jerusalem and Back*, reprinted in *Towards a New Cold War*, a review that aroused such anger that it caused the suspension of the journal in which it originally appeared, so I was informed. For many more examples, see other chapters in the same book, my *Peace in the Middle East?* (Pantheon, 1974, chapter 5), and *Fateful Triangle*.

22. See appendix V, section 4.

23. "Statement by the AFL-CIO Executive Council on Israel, Feb. 16, 1988.

24. Wiesel, Op-Ed, *NYT*, June 23; Reuven Padhatzur, *Ha'aretz*, May 16, 1988. On Wiesel's long-held doctrine that it is obligatory to maintain silence in the face of atrocities of the state one loves, and that only those in power are in a position to know so that he must refrain from comment on atrocities, see *Fateful Triangle* and *Turning the Tide*. For his reiteration of the obligation of silence at the peak of the recent repression, see his article in *Yediot Ahronot*, Jan. 22, 1988, where he explains: "I refuse to criticize Israel, I have always refused to do this," among other similar sentiments, familiar from apologists for other states in earlier days. It would be unfair, however, to note Wiesel's practice without reference to those who now condemn him for his silence while effacing their own much worse record over many years. On the unacceptable facts, see the references of note 21. Wiesel, at least, had the integrity to adhere to his long-held position when it became unpopular.

25. Ze'ev Sachor, "Getting Accustomed to Atrocities," April 1, 1988, *Hotam*, one of many items translated from the Israeli press in the 1988 *Report* of the Israeli League for Human Rights, Tel Aviv, which give the flavor of the pogroms organized by the Defense Ministry to teach the beasts of burden a lesson. This highly informative material is next to unknown in the United States, though it is arguably of some relevance to those who are expected to pay the bills.

26. *Ha'aretz*, July 15, 4; *Jerusalem Post*, July 6; Ya'akov Lazar, *Hotam*, July 15, reporting from Jabaliya; William Montalbano, *Los Angeles Times*, May 31, 1988, AP, May 30, on Dahariya, one of the atrocities reported by Dedi Zucker based on testimony by reservists, *Yediot Ahronot*, June 10; *Yerushalayim*, June 17, on Jericho; *JP*, June 24, 22, citing charges by Knesset member Ran Cohen;

JP, Aug. 3, 1988, on the release of Mohammed Dari after three months in prison. For extensive documentation, see *Punishing a Nation: Human Rights Violations During the Palestinian Uprising, December 1987 December 1988* (Al Haq—Law in the Service of Man, Ramallah, December 1988).

27. Yizhar Be'er, *Kol Ha'ir*, Aug. 26, 1988; Joshua Brilliant, *JP*, Aug. 26, 1988.

28. Eitan Rabin, *Ha'aretz*, Sept. 23, 1988.

29. Shimon Elkavetz, *Hadashot*, Sept. 28; Tali Zelinger, *Jerusalem Post*, Sept. 29, 1988.

30. *JP*, Nov. 17; *Ha'aretz*, Dec. 2, Nov. 15, 16; Yariv, *Yediot Ahronot*, Nov. 18, 1988. Michal Sela, *JP*, Jan. 26, Feb. 3; *JP*, Feb. 10, 1989. See also Glenn Frankel, *WP*, Feb. 12; George Moffett, *CSM*, Feb. 15, 1989.

31. Reuven Padhatzur, *Ha'aretz*, Nov. 30, 1988. See also Eitan Rabin, *Ha'aretz Supplement*, Dec. 2, 1988, making the same points.

32. *Hadaf Hayarok*, supplement to *Al Hamishmar*, Aug. 23, 1988.

33. Almagor, *Ha'ir*, Dec. 16, 1988; *NYT*, March 18, 1968.

34. Gilat, *Hadashot*, Dec. 16; Gissen, Joel Brinkley, *NYT*, April 28; AP, *NYT*, Dec. 15; special, *NYT*, Dec. 5, 1988. Eiran Taus, *Al-Hamishmar*, Nov. 19; Judith Green, *News from Within*, Dec. 14, 1988. Green, a Jerusalem architect working with the "Beita Committee" that hopes to reconstruct the houses destroyed by the army, visited the village with a member of the U.S. consulate on the day when the child was killed, and reported this story as well as the destruction caused by rampaging soldiers in a village that was quiet, with almost no villagers on the streets when the soldiers entered with riot control equipment. See my article in *Z Magazine*, July 1988, for more on the background, based in part on a personal visit a week after the incident with the hikers in April, while the village was still under military siege.

35. Gad Lior, *Yediot Ahronot*, July 10, 1988.

36. For a few references to current discussion on transfer, see my article in *Z Magazine*, May 1988. Poll, *Ha'aretz*, June 8, 1988; the poll, excluding settlers and kibbutz members, found 41 percent in favor. A poll taken shortly after found 49 percent favoring "transfer" of Arabs from the occupied territories; *JP*, Aug. 12, 1988. Rav Kook, quoted by Eyal Kafkafi, *Davar*, Sept. 26, 1988. See Yehoshafat Harkabi, *Israel's Fateful Hour* (Harper & Row, 1988), the first readily available source to deal with these important matters.

37. Michael Walzer, "Nationalism, internationalism, and the Jews," in Irving Howe and Carl Gershman, eds., *Israel, the Arabs and the Middle East* (Bantam, 1972); Cockburn, *Nation*, Nov. 21, 1988.

38. Addendum to p. 84.

39. *Extra!*, Dec. 1987.

40. CBS News, 6:30 P.M., Dec. 7, 1987. The phrase in quotes is either an exact quote or a very close paraphrase; I do not have the transcript available.

41. Many did, however; see chapter 2.

42. *NYT*, Dec. 4, 1987.

43. Steven Roberts, *NYT*, May 31; editorial, *NYT*, June 1.

44. Alexander Cockburn, *Nation*, June 18, 1988.

45. Editorial, *Globe and Mail*, June 10, 1988; James LeMoyne, *New York Times Magazine*, June 5, 1988. With regard to Father Carney, LeMoyne notes only the report that he was executed. On the follow-up to LeMoyne's account of torture, see appendix V, section 6.

46. *New Statesman*, June 3, 10, 1988. For some exceptions, see a forthright editorial in the *Boston Globe*, June 1, and Michael Parks, *Los Angeles Times*, May 28, 1988.

47. Addendum to p. 89.

48. *American-Arab Affairs*, Winter 1987-88.

49. Paul Lewis, *NYT*, Nov. 4, 1988.

50. "The U.N. versus the U.S.," *NYT Magazine*, Jan. 22, 1984.

51. Shirley Hazzard, *Defeat of an Ideal* (Atlantic Monthly Press, Little, Brown, 1973, 201). The only exceptions, she notes, were a Lao government initiative of 1959 and the Tonkin Gulf incident of 1964, when Adlai Stevenson falsely claimed that the alleged attacks on U.S. naval vessels were "a calculated, a deliberate act of military aggression against the United States."

52. *Times Literary Supplement* (London), Sept. 17, 1982.

53. *Defeat of an Ideal*, 9, 14ff., 60f., 65, 71.

54. Here named "General Ortega," in a slip of the pen; David Johnston, *NYT*, June 25, 1988. Lindsey Gruson, *NYT*, Nov. 14, 1988.

55. Paul Lewis, *NYT*, Oct. 16, 1987; AP, Feb. 28, 1988.

56. AP, March 22; *Christian Science Monitor*, March 25, 43 words; Treaster, *NYT*, March 27, 1988. See also Mary McGrory, *Boston Globe*, March 23, noting that Honduras refused to admit a U.N. observer team.

57. Addendum to p. 90.

58. For discussion of how the problem was addressed in the case of Indochina from 1950 until today, see *Manufacturing Consent*, chapters 5, 6. On similar problems with regard to the Arab-Israeli conflict, see appendix V, section 4.

59. *New Republic*, Aug. 29, 1988; my emphasis. Christian, regarded as a specialist on Nicaragua, goes on to argue that the contras are a typical Latin American guerrilla movement, "largely a Central American creation," since "aside from a few individual Americans with nebulous government ties the key players were the Argentine colonels" (transmuted into Central Americans), the Honduran military chief Gustavo Alvarez, a noted killer, "and an assortment of former Nicaraguan National Guardsmen." Plainly, "the classic pattern of guerrilla armies in Latin America," even putting aside a few

notable omissions. She does not elaborate on the significance of this interesting collection of "key players." Such contributions are apparently taken seriously.

60. Michael Allen, *Wall Street Journal*, Aug. 10; *Central America Report* (Guatemala City), Aug. 14, 1987. See *Culture of Terrorism*, 141f., 18-19, on the events and the media reaction.

61. Here and below, I will use the Guatemalan version of the English translation; Special Document, Esquipulas II Accord, *Central America Report*, August 14, 1987.

62. LeMoyne, *NYT*, Aug. 6, 7. On the actual reaction of Presidents Cerezo and Arias, see *Central America Report*, Aug. 14. See *Culture of Terrorism*, 141f., for further details.

63. Rosenthal, *NYT*, Aug. 21, 1987.

64. Brian Barger, UPI, *Philadelphia Inquirer*, Oct. 22, 1987; *Excelsior* (Mexico City), Oct. 22, 1987. On the supply flights and other matters, see the footnoted versions of my articles in *Z Magazine*, January, March, 1988.

65. For some exceptions, see chapter 4, notes 34, 37.

66. Note that this review is based on the library edition of the *Times*. The earlier (Boston) edition sometimes differs. Thus in the last paragraph (par. 25) of an October 24 story on contra attacks, omitted in the library edition, Kinzer mentions that the contras are using Redeye missiles and other supplies provided by "clandestine" CIA flights from Honduras, which Nicaragua cannot intercept without jet fighters.

67. In a December 6 interview with a contra commander, Kinzer quotes him as saying that the contras cannot supply themselves within Nicaragua (the sharp contrast with El Salvador is unmentioned, following standard convention), and have received, intact, 52 CIA supply drops. In a report the following day, he cites a Nicaraguan government report of 82 supply flights and 21 surveillance missions from November 5 to December 5. A January 25 story notes that "clandestine night supply flights into Nicaragua are a vital lifeline for the contras," citing an American official who says that there were more than 350 such flights in 1987. A brief AP report on October 30, 1987, notes the crash of a contra supply plane in Honduras.

68. Neil Lewis, *NYT*, Nov. 12, 1987. Others stated the facts correctly. See references cited in note 64.

69. U.N. General Assembly, A/42/PV.67, Nov. 16, 1987. On the reporting of this U.N. session, see chapter 4.

70. Stephen Kinzer, *NYT*, Oct. 15, 1987. He claims that President Arias "said Honduras could not be expected to close contra camps and ban clandestine supply flights if the Sandinistas do not negotiate a cease-fire with the contras and issue a broad amnesty." The Esquipulas Accord set no such condition on cessation of contra aid. Neither Arias nor anyone else has held that foreign

aid to the guerrillas in El Salvador and Guatemala is legitimate until the governments negotiate a cease-fire with these indigenous forces or live up to the terms of the accords. If Kinzer's statement is correct, it follows that Arias too was committed to the failure of the accords that are mislabeled "the Arias plan." There are repeated references in the *Times* to alleged positions of Arias which lead to the same conclusion, but it is difficult to know how much is accurate, how much wishful thinking. For more on Arias's role and the reason for his relative acceptability in the United States, see my article in *Z Magazine*, November 1988. For comment on his "shocking record" in "only superficially promoting his own plan" while responding to pressures from Washington and the powerful right-wing elements within Costa Rica, see Council on Hemispheric Affairs, "News and Analysis," Feb. 10, 1989.

71. Questions also arise about Costa Rica, generally regarded as exempt from the accords. Thus the Spanish-language press is firmly under right-wing control, barring access of "all ideological groups," among other questions that would arise if Costa Rican affairs were reported. See appendix V, section 6. Also, *Culture of Terrorism*, 243, for one critical case.

72. COHA, *Washington Report on the Hemisphere*, Feb. 3, 1988; *Update*, Central American Historical Institute, Dec. 28, 1987; *Cultural Survival*, vol. 12, no. 3, 1988.

73. Jonas, *San Francisco Bay Guardian*; Cockburn, *Anderson Valley Advertiser*; both June 8, 1988.

74. Human Rights Watch (Americas Watch/Asia Watch/Helsinki Watch) and Lawyers Committee for Human Rights, *Critique: Review of the Department of State's Country Reports on Human Rights Practices for 1987*, June 1988. The review particularly condemns the State Department reports on the Central American countries, and their denigration and misrepresentation of the work of the "highly respected" Tutela Legal. These have been regular features of State Department productions.

75. COHA *Washington Report on the Hemisphere*, Feb. 17, 1988; *Latinamerica press* (Peru), Nov. 19, 1987.

76. See my article in *Z Magazine*, March 1988, for further details; U.N. testimony, *La Voz*, CDHES, March 24, 1988.

77. AP, Nov. 15, 1987; the Archbishop also noted other death squad killings. On February 20, the *Times* ran a brief AP report noting that the Archbishop attributed the murder to death squads and that the alleged killer retracted his confession.

78. LeMoyne, *NYT*, Nov. 29, 1987; COHA *Washington Report on the Hemisphere*, Feb. 17, 1988. Access to radio and TV later became much more free, but to speak of "free access to the press" in November 1987 was outlandish, and there has never been anything corresponding to the U.S.-funded pro-contra journal *La Prensa*. On the media in Central America, see appendix V, section 6.

79. *NYT*, Nov. 29, 1987; June 5, Feb. 22, 1988.

80. See appendix V, section 6.

81. *Ibid*. On Chamorro's return, see COHA, *News and Analysis*, Feb. 20, 1988.

82. See *Turning the Tide*, 109-10.

83. *El Sol* (*El Salvador On Line*, Center for Central American Studies, Washington), Aug. 29, 1988; Sam Dillon, "El Salvador's Violent Past Returns in Poverty, Death," *Miami Herald*, Sept. 6, 1988.

84. LeMoyne, *NYT*, Nov. 21; Stephen Kinzer, *NYT*, Nov. 16, 1987. LeMoyne duly noted the risks that Zamora and Ungo faced from "extreme leftists and rightists" who "enforce their views with bullets and bloodshed," concealing the fact that the major risk by far has always been the behavior of the state security services and their associates. The "terror of left and right" technique is a common literary device to conceal the terror of the "centrists" whom the U.S. supports.

85. *El Norte* (Mexico), July 17, 1988; *Central America NewsPak*.

86. His party is the Social Christian Popular Movement. For his assessment of the current situation, with no "functioning democracy" or even "a democratic opening," see COHA's *Washington Report on the Hemisphere*, Aug. 31, 1988.

87. LeMoyne, photo, *NYT*, Nov. 4, 1987; *NYT*, October 28, 1987.

88. For further information, see references of note 64.

89. *Central America Report*, July 15, 1988; *Latinamerica Press* (Peru), July 21, 1988, datelined Tegucigalpa.

90. Reuter and AP, Toronto *Globe and Mail*, March 23; Pamela Constable, *Boston Globe*, March 20, 1988. *El Tiempo*, July 14, 1987.

91. Toronto *Globe and Mail*, March 23, 1988. See appendix III on the integrity of the concerns angrily expressed over the Sandinista border violation. On the aid proposal, see Susan Rasky, *NYT*, March 19, 1988.

92. From Tegucigalpa, Joseph Treaster reported only that "ordinary Hondurans" generally feel that with the contras out of Honduras, tensions between the two countries will end, referring to the fear in Honduras that they will "get stuck with" the contras; *NYT*, March 21, 27.

93. See p. 221. Peter Ford, *Christian Science Monitor*, Jan. 15; Richard Boudreaux, *Los Angeles Times*, Jan. 14; LeMoyne, *NYT*, Jan. 16; Kinzer, *NYT*, Jan. 25, 1988.

94. *NYT*, Nov. 10, 1987.

95. *San Francisco Bay Guardian*, Jan. 6, April 20, 1988.

96. *Ibid*., and FAIR Questionnaire submitted to *Times* editors on their Central America coverage, Jan. 23, 1988. Gutman, *WP*, Aug. 7, 1988.

97. AP, Feb. 2, 3; *Globe and Mail*, Feb. 3, 1988; Amnesty International, *El Salvador: 'Death Squads'—a Government Strategy* (October 1988). See my article in *Z Magazine*, Jan. 1988, for further details.

98. Douglas Farah, *WP*, Jan. 4; COHA *Washington Report on the Hemisphere*, Jan. 20, 1988.

99. AP, Feb. 26, 23, 1988; *Congressional Record*, House, Dec. 8, 1987, H11037f. See *Envío*, Jan. 1988, for a reaction by Jesuits in Nicaragua.

100. Feb. 18; March 20; April 20, 1988. On the credibility of LeMoyne's reports of guerrilla atrocities, see appendix V, section 4.

101. March 20; March 20, "Review of the Week"; Feb. 29, 1988. LeMoyne's successor Lindsey Gruson follows basically the same script. Thus a dispatch with the headline "Rebel Attacks on the Rise in Salvador" begins with ten paragraphs on the violence of the "Marxists committed to redistributing the nation's wealth and overthrowing the American-backed government," including attacks on army headquarters, ambushing police, and two car bombs in a wealthy neighborhood; and in paragraph eleven, we learn that human rights monitors report "a sharp increase in terrorism and massacres attributed to right-wing death squads, the army and the guerrillas" (*NYT*, Oct. 20, 1988).

102. Editorial, *Observer* (London), Feb. 7, 1988.

103. For details, see my articles in *Z Magazine*, January, March 1988.

104. Editorial, *NYT*, Jan. 31.

105. LeMoyne, *NYT*, Jan. 22, 1988.

106. LeMoyne, *NYT*, Jan. 18; *Globe and Mail*, Feb. 5, 1988.

107. Editorial, *El Tiempo*, May 5, 1988; reprinted in *Hondupress*, May 18.

108. *Central America Report*, June 17, 1988.

109. Human rights monitors have repeatedly condemned this technique of ideological warfare, but to no avail. See my article in *Z Magazine*, Jan. 1988, for details.

110. Reuters, *NYT*, Nov. 9, 1987, citing the CIVS report of November 8 and Latin American officials; Amnesty Law and Bill to suspend the State of Emergency, promulgated in November 1987, Unofficial translation, Nicaraguan Foreign Ministry, given to me in December by Foreign Minister Miguel D'Escoto, who appeared genuinely to believe that the Accord would be permitted to survive.

111. Nov. 18, 1987.

112. Lindsey Gruson, *NYT*, Oct. 29; LeMoyne, Nov. 29, 1987.

113. Chris Norton, *Globe and Mail*, Feb. 10, 1988.

114. Chamorro, *Packaging the Contras*.

115. *Harper's*, Oct. 1987.

116. Lindsey Gruson, *NYT*, Dec. 15, 1987.

117. Tad Szulc, *Parade Magazine*, Aug. 28, 1988.

118. Julia Preston notes that the Sandinistas have captured "state-of-the-art equipment, so modern that not even all U.S. units have them" (*WP*, Feb. 4, 1988), quite apart from the sheer mass of regular supply and the crucial assistance of U.S. aerial and naval surveillance. On the high quality of contra military and communication systems, extraordinary by the standards of the region, see *Culture of Terrorism*, 91. The illegal "humanitarian" aid sent to the contras in their Honduran bases provides them with a level of sustenance beyond what they could find within Nicaragua, not only food and supplies but even first class sports equipment (see Joe Gannon, *Christian Science Monitor*, Feb. 13, 1989). The "humanitarian" aid is presumably designed not only to maintain the terrorist forces in the field but also to draw people from Nicaragua as the economic situation worsens.

119. *Interamerican's Public Opinion Series*, no. 7, June 4-5, 1988, Interamerican Research Center, Los Angeles. *Alert!* (CISPES), March 1988.

120. See p. 16.

121. William Bollinger and David M. Lund, *Latinamerica Press* (Peru), Sept. 22, 1988. Bollinger is the director of the Interamerican Research Center; Lund is chair of the history department at the Universidad Autónoma in Mexico City. Both are involved in polling in Central America, including the polls they discuss.

122. *Conclusions of the National Debate for Peace in El Salvador*, Called by Archbishop Arturo Rivera y Damas, Sept. 1988. Distributed by National Agenda for Peace in El Salvador, Box 192, Cardinal Station, Washington DC 20064.

123. Katherine Ellison, Knight-Ridder Service, *BG*, Aug. 1, 1988. Others understand that "Nicaragua has gone further in complying with the Arias peace plan than Guatemala, Honduras and El Salvador," but Nicaragua's ties to the Soviet bloc provide "a reason, if not an excuse," for ignoring the fact, and recognition of it in no way influences continuing news coverage or opinion; editorial, *NYT*, March 11, 1988.

124. In El Salvador at least; in Guatemala, evidence is not available. Ellison's report is unusual in at least acknowledging that Guatemala "broke off talks" with the guerrillas.

125. COHA *News and Analysis*, Jan. 14, 1988. The FDR is the political group allied with the FMLN guerrillas.

126. *Excelsior*, Feb. 9; *Central America Report*, Feb. 26. There were brief notices in *BG*, Feb. 9, 11; *CSM*, Feb. 10, 1988.

127. *El Sol*, Feb. 22; editorial *WP Weekly*, March 28; AP, May 13; *BG*, May 14; Tad Szulc, *LAT*, May 22, 1988.

128. *Central America Report*, March 4, June 24; AP, Feb. 24, March 30, 1988.

129. *Congressional Quarterly,* June 25, 1988.

130. To be precise, we refer now to the revised accords, modified by the dictates of the U.S. government, and relayed by the media in conformity to these dictates.

131. COHA press release, June 11, 1988.

132. Kinzer and editorial, *NYT,* June 25; LeMoyne, *NYT,* June 7, 1988.

133. COHA's *Washington Report on the Hemisphere,* July 20, citing Tutela Legal. Archbishop Rivera y Damas, May 29, Bishop Chávez, denouncing April 14 killings; *Alert!* (CISPES), July, June. *El Sol,* Aug. 8. Orellana, *El Sol,* Aug. 1; *Guardian* (New York), Aug. 17. *El Sol,* Aug. 29, 1988. European Parliament, *Excelsior* (Mexico), Oct. 7, 1988; *Central America News Update.*

134. Brook Larmer, *CSM,* Aug. 16. Zamora, NPR, July 19. *El Sol,* July 25; AP, *BG,* June 22, 100 words. *El Sol,* July 18; AP, *NYT,* July 14, 125 words. Joel Bleifuss, *In These Times,* May 18. *Hondupress,* May 4; editorial, *El Tiempo,* May 4; *Hondupress,* May 18, June 15; *Central America Report,* Nov. 18, 1988. María Verónica Frenkel, reporting on a visit to striking farmers in Costa Rica, *Nicaragua Through Our Eyes* (Americans working in Nicaragua), July 1988.

135. *WP Weekly,* Aug. 15-21; *NYT,* Aug. 19; COHA's *Washington Report on the Hemisphere,* Aug. 31, 1988.

136. *NYT,* July 11, 1988.

137. Robert Pear, *NYT,* July 15, 1988, and many further references.

138. See p. 57.

139. Editorials *NYT,* July 18, Aug. 7; Kinzer, *NYT* "Week in Review," July 17, 1988.

140. *WP Weekly,* July 18-24, 25-31; COHA press release, July 14; *Update,* Central American Historical Institute (Georgetown U., Washington), Aug. 17, 1988.

141. *The National Interest,* Fall 1988.

142. COHA, "News and Analysis," Sept. 8, 1988.

143. Reuter, Toronto *Globe and Mail,* Oct. 26; *Miami Herald,* Oct. 26; a briefer report appears in the *Boston Globe,* AP, same day. See also Americas Watch, *Nightmare Revisited,* September 1988.

144. Pamela Constable, *BG,* Oct. 27, 1988.

145. *Central America Report,* Oct. 14, 1988.

146. *NYT,* Nov. 13, 1988.

147. *LAT-BG,* Nov. 25, 1988.

148. Chris Norton, *CSM,* Jan. 13; *El Sol,* Jan. 9, 1989.

149. UPI, *BG,* Sept. 14; *El Sol,* Sept. 19, *Central America Report,* Sept. 23; Sam Dillon, *MH,* Sept. 20; COHA "News and Analysis," Oct. 19, 1988.

150. Preston, *WP*, Nov. 8, 1988.

151. Sam Dillon, *MH*, Oct. 1, 1988.

152. *Excelsior* (Mexico City), Aug. 31, *Central America NewsPak*. AP, Nov. 15; a few words were excerpted in the *Boston Globe*, noting that there had been a march for unstated purposes, Nov. 16, 1988.

153. Lindsey Gruson, *NYT*, Nov. 18, 1988.

154. *Excelsior*, Oct. 19, 21, 1988; *Central America NewsPak*.

155. Kinzer, *NYT*, Aug. 2, 1988.

156. See note 138.

157. Rasky, *NYT*, Aug. 2; AP, *BG*, Aug. 3, 1988.

Appendix V

1. Addendum to p. 113.

2. Unless otherwise indicated, the material that follows is drawn from *Foreign Relations of the United States*, 1955-7, VII, 2ff., 198f.

3. "Memorandum by the Director of Central Intelligence (Smith) to the Under Secretary of State (Bruce), Dec. 12, 1952; NIE-84, May 19, 1953. *FRUS* 1952-1954, vol. IV, 1055, 1061ff.

4. Sol W. Sanders, *The Costa Rican Laboratory* (Twentieth Century Fund, Priority press, 1986).

5. Feb. 26, 1953; cited by Stephen G. Rabe, *Eisenhower and Latin America* (North Carolina, 1988, 33).

6. See pp. 67-8 and references of note 58.

7. See Tom Barry and Deb Preusch, *AIFLD in Central America* (Resource Center, Albuquerque, 1986); Daniel Cantor and Juliet Schor, *Tunnel Vision* (South End, 1987); Al Weinrub and William Bollinger, *The AFL-CIO in Central America* (Labor Network on Central America, Oakland, 1987). See also references of *Turning the Tide*, 273, note 61.

8. Ameringer, *Don Pepe*.

9. Richard Boudreaux, *Los Angeles Times*, Aug. 5, 1988.

10. COHA "News and Analysis," Aug. 18, 1988.

11. Sanders, *Costa Rican Laboratory*.

12. LaFeber, *Inevitable Revolutions*; *Mesoamerica*, July 1988; *Central America Report*, Nov. 1988; COHA's *Washington Report on the Hemisphere*, Nov. 23, 1988. See also Donald Dye, *In These Times*, Nov. 23, 1988. Some of the figures are reported to be only estimates because in the early 1980s external debt was declared a state secret.

13. Linnea Capps, *Links*, Central America Health Report (NCAHRN), Summer 1988. On Hull, see Leslie Cockburn, *Out of Control* (Atlantic Monthly Press, 1987). Hull was arrested in Costa Rica in January 1989 and held for questioning in connection with his alleged role in narcotics and weapons smuggling; Stephen Kurkjian, *Boston Globe*, Jan. 14, 1989.

14. Sanders, *Costa Rican Laboratory*.

15. COHA "News and Analysis," Aug. 18, 1988.

16. Interview, *World Policy Journal*, Spring 1986.

17. Addendum to pp. 114.

18. See sources cited in note 25, chapter 5, for much more extensive discussion and specific references where not given here.

19. *US Army Operational Concept for Terrorism Counteraction* (TRADOC Pamphlet No. 525-37, 1984); Robert Kupperman Associates, *Low Intensity Conflict*, July 30, 1983. Both cited in Michael Klare and Peter Kornbluh, eds., *Low Intensity Warfare* (Pantheon, 1988, 69, 147). The actual quote from Kupperman refers specifically to "the threat of force"; its use is also plainly intended.

20. See *Culture of Terrorism*, 77, and my article in *Z Magazine*, January 1988.

21. Shultz, "Moral Principles and Strategic Interests," U.S. Department of State, Current Policy No. 820, speech of April 14, 1986.

22. *Pirates and Emperors*, 136; Cockburn, *Out of Control*, 26.

23. Woodward, *Veil* (Simon & Schuster, 1987, 396f.).

24. See chapter 5. Recall that aggression is a far more serious crime than international terrorism.

25. For details, see my "Libya in U.S. Demonology," *Covert Action Information Bulletin*, Summer 1986, expanded in *Pirates and Emperors*, chapter 3; William Schaap, *CAIB*, Summer 1988. Dave Griffiths, *Business Week*, Sept. 19, 1988. Though no credible information about the terror attack at the disco has been forthcoming, suspicions have been voiced in Germany that the bombing at this Third World bar, killing a Turkish woman and a Black GI (later a second Black American soldier died), may have been drug-related or even perhaps a Klan operation.

26. The first exposure of a "disinformation" campaign was in *Newsweek*, Aug. 3, 1981.

27. Turner, testimony before House Subcommittee on Western Hemispheric Affairs, April 16, 1985, cited by Peter Kornbluh in Walker, *Reagan vs. the Sandinistas*.

28. Fred Barnes, *TNR*, May 30, 1988; editorial, *TNR*, April 2, 1984. For a longer excerpt see *Turning the Tide*, 167-68; and notes, on the efforts by editor Hendrik Hertzberg to evade the facts. Hertzberg, *TNR*, Feb. 6, 1989. Recall also the laudatory comments on Reagan's dedication to human rights during the propaganda exercises at the Summits, already discussed.

29. Raymond L. Garthoff, *Reflections on the Cuban Missile Crisis* (Brookings Institution, 1987, 17).

30. *Ibid.*, 16f., 78f., 89f., 98; *International Security*, Winter 1987-88, 12. For more on these terrorist operations, see the references of chapter 5, note 25; also U.S. Army Captain Bradley Earl Ayers, *The War that Never Was* (Bobbs-Merrill, 1976); Warren Hinckle and William Turner, *The Fish is Red* (Harper & Row, 1981); William Blum, *The CIA* (Zed, 1986); Morris Morley, *Imperial State and Revolution* (Cambridge, 1987).

31. *Jerusalem Post*, Aug. 16, 1981; see *Fateful Triangle*, chapter 5, sections 1, 3.4, for further quotes, background, and description.

32. Glass, text of talk at Middle East Studies Association Conference, Los Angeles, Nov. 4, 1988, published in *Index on Censorship* (London), January 1989.

33. Yaniv, *Dilemmas of Security*, 70. The October 1973 war brought home the lesson that Egypt could not be disregarded. The U.S. then turned to the obvious strategy: remove it from the conflict. See my 1977 article reprinted as chapter 11, *Towards a New Cold War*. Camp David consummated this strategy.

34. See *Towards a New Cold War* and *Fateful Triangle* on the events, and *Pirates and Emperors* on how they have entered into memory. For a brief review from an expert Israeli perspective, see Schiff and Ya'ari, *Israel's Lebanon War*. It is difficult to know just what their original manuscript might have contained, since much was excised by the Israeli censor; 20 percent according to Ehud Ya'ari, 50 percent according to a "respected correspondent" cited by Middle East historian Augustus Richard Norton of the West Point Military Academy (*Kol Ha'ir*, Feb. 10, 1984; *Middle East Journal*, Summer 1985).

35. Editorial, *Washington Post*, April 22, 1982; see *Fateful Triangle* for further background; and Yaniv, *op. cit.*, for justification of these operations. See also appendix I, section 2, above.

36. Harkabi, *Israel's Fateful Hour*, 100-1. See appendix I, section 2.

37. *NYT*, Sept. 7, 1987.

38. Laqueur, *The Age of Terrorism*. Citations that follow are from pp. 8, 91-92, 218, 215, 139, 166, 232, 141, 106, 21-22, 291-92, 204, 262, 245, 296-97, 310, 300.

39. Laqueur and Charles Krauthammer, *New Republic*, March 31, 1982.

40. On the facts, and the numbers game, see appendix I, section 2.

41. Ehud Ya'ari, *Egypt and the Fedayeen* (Hebrew) (Givat Haviva, 1975, 27f.), a study based on captured Egyptian and Jordanian documents. At the same time, Salah Mustapha, Egyptian military attaché in Jordan, was severely injured by a letter-bomb sent from East Jerusalem, presumably from the same source; *ibid.*

42. Israeli military historian Uri Milshtein, *Hadashot*, Dec. 31, 1987, referring to Eliav's 1983 book *Hamevukash*.

43. See, among others, Jeffrey Race, *War Comes to Long An* (California, 1972, 197, and particularly chapter 3).

44. See Alfred W. McCoy et al., *The Politics of Heroin in Southeast Asia* (Harper & Row, 1972). For some recent discussion, see Jonathan Kwitny, *The Crimes of Patriots* (Norton, 1987). Stone, "Is the Cold War really over?," *Sunday Telegraph* (London), Nov. 27, 1988.

45. On these matters, also virtually ignored in the U.S. media, see Herman and Brodhead, *Rise and Fall of the Bulgarian Connection*, 81f.

46. For critical discussion of the Weathermen at the time, see Harold Jacobs, ed., *Weatherman* (Ramparts, 1970).

47. Addendum to p. 120.

48. On U.S.-Iranian relations, see James A. Bill, *The Eagle and the Lion* (Yale, 1988).

49. *Ibid.*, 55-56.

50. The maneuverings are of some interest; see *Towards a New Cold War*, 313f.

51. Dorman and Farhang, *The U.S. Press and Iran*. Quotes below are from this book, unless otherwise indicated.

52. Editorial, *NYT*, Aug. 6, 1954; for a longer quote and more context, see *Towards a New Cold War*, 99, and the discussion there and in chapter 11.

53. *U.S. Press and Iran*, 33ff., 123, 164, 91f., 120, 54, 148, 157. For an insider's account of how the *Times* looked the other way on the CIA role in the coup, and on "sanitizing" copy on Vietnam in which he was personally involved as a senior rewrite editor, see John Hess, *Grand Street*, Winter 1989. Hess's interesting comments reveal illusions of their own, however. Thus he writes that while *Times* correspondents David Halberstam and Neil Sheehan originally criticized the conduct of the U.S. war in Vietnam on tactical grounds, they "gradually...came to see the war as evil in itself, and they helped to persuade many fellow Americans that it was." In reality, they were far behind not only the peace movement (which did the work that they failed to do) but even the majority of their fellow Americans in this regard, and at least their published criticism remained well within the dove-hawk consensus that adopted unquestioningly the basic doctrines of the propaganda system.

54. Bill, *op. cit.*, 283-84.

55. Saeedpour, "Kurdish Times and the New York Times," *Kurdish Times* (Brooklyn), published by Cultural Survival, Summer 1988. Other journals are also sampled.

56. Addendum to p. 122.

57. There has been a most remarkable campaign in the United States to justify this stance by denying that the Palestinians are more than recent immigrants,

occasioned by a book by Joan Peters that received almost unanimous applause in a euphoric reception among American intellectuals. For discussion of this most illuminating episode of recent intellectual history, which actually merits much closer study, see essays by Norman Finkelstein and Edward Said in Said and Hitchens, *Blaming the Victims*. Finkelstein's important study exposing the fraud, which was well known early on in the propaganda campaign, was unpublishable in the United States. It was only after the book appeared in England, and was utterly demolished by reviewers (in part, relying on Finkelstein's unpublishable analysis), that its American enthusiasts, or at least the less audacious among them, broke ranks and dropped the matter, some claiming falsely that they had not known before about the fraud that was being perpetrated with their assistance. This is a revealing story that has yet to be properly told.

58. Like any historical comparison, this one is inexact in some ways. To mention only the most obvious discrepancy, and the one least likely to be recognized, support for the PLO among the Palestinians, by all available evidence, is far beyond support among Jews for the Zionist organizations in the mid-1940s.

59. For further details and the background factors, see *Fateful Triangle; Pirates and Emperors*; and my articles "The Palestinian Uprising," *Z Magazine*, May 1988, and "The U.S. and the Middle East" (see chapter 3, note 23). The latter also reviews some important documentation from the Israeli diplomatic record. See the same sources for references, where not cited below.

60. Mary Curtius, *Boston Globe Magazine*, Aug. 14, 1988. The example is more interesting than most, because Curtius is an independent and knowledgeable Middle East correspondent. For a sample of many other cases, see *Fateful Triangle*, chapter 3, 2.4.2. Major journals have even rejected letters to the editor correcting false statements on this matter.

61. Friedman, *NYT*, Aug. 7, 1988.

62. For details, see *Pirates and Emperors*, chapter 2, note 58 and text, and sources cited.

63. Friedman, "The Power of the Fanatics," *NYT Magazine*, Oct. 7, 1988.

64. Editorial, *NYT*, June 13, 1988.

65. See references of note 59.

66. *NYT*, March 17, 21; June 2, 1985.

67. Peace Now had never clearly separated itself from Labor Party rejectionism. On its unclear and vacillating positions, considerably misunderstood in the United States, see below.

68. Friedman, *NYT*, Dec. 10, 1986; March 27, 1987.

69. Yitzhak Ben-Horin, *Ma'ariv*, Dec. 4; *Ma'ariv*, Dec. 5; Eyal Ehrlich, *Ha'aretz*, Dec. 19, 1986.

70. AP, April 1, 1988. In the *New York Times*, these events were reported accurately by John Kifner, a fine journalist for many years, and by other media, in the early months of the uprising.

71. "The Man who Foresaw the Uprising," *Yediot Ahronot*, April 7; *Hotam*, April 15.

72. Friedman, *NYT News in Review*, Jan. 29, 1989.

73. *Hadashot*, Jan. 7, 1988; *Ha'aretz*, Dec. 31, 1987.

74. Interview, *Nouvel Observateur*, Jan. 7, 1988.

75. AP, Jan. 15; Toronto *Globe and Mail*, Jan. 15, 1987; also published in several local newspapers in the United States.

76. *NYRB*, June 25, 1987. U.N. English translation, quoted in *The Other Israel*, Newsletter of the Israeli Council for Israeli-Palestinian Peace, Nov.-Dec. 1987.

77. To be precise, the PLO support for the nonrejectionist political settlement vetoed by the United States at the United Nations in January 1976 was reported (*NYT*, Jan. 27, 1988), but then disappeared from history.

78. *NYT*, March 12, 1988.

79. "Israeli Supreme Court lets two extremist parties run," *Christian Science Monitor*, June 29, 1984.

80. *Ha'aretz*, April 12; *Jerusalem Post*, April 13; Shamir, *Ha'aretz*, April 7; Herut, Dorit Gefen, *Al-Hamishmar*, Feb. 29, 1988; Milo, then chairman of the Likud bloc in the Knesset, *Maariv*, Jan. 3, 1984; *Globe and Mail*, April 26; Rabin, Tony Banks, *Jane's Defence Weekly*, May 7; Eban, *Jerusalem Post*, Dec. 3, 1988.

81. See my articles in *Z Magazine*, May, July 1988. I found no other mention.

82. Sciolino, *NYT*, April 6, 8, 1988.

83. *In These Times*, June 22, distributed several days earlier; *New York Times*, June 22, 1988. In subsequent weeks, there were continued indications of controversy within the PLO over the Abu Sharif initiative.

84. As of 1988, Peace Now—unlike the PLO—had never proposed a non-rejectionist peace settlement. Individuals associated with the group have done so, while others (notably Abba Eban) maintained an association with it while clearly advocating Labor Party rejectionism (see, e.g., his "The Central Question," *Tikkun* 1.2, 1986). As of April 1988, leading activists in Israel were unable to provide me with a single textual example of support for a two-state settlement, and I can find none. Funding literature of November 1988 cites Peace Now's willingness to "talk to Palestinians" who advocate a non-rejectionist political settlement, so that other Palestinians can be "encouraged to renounce violence and fend off rejectionists." But there is not a word to indicate that Peace Now joins their Palestinian interlocutors (specifically, Faisal Husseini) in adopting a nonrejectionist position. See below for further confirmation of this conclusion.

85. In the intellectual climate in the United States, often semi-hysterical on these matters, it is perhaps worth adding that the review of the factual record does not entail that the PLO is an admirable organization. In fact, it has proven over the years to be incompetent, corrupt, foolish, and often murderous, particularly in the early 1970s. These are matters that I have often discussed for the past twenty years. They have no relevance in the present connection, just as the long record of Zionist violence was not relevant to evaluating the right of Jews to be represented by the Zionists in 1947, or their right to national self-determination in Palestine.

86. *Jewish Post and Opinion*, Nov. 16, 1988.

87. See chapter 4. Editorial, *NYT*, Nov. 16, 1988.

88. Editorial, Dec. 8, 1988; Steve Lohr, "Arafat says P.L.O. Accepted Israel, *NYT*, same day; official statement, same day.

89. Editorials, *LAT*, Nov. 16, *WP*, Nov. 15, 1988.

90. Will, *BG*, Nov. 20; Kipper, Lewis, *NYT*, Dec. 1, 1988; Weinstein, *BG*, Dec. 4, 1988.

91. *CSM*, Dec. 8, 1988.

92. Peter Steinfels, Dec. 8, 1988.

93. Aryeh Dayan, *Kol Ha'ir*, Nov. 25; Peace Now advertisement, Nov. 23; poll, *Yediot Ahronot*, Dec. 23, 1988.

94. An exception is a column by William Raspberry, pointing out that Israel's commitment to terror continues unabated and that "the real sticking point for Israel is not PLO 'ambiguity' but insistence that the Palestinians no less than Israelis have a right to a homeland" (*WP*, Dec. 14, 1988). With regard to terror, the same can be said about the United States. It is difficult to overlook the fact that this near-unique recognition of reality was written by one of the few Black columnists in the United States.

95. Editorial, *NYT*, Dec. 21, 1988; Friedman, "Reality Time in Mideast," *NYT*, Dec. 19, 1988. On Friedman's version of "reality," see below.

96. On the actual record of apologetics for Israel and venomous attack on anyone who departed from the party line, quickly effaced from history when the conditions of respectability changed, see *Peace in the Middle East?*, chapter 5; *Fateful Triangle*, 146f., 263f., 378f. Some of the transitions are startling.

97. State Department conditions, *NYT*, Dec. 14; Marie Colvin, *NYT Magazine*, Dec. 18; Chancellor, NBC evening news, Dec. 13, 1988, reported to me by Marilyn Young. For a succinct legal analysis of the U.S. obligations to the U.N., see Alfred P. Rubin, *CSM*, Dec. 15, 1988.

98. Richard Strauss, *BG*, Dec. 14; Charlotte Saikowski, *CSM*, Dec. 15, 1988.

99. On the early stages of the Israel-Jordan alliance, see Avi Shlaim, *Collusion across the Jordan* (Columbia, 1988). Van Creveld, *Jerusalem Post,*, Feb. 1, 1989.

100. Editorial, *WP Weekly*, Dec. 19, 1988, lauding Shultz for having "hung tough on the principled conditions of 1975" and for denying Arafat a visa, a "useful signal." The editors state that "the 1975 conditions were drafted at a time when Israel had a government prepared to exchange territory for peace if there were a negotiating partner." The facts, however, are that Israel's Labor government explicitly refused to deal with any Palestinians on any political issue, and the U.S. and Israel rejected the land-for-peace offer at the U.N. Security Council. See *Fateful Triangle*, and for more detail on the Israeli government attitude at the time, *Towards a New Cold War*, 267f. Israel's reaction to the U.N. session was a gratuitous bombing of Lebanon, with over fifty killed. The U.S. reaction was to veto the resolution. The media reaction has been to deny the facts, as in this editorial.

101. H.D.S. Greenway, *BG*, Dec. 15; see also Randolph Ryan, *BG*, Dec. 16, 1988, the only example I found where the elementary facts about the State Department conditions are recognized.

102. Alan Cowell, *NYT*, Dec. 19; Robert Pear, *NYT*, Dec. 15; editorial, *WP Weekly*, Dec. 19; "Palestinian Semantics: Arafat's Changing Words," *NYT*, Dec. 15; editorial, *NYT*, Dec. 16; editorial, *BG*, Dec. 16; Pipes, "How the U.S. Should Handle Arafat," Dec. 20; Friedman, "Reality Time," *NYT*, Dec. 19, 1988. On the facts concerning the 1971 negotiations, which Friedman has always suppressed or denied, see *Fateful Triangle*, chapter 3.

103. Bush News Conference, *NYT*, Jan. 28; Brinkley, Jan. 29, 1989.

104. "Palestinian Semantics," *NYT*, Dec. 15; Alan Cowell, *NYT*, Dec. 19, 1988.

105. Safire claims that "Mr. Arafat, by accepting the hated word *renounce*, promised to cut out what his organization had been doing in the past," by which he apparently means that Arafat promised to cut out what he, Safire, considers to be terrorism. That, however, plainly does not follow; it only follows that Arafat promised to cut out what he, Arafat, considers terrorism. The issue turns again on the right of struggle for self-determination against colonialist and racist regimes and foreign occupation, accepted by the entire world apart from the United States and Israel. Safire's contorted argument misses this point and thus collapses.

106. Safire, *NYT Magazine*, Jan. 1; Berman, "What is a Jew?," *Village Voice*, Jan. 3, 1989. On Howe's actual role over many years, see the references of note 96.

107. *BG*, Dec. 19; *NYT*; Peres, Op-Ed, *NYT*, Dec. 21; John Kifner, *NYT*, Dec. 20, 1988. On casualties, see Daoud Kuttab, *Middle East International*, Jan. 20, 1989, citing figures of thirty-one killed (including children) from mid-December to mid-January, the highest monthly total since the preceding March, and 1,000 injured. The horrifying details are regularly reported in the Hebrew press. See, for example, Yizhar Be'er, *Kol Ha'ir*, Dec. 30, 1988, reporting the results of an intensive investigation of the "day of slaughter" in Nablus on December 16, two days after Arafat allegedly said the magic words. For some details, see my article in *Z Magazine*, March 1989.

108. *Hadashot*, Feb. 14; Rabin, Nahum Barnea, *Yediot Ahronot*, Feb. 24; *JP*, Jan. 6, 1989. Emphasis in *JP*. It is not impossible that U.S. and Israeli intelligence actually believe that the Intifada was initiated by the PLO and is directed by it. There is ample evidence from the documentary record of the incapacity of intelligence, the national political police, or the political leadership to comprehend the reality of popular movements and popular struggles. The idea is simply too threatening, and cannot be faced or comprehended. It is also necessary to bear in mind the ideological fanaticism that often colors intelligence reports and the higher-level interpretation of them, also amply documented.

109. See references cited earlier; *NYT*, Nov. 6, 1982.

110. Wilkie, *BG*, Dec. 1, 1985.

111. *NYT Magazine*, Oct. 30, 1988.

112. Klein, "Our Man in Managua," *Esquire*, Nov. 1986; Howe, *NYT Book Review*, May 16, 1982; Peretz, *New Republic*, Aug. 29, 1983, May 7, 1984, among many examples; Brooks Jackson, *Wall Street Journal*, March 23, 1984; Matt Moffett, *WSJ*, Aug. 30, 1984; Safire, *NYT*, Sept. 5, 1988; Ruth Wisse, Professor of Yiddish Literature at McGill University, *Commentary*, May 1988.

113. Eban, *Congress Bi-Weekly*, March 30, 1973.

114. Nathan and Ruth Perlmutter, *The Real Anti-Semitism in America* (Arbor House, 1982); see *Fateful Triangle*, 14f., for more extensive quotes and discussion.

115. Colin Campbell, *NYT*, Jan. 30, 1985. See *Fateful Triangle* (11f.) and *Pirates and Emperors* (29f., 46n) for some references to the condemnations by Israeli doves of the hysteria, fanaticism, Stalinist-style methods and sheer cynicism that they see—correctly, in my view—as profoundly harmful to the interests of their country.

116. Seven were discharged from the Bush campaign after the revelations, four of them retaining their leadership positions in the Heritage Groups Council, the ethnic outreach arm of the Republican National Committee. See Russell C. Bellant, "Will Bush Purge Nazi Collaborators in the G.O.P.?," Op-Ed, *NYT*, Nov. 19, 1988.

117. Judis, *In These Times*, Sept. 28; *New Republic*, Oct. 3, 1988. See David Corn, *Nation*, Oct. 24, 1988, for more on the "haven" for "anti-Semites and fascist sympathizers" in the Republican party. Also Holly Sklar, *Z Magazine*, Nov. 1988; Charles Allen, *Village Voice*, Nov. 1, 1988. On the downplaying of the story by the *New York Times*, see FAIR, *Extra!*, Sept./Oct. 1988.

118. Ed Vulliamy, *WP Weekly*, Oct. 24-30. See also Christopher Kenneally, *BG*, Oct. 16; David Korn and Jefferson Morley, *Nation*, Nov. 7, 1988.

119. Spector, Op-Ed, *NYT*, March 17, 1988, noting that not a single question was raised to Prime Minister Shamir about this matter in his press conference

in Washington and TV interviews; *LAT-BG, NYT,* Oct. 31, 1984; *BG, NYT,* Feb. 25, 1987.

120. Abraham, AAUG *Mideast Monitor,* April 1987.

121. See *Fateful Triangle,* chapter 7, section 4.2.

122. *Sunday Times,* Aug. 9, 16; *NYT,* Aug. 31, 1987. Also *Jerusalem Post,* Aug. 9, reporting the *Sunday Times* story. On media unwillingness to report "unflattering stories about Israel that are routinely covered" in the Israeli press, and the reasons for it, see Robert I. Friedman, *Mother Jones,* Feb.-March, 1987.

123. AP, Sept. 19, 1987.

124. Victoria Brittain, *Guardian* (London), June 6; Anthony Robinson, *Financial Times,* June 7; *Economist,* June 14, 1987; also BBC world service.

125. Addendum to p. 123.

126. See p. 316. Sarah Honig, *JP Magazine,* Sept. 23, 1988.

127. Transcript, ABC NEWS VIEWPOINT Show #1794, ABC, April 7, 1988. Coverage of South Africa and some other matters are also mentioned, but the focus is on coverage of Israel.

128. Wieseltier, *New Republic,* Sept. 23, 1981; Pipes, *NYT,* Aug. 3, 1988; Herzog, *LAT,* July 9, 1988.

129. Shah cited in Dorman and Farhang, *The U.S. Press and Iran,* 24; *FRUS, 1952-1954,* vol. IV, 1132, Memorandum of NSC discussion, May 27, 1954; Harrison E. Salisbury, *Without Fear or Favor* (Times Books, 1980, 479); Thomas P. McCann, *An American Company* (Crown, 1976, 47). See McCann and *Turning the Tide,* 164f., on *Times* coverage and commentary during the period.

130. Brzezinski, *The National Interest* (Fall, 1985); Tucker, *Commentary,* Oct. 1982. On Shawcross's intriguing construction and its influence, see *Manufacturing Consent,* chapter 6, section 2.8. The alleged quote was left unidentified and undated to obscure the evident absurdity of the charge and the fact that it was fabricated for the occasion. *Ibid.,* for details.

131. Hollander, *Wall Street Journal,* Dec. 24, 1985; Diggins, *NYT Book Review,* Oct. 20, 1985; *NYT* Op-Ed, Aug. 22, 1988.

132. Addendum to p. 127.

133. The CIA-appointed press spokesman for the contras, Edgar Chamorro, describes Stephen Kinzer as "like an errand boy" for the Reagan administration, "building up those stories that fit in with Reagan's agenda," "just responding to what the White House is saying." In his monograph on the contras, the CIA, and the media, Chamorro describes cases in which correspondents readily accepted contra manipulation, and quotes James LeMoyne as telling him: "The *contra* leaders won't invite you on trips, won't take you into their camps, and won't talk to you, if your articles are too critical" (Interview, *Extra!* (FAIR), Oct./Nov. 1987; *Packaging the Contras*).

134. Michael Massing, *Columbia Journalism Review*, July/August, 1987. Also *Update*, Dec. 29, 1987 (Central American Historical Institute, Georgetown University, Washington).

135. Eleven issues were missing in this collection.

136. There is no report of the endorsement by the International Verification Commission (CIVS), a few days later, of the Sandinista position that the state of emergency can be maintained until the aggression ends.

137. AP, Nov. 24, 1986.

138. *NYT*, Jan. 31, 1988.

139. AP, Oct. 20, 1987; *BG* and *La Prensa*, same day.

140. Kinzer, *NYT*, Oct. 20, 22, 25; LeMoyne, Nov. 5, 1987.

141. "Sad Tales of La Libertad de Prensa," *Harper's*, Aug. 1988.

142. Chamorro, *Packaging the Contras*.

143. Though Goldman does not discuss the point, it is worth noting that by mid-1988 TV and radio in El Salvador were quite open to a range of positions, more so than the United States, I suspect, and that parts of the press would publish paid advertisements over a wide spectrum. The situation, of course, is radically different from Nicaragua, where a major journal, funded by the foreign power attempting to overthrow the government of Nicaragua, openly supports that effort.

144. Council on Hemispheric Affairs and The Newspaper Guild, *A Survey of Press Freedom in Latin America 1985-1986* (Washington, Dec. 1986).

145. For discussion of many examples, see Mario Zeledón, ed., *La Desinformación de la Prensa en Costa Rica: Un grave peligro para la Paz* (Istituto Costarricense de Estudios Sociales, Costa Rica, 1987).

146. Kinzer, *NYT*, Oct. 3, 1987; on the polls, see p. 242.

147. "Full Amnesty Seen as Test for Managua," Sept. 10, 1987; "Life on a Cooperative: 'A Little Better Off'," Sept. 7, 1987. On fact and fancy concerning political prisoners, see my article in *Z Magazine*, Jan. 1988.

148. Gutman, *Banana Diplomacy* (Simon and Schuster, 1988, 371).

149. *NYT*, Nov. 8, 1987.

150. *Christian Science Monitor*, Nov. 9, 1987.

151. Kinzer, *NYT*, Jan. 31, 1988.

152. See appendix IV, section 5. LeMoyne, *NYT*, June 15, 1988.

153. *NYT*, Nov. 10, 1985.

154. Kinzer, Dec. 4; Jonathan Steele, interview with Arias, *Guardian* (London), Nov. 17; Kinzer, Nov. 15, 1987.

155. Michael Emery, *San Francisco Bay Guardian*, Dec. 3, 1988, quoting *La Penca: Pastora, the Press and the CIA* by Tony Avirgan and Martha Honey,

reporting their two-year investigation of the bombing in which Avirgan was wounded and eight people were killed. "Ironically," Emery observes, "Honey's story on Pastora, citing the CIA pressure, had run on the front page of The New York Times May 31st [1984]."

156. For many others, see *Culture of Terrorism* and my articles in *Z Magazine*, January, March 1988.

157. *NYT*, Dec. 25, 1987; Cook, "Nicaragua: the Show Goes On," ms., Managua, Dec. 28, 1987; Cockburn, *Nation*, Jan. 30, 1988. Letters, *Nation*, July 2/9, 1988. Background on this remote region, where the war had caused 17,000 people to seek refuge in the towns that were attacked and where the U.S.-run propaganda radio in Honduras is virtually the only source of information, appears in *Excelsior* (Mexico), Dec. 12, 1987; *Central America NewsPak*.

158. LeMoyne, *NYT*, June 26, 1988; Cockburn, *Nation*, July 30/Aug. 6, 1988.

159. Chris Norton, *Extra!* (FAIR), July/August 1988. Alexander Cockburn, *Nation*, Aug. 27/Sept. 3, 1988, citing a story by journalist Marc Cooper, *Los Angeles Weekly*, May 27-June 2. After Cockburn's column appeared, the *Times* published an "editors' note" (Sept. 15) stating that the story "fell short of The Times's reporting and editing standards" because it gave the impression of firsthand interviewing while in fact it "was based on a report in El Mundo, a center-right newspaper, which attributed the information to the Salvadoran military command," and on "a representative of a leading human rights organization," unidentified and unmentioned in LeMoyne's story (and probably nonexistent), who allegedly said she believed the report to be true, later retracting this judgment. The editor's note refers to unnamed "freelance journalists in Central America" who determined that the story was false, and to the *LA Weekly* account. Interviewed by *Newsday* (Sept. 21), foreign editor Joseph Lelyveld said that the correction was motivated by Cockburn's story, which is not mentioned in the editor's note. He accused Cockburn of "waging a vendetta against LeMoyne." LeMoyne himself conceded that he was not in the country at the time, but on returning had "noticed a tremendous number of political killings, both by guerrillas and by what they call right wing death squads." On his falsification of the figures for the May Day rally, LeMoyne said his estimate "came from a member of a pro-guerrilla group" whom he would not name because Cockburn would denounce this alleged informant for having "betrayed the cause."

160. LeMoyne, "Testifying to Torture," *NYT Magazine*, June 5; letters, Sept. 18, 1988. See also Murillo's accompanying letter to the *New York Times* editors with further clarifications, in which she offers to appear for personal discussion to resolve the issues, printed in *Honduras Update*, June/July 1988. The *Times Magazine* editors deserve credit for publishing Murillo's letter. Often, journals do not permit the right of response to dissidents, even in response to direct personal attacks.

161. Addendum to p. 130.

162. See special, *NYT*, Oct. 26, 1988, where the facts are acknowledged in a story on the suspension of press credentials for three foreign correspondents who had reported operations of Israeli death squads in the occupied territories.

163. Al-Haq *Newsletter*, March/April 1987, July/August 1987; Marty Rosenbluth, "Harassing Palestinian unions," *Middle East International*, Nov. 7, 1987; Amnon Barzilai, "Danger: a Painter," *Ha'aretz*, Dec. 21, 1984. See also, among others, Shirley Eber, "Censorship in the Middle East," *Third World Affairs*, 1988, with many examples. Shyam Bhatia, *Observer* (London); *Jerusalem Post*, Nov. 17; Avigdor Feldman, *Hadashot*, Nov. 18; Daniel Williams, *LAT*, Nov. 20, 1988. See also Committee to Protect Journalists, *Journalists Under Occupation* (New York, 1988).

164. Irit Nahmani, *Hadashot*, Aug. 29, 1988; Khaled Abu-Tuama, *Yerushalayim*, Nov. 11, 1988. The policy of supporting fundamentalist extremists has come under severe criticism. Pinhas Inbari writes that Israel is making the same mistake in the occupied territories that it made in southern Lebanon, where "the sapping of Palestinian nationalism's strength led to the emergence of Islamic fundamentalism," a far more dangerous force. In the occupied territories, he warns, Israel may undermine the PLO, but "those who didn't want to talk with Arafat will have to do battle with Khomeini" (*Al Hamishmar*, Sept. 15, 1988).

165. Inbari, *Al-Hamishmar*, Nov. 27, 1987.

166. Appeal, Attorney Avigdor Feldman.

167. *NYT*, Feb. 18, 1987.

168. Oren Cohen, *Hadashot*, March 24; Peretz Kidron, *Middle East International*, May 14; AP, May 25; *News from Within* (Jerusalem), July 10, 1988.

169. Statement by the defendants, July 1988.

170. Aryeh Dayan, *Kol Hair*, Aug. 5, 1988; *LAT*, Aug. 1; *NYT*, Aug. 1; Joel Greenberg, *Christian Science Monitor*, Aug. 3; Geraldine Brooks, *Wall St. Journal*, Aug. 26, 1988.

171. Dayan, *op. cit.*; *The Other Israel*, Nov./Dec. 1987; Porath, *Ha'aretz*, Aug. 9, 1988.

172. Reuters, *NYT*, Nov. 13, 1986; EEC reaction, *Manchester Guardian Weekly*, Jan. 4, 1987; "Natan Sharansky Clarifies," advertisement, *Jerusalem Post*, *Ma'ariv*, Nov. 13, 1986; Interview with Louis Rapoport, *JP*, Dec. 5, 1986; Award, Samson Krupnick, *Jewish Post & Opinion*, Dec. 3, 1986; William Claiborne, *Washington Post*, Feb. 19, 1986; Robert Stone, *NYT Book Review*, June 5, 1988. *New Republic*, Feb. 27, 1989.

173. *NYT*, July 1, 1988.

174. Ihsan Hijazi, *NYT*, Aug. 10, 1988, 190 words.

175. *NYT*, April 24, 1988.

176. *El Pais* (Madrid), May 3; *Egin* (San Sebastian), June 28, August 2, June 22, July 24, 28, 1988.

177. Addendum to p. 131.

178. Without pursuing the matter, I should at least note here that in other industrial democracies, the situation is often far worse.

179. Rocker, "Anarchism and Anarcho-Syndicalism," in Paul Eltzbacher, ed., *Anarchism* (Freedom Press, 1960). This is excerpted from Rocker's important 1938 book *Anarcho-Syndicalism* (Pluto Press, London, 1989).

180. Hughes, in *Near v. Minnesota*, 1931, cited by Jerome Barron, "Access to the Press."

181. Kairys, "Freedom of Speech," in David Kairys, ed., *The Politics of Law* (Pantheon, 1982).

182. Jamie Kalven, editor's introduction to Harry Kalven, *A Worthy Tradition: Freedom of Speech in America* (Harper & Row, 1988); Brennan's opinion cited on p. 66. Note that Kalven's interesting book is mistitled; the actual tradition he surveys is far from worthy.

183. *Ibid.*, 63.

184. "Espionage Act of 1917," reprinted in Harold L. Nelson, ed., *Freedom of the Press from Hamilton to the Warren Court* (Bobbs-Merrill, 1967, 247f.)

185. Cited by Kairys, *op. cit.*

186. Burleson, cited in introduction, Nelson, *op. cit.*; William Hard, *New Republic*, May 10, 1919, in Nelson, 253f.

187. For a review of hundreds of cases from April 1917 through June 1918, see the 1919 report of the National Civil Liberties Bureau, which became the ACLU a year later, reprinted in Nelson, *op. cit.*, 307f.

188. Robert J. Goldstein, *Political Repression in Modern America* (Cambridge: Schenkman, 1978). See also appendix II, section 2.

189. Chafee, *Free Speech in the United States* (Harvard, 1941), cited by Kairys, *op. cit.*

190. ACLU *Review of the Year* (to June 1943), reprinted in Nelson, *op. cit.*, 264.

191. A "sweeping federal sedition law," Harry Kalven observes, making it a crime "to knowingly or willfully advocate, abet, advise, or teach the duty, necessity, desirability, or propriety of overthrowing or destroying any government in the United States by force or violence," to organize or help to organize any group that teaches, advocates or encourages such doctrines or "to be or become a member of, or affiliate with, any such society, group, or assembly of persons, knowing the purposes thereof." The membership clause of the Smith Act was upheld by the Supreme Court in *Scales v. United States* in 1961. Kalven, *op. cit.*

192. Goldstein, *Political Repression.*

193. *Ibid.*, citing the *New Republic, New Leader, Nation*; Fox, *Reinhold Niebuhr*, 293.

194. Richard Polenberg, *Fighting Faiths* (Viking, 1987, 367).

195. See the review of his *America in Vietnam* reprinted in *Towards a New Cold War* (co-authored with Edward Herman).

196. Lewy, "Does America Need a Verfassungsschutzbericht?," *Orbis*, Fall 1987.

197. Among their dramatic exposures is the fact that Marcus Raskin of the Institute of Policy Studies and I are "terrorist commanders" who, working with the CIA, the KGB, and other cohorts, control the international terror network, planned to set off atom bombs in American cities to disrupt the bicentennial, etc., while our colleagues such as the Queen of England control the international drug racket, linked with international Zionism and other nefarious elements. All of this, of course, is "hidden agenda," though penetrable by the skilled investigator.

198. Emphasis added.

Index

413

About South End Press

S outh End Press is a nonprofit, collectively run book publisher with over 200 titles in print. Since our founding in 1977, we have tried to meet the needs of readers who are exploring, or are already committed to, the politics of radical social change. Our goal is to publish books that encourage critical thinking and constructive action on the key political, cultural, social, economic, and ecological issues shaping life in the United States and in the world. In this way, we hope to give expression to a wide diversity of democratic social movements and to provide an alternative to the products of corporate publishing.

Through the Institute for Social and Cultural Change, South End Press works with other political media projects—Z Magazine; Speakout, a speakers' bureau; Alternative Radio; and the Publishers Support Project—to expand access to information and critical analysis. If you would like a free catalog of South End Press books, please write to us at: South End Press, 116 Saint Botolph Street, Boston, MA 02115. Visit our website at http://www.lbbs.org.

Related Titles by Noam Chomsky

Powers and Prospects
Reflections on Human Nature and the Social Order
$16.00 paper; $40.00 cloth

Year 501
The Conquest Continues
$16.00 paper; $30.00 cloth

Rethinking Camelot
JFK, the Vietnam War, and U.S. Political Culture
$14.00 paper; $30.00 cloth

The Culture of Terrorism
$18.00 paper; $35.00 cloth

On Power and Ideology
The Managua Lectures
$12.00 paper; $25.00 cloth

Liberating Theory
(co-authored with Michael Albert, Leslie Cagan,
Mel King, Lydia Sargent, and Holly Sklar)
$14.00 paper; $25.00 cloth

Turning the Tide
U.S. Intervention in Central America and the Struggle for Peace
$16.00 paper; $35.00 cloth

Fateful Triangle
The United States, Israel, and the Palestinians
$22.00 paper; $40.00 cloth

After the Cataclysm
Postwar Indochina and the Reconstruction of Imperial Ideology
(co-authored with Edward Herman)
$18.00 paper; $40.00 cloth

The Washington Connection and Third World Fascism
(co-authored with Edward Herman)
$16.00 paper; $40.00 cloth

Other Related Titles from South End Press

Beyond Hypocrisy
Decoding the News in an Age of Propaganda
Edward Herman
$16.00 paper; $35 cloth

Networks of Power
Corporate TV's Threat to Democracy
Dennis Mazzocco
$14.00 paper; $30.00 cloth

When ordering, please include $3.00 for postage and handling for the first book and
75 cents for each additional book. To order by credit card, call 1-800-533-8478.